Reading: Research and Classroom Practice

Proceedings of the thirteenth annual course and conference
of the United Kingdom Reading Association
University of Durham 1976

Editor John Gilliland

Ward Lock Educational

ISBN 0 7062 3630 0

First published 1977

Set in 10 on 11 point Times by Amos Typesetters and printed by
Willmer Brothers, Birkenhead
for Ward Lock Educational
116 Baker Street, London W1M 2BB
A member of the Pentos Group
Made in Great Britain

Contents

Foreword

The thirteenth annual course and conferences of the United Kingdom Reading Association was held at the University of Durham in the fine summer of 1976.

The conference took as its major theme the relationship between research and classroom practice. This relationship has long been a matter of concern but seemed particularly appropriate at a time when there is current concern over standards and progress in reading and when large amounts of research are being published. Opportunities were provided for researchers and teachers to consider how the problems facing teachers of reading can be more effectively researched and also to consider and discuss ways in which research findings may be implemented. It is hoped that this selection of papers reflects the blend of theoretical statements, research findings and practical proposals contained in the conference programme, and that they will generate further improvements in reading research and teaching.

I should like to thank the contributors for the time, effort and experience which they have invested in this book. My thanks are due also to many friends and colleagues for their support and assistance. In particular, I should like to thank Betty Fairley for her patience and help in the preparation of the manuscripts. Finally, I should like to acknowledge the tacit but significant support provided by Marian, David and Catherine.

John Gilliland

Part 1

Realities of reading

1 Improving classroom practice and research in reading

John Gilliland

One currently held notion is that we all construct our own realities. For example, a class teacher organizing and analysing his or her experience comes to a conclusion as to what classrooms are *really* like, and what children are *really* like. Similarly, research workers and theorists come to conclusions as to what classrooms are *really* like, what children are *really* like. All too often the realities do not appear to coincide and many teachers feel frustrated, even annoyed, at the apparent irrelevance of research findings. Also researchers feel frustrated, even annoyed, at the reluctance of teachers to find practical applications for their research findings.

The two realities of concern at this conference are exemplified in the mentality and behaviour of Cervantes' Don Quixote and Sancho Panza. The learned man of ideals and the down-to-earth practical man show contrasting techniques for defining and dealing with problems and deciding upon actions. Although stereotypes, these two characters do provide us with a means of examining the value of 'theoretical scientific knowledge' and 'commonsense practical knowledge'. We tend to be struck by the contrast between the points of view and behaviour stemming from these types of knowledge (Olson 1975). We are dealing with different 'minds' and any attempt to understand these minds within the sphere of classroom practice and teaching reading is likely to be complex and difficult. We can all probably recall occasions in which researchers and teachers seemed to be not only speaking different languages but wandering around different universes! Although Don Quixote and Sancho Panza viewed their experiences differently, each drew from the other's thinking and contributed to the other's welfare, even survival. In the same way, this conference brings together theoretically orientated and practically orientated people whose mutual cooperation is so necessary to any significant improvements in classroom practice, and whose minds may not be so at variance as we at first imagine.

Three aspects of theoretical scientific research seem to hamper communication between teachers and researchers. Researchers attach importance to their methods, that is hypothesizing, fact finding and generalizing. From our appreciation of the enormous strides in understanding made by researchers in the natural sciences, we see normal science as the solution of puzzles based upon some acknowledged past achievements and some general theoretical viewpoints. Such researchers are proceeding on the basis of calculated rather than haphazard guesses which are checked against the data. A process not dissimilar from that undertaken by thoughtful teachers dealing with children's learning difficulties? On the other hand, educational research and much research into reading has been regarded as superficial, or, in the eyes of some scientists, 'pre-pubertal'. It lacks the stable foundations of acknowledged theoretical and methodological paradigms necessary for qualification as *real* science. In attempting to render their work more scientifically respectable, researchers in education have utilized theories from, for example, psychology, sociology and analytical philosophy, or have attempted to establish an 'empirical truth capturing machine' which will collect sufficient observations so that generalizations will emerge. Either approach poses difficulties for the teacher wishing to improve his or her practice. In the first case, the necessity to be conversant with the theories of, say, Gestalt Psychology or Structural Functionalism is daunting – particularly at the end of a working day. In the second case, large amounts of description including descriptive statistics are daunting – particularly at the end of a working day! In such situations, our preconceptions about the value of research can easily become negative and antipathetic.

A second aspect of scientific research which affects the implementation of findings and generalizations, lies in the observation that major scientific changes are characterized not necessarily by novel experiments or findings but by major perceptual reorganization. A major change in thinking precedes major advances in knowledge. Also, such scientists as Galileo or Newton generated ideas, later upheld by experiment, which would be difficult to derive simply from observation. For example, the idea of a body continuing indefinitely at constant speed is only loosely related to common and frequent experiences of motion. In teaching reading the problems of reconciling knowledge based upon experience of the senses and knowledge derived from argument and reasoning based upon the use of logic stem from the fact that teachers do not stand in complete ignorance of the phenomena in which they and other researchers are interested. In fact, one of our most disabling sources of preconception comes from an over-familiarity with the phenomena which we are trying to explain and understand. These preconceptions stand in the way of our desire to probe beneath the surface of what we see. Unfortunately, when we do probe beneath the surface, we find researchers confusing. For example, Bennett (1976) found that while in general teachers using 'traditional' methods were more effective in teaching certain subjects, the most effective teacher used 'progressive' methods. How do we use such conclusions as a means of improving practice? Criticisms by researchers of such studies tend to refer to aspects of methodology or conceptual confusion. Some confusions and difficulties faced by researchers are the result of attempts to meet such criticisms, but the researcher may often be in a muddle because teachers put him there by asking him questions which he cannot answer. Scientific research will tend to be confused when the questions posed are confused. And we need perhaps to remind ourselves constantly that while researchers may help us to understand what we do and to understand what we *could* do, they will not tell us what we *should* do. From this we can see why so often practical problems and research methods pass one another by.

The third aspect of scientific research to be commented upon is terminology or use of words. Researchers seem to love long words – lots of them. Any definitions of long words usually seem to involve the use of even longer ones! That this may be a deterrent to many teachers is accepted, but also the need in research for careful categorization and description is recognized and with it the need for an appropriate vocabulary. Implications and meanings of words are important, both for researchers and teachers. If we consider the words *length*, *height*, *width* or *depth*, they can be seen as descriptive of the same *phenonemon* – the extension of space in one dimension. On the other hand, if we take a collection of words such as *reading disability*, *reading retardation*, *reading difficulty*, *reading impairment*, *arrest in reading*, *illiteracy*, *semi-literacy*, and *dyslexia*, we can appreciate that though they refer to the same *phenomenon*, the different words imply differences which may be difficult, even impossible, to grasp. However, when it comes to *doing something* teachers often feel that the differences do not *really* matter. Increasingly, teachers and researchers seek to use a common language but may seem to be separated by that same common language.

Just as the experience and reality of the scientific researcher pose difficulties for teachers, so the expectations of teachers may pose difficulties for researchers. Teachers seeking to improve their practice who expect researchers to give them clear evidence or conclusive proof about particular tactics or materials invite disappointment, which is regrettably often a prelude to dislike and rejection. Researchers seek to examine the effectiveness of teachers and materials by looking at classrooms objectively. Educational outcomes are related to the frequency of occurrence of a range of verbal and non-verbal behaviours. At worst, teachers come to be seen as 'expensive automatic material reward dispensers for use with children'! Nevertheless, such studies provide the basis for improvement and change since they enable teachers to 'see' their actions more clearly, and to match the reported behaviour against what they believe they do. However, there is a suspicion in the minds of many of us that to view children objectively implies that they will be treated as *objects*. While some teachers are happy to do this and improve standards in the process, others wish to treat children as *subjects*. They concern themselves with the human qualities of the children rather than mere behaviour. They exemplify a view that children become *readers* by being recognized and valued as *readers*. Here we are dealing with the 'reality' of reading and that reality causes teachers concern. To some children the reality of reading may be pronouncing isolated words correctly, to others reading all the words on every page, to others reading ten pages a day or answering thirty questions after a 'read'. The speed with which most children learn what is expected of them is easy to see, and much research on expectations and self-fulfilling prophecies is available. Teachers appreciate the importance of developing a concept of what being a reader can involve and to evoke appropriate attitudes and expectations as well as ensuring that certain reading behaviours are acquired. Of the various theories and explanations relevant to this aspect of the reality of reading, the views of Kelly have been found useful.

Kelly (1955) argues that we are *all* scientists – researchers who attempt to predict or construe events in the light of analysis of previous experience. Perhaps he offers a means by which the realities of researchers and teachers may be more clearly understood and communication improved. Kelly applied his ideas to clinical settings, but they may be of value to researchers and teachers alike. If researchers are to be helpful, it seems they must:

  define clients' (teachers') problems in usable terms
  reveal pathways or channels along which the client is free to move
  furnish hypotheses which may subsequently be tested and put to use
  reveal those resources of the client which might otherwise be overlooked by the clinician
  reveal those problems of the client which might otherwise be overlooked by the therapist.

Taking Kelly's view of man requires that we see research not as something closed and conclusive, but as something tentative and open-ended. I argue that such a view can, in fact, offer liberating and constructive means of analysing and improving classroom practice. In the same way the conference programme should be seen as a vehicle for promoting enquiry and speculation and an increased awareness rather than a vehicle for sets of conclusions to be absorbed and implemented.

The problems and difficulties discussed here all stem basically from the value which we place upon theoretical scientific knowledge or practically based knowledge. They come to be regarded as forms of authority to which we turn. The improvement of classroom practice and research is influenced by the regard which we have for authority, be it in the form of intuition, formal logic, scientific research or expert opinion. Each of these forms of authority is used as a basis for tackling problems in teaching reading and each falls into disrepute and is rejected from time to time. Increasingly, the roles of teacher and researcher are becoming fused rather than confused. For example, many of the speakers at this conference who may now be viewed as researchers have a considerable amount of teaching experience to utilize in their work and many of us in fact come to think like researchers as a result of our teaching experiences. The potential benefits of reading research and undertaking research in the classroom are recognized by more and more teachers willing to admit the limitations of the forms of authority referred to. It is encouraging to find that research work is taken more and more seriously by teachers and the shop-floor problems of teachers are becoming the starting point of promising pieces of research. A positive, if cautious, view of research is replacing inertia, indifference and ignorance as an increasing proportion of teachers of reading become reading teachers.

In conclusion, it appears that the differences between researchers and teachers are often unnecessarily exaggerated and that there are similarities which may be exploited. Whatever preconceptions each may bring to the phenomena which they are seeking to understand and control, there is agreement that the phenomena are complex. The children, teachers, and situations are all complex. As researchers and teachers together analyse and appreciate this complexity, so simplistic but convenient and attractive practices will be abandoned. In their place I hope that improved research and improved classroom practice will bring to adults and children alike a quality of experience and discoveries in reading to which we obviously think they are entitled.

References
BENNETT, N. (1976) *Teaching Styles and Pupil Progress* Open Books
KELLY, G. A. (1955) *The Psychology of Personal Constructs* New York: Norton
OLSON, D. R. (1975) The language of experience: on natural language and formal education *Bulletin of the British Psychological Society* 28, 363–73

2 Mother tongue and father tongue

Joyce M. Morris

Great writers tend to be avid readers, acute observers and astute thinkers. In consequence, their views on reading are generally very illuminating, whether considered simply as reflections of a particular life and times or as insights into truths of universal validity. Moreover, as masters of written language, they provide us with a rich source of inspiration in a wide variety of linguistic styles.

My title, *Mother tongue and father tongue*, epitomizes the differences as well as the relationships between spoken and written language which must be fully appreciated by all concerned with the cause of literacy. It is taken from Henry Thoreau's discourse on 'Reading' in his book *Walden*, first published in 1854, and now widely acclaimed as a masterpiece of American literature. I recommend to you the whole of his discourse because, among other things, it is pertinent to current controversies about definitions of illiteracy, the relevance of classical literature in the school curriculum, and so on. Meanwhile, in the space available, the following extract will have to suffice as a literary introduction to a number of critical issues.

Thoreau was concerned about the illiteracy of adults who have learned to read only what he considered appropriate for 'children and feeble intellects'. He deplored the ignorance and stagnation which comes from neglecting works of genius in the 'select language of literature'. Hence, he wrote:

> To read well, that is to read true books in a true spirit, is a noble exercise, and one that will task the reader more than any exercise which the customs of the day esteem. It requires a training such as the athletes underwent, the steady intention almost of the whole life to this object. Books must be read as deliberately and reservedly as they were written. It is not enough even to be able to speak the language of that nation by which they are written, for there is a memorable interval between the spoken and the written language, the language heard and the language read. The one is commonly transitory, a sound, a tongue, a dialect merely, almost brutish, and we learn it unconsciously, like the brutes, of our mothers. The other is the maturity and experience of that; if that is our mother tongue, this is our father tongue . . .

As will be seen, it is reasonable to suppose that, had Thoreau been alive today, he would have applauded the emphasis placed by the Bullock Report (DES 1975) on reading as a developmental process requiring, for its mature application, a life-time of training and constant use. At the same time, his views on how worthwhile books must be read suggest that he would have rejected, or at least had serious reservations about, Goodman's (1970) theoretical model of reading as a 'psycholinguistic guessing game' (a notion to which I will return). Most certainly, Thoreau would have been astonished, if not as disturbed as I am, by recent professional literature which focuses attention on relationships between spoken and written language whilst playing down, dismissing, or even totally ignoring significant differences not only between the two media of communication but between varieties of each: in other words, publications which fail to highlight differences which have important implications for classroom practice, preschool provision, and published materials for learning and teaching reading.

Of course, as a literary masterpiece, *Walden* exemplifies some of the fundamental differences between 'mother tongue' and 'father tongue' to which the author explicitly drew attention. Likewise, by reading this paper instead of talking freely, I am illustrating some of these differences; but, obviously, far from enough to achieve my principal aim of alerting teachers (with neither time nor energy for broadly-based, intensive study) to the dangers of ignoring these differences, and of following 'trendy' advice about the relative unimportance of training children to be 'accurate' readers.

Accordingly, still using Thoreau's analogue of family relations, my plan is to present salient points about language and reading under four main headings, namely, 'Mother tongue', 'Father tongue', 'Parental discord' and 'Parental harmony'. Other points to consider will then be summarized under 'Practical implications'.

Mother tongue
Since the early 1960s, there has been a marked increase in the amount of linguistic, psychological and neurophysiological research devoted to specific aspects of children's acquisition of their mother tongue. As in the case of the now voluminous reading research, much of it is fragmentary, poorly designed and inconclusive. Nevertheless, whilst revealing how much we still need to know (and could know with a greater coordination of rigorous, professional effort), the conflicting evidence gathered so far in support of various hypotheses provides interesting food for thought.

1 How acquired
Thus, if we start by considering *how* children acquire their mother tongue because we want to know how parents and teachers might best

encourage this acquisition, we are immediately faced with strongly-opposed theories such as those of the behaviourist psychologist Skinner (1957) and the linguist Noam Chomsky (1965). On the one hand, we have a modern *empiricist* approach to language which lends support to conditioning or programming techniques like those applied by Bereiter and Engelmann (1966) in their efforts to improve the oracy of disadvantaged children. On the other hand, we have Chomsky's *rationalist* approach which claims that human beings have innate mental structures specific to language and, hence, children acquire their mother tongue largely as a result of hidden processes of the mind rather than experience and environmental factors.

Evidence cited for this claim includes the fact that young children are able to produce well-formed sentences they cannot possibly have heard before, and words such as 'growed' which, though incorrect, nevertheless conform to the inflection rules of English. In other words, they acquire the 'creative' use of their language rapidly, with only a small amount of data and without explicit instruction. Accordingly, although Chomsky's theories have few direct educational implications, it is argued by some authorities that teachers are, to say the least, 'misguided' if they relegate pupils to a passive role and try to improve their oral language facility by tightly-controlled instructional techniques.

2 What is acquired

Be that as it may, when we consider precisely *what* is acquired, there is reliable evidence that normal-hearing children have developed the complete, adult, phonemic system of their language by the age of five or thereabouts (Fry 1968). Whereas, with regard to the acquisition of syntax, there is now a growing body of conflicting evidence from dialect studies and as a result of recent research not confined, as before, mainly to studying preschool children. For example, Carol Chomsky (1969) states, 'Contrary to the commonly held view that a child has mastered the structures of his native language by the time he reaches the age of six, we find that active syntactic acquisition is taking place up to the age of nine and perhaps even beyond.'

3 Theories of syntactic acquisition

This is probably closer to what primary-school teachers would conclude from their own subjective experience of children talking. Even so, it must be remembered that modern linguistic studies and theories of syntactic acquisition yield a somewhat biased picture of language. As Olsen (1975) points out, they claim to be describing a mother tongue, 'ordinary' or 'natural' language, yet, in actual fact, their descriptions are often those of logical written prose; that is, the language of a literate culture spoken spontaneously by nobody. This is certainly true of studies such as Carol Chomsky's which set out to test

16

children's interpretations of selected syntactic structures. According to Olson's reasoning, there is also a good case for stating that the formal syntactic theory of Noam Chomsky is 'valid only for the analysis of logical prose. But it is not a model of a mother tongue.'

Admittedly, Chomsky (1971) draws attention to the fact that 'Normal speech consists in large part of fragments, false starts, blends, and other distortions of the underlying idealized forms.' Other scholars too have highlighted the 'mazes' characteristic of spoken language; that is, the many hesitations, false starts and meaningless repetitions which Loban (1963) describes as resembling:

> the physical behaviour of a person looking for a way out of an actual spatial maze. He thrashes about in one direction or another until, finally, he either abandons his goal or locates a path leading where he wishes to go. Sometimes he stumbles upon a way out; sometimes he has the presence of mind enough to pause and reason a way out.

4 'Natural' language

Teachers are well aware of these 'mazes' in children's speech and, indeed, in their own oral expression. They are also aware of the wide varieties of language spoken by their pupils; for instance, the many dialects of English which operate at the levels of phonology, lexis, grammar and semantics. The distinctive styles of speaking are closely related to personality which, for the purposes of studying children's language, Loban analysed into eleven outstanding features, each scaled on a continuum from 'fluent to halting, deliberate to impulsive', and so on. There are also other differences which reflect influences such as the specialized languages of parental occupations and hobbies as well as those of peer groups recorded, for example, in *The Lore and Language of Schoolchildren* by Iona and Peter Opie (1959).

In short, today's teachers realize that each child develops a language very much like that of the people in his community, yet somehow uniquely his own. So why, to my knowledge, are some of our most experienced teachers falling into the trap of current popular mythology about a single entity called 'natural' language, which could and should be the language used in published schemes for beginning readers? Why don't they challenge those who write simplistically about 'natural' language to explain 'whose natural language' they are discussing?

Father tongue

I could offer an explanation for this disturbing phenomenon, but it is perhaps best to turn now to the characteristics of written language which, in Thoreau's words, constitute our 'father tongue'. Clearly, in the space available, it is impossible even to mention all of them and, in any case, some are very obvious – such as the *logical* structure of written discourse marked by such words as 'therefore' and 'nevertheless'.

1 Types of written material

Of course, all teachers of reading, however immature their pupils, should bear in mind the goal of mature, effective reading and, hence, the wide variety of written material their charges will be expected to read or, simply, may wish to read at later stages in their lives. Accordingly, I draw attention to the categories of written material distinguished in the ongoing, large-scale, 'Survey of English Usage', conducted at University College, London.

Quirk (1974) informs us that he and his colleagues have recognized three major classes of material for reading, each with several subclasses. The most important class is printed material which is divided into 'learned writing (subdivided between artistic and physical studies), instructional writing (that is, popular arts – the 'how to do it' books), general non-fiction (such as biography, travel), printed news, administrative and official language, statutory language, persuasive writing (as in essays and sermons, for example), and finally prose fiction'. The second major class is 'manuscript and typewritten material, with chief subdivisions into letters, continuous composition and private journals (including those written for ultimate publication)'. Finally, there is 'the class of material which takes shape originally in the written medium, but which is written in order to be heard – drama especially, of course, but also radio talks and news'.

Even this summary of types of material for reading indicates the enormity of the task facing schools if children are to master all the skills necessary to cope with written material in the curriculum and, later, in the world at large. Of course, it might be argued that, in our society, only a tiny minority are ever called upon to read radio news and sermons. But think of the huge army of clerical workers who have to cope daily with letters, manuscripts and typescripts, not forgetting the millions of tax-payers and car-drivers etc., who must read and respond to the official language of government! Furthermore, although reading prose fiction, newspapers and do-it-yourself books etc., is not absolutely essential, children who live in a literate society should be given the best possible opportunities to develop the reading skills necessary to keep their options open. As adults, they may elect to read material fit only for 'children and feeble intellects', but it should be a matter of choice, not of necessity.

2 Styles of written language

All this means that teachers must know a great deal about the many styles of written language with their different modes of expression, thought and, of course, specialized vocabularies. In the words of Harry

Lee Smith (1966), they must understand 'the various levels of style in the written language, all the way from a note to the milkman to a sonnet by Milton'. Most importantly, they must also be fully alert to the problems of pupils who, in the course of a school day, have to switch from language style to language style; a constantly demanding activity particularly in these days of integrated studies. Here, naturally, difficulties loom especially large for children trained to regard reading as a 'psycholinguistic guessing game' and, in later life, they can become crippling handicaps. For instance, accuracy in word recognition is absolutely essential in the low-redundancy texts of mathematics and science. Likewise it is vital in reading directives. (We all know what can happen to a motorist who reads 'slow' for 'stop'.)

Young children also have to cope with the problem of adapting to different styles of their father tongue long before they can read themselves. Consider, for example, how they must try to understand the archaic language of nursery rhymes, fairy stories and fables preceded or followed by children's modern fiction which, though deceptively simple, draws on the full resources of our language.

Parental discord
This brings me back to the differences or 'parental discord' between mother tongue and father tongue which are the root cause of many problems in teaching beginners to read.

Nowadays, parents and teachers are exhorted to foster children's oracy as a prelude to literacy. At the same time, they should be encouraged to value oral language ability for its own sake, because it does not necessarily guarantee even a successful start with learning to read and write.

1 Reasons for discord
There are many possible reasons for this within the learning task itself. In the first place, children must learn a new role as readers and writers. They must learn new cues for a 'silent' printed language which differs from their own idiolect and neighbourhood dialect, and involves the mastery of new conventions and some new grammar. At least in the initial stages of learning to read, children must accept that the language of basal texts is less advanced than their spoken language, and yet is more rigidly structured. They have also to accept that written language breaks the tie of context and expectancies in a profoundly significant way. Furthermore, young learners must realize that, although what they say in casual conversation can be recorded in writing, replicas of their language are not to be found in published books, because it is 'believed' not 'actual' usage which authors put on paper to represent spoken English. Perhaps this is as well, for, after struggling to read a printed page, beginners have the right to expect something more interesting than what they normally hear and say themselves; a right,

alas, which the bland banalities of most basal reading schemes fail to recognize!

2   Research findings

In 1962, Strickland reported her study of the language of elementary school children and its relationship to the language of books used for teaching them to read. She concluded that evidence was needed as to 'whether children would be aided or *hindered* (my italics) by the use of sentences in their books more like the sentences they use in their speech'. As yet, such evidence is not available, although attempts have been made to produce basal readers of the kind she had in mind and which, obviously, could be used to test her hypotheses, for example the early books in *Link-Up* (Reid and Low 1972).

From this it follows that there is no real justification from research for the Bullock Report to conclude that 'Unless there is a close match between the syntactic features of the text and the syntactic expectancies of the reader there will be a brake on the development of word identification.' In any case, as Crystal (1975) points out: 'How *does* one make a 'close match' between two phenomena whose differences are fundamental?'

The relationship between facility in oral expression and reading achievement, likewise, has not been clearly demonstrated, partly because investigations such as that reported by Loban in 1963 have since been few and far between. Most American studies in this area have concentrated on the possible *interference* of non-standard English speech, especially that of black children. However, as Miller (1973) points out: 'The matter of dialect interference with reading is a complicated one, complicated primarily by the fact that children – particularly older children – are capable of code switching; thus they cannot be said to be monodialectal speakers.' This also applies to the social class codes highlighted by Bernstein (1971).

Pending further research, experts remain divided on the issue of dialect and class code interference in reading. Understandably, they also remain divided about the use of dialect and context-tied resource material for beginning reading. At the same time, there is general agreement among research workers about the need to improve teacher-training and preschool provision, so that by the time nonstandard speakers start school they will be better prepared to learn to read, and will also enter a learning situation where the most important variable – the teacher – is well equipped and keen to teach.

Parental harmony

A vital task for teachers is to help beginning readers to build a bridge between speech and print. As already indicated, they can only do this successfully by understanding fully the respective natures of our mother tongue and father tongue, and the fundamental differences between them. They must also appreciate the degree to which 'parental harmony' exists, and use it to help pupils build up confidence in their approach to print which, at first sight, may seem to them 'a meaningless jumble of black squiggles'.

Because the English writing system is alphabetic, there is a direct relationship between written and spoken language. This is not a single small set of letter-to-sound correspondences (as traditional 'phonic' approaches assume), but relationships between patterns of letters and sounds. Accordingly, once one recognizes that vowel and consonant *letters* are not synonymous with vowel and consonant *sounds,* one is well on the way to realizing that English orthography is not hopelessly chaotic, as Bernard Shaw and other spelling reformers would have us believe.

It is also important to recognize that, to some extent, the three distinct aspects of intonation which convey meaning in speech, i.e. stress, pitch, and what can be called the 'chunking' of utterances, are represented in writing by punctuation and capital letters. Furthermore, the main rules of syntax apply both in speech and print with only a few exceptions (notably poetry) which allow the rearrangement of normal word order and usage. Similarly, combinations of words known as 'collocations' occur in both media.

Practical implications

What then are the practical implications of all this? Briefly, the differences between oral and written language are such that, in general, children will not learn to read effectively or make good use of their reading ability at all stages unless they are highly motivated to do so initially, and throughout their school course. Ideally, responsibility for motivating them should be shared by home and school but, realistically, it is the teaching profession which must bear the ultimate responsibility.

A small minority of exceptional children, such as those involved in Clark's (1976) study, start school already aware of the basic purposes of reading, and their early success and pleasure create an appetite for more. However, the vast majority need expert teachers to lead them to this awareness initially through the use of language-experience approaches to literacy, but, more important, through frequent exposure to literature which introduces them to the rich possibilities of their language beyond the utilitarian purposes of the language heard in everyday communication.

Children who have achieved some competence in reading their own recorded utterances, and have a feel for the peculiarities of literary language, can begin to read it with a reasonable chance of success *if* they have also been taught to recognize spelling patterns and to use context cues as aids to word recognition, not forgetting punctuation and capitalization as clues to intonation and, hence, to meaning. In other words, children can make a successful start if their teachers have made the most of the relationships between oral and written language, whilst drawing attention to important differences where appropriate.

Bearing in mind the wide variety of written language, considerable preparatory work is also necessary if pupils are to cope successfully with the unusual language cues of textbooks, and the distinctive writing styles of reference books. In short, it is vitally important that teachers help children to develop independence in using appropriate reading strategies and techniques with different types of written material for different purposes.

Meanwhile, as previously indicated, all teachers should beware of current mythology about a single entity called 'natural' language, and should be sure to ask, 'Whose natural language?' They need also to study the reasons behind the current heated controversy about whether reading should be taught as a single, 'holistic' process, or as a complex process involving the mastery of a hierarchy of interrelated skills. For, if either theory is followed exclusively, it has very different implications for classroom practice and for the development of children as readers.

At present, it is the development of children as talkers which is receiving the lion's share of research grants and teachers' attention. This is all very well provided that attention is not too long deflected from the more difficult task of ensuring that children become literate.

For me and, I suspect, for most of you, it is literacy that is the main concern. As I recall, it was likewise for Thoreau who said:

> the noblest written words are commonly as far behind or above the fleeting spoken language as the firmament with its stars is behind the clouds. *There* are the stars and they who can may read them.

Let us, therefore, be inspired by his words. Let us recognize fully the discord as well as the harmony between our mother tongue and father tongue. Let us reach for the stars, and make it possible for many more of our fellow human beings to join us in reading them.

References

BEREITER, C. and ENGELMANN, S. (1966). *Teaching Disadvantaged Children in the Preschool* Englewood Cliffs, New Jersey: Prentice Hall

BERNSTEIN, B. (1971) *Class Codes and Control* Routledge and Kegan Paul

CHOMSKY, C. (1969) *The Acquisition of Syntax in Children from 5–10* Cambridge, Mass: MIT Press

CHOMSKY, N. (1965) *Aspects of the Theory of Syntax* Cambridge, Mass: MIT Press

CHOMSKY, N. (1971) 'Language and the mind' in A. B. Adon and W. F. Leopold (eds) *Child Language* Englewood Cliffs, New Jersey: Prentice Hall

CLARK, M. M. (1976) *Young Fluent Readers* Heinemann Educational

CRYSTAL, D. (1975) Linguistic perspectives *Reading* 9, 2, 37–49

DES (1975) *A Language for Life* (Bullock Report) HMSO

FRY, D. B. (1968) The phonemic system in children's speech *British Journal of Disorders of Communication* 3, 1, 13–19

GOODMAN, K. S. (1970) 'Reading: A psycholinguistic guessing game' in H. Singer and R. B. Ruddell, (eds) *Theoretical Models and Processes of Reading* Newark, Delaware: International Reading Association

LOBAN, W. D. (1963) *The Language of Elementary School Children* Champaign, Illinois: National Council of Teachers of English

MILLER, G. A. (1973) *Linguistic Communication: Perspectives for Research* Newark, Delaware: International Reading Association

OLSON, D. R. (1975) The language of experience: on natural language and formal education *Bulletin of the British Psychological Society* 28, 363–73

OPIE I. and OPIE, P. (1959) *The Lore and Language of Schoolchildren* Oxford University Press

QUIRK, R. (1974) *The Linguist and the English Language* Edward Arnold

REID, J. F. and LOW, J. (1972) *Link-Up* Holmes McDougall

SKINNER, B. G. (1957) *Verbal Behaviour* New York: Appleton-Century-Crofts

SMITH, H. L. (1966) *Linguistic Science and the Teaching of English* Cambridge, Mass: Harvard University Press

STRICKLAND, R. G. (1962) The language of elementary school children: its relationship to the language of reading textbooks and the quality of reading of selected children. Indiana University: *Bulletin of the School of Education* 38, 4

THOREAU, H. (1968) *Walden* Prentice-Hall

3   A question of standards

John E. Merritt

This paper is concerned with identifying myth and reality in assessing reading performance, and with the development of a more realistic approach towards monitoring. It will be argued first that current ideas about tests and test scores need radical revision and that schools should in any case develop their own assessment instruments. Next it will be argued that the purposes of monitoring should be more clearly defined and that the results should always be seen as part of an evaluation and development process.

Any assessment of performance presupposes the existence of valid tests. In the case of reading, a valid test is not one which simply measures word recognition, or the ability to underline the correct answer in a multiple choice test. It is one which measures functional literacy; that is to say, the ability to achieve a satisfactory reading outcome in the range of reading situations which adults actually encounter. Current tests of reading are therefore deficient in two ways:

1   *Current tests do not cover the complex range of skills involved in functional literacy*
In everyday encounters with printed media we skim for general impressions, scan for specific items of information, and read intensively to satisfy our own particular purposes.

Our current tests provide a very limited measure of these abilities. They relate to functional literacy in much the same way as tests of trapping a ball, or of shooting at an empty goal, relate to the competence of a professional footballer. Competence in a limited array of isolated skills is no guarantee of competence in using skills in real-life situations.

2   *Test scores do not tell us anything about functional literacy*
Even if average scores in national surveys had risen steadily for the last ten years it could still be the case that large numbers of people were not functionally literate. It would still be necessary in this case to devote additional resources to reading development. Conversely, a levelling-off of scores, or even a slight decline, would be perfectly acceptable if standards were already well ahead of the minimal requirements for functional literacy. In this case, scarce

resources could more profitably be devoted to other aspects of education. We must therefore shift our attention from statistical averages to more appropriate criteria.

There is an ever increasing amount of empirical evidence which demonstrates the practical significance of the above observations.

First, the application of a readability formula to everyday reading material shows that a reading age of 14.0 to 18.0 is commonly required. This suggests, as the Bullock Report (DES 1975) pointed out, that '. . . standards need to be raised to fulfil the demands that are being made upon them' (*para. 1.3*).

Next, there is the kind of evidence reported by Bormuth (1973–4) following a study of reading standards in a middle-class residential suburb in the United States. Here, one third of the eighteen year olds tested achieved scores indicating that they could 'gain little or no information' from newspaper articles on which they were tested. This provides more direct corroboration of the conclusions drawn from the readability studies cited above, for there is little doubt that broadly similar results would be obtained if this kind of assessment were to be replicated in this country.

Table 1
(From PE231 Reading Development, Units 5 and 6)

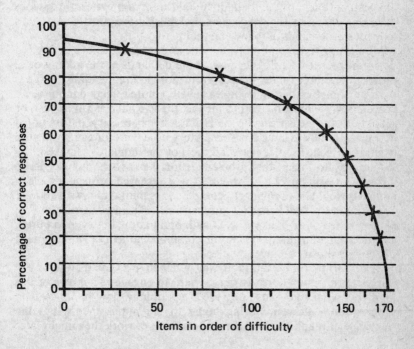

25

Additional evidence comes from a study reported by Murphy (1973). In this research, the daily reading diet of a large sample was surveyed; tests were then constructed to reflect the different types of material read and the kind of reading that was normally involved. The following table shows the proportion of errors made on the various items by the experimental sample.

This is not too alarming – until we recognize that each mistake could represent, for example, a missed bus, a course unnecessarily taken (in the case of an Open University student), a badly assembled bit of equipment; or, in a recently reported tragic case, millions of people poisoned. (*The Observer,* 5 December, 1976, reported that 'Nine million residents of Michigan may be harbouring a deadly chemical in their bodies for which there is no known antidote. This was due to a mistake by an illiterate lorry driver who mistook "Neutromaster" for "Firemaster". A chemical used as a fire retardant was consequently used in animal feed.')

Little wonder, therefore, that employers and politicians complain about standards of reading. Their only mistake is to assume that the situation was ever any better.

The comments of employers on current standards reported in the Newbolt Report in 1921 could equally well have been included in the Bullock Report of 1975 – and were in fact cited to make this very point. It is this serious lack of perspective that leads some educationists to advocate a return to the inadequate educational practice of previous decades rather than the development of much more effective practices to meet the demands of today and tomorrow.

Monitoring techniques must provide an appropriate perspective. To do so they must take full account of the demands of the adult world, rather than simply reflect the currently more limited reading demands of the school. Further, in trying to develop more effective monitoring procedures, we must face up to the fact that we have as yet no test, or set of tests, for measuring the kinds of reading necessary for functional literacy. Nor do we have any satisfactory base lines for estimating the extent to which school leavers fall short of the standards required.

One way to tackle this problem is for the schools themselves to include assessment of performance as a research project for older pupils. It would be particularly suitable for pupils taking CSE, Mode 3.

The first task would be to identify the kinds of printed media they are likely to encounter. This will vary with occupation, but even in purely vocational reading there are certain common features as Table 2 (page 27) clearly shows.

The information for this table was obtained in a Canadian survey of thirty-seven occupations. If pupils were to engage in surveys of this kind this would not only provide a continuing flow of up-to-date information – it would bring home to the pupils themselves the relevance of reading competence to the kind of work they might later

Table 2
('Taken from Smith, A. DeW. (1974) 'Reading Skills – What Reading Skills?' in J. E. Merritt (ed) *New Horizons in Reading* Proceedings of the Fifth IRA World Congress on Reading, Vienna, Austria)

Roman numerals	Books, manuals	Charts, tables	Notes, letters, memos	Forms	Selected communications skills * — skill required o — skill optional
*	*	*	*	*	Policeman
*	*	*	*	*	Draftsman
*	*	*	*	*	Insurance salesman
o	*	*	*	*	Farmer
*	*	*	*	*	Packaging machine mech.
*	*	*	*	*	Sheet metal worker
	*	*	*	*	Radio and TV serviceman
*	*	*	*	*	Lineman
*	*	*	*	*	Sales representative
o	*	*	*	*	Electrician
o	*	*	*	*	Motor vehicle mech.
*	*	*	*	*	Hardware sales person
*	*	*	*	*	Nursing assistant
	*	*	*	*	Small engine mech.
	*	o	*	*	Cook
*	*	*	*	*	Accountant clerk
	*	*	*	*	Sales clerk
o	*	o	*	*	Painter
*	*		*	*	Nurse aide
	*	*	*	*	Bookkeeping clerk
	*	*	*	*	Bookkeeping, clerical
	*	o	*	*	Truck driver
	*	*	*	*	Carpenter
o	*	*	*	*	Machinist
	*		*	*	Taxi driver
*	*	*	*	*	Metal assembler
o	*	o	*	*	Secretary
	*		*	*	Janitor
	*		*	*	Receiving clerk
	*		*	*	Construction labourer
	*	*	*	*	Cashier
o	*	*	*	*	Clerk typist
o	*	o	*	*	Welder
	*			*	Driver salesman
	*			*	Storeman
	*			*	Heavy equip. operator
	*			*	Waiter, formal service

27

wish to undertake.

A survey limited solely to reading in occupational roles would, of course, provide an unduly narrow focus. A similar survey needs to be carried out for various other roles – home and family roles, more general social roles, consumer roles, and leisure roles (the latter term needs to be broadly interpreted and would include, for example, personal reading and continuing education as well as hobbies, sports, holiday travel, etc.).

Next, there is no reason why pupils should not construct realistic tests of functional literacy. They can learn, for example, that the way to test the ability to read a timetable is to set a question such as, 'What is the time of the first through train to X after 11 am on Friday?' or, 'Can you get a meal on the 10.20 am train to Y?' Indeed, they are perhaps more likely to set realistic questions than the teacher, who might prefer to ask, 'What is the conventional sign for "Saturdays only", or "restaurant car"?'

With such tests, norms are irrelevant so there is no standardization problem. Pupils must achieve 100 per cent correct solutions. The only problem is to cover a sufficiently wide array of reading tasks, and here, schools could well combine their efforts to produce a common pool.

This still leaves open the question of testing younger pupils. Here, too, the older pupils could help, for by constructing tests for younger pupils they would automatically develop their own reading skills in that area.

At this stage it would be helpful, perhaps, to recall the main reasons for monitoring, whether at national, local, or school level. These may be broadly summarized as follows:

1 to find out whether or not the general level of achievement is acceptable so that time and resources can be allocated accordingly
2 to find out where standards are high, and where they are low, so that available resources can be directed to where the need is greatest
3 to find out which methods of using resources are most beneficial.

With tests of the kind discussed above the school has a more realistic basis for deciding on the resources that need to be allocated to reading development. It is also possible to see which classes, or which teachers, need most help. The same information can also be used in deciding which aspects of the reading curriculum most need attention, and follow-up tests of the same kind can be used to decide whether the form of help given was effective.

A checklist covering all the different kinds of reading to be examined can then provide a means for monitoring what is included in the reading curriculum, and for ensuring that there are no significant omissions over a period of time.

All of this information should, of course, be made available to all members of staff who can then participate in diagnosing the needs of the school. By sharing their ideas they can develop a more effective reading curriculum.

Monitoring reading progress can thus be seen not as a bureaucratic imposition – but as an essential aspect of a continuous evaluation and development cycle.

References

BOARD OF EDUCATION (1921) *The Teaching of English in England* (Newbolt Committee Report) HMSO

BORMUTH, J. R. (1973-4) Reading literacy: its definition and assessment *Reading Research Quarterly* 9, 1, 7-66

DES (1975) *A Language for Life* (Bullock Report) HMSO

MURPHY, R. T. (1973) *Adult functional reading study. Project 1: Targeted research and development reading program objective, sub-parts 1, 2 and 3. Final report.* Project No. 0-9004. Grant No. OEC-0-70-4791 (508). Princeton, New Jersey: Educational Testing Service

OPEN UNIVERSITY (1977) *PE231 Reading Development, Units 5 and 6, Higher Order Skills* Open University Press

SMITH, A.De.W. (1974) 'Reading skills–what reading skills?' in J. E. Merritt, (ed) *New Horizons in Reading* Proceedings of the Fifth IRA World Congress on Reading, Vienna. Newark, Delaware: International Reading Association

4 Teachers' perceptions of children's performance: problems of research and implications

Alan Cohen

The research area to do with teacher perceptions, teacher expectations and their effects on children's performance in schools has received a great deal of attention from investigators in America (for example, see Brophy and Good 1974). Increasingly in this country educational researchers are directing their activities towards the classroom itself and the interactions between teachers and taught in their attempts to answer, for example, the seemingly simple question, 'Do teachers' attitudes toward their pupils influence the children's performance in schools? – and if so, how? and why?'

This paper aims both to offer an overview of the research findings and also to attempt a critical appraisal of the state of the field, pointing to the urgent need for particular kinds of research which have yet to be done. The very magnitude of the topic as well as the abundant research evidence (particularly from America) impose some necessary limitations on the paper – hence the observations and remarks are largely confined to the primary age range. However, the use of the concept of children's performance will be seen to include all those attributes (both cognitive and affective) which have been found to influence teachers' perceptions of children and hence their patterns of interacting with them in the classroom. For example, the teacher's perceptions of a child might well be influenced by the child's social class background, or race, or sex, as well as by very many personal qualities the youngster may (or may not) possess, such as high intelligence or sociability or physical attractiveness.

In an earlier study, Jackson (1968) demonstrated that 'life in classrooms' is very different for different children; teachers interacting in widely differing ways with their pupils, and the pupils with their teachers. Praise, encouragement, affection, hostility, punishment and reward are *not* distributed evenly in any classroom, and evidence about the vastly uneven patterns of teacher-child contact in the classroom has been demonstrated over and over again both in American schools and in schools in this country (Jackson and Lahaderne 1967). In short, the teacher's perceptions of his pupils are influenced by a whole range of attributes which the teacher, rightly or wrongly, ascribes to his charges.

To illustrate how the social class background of children can influence teachers' perceptions and hence their expectations for their pupils, Rist (1970) demonstrated that on the sole basis of teachers' estimations of the socioeconomic background of kindergarten children, teachers separated the youngsters into three groups on their entry into school at the age of six years and began immediately to treat the groups very differently. 'Higher status' children were quickly identified as 'fast learners' whose teachers were very much concerned with 'instructing' them, as contrasted with 'low status' pupils, perceived as 'slow learners' whose teachers concerned themselves much more with 'controlling' and 'disciplining' their pupils. Furthermore, the initial groupings tended to remain fixed and rigid *regardless* of the actual performance of the children. In Great Britain, the researches of Douglas (1964), Morrison and McIntyre (1969), Goodacre (1967), Burstall (1968), Pidgeon (1970), Garner and Bing (1973) and Barker-Lunn (1970) (to quote only a few), largely confirm similar American findings – that in very many schools, the child's subsequent educational path is somewhat determined from his first entry into school on the basis of factors related to the socioeconomic status of his family but not necessarily to his ability or potential.

Similarly, the sex of the child (particularly at the primary-school stage) may have a considerable influence upon the teacher's perceptions of and expectations for the child. Barker-Lunn's research has shown that (at primary school) girls have a more favourable attitude to school than boys, that girls are more interested in school work than boys, that doing well at school is more important to girls than to boys, that girls have a more favourable attitude to their class than boys, that girls have a more favourable 'other image' of their class than boys ('other image' being a measure of what the child believes others think of his class), that girls are more conforming than boys, that girls perceive their teacher relationship as more positive than boys, and that girls are more anxious in the classroom situation than boys. It would seem to follow that teachers tend to perceive girls more favourably than boys and that in the classroom situation boys tend to receive more teacher disapproval and criticism than girls! In general, then, teachers tend to prefer conforming and acquiescent children and to reject the more active and assertive child. Whilst not pretending that the list is endless, we could add that intellectually bright children, high achievers, children whose personalities please teachers, children who are physically attractive, who write neatly and speak nicely, whose names are Jason, Jeremy, Amanda or Dawn, compared with their opposites, all tend to be the objects of higher teacher expectations, all tend to receive more frequent, more reinforcing and more appropriate interactions with their teachers: in short, that inequality is the rule rather than the exception for teacher-child relationships and interactions in the same classroom (Brophy and Good 1974).

The argument so far, then, is that expectations held by teachers affect their behaviour and patterned interactions with their pupils, which in turn influence and sometimes alter the children's behaviour. Expectations are simply the inferences that teachers make about the present and predicted future behaviours of their pupils and are most often based both on information gathered about the children (in the form of reports, reading ages, IQ scores, etc.) as well as assessments which teachers make concerning their experiences and contacts with the children in the classroom setting.

As Brophy and Good point out, teachers' expectations may be 'generalized' and apply to a whole class or group of children – for example when a teacher holds low generalized expectations for a group of children whom he perceives as 'slow learners' or for children from a particular social class background. Quite a lot of data from Barker-Lunn's research show clearly the effects of general teacher expectations on pupil attainment. Although Barker-Lunn found, for example, that the reading performance of children of lower social class origin fell off in relation to higher social class children she hypothesized that this effect was possibly related to the teachers' 'generalized' lower expectations for children from lower social class groups and not just to factors in the home environment (Morrison and McIntyre 1969). The teachers in this study consistently tended to *overestimate* the upper social group and to *underestimate* the lower social group. From the findings of this and many other studies (at secondary level as well as primary), it would seem a reasonable hypothesis that the *underestimation* of the abilities of lower working-class children (a 'general' expectation of some teachers) is influential in determining their decline in performance. Clearly not *all* teachers share these particular general expectations and it would be manifestly untrue to suggest that teachers' perceptions of their pupils, and hence their expectations for them, are invariably biased, prejudiced or illogical. Nevertheless, there is a wealth of research evidence to suggest that teachers, like any other group, *are* influenced by many of the factors mentioned above and *do* differ in the accuracy of their perceptions and expectations. It is true, therefore, that expectations based on perceptions which are inaccurate, biased and rigidly held *can* be instrumental in causing changes in children's performance since inaccurate expectations often tend to act as self-fulfilling prophecies. Thus, teachers who hold high expectations for the children whom they consider very bright tend to behave differently towards them, creating much more favourable learning conditions by acting more positively, praising and encouraging more frequently and generally expecting more from such children. Equally, however, Hargreaves (1967) demonstrates the opposite. When expectation acts as a self-fulfilling prophecy it functions as an *antecedent* of children's performance rather than as a *result* of observed children's performance. It is, by definition, an expectation based on inaccurate initial perceptions which initiates very different teacher treatment of the child, causing the original prediction to come true. There is abundant research evidence to suggest that in classrooms where inappropriately low expectations exist, children's interest in school work, their attitudes and self-confidence, their motivation and levels of aspiration are consistently diminished.

So far, a number of ideas to do with perceptions and expectations from the point of view of the teacher have been discussed. It would seem logical now to consider some of their concepts from the point of view of the child, since, clearly, the teacher is not the only source of expectations which influences the child's behaviour. There are also his classmates who convey to him in terms of group pressures, sanctions, status hierarchies, approvals, etc., *their* expectations. We are apt to forget, as teachers, that children in our classrooms, like us, are busily engaged in inducing behaviour on the part of others (the others being their peers) and their teacher! Furthermore, when engaged in this kind of activity they utilize, often very expertly, the same kinds of strategies that their teachers employ. Modelling one's behaviour on the teacher is an infinitely wide concept. Jackson (1968) uses the phrase 'crowds, praise and power' to indicate the shaping force of expectations which impinge on the child – the crowds of other children, the constant assessment and evaluation of the child's work and behaviour by the teacher and by peers which may produce praise or blame; and the power embodied in the teacher – the ultimate and final authority. In some classrooms for some children these sources of expectations 'create the anticipation that the child shall work, not at his own pace, but at that of the class; not for the satisfaction of having learned, but for the compliments of others; and not because he deems the activity worthwhile, but because an "authority" so deems' (Finn 1972). Here, it seems, we have, for at least some teachers, a 'common denominator' of expectations. To pursue this analogy of a common denominator of general teacher expectations Nash (1973) has observed, with penetrating insight, that in the same way that sociologists have shown that the staff of almost any institution (hospital, prison, asylum, etc.) evolve some kind of collective theory of human natures, teachers' perceptions of their pupils, distilled into general expectations, embody a common denominator of intuitive theory about the nature of the child. Nash writes that Erving Goffman, in his study of asylums, proposed a number of roles or attitudes which the inmate of a mental hospital could adopt. The inmate can take an 'intransigent line' and rebel against the authority around him; he can become 'colonized' and lead a stable and contented existence; he can become 'converted' and act out the role of the ideal patient; he can 'play it cool' which offers the maximum chance of getting out physically and psychologically undamaged; or he can pursue the line of 'situational withdrawal' and opt out of any significant interaction with the environment. Nash suggests that this is a very useful way of looking at the sorts of adjustments which children make to their institution – the school, and he argues that most children 'play it cool' – that is, they keep out of trouble, and while not volunteering for activities or taking a major part in things, they give the impression of having just enough involvement to avoid being seen as intransigent.

The picture which emerges, then, is that of the gradual building up of a very complex network of expectations to which the child is continuously exposed – a network which constitutes the child's educational environment and which is made up of all aspects of the milieu which set expectations for the individual's educational attainment – cognitive or otherwise. It follows, then, that to the extent that the child's own behaviour is a response to this network he is 'selecting, integrating and reacting to those aspects which are of particular significance to him' (Finn 1972, page 393). Thus, the expectations which significant others hold for the child are largely instrumental in the forming of his own self-expectancies (his self-concept), and it follows that the quality and quantity of the child's achievement experiences in school will come more and more to influence his expectations for future achievement.

The final section of this paper attempts a critical appraisal of the field of research and suggests some of the major implications.

It would be somewhat naive to imagine that because of the enormous output of educational research we are necessarily very much the wiser about what goes on in classrooms, or that we have at last produced a blueprint for teacher effectiveness. In fact the picture is rather the opposite. The more research we do, the more we are led to realize how little is known about the complex network of interactions which go on between teachers and children – and even less about the effects of such interactions. Very often, too, the results of much educational research have been found to offer little prescriptive, practical help to the teacher, because the 'findings' have been overgeneralized and thereby made largely inapplicable or even inappropriate to specific classroom situations for specific children. Indeed, it has been argued that many of the 'findings' of research have provided comfortable 'reasons' to explain failures, so that we are tempted to rationalize some children's lack of success and progress by turning to research findings on social class or restricted codes or personality defects, or better still, any seemingly immutable factor we can lay our hands on, rather than concentrating our attention on diagnosing the individual child's present learning problems and working out remedial programmes which are likely to help him. Generations of students have been turned out of the colleges impressed with the importance of catering for the individual differences in children, yet very little educational research to date has systematically focused on the individual child in the class situation. This, then, would seem to be an urgent and immediate priority for research, since most of the evidence we have, for example from classroom interaction analysis research, has concentrated either on the teacher, or upon teacher-class interaction patterns where the class is treated as an undifferentiated whole group – which effectively masks and obliterates the fact that the class is a group of individuals and that teachers interact (certainly at primary-school level) much more with individuals than with whole groups. We need to know a great deal more about the kinds of individual differences in teachers and those they teach which are responsible for the expectation effects already discussed. We need to know more about the personality profiles of teachers in order to study those who are more likely to allow expectation effects to influence their treatment of particular children. We need to know more about the particular personality profiles of children who are more likely to influence their teacher's perceptions and expectations. Finding answers to questions like these may be part of the way towards designing successful classroom environments for different children taught by teachers who have *appropriate* expectations for them.

References
BARKER-LUNN, J. (1970) *Streaming in the Primary School* NFER
BROPHY, J. E. and GOOD, T. L. (1974) *Teacher-Student Relationships: Causes and Consequences* Holt, Rinehart and Winston
BURSTALL, C. (1968) *French from Eight: a national experiment* NFER
DOUGLAS, J. W. B. (1964) *The Home and the School* MacGibbon and Kee
FINN, D. J. (1972) Expectations and the educational environment *Review of Educational Research* 42, 3, 387–410
GARNER, J. and BING, M. (1973) Inequalities of teacher-pupil contacts. *British Journal of Educational Psychology* 43, 3, 234–43
GOODACRE, E. (1967) *Teachers and their Pupils' Home Background* NFER
HARGREAVES, D. H. (1967) *Social Relationships in a Secondary School* Routledge and Kegan Paul
JACKSON, P. (1968) *Life in Classrooms* New York: Holt, Rinehart and Winston
JACKSON, P. and LAHADERNE, H. (1967) Inequalities of teacher-pupil contacts *Psychology in the Schools* 4, 204–211
MORRISON, A. and MCINTYRE, D. (1969) *Teachers and Teaching* Penguin
NASH, R. (1973) *Classrooms Observed: the teacher's perception and the pupil's performance* Routledge and Kegan Paul
PIDGEON, D. (1970) *Expectation and Pupil Performance* NFER

Rist, R. (1970) Student social class and teacher expectations: the self-fulfilling prophecy in ghetto education *Harvard Educational Review* 40, 411–51

5 The realities of remedial reading

Margaret M. Clark

Remedial and special education

To some, the term remedial education suggests a certain kind of teaching for children with difficulties; these may be of long-standing or of shorter duration and may be general or specific. Others see remedial education as a euphemism for the teaching of children of low ability and little promise of success – 'opportunity' and 'adjustment' classes for slow learners. It is perhaps pertinent to consider the extent to which remedial and special education differ. There is certainly overlap of the populations of slow-learners in receipt of remedial education and the mentally handicapped receiving special education. In a recently completed study of special education in Scotland, as in other studies elsewhere, it was found that approximately a third of those ascertained as mentally handicapped and in need of special education had an IQ of over 70; it is also true that many children with measured IQ below 70 are in ordinary schools, some well motivated and functioning adequately (Clark and MacKay 1976). Where the proportion of children segregated in special schools and units from an early age is high, this will influence the extent of need for assistance and the type of children requiring remedial help in the ordinary school. The present trend towards considering special education as temporary, and of encouraging the integration or 'mainstreaming' of handicapped children clearly has implications also for remedial teachers. In the present economic crisis there is danger that while special education will be protected to some extent, remedial education, seen by some administrators as an expensive luxury or a 'frill', will be doubly affected both by a cut in services and by the addition, and re-integration, of some children previously in special education. Some would suggest that no child should be referred for special education on account of low intelligence who has not had the benefit of remedial education after which he has still failed to make progress.

While special education is normally full-time, remedial education may be full- or part-time, group or individual, and arranged in a variety of ways. There seems at present a disappointing lack of integration of the services for special and remedial education – or even awareness of the extent of overlap of their populations. It is as pertinent to question the extent to which special education is 'special' in the sense of different as to question whether remedial teachers have, or indeed need, special skills. Some would insist that a sensitive 'counselling' role is that of the remedial teacher, and provided she progresses more slowly and uses a different approach from that on which the child failed that is adequate. Lawrence in the Times Educational Supplement, in arguing this point of view, stresses the extent to which remedial teachers discover that 'the group selected by the head for remedial work has been selected on its nuisance value' (TES, 2nd July 1976). In order to explore the issues of the necessary skills in the remedial context it is important to consider both the children with whom the remedial teacher is working *and* the organizational structure within which she is expected to operate. It must be accepted, however, that the skills displayed by a particular individual will influence the role she is permitted to play.

Special services and the educational system
It is pertinent to consider not only the relationship between special and remedial education, but also the effects on the educational system of the very existence of remedial and indeed of special services. The existence of special services will inevitably lead to some form of assessment of failure to meet a pre-set standard, either implicit or explicit, in terms of, say, reading age on a particular test, IQ or some other arbitrary measure. The class teacher for whom 'remedial' and 'special' pupils are a reality is more likely to find them, and even perhaps to 'create' them, by her very attitude. It would, however, certainly not be correct to assume that the abolition of such services would necessarily lead to a more tolerant attitude in schools: it may be, nevertheless, that the necessity for a remedial or special service is evidence of *our failure* rather than the children's. Bernstein (1970) has questioned the use of the term 'compensatory education' arguing that:

> The compensatory education concept serves to direct attention away from the internal organization and the educational context of the school, and focus our attention upon the families and children. Compensatory education implies that something is lacking in the family, and so in the child, and that as a result the children are unable to benefit from schools (53-4) . . . we should stop thinking in terms of compensatory education but consider instead most seriously and systematically the conditions and contexts of the educational environment (page 55).

A similar comment has been made about remedial education that: 'it has escaped our attention that our curriculum and instructional methods were formulated when only the most able and willing attended school', and that reforms tend to give priority to remedial measures rather than revising the curriculum and our teaching in order to make remedial measures unnecessary (Taba and Elkins 1966, pp. 14-15). These are not necessarily alternative decisions; on the contrary, an awareness of the interrelatedness of ordinary and remedial education is essential.

There is growing evidence of the importance of both teacher competence and teacher expectation on level of functioning. It might also be rewarding to study the influence of parent expectation with more refined instruments than social class, number of books in the home or frequency of visits to the school. Not all those in my recent study of children who were already reading fluently on starting school were from professional homes; not all the homes were well stocked with books and some of the parents rarely visited the school and would indeed have been embarrassed to do so (Clarke 1976). It would have been so easy to take these parents at their own modest evaluation and yet they were a crucial variable in the continuing success of these children – and many of their brothers and sisters who were not reading when they started school.

There is evidence that few teachers pay attention to the findings of educational research and that fewer read the original researches; some blame must rest with the research worker who fails to present the results in a way that communicates and interprets in terms of educational relevance. There are dangers in research workers communicating only with other research workers and teachers seeing only summarized, over-simplified reports in the more popular journals or the media. The limitations in methodology and the sample are then not evident; also the results are presented in terms of means and generalities while the extent of overlap between groups – and the exceptions to the general trend – cannot be identified. The exceptions are at least as important as the generalizations: the child for whom the reading readiness battery predicted failure who succeeds, or the child of low IQ who is functionally literate.

Remedial reading: the reality of the research worker
My early research, *Reading Difficulties in Schools* (Clarke 1970) was an attempt to understand from a community study of 1544 children the extent and nature of severe and prolonged reading difficulties in children of average intelligence. There were relatively few such children found in the community studied, but significant was the diversity of their difficulties, not the similarity. This study highlighted the need for those dealing with such children to be sensitive in diagnosis and to have a working knowledge of a variety of remedial techniques. It should be noted that evidence on community incidence figures still means that certain individual schools, even within that community, may have a much higher proportion of such children than the general figures would have predicted – a very different reality exists therefore for these teachers.

At the same time as my community study was underway in Dunbartonshire, the famous Isle of Wight survey was taking place, one aspect of which was also a study of the incidence of severe reading difficulty (Rutter, Tizard and Whitmore 1970). Both these studies coloured the recommendations of the Tizard Report, *Children with Specific Reading Difficulties* (DES 1972). That report is more often quoted for its negative statement that dyslexia is not a useful term for educational purposes than for its valuable positive recommendations aimed to ensure that:

all children with reading difficulties would early be identified
their progress would be monitored
remedial and advisory services would be available in primary and secondary schools
and finally, that oral methods of teaching and alternative methods of assessment would be made available to such children.

Since the publication of the Tizard Report in 1972 there has been little evidence of a change in the provision of specialist help or the coordination of remedial services. Many administrators preferred to await the publication of the findings of the Bullock Enquiry, published as *A Language for Life* (DES 1975). Among its recommendations were some similar to those in the earlier Tizard report, but with its wider brief the Bullock Report also stressed the need for a link between language and reading, and for a specialist teacher coordinating all the work of reading in the school. Unfortunately, although the government provided the finance for the enquiry, there were no resources available for implementation, its publication coming as it did at the beginning of the economic crisis.

The reality?
Sampson, in her book *Remedial Education* (1975), describes the remedial organization in secondary schools in England. Most schools were found to have a remedial department, but the proportion of children catered for varied from school to school, as did the organization. In many cases the remedial department provided full-time classes for slow learners; in many the classes were of twenty or so although some schools operated a withdrawal system for at least some of the children who attended in small groups or individually. Many remedial teachers had, however, no specialist qualifications.

A working party in Scotland based on the Scottish Central Committee on Primary Education recently undertook a study of the policy in the 35 local education authorities for the organization of remedial education in the primary schools. The report *Remedial Education in the Primary School* (1974) indicated that because of a persistent and serious teacher shortage in some authorities, there was little evidence of remedial provision which was confined to employment of a limited number of part-time teachers. In other areas there was a conscious policy organized at a central level with deployment of teachers, resources and possibly screening of children in need, centrally planned. Some authorities equally committed to remedial education operated a school-based service with encouragement but considerable autonomy to headteachers regarding whether and how they organized remedial assistance in their schools, the allocation of resources and the selection of children. In Scotland until 1975, education was the responsibility of thirty-five local authorities, each with considerable autonomy in the deployment of resources. With reorganization the responsibility for education is now vested in twelve regional authorities but with, as before, considerable autonomy left to headteachers in the management of their schools – the role of the Scottish Education Department being, as previously, advisory rather than dictatorial.

Over the two years immediately prior to reorganization (1973–5), together with Morag Hunter who had wide experience of work with children with learning difficulties, I have undertaken an 'action' research of one school-based remedial service. The aim of the research was to give advice to the authority on the development of its remedial provision within the school-based structure which it favoured. Our role was to monitor and evaluate the service as participant, but detached, observers. This involved an experimental screening, an analysis of the timetables of the remedial teachers and of the characteristics of children in receipt of remedial assistance. Additional remedial resources were also made available within the research budget. These resource materials were shared and evaluated by the teachers. The project was jointly financed by the authority and by the Scottish Education Department. Frequent research meetings were held with the remedial teachers. Meetings were also held with headteachers and these were attended by representatives of the directorate and the inspectorate. The research was inevitably, but perhaps in this study legitimately, 'contaminated' by any influence which our presence and views had on the teachers and the administrators. Unfortunately, both reorganization and the economic crisis coincided with the presentation of our report for development of the service. Any plans for implementation were affected adversely by loss of autonomy by the local authority upon its absorption into the regional structure and by a cut-back in remedial provision in order to improve staffing in other areas of the region.

The importance of studies such as these is the ongoing nature of the interaction with the practitioners who were throughout being encouraged to evaluate their own practice and to improve lines of communication both within and across primary schools and also to develop links with secondary schools.

A further study with which I have been involved simultaneously in the same authority, but with preschool children, has brought home to me very forcibly the shifting nature of readiness for school and for learning and also the extent to which the potential failures can be identified at an early age. A study of children with high and low interest in books in the nursery school gave evidence of the strategies of some children in persuading adults to read to them what they wished, when they wished, and also the specificity of some children's choices. One fascinating sidelight was the ability of even very young children in the researches to retell some of the stories read to them in a simulation of the language of the original. Even when they did not remember the precise language, they could use sentences as complex as the original, a vocabulary as varied. Furthermore many were sensitive to a further aspect of the 'read' as distinct from the 'told' story – namely, the invariant nature of text. What are the crucial features of print, and to what extent have remedial children ever learned to appreciate these, and do they experience this even in the remedial situation? Observation of young children aged three to five years in the nursery-school setting also highlighted for me the need for these children's development to be monitored over a period of time if their education was to meet their needs.

Whether a particular level of difficulty in reading or written work results in remedial or additional assistance will depend on many factors:

1 the area in which the child lives, or where there is a school-based service; even the school he attends
2 his age or stage in school
3 his considered level of intelligence which may permit him to have assistance, prevent him or determine what type he is permitted
4 his score on a screening test, different types of tests identifying different children
5 diagnosis by a particular expert.

It is important that there is some classification of the criteria which necessitate remedial assistance and that this takes account of the growing child, his needs and his background of previous experience. For this some recording of progress which enables communication within and between schools is crucial – a communication which includes the parents as providers of information as well as recipients. Channels of communication must be more effective if remedial education is to be a reality within the education system which helps a child not only to overcome his weaknesses but also to develop his strengths.

References

BERNSTEIN, B. (1970) 'A sociolinguistic approach to socialization with some reference to educability' in F. Williams (ed) *Language and Poverty* Chicago: Markham pp. 25–61

CLARK, M. M. (1970) *Reading Difficulties in Schools* Penguin Papers in Education. Penguin

CLARK, M. M. (1976) *Young Fluent Readers* Heinemann Educational

CLARK, M. M. and MACKAY, T. A. W. N. (1976) *Ascertainment for Special Education in Scotland* unpublished report for Scottish Education Department

DES (1972) *Children with Specific Reading Difficulties* HMSO

DES (1975) *A Language for Life* (Bullock Report) HMSO

LAWRENCE, D. (1976) 'Same, but different' *Times Educational Supplement* p.17, 2nd July 1976

RUTTER, M., TIZARD, J. and WHITMORE, K. (eds) (1970) *Education, Health and Behaviour* Longman

SAMPSON, O. C. (1975) *Remedial Education* Routledge and Kegan Paul

SCOTTISH CENTRAL COMMITTEE ON PRIMARY EDUCATION (1974) Paper 2 *Remedial Education in the Primary School* A survey of Education Authority Policy and Provision. HMSO

TABA, H. and ELKINS, D. (1966) *Teaching Strategies for the Culturally Disadvantaged* Chicago: Rand McNally

6 Reading research – a problem for teachers

James Maxwell

The data on which this discussion is based were obtained as part of an investigation into the teaching of reading in Scottish schools, financed by the Social Sciences' Research Council and sponsored by the Scottish Education Department; neither of these bodies, however, are responsible for any opinions expressed herein.

The unit of the aspects of the inquiry discussed here was the primary school class. About one hundred classes in Primary 4 were selected and tested by the Edinburgh Reading Test Stage 2. These classes were followed through the primary school and tested again when they reached the Primary 7 stage, this time by Edinburgh Reading Test Stage 3. As the two tests were not the same, the amount of progress in reading by each class could not be directly measured; relative progress could however be assessed, and part of the investigation was aimed at establishing whether any teaching practices, policies or materials were associated with more reading progress than others. The period of schooling covered is P4 to P6 inclusive.

Table 1

(a) *Incidence of homework involving reading*

	P4	P5	P6
Regular	61	54	49
Occasional	18	11	19
None	19	37	38
Total no. classes	98	102	106

(b) *Teachers' aims in teaching reading (percentages)*

	P4	P5	P6
Interest/enjoyment	33	42	51
Comprehension	21	18	23
Skills	46	40	26

Two items of practice and attitude are taken here as examples.

Teachers were asked about their practice in setting homework involving reading, and what their main aims were in the teaching of reading. Data were obtained from interviews with teachers of P4, P5 and P6 classes. The information so obtained is presented in Table 1. The table indicates that the incidence of homework decreases from P4 to P6, and that the emphasis of the teachers of reading tends to shift from interest and enjoyment at the expense of skills over the same span of primary schooling. This gives a fair enough picture of teachers' practices in the upper primary classes.

When, however, the question is asked whether the classes receiving regular homework show more or less progress in reading than those having no homework, no clear answer is possible. The same applies to the question of whether stress on enjoyment, comprehension or skills is associated with greater or less progress in reading attainment. The reason for the inability to relate reading progress to these two aspects of teachers' practices is shown in Table 2. This table is compiled from a set of 'class histories' which recorded teachers' practices for each class for the three consecutive years from P4 to P6.

Table 2

Class consistency from P4 to P6

		No. of consistent classes
(a)	Homework	
	Regular	16
	Occasional	1
	None	0
(b)	Teachers' aims	
	Interest/enjoyment	8
	Comprehension	0
	Skills	0

Of the one hundred or so classes whose practices were observed, only sixteen received regular homework over the three years, and no classes spent three years without some homework. In the same way, eight classes were consistently taught reading with emphasis on interest and enjoyment, but none received consistent teaching which stressed comprehension or skills. Even if the eight classes were accepted as a sufficient number on which to base conclusions, it still remains that there are no corresponding classes with which comparison can be made. The rule appeared to be variety of practices and attitudes, with consistent teaching very much the exception. Nor is the difficulty confined to the two aspects of teaching practice; other components of teaching practice, such as oral reading and class organization show similar features.

The research approach used here may be called descriptive research. It has the advantage of being firmly based on what is actually happening in classrooms but, as has been shown, interpretation is difficult. Not only is there a lack of information about how long any practice needs to be followed before it has any impact on pupils' development of reading attainments, but also there is little or no evidence available about the effects of one practice upon succeeding practices – whether they reinforce, neutralize or conflict with each other. Finally there is the practical difficulty that, in order to obtain sufficient evidence from consistent practices, a very large initial sample would be needed, and in any case findings would be based on the minority of consistently taught pupils rather than on the majority. Studies based on single school sessions can be deceptively conclusive; the more long-term the investigation the more acute does the difficulty of interpretation become.

The alternative is prescriptive research, in which prescribed practices are used by parallel groups of teachers for a prescribed period of time, and the reading progress of the pupils compared. This gives little difficulty to the researcher, as the techniques are well established. But it does present the teachers with a problem. If it is assumed, as it reasonably can be, that an effective method of teaching reading is effective when used by any teacher, it is possible by such prescriptive research to establish the effects on the pupils' reading progress of different teaching practices. There are, however, teachers who do not believe in homework, or teachers who believe that reading development should be based on stimulating interest and pleasure in reading. Such views are often strongly held by teachers, and it is difficult for some teachers to accept that these views are not founded on firm evidence. Prescriptive research would, in the long run, provide such evidence. But the price the teachers would have to pay is suspension of their beliefs and the conscientious application of teaching practices which may not have their personal approval. The problem for teachers is to decide whether they are prepared to pay that price for firm evidence about teaching practices.

Part 2

Language and reading development

7 The evaluation of reading materials

Donald Moyle

Introduction

As a race the British seem to be over-concerned with their failures and problems and rarely, unlike many other nations, with their inventions, achievements and successes. This is nowhere more clearly shown than in the reaction of the national press to the Bullock Committee's suggestion in its report *A Language for Life* (1975) that there was no proof of a decline in reading standards in England. The newspaper editors were disbelieving, even angry, and suggested that the report was a 'whitewash' job.

The suggestions made were numerous, from a return to teaching methods of past eras to the massive investment in each person's favourite teaching method, media or materials. Behind all of the suggestions, however, was the indication that panic measures were in order to put the situation right. On the evidence of a good many surveys, however, and perhaps most notably Thorndike (1973) standards of reading in Britain would appear to compare well with those of other countries. There would seem, therefore, no real need for panic, but a careful and constructive appraisal of current and possible future needs.

The controversy concerning whether or not reading standards had declined unfortunately drew attention away from the suggestions for the future made by the Bullock Committee; namely, that the needs of society currently demanded higher levels of reading ability on the one hand, and a reappraisal of the appropriateness and quality of reading resulting from current methods and materials on the other.

Surveys of adult functional reading such as Murphy (1973) have suggested that instruction should be re-examined for adults who on traditional tests of reading comprehension had acceptable scores but who proved ineffective readers on many ordinary, everyday tasks of reading in real-life situations. Equally, though less than 4 per cent of children on average have left school with a reading age level of less than 9.0 years since 1948, it is suggested that only 50 per cent of our adult population ever read a book. This is not of course to say that the other half of the population do not read, but rather that they have no contact with the major classification of types of reading media.

Attitudes in the recent past

The belief that some discovery in terms of a teaching method, a change of medium or bigger and better materials would result in an end to all the problems experienced by children in learning to read, has dominated much of the thinking concerning reading over the years. Teachers and research workers alike have sought for such a panacea, but of course have sought in vain. It is not unusual to hear at reading courses the comment overheard from an experienced teacher prior to the last session of a short course on remedial teaching, 'I hope that at last we shall hear the secret of how it is done tonight.'

A vast amount of our research literature in reading over the years has reinforced this attitude. Time after time one teaching method has been compared with another and one set of materials with another set. Usually in short-term experiments one approach or set of materials has been shown to produce a slightly superior level of attainment than the other. However the gains have been minimal and not sufficiently convincing to encourage teachers to change their approach or invest exclusively in new materials. It is not surprising therefore that the teaching of reading and the selection of reading materials by teachers has not been extensively influenced by research results.

It may be that there is an underlying truth arising from all such research projects and one which may be far more important; namely, that though there are undoubtedly inferior and superior materials it is the use made of them by the teacher which is the most significant factor in bringing about reading success. This is pointed to by Bond (1967) in the First Grade Reading Study in the USA where factor analysis was used to try to discover which factors appeared to be related to reading success. After partialling out factors within the child and his home environment, it was suggested that only 20 per cent of the variance of success appeared to be related to teaching methods and materials, whereas 80 per cent appeared to arise from the qualities of the teacher. Gray (1977) has pointed out the difficulties of making such statements with confidence owing to our lack of knowledge of all the variables and their interaction in the teaching/learning situation, but there is little doubt that everyday observation seems to confirm the validity of the importance of the teacher. It is not surprising therefore that the Bullock Committee suggested that the expertise of the teacher was the most important area for the investment of effort.

Brief historical survey of reading materials

This survey must for want of space be a rather simplistic overview, but is necessary to realize fully how the design and content of materials reflect the definition and nature of the reading process as it appeared in each successive era. In the age of payment by results, phonic teaching seemed to offer the teacher the best chance of ensuring that their children performed well in the tests. Thus before the end of the nineteenth century the first reading schemes written from a phonic base began to appear. It is interesting to note, however, that the older alphabetic and story methods were also reflected in these new materials. Certainly the scheme produced by Nellie Dale (1899) included opportunities for language development, auditory discrimination, support from story method, drama and choral speech as well as the first known scheme to employ a colour cueing system to aid the child in overcoming some of the inconsistencies of the English spelling system.

Over the years, materials for reading development via phonic methods have tended to become progressively narrower in their approach as they became more sophisticated in the selection of vocabulary to illustrate certain rules. The strange fact emerges that, whilst the vast majority of materials for the early stages of reading had a base in phonics, the colleges from the turn of the century taught their students to use whole-word methods at least in addition to, if not to the exclusion of, phonic methods.

The phonic era is typified in the *Beacon Reading Scheme* first published in 1922 and still widely used today. Its content, however, still has a relationship with story-method approach with its folk tales embodying rhythm and repetition, whereas the *Chelsea* readers, so popular in the thirties, were much more obviously created for the mastery of phonic rules.

Although a good deal of discussion about the supposed merits of whole-word methods in comparison to phonic methods had been a feature of literature on the teaching of reading for many years, it was not really until after 1945 that schemes based entirely on whole-word approaches such as *Janet and John* were widely published in Britain. Even so, most materials prepared in this era professed a mixed-methods base usually commencing with whole words and then continuing with phonics after the establishment of a sight vocabulary. This mixture claimed a certain amount of research support notably in England from Schonell (1949). Most of the evidence from research on the question of mixed methods is suspect, however, for there is little description of how the work was undertaken and the balance of the elements in the mixture.

In parallel with the production of whole-word reading schemes came a number of schemes, for example *John and Mary,* based upon sentence methods. Decroly had suggested the viewing of the sentence as the basic 'whole' in learning to read and it had long been used in infant schools, though without specific materials (Jagger 1929).

The sixties saw a flood of materials and new editions of existing ones and a number of factors seemed to be attracting increasing attention including:

the simplification of type faces

increasing the attractiveness of illustrations

enlarging the amounts of graded material within schemes in the form of supplementary and extension readers

the provision of related readiness materials

a change in the type of story in an endeavour to make the content nearer the everyday experience of children

an attempt to link reading schemes to language-experience work.

One reservation to the general trend was that some schemes, particularly those for remedial reading work, began to explore the area of fantasy which had been given little place in reading schemes in recent years despite the obvious interest in it shown by children – as evidenced by the immense sales of books by Enid Blyton.

Until this point in time the overriding principle governing the construction of schemes had been the controlled rate of the introduction of new words and the establishment of high repetition rates. Gates (1930) had suggested that the child of average ability needed thirty-five repetitions of a word on average within a short space of time in order that it should be committed to memory. This level of repetition is achieved for few words within total reading schemes.

As we move into the seventies, materials for the early stages of reading seem to show a more direct influence of research and theoretical positions. This is particularly so in the effects of linguistic science. There had been a few forerunners of this period of development and Daniels and Diack (1956) provided strong evidence from research to show that a linguistic approach appeared to be successful in enabling children to master the spelling patterns of English.

Linguistics has produced two major directions in the production of schemes. The first, the progressive mastery of the spelling of English, is seen in *Language in Action* (Macmillan Education), whereas the second, the grading of sentence structures, is seen in *Link-Up* (Holmes-McDougall).

A further influence of structural linguistics is exemplified in *Breakthrough to Literacy* (Longman). Here there is a major attempt to use the child's own language as a basis for the learning of words and the spelling patterns of English. This scheme contains only supplementary readers and marks a break with the idea of the use of a vocabulary-controlled scheme as a necessity for beginning-reading success.

Increasingly teachers have been looking for a wider base than a single reading scheme in their selection of materials for early reading. The rise of language-experience work and centres of interest resulted in the provision of graded and readability controlled non-fiction material such as *Zero's* and *Starters* (Macdonald). The sixties also saw the introduction of reading laboratories and workshops into Britain. This was the first influence of behaviourist theories upon reading materials in Britain, but also the first major attempt to extend materials for the teaching of reading beyond the beginning-reading stage. Research, for example Moyle (1966), has strongly supported the effectiveness of such materials, but it must be acknowledged that the research results may show little more than the fact that action was being taken to develop comprehension whereas prior to the introduction of such materials there was little evidence of constructive attempts to extend reading ability after fluency had been achieved.

The major problems with the laboratory-type material and the extensive schemes such as the Scott Foresman Reading System and the Holt Basic Reading Scheme are to be found in the division of reading into a multiplicity of subskills and that of the transfer of learning. The mastery of the subskills of reading seems to be possible by a variety of routes largely dependent on the personality, abilities and interests of the learner, and transfer of learning of skills from the situation where they are learned to other situations where they may be usefully applied appears to require special legislation on the part of the teacher.

Some difficulties which remain

Historically, reading has been viewed as the simple equation of graphic symbols with speech sounds, i.e. word recognition through either memorization of whole words or the mastery of the relationship between sounds and symbols. There is little doubt that to some people reading is still defined in these terms. Even when definitions are somewhat more extensive, the suggestion is usually maintained that attention to the message conveyed by text should be left until fluency in the recognition of words has been achieved.

It is unfortunate that such views have persisted so long and have influenced our reading materials so deeply, for even today many materials ill-prepare the child to use his abilities to recognize linguistic forms and meaning units in text as a major word-identification skill.

There is still an atmosphere which suggests that reading is a relatively simple task and growth in attainment follows a clearly defined route through a number of subskills. There appears, however, to be no one set route for the mastery of reading, and materials must take into account individual variations in learning style, interests and linguistic development.

The nature of reading skill varies considerably from task to task; it is not simply a matter that the same skills are practised on different types of content. The work of Murphy (1973) shows a poor relationship between reading tests and real-life reading tasks and also a low correlation between success in, say, the reading of a newspaper and the reading of a recipe. We must acknowledge this low relationship if we are to improve the quality and appropriateness of reading skill among our children.

Let us examine the possible effects of the narrow usage of one basic reading scheme. On average in the first three main readers of British reading schemes there are forty words to a page, some three of which are likely to be new words. Such a learning load is heavy even for the bright child, so if no further support is given the child is likely to have to pay such great attention to the words that he can have little hope of extracting the story line. If this is allowed to persist then the child begins to feel that reading is about word calling and not about the thoughtful consideration of meanings expressed by an author. Further, he will feel it is hard work for little result and not an activity which can bring about personal development and enjoyment. Most children will work hard in the early years simply to please the teacher, but eventually they will reject reading as an activity unless it fulfils some conscious need within them.

In recent years the importance of recognizing individual needs has been partially catered for by adjusting the rate of progress through schemes and laboratories to the speed set by each child. There is much to be said for this position, but it also has an unfortunate result in isolating the child. Opportunities for discussion or joint usage of the results of reading among groups tend to divorce reading from other forms of communication and make reading a relatively passive pursuit.

Conventional wisdom has tended to hold back research and the development of materials, for opinions are so deeply rooted that change is inhibited. This is often supported by the fact that, in terms of the results from current tests, many teachers produce good results from outmoded materials and teaching techniques. One must ask whether these good results are paralleled by effective reading in later life and also what new ground might be broken if these successful teachers became more adventurous.

Again, research and the development of materials is hampered by the application of opposite but widely accepted views, for example 'everybody knows that the way to teach reading is through phonics' and 'the English spoken and written language forms are so unrelated that phonic teaching is pointless'. Thus there is a tendency to force people into particular camps which results in a narrow approach.

Research and development work are helped if they can be based in theories or models of the reading process. Within such a framework predictions and hypotheses can be tested and thus supported or rejected. Unfortunately, the models of the reading process produced to date appear to restrict rather than open up the field. In the second edition of a book of some 800-plus pages dealing with reading models (Singer and Ruddell 1976), not one model acknowledges that reading is a need-related activity. Every model is restricted to eyeball-to-print contact and ignores the purposes and outcomes related to the use of reading skills. It is little wonder, therefore, that authors of reading materials, and teachers, gain the impression that reading can be mastered within one set of materials and the skills will automatically transfer to all other reading tasks.

Suggestions for improvements

In order to achieve effectiveness as a reader the child must also develop the abilities and skills of the independent learner. He must be able to guide and control the whole of the reading process. This means that he is not only to become capable of identifying words and processing meaning, but also develop his ability to set and analyse his reading purposes, select appropriate reading materials, decide upon the mental set and type of read which is most appropriate and finally collate, evaluate and appraise the outcome of his efforts.

The majority of reading materials currently available delete both ends of the reading process by setting the purpose and defining which outcomes are required. What is needed is material capable of use in a variety of ways so that the child may make selections as to which procedure satisfies some personal need. Such materials would involve closer links with content and the other language arts.

The current isolation of reading could be overcome to a large extent by providing materials more worthy of discussion. The use of comparative and cooperative reading is possible on all types of written material, and reading/thinking activities and discussions based upon alternative responses to cloze exercises are especially helpful within story-type material.

The struggle experienced by many children in the early stages could be overcome to some extent by the use of story-method materials where a voice on tape supports the reading or the child reads a summary of a story he has previously heard. In the early stages, rhymes and even popular songs might precede the story because of the lower demand upon memorization. At the moment few of our graded schemes provide material with a sufficiently strong story line for this type of work.

Vocabulary control, though it provides the child with a certain security, also means that for some length of time the child is limited in his reading largely to one reading scheme and also emphasizes words rather than meaning. Somewhat looser grading carefully checked by readability assessment could be achieved and this could then facilitate the matching of books at equivalent levels of reading demand from both fiction and non-fiction – not to mention the immense range of other types of media.

British reading materials have the advantage that no one scheme is sufficient to provide for the growth of a child's reading ability and therefore the inventiveness of the teacher and the use of other materials is encouraged. However, though the larger American schemes are rather more inhibiting, they are usually much more thoroughly researched and evaluated. The following guidelines for the effective validation of materials suggested by Squire (1976) might usefully be considered by British authors and publishers:

1 Select authors with practical classroom experience and familiarity with classroom applications of research.
2 Engage experienced and successful writers of literature for children, hoping that the writers' demonstrated sensitivities to the interests of children will provide a reservoir of insights useful in writing or choosing selections for reading.
3 Rely on the judgment and insights of professional reading editors – the large majority of whom have devoted their careers to teaching and education – and on the experienced and highly qualified staffs in some publishing houses.
4 Depend, in initiating new programmes, on the accumulated background of studies on previously published programmes – both on the programmes that worked and those which did not work. It is no accident that the majority of publishers who were strong in reading twenty years ago continue to be strong today.
5 Build on small-scale experimental projects initiated by individual schools and school systems, attempting to make the innovative dimensions of an isolated experiment usable by all teachers.
6 Call on professional scholars and successful teachers to review manuscripts prior to publication and, today especially, consult qualified and sensitive educational leaders on problems of cultural pluralism and sexism in content and graphics.
7 Check the readability level, the concept density, and the interest level of particular manuscripts prior to publication, just as the content authenticity is checked.
8 Ask selected groups of children to read and use materials prior to publication to obtain an indication of pupil response.
9 Field test materials prior to publication.

Postscript
Increasingly, materials specifically prepared to develop reading skill are being intermixed with other materials by teachers to gain a wider and more effective base. With the problems of large classes it is unlikely that the teacher will be able to satisfy the needs of her children without the help of structured materials. It is hoped, however, that increasingly teachers and designers of materials will realize that they are to be used by teachers and children and not vice versa. The route through the maze of skills is probably best directed by the needs and interests of the child so that skills are learned when they are required. In this atmosphere the child should be able to realize the value of skill mastery and become one who not only can read but does so with enjoyment and personal satisfaction.

References

BOND, G. L. (1967) First Grade Reading Studies: An Overview *Elementary English* 43, 464–70

DALE, N. (1899) *On the Teaching of English Reading* Philip

DANIELS, J. C. and DIACK, H. (1956) *Progress in Reading* University of Nottingham

DES (1975) *A Language for Life* (Bullock Report) HMSO

FARR, R., WEINTRAUB, S. and TONE, B. (1976) *Improving Reading Research* Newark: International Reading Association

GATES, A. I. (1930) *Interest and Ability in Reading* New York: Macmillan

GRAY, J. (1977) Teacher competence in reading tuition *Educational Research* Vol. 19, No. 2, pp. 113–21

JAGGER, J. H. (1929) *The Sentence Method of Teaching Reading* Grant

MOYLE, D. (1966) SRA Laboratory IIA *Bulletin of the United Kingdom Reading Association*

MURPHY, R. (1973) *Adult Functional Reading Study: Final Report* Princeton: Educational Testing Service

SCHONELL, F. J. (1949) *(4th ed.) Backwardness in the Basic Subjects* Oliver and Boyd

SINGER, H. and RUDDELL, R. (1976) *Theoretical Models and Processes of Reading* Newark: International Reading Association

SQUIRE, J. R. (1976) 'How publishers develop instructional materials' in L. Courtney (ed) *Reading Interaction* Newark: International Reading Association

START, K. B. and WELLS, B. K. (1972) *The Trend of Reading Standards* NFER

THORNDIKE, R. L. (1973) *Reading Comprehension Education in Fifteen Countries* New York: J. Wiley

8 Comprehension: an elusive concept

H. Alan Robinson

For a number of years, at least across my professional lifetime, some American 'reading experts' (myself not exempted) have wondered what was wrong with other countries. Why didn't they possess our wisdom about reading skills? Why didn't they teach all of these skills in sequence from the first year of schooling upward? Why didn't they realize that reading comprehension could be broken down into many component parts and each could be taught?

Oh, there have been American doubters and questioners, but since it seemed easier to programme lists of skills than tangle with a concept as elusive as comprehension, we have gone ahead to 'teach' the skills even as doubts intruded upon our efforts. The temptation and execution were understandable – do something rather than sit and ponder.

Although voices throughout the years have suggested that a holistic approach rooted in the curriculum content might be more viable, it is only quite recently that we are giving serious consideration to the possible modification of the 'piece-by-piece' view of reading instruction. In the United States long lists of skills still prevail and too many teachers assume 'exposure' is learning.

But there is a trend toward humility. Maybe we don't know as much as we thought. Maybe we have not facilitated learning for a rather large body of students. Maybe, before we proceed on the assumption that we know how to teach reading comprehension, we had better try to learn more about it.

Definitions of reading comprehension

Prior to 1908 little attention was paid to reading comprehension; emphasis was placed on accuracy of oral presentation and elocution. Experimentation concerned with meaning focused on the isolated word. Huey (1908), in his germinal work on reading research and instruction, reported experiments with isolated words but indicated a dissatisfaction with such measurements. He consciously 'lifted' the concept of *meaning* beyond the word level:

> When a single word is presented, therefore, it suggests but a part
> or an aspect of this total meaning and is felt as inadequate and

artificial unless given in its sentence context. With meanings, as with vocal utterance, the sentence-meaning is the natural unit, and smaller divisions considered apart from this are felt as *disjecta membra* (page 167).

By 1916, Judd, as cited by Cleland (1968), was referring to comprehension of continuous discourse as the 'quality of reading'. In 1917, Gray, as cited by Cleland (1968), spoke of comprehension as 'the obtaining of meaning through reading'. Also in 1917, Thorndike (1971) spoke of reading as '. . . a very elaborate procedure, involving a weighing of each of many elements in a sentence, their organization in the proper relations one to another, the selection of certain of their connotations and the rejection of others, and the cooperation of many forces to determine final response' (page 425).

Although a number of definitions were generated between 1917 and 1955, Yoakam, as cited by Cleland (1968), included most of the ingredients as well as the doubts from the varied definitions when he stated:

> The term *comprehension*, which is used to represent the general comprehension of meaning in reading, has never been completely described. . . . It seems likely that comprehension is a complex which involves the mental process of recognition, or association of meaning, evaluation of suggested meaning, selection of the correct meaning, and generalization based on the meanings of details involved in a context. Some writers would add the anticipation of meaning to this complex (page 18).

Gray (1960) summarized his notion of comprehension as '. . . the attainment of competence in understanding what is read requires steady growth in ability to read the lines, to read between the lines and to read beyond the lines'. Cleland (1968) suggested that comprehension is a '. . . complex process of bringing meaning to the printed page so that the reader can establish rapport with the author' (page 16). Smith (1971) said: 'I shall define comprehension – or the extraction of meaning from the text – as the reduction of uncertainty' (page 185).

Obviously these definitions of reading comprehension, but representative of a host, raise more questions than they answer. Simons (1971) suggested that Thorndike's description of reading comprehension reported in 1917:

> . . . still almost exhausts the accumulated knowledge of this fundamental intellectual process. The workings of the mind during reading comprehension remain a great and profound mystery (page 340).

Miller (1976), in his role as chairperson of a panel of the National Institute of Education Conference on Studies in Reading (U.S.), stated:

> Work on text comprehension is not yet far-advanced. There are major gaps in our understanding of the anatomy of the text comprehension process, and in our knowledge of the skills that make comprehension possible (pages 709-10).

Missing emphases

Although Thorndike (1971), Yoakam (1955), Cleland (1968), Smith (1971) and others not cited strongly suggest the interaction of the reader and the writer as vital factors in reading comprehension, the significant role played by the quality and quantity of pre-knowledge of the reader is not seriously considered. In my opinion – partially formulated with the help of the ideas of Kellogg Hunt and others – reading comprehension is the difference between what someone knew about a topic prior to the reading and what he or she 'winds up with' or possesses following the reading. This information gain is always modulated by the individual reader. Factors which influence information gain are the nature of the learner, the nature of the material, the nature of the purposes for reading, and the means used for measurement.

Nature of the learner

Since the individual learner is a being different from all other beings, there is little doubt that reading comprehension will be affected by cultural background, specific background experiences, linguistic knowledge and flexibility, general knowledge and attitudes. As has been said so often, *the printed words mean nothing unless the reader brings meaning to them.* It would appear that comprehension should be better for a given reader when background factors more closely match those represented in the graphic display. When you know about something in advance, the task – even with new information added – is less formidable and comprehension of the new is much more certain. When language patterns of reader and writer are similar, the message has a far better chance of being understood. As Smith said, uncertainty can be reduced. When the reader meets language very distant from his or her own – no matter how simple the information presented – reducing uncertainty becomes a great struggle.

Nature of the material

As already indicated, the distance between the reader and the writer is a vital factor in reading comprehension. When the written language patterns are far different from that of the reader, when the information being presented is largely unknown to the reader, and when the writer's attitudes diverge widely from those of the reader, comprehension becomes difficult. Hence, a given reader's comprehension may differ widely from week to week, day to day, moment to moment, dependent upon the nature of the content and the attitudes of the writer.

Purposes for reading
Although many of the theorists and some of the research focus on the importance of purposes in reading, actually little attention has been paid to this aspect of reading comprehension. Readers do tend to adjust comprehension to their purposes. They appear to be at the greatest loss when they are asked to contend with amorphous purposes such as, 'Read pages 230-276 for tomorrow.' Or, and this is in the form of conjecture, when they are asked to deal with external purposes having little real meaning for them: 'Today you are going to take a standardized reading test to see how well you read.'

Means used for measurement
In our quest to ascertain reading comprehension, we administer many types of quizzes or tests or examinations. Aside from needing to have more information about pre-knowledge of students – linguistic, experiential, attitudinal – we need to consider the nature of the measurement. We are not evaluating the same kind of understanding when we ask students to state main ideas at times, details at other times, and inferences at others. We are asking for different types of performances when we use multiple-choice, cloze, essay, sentence completion, paraphrase, summary, etc. Some students may 'comprehend' better when faced with one type of test format than another. Some may do better with a given format dependent upon the nature of the material, the testing conditions, the expectations of the instructor.

Comprehension versus retention must also be considered. When an open-book test is administered, that is probably a test of comprehension as long as the instructor considers what the reader knew prior to reading. On the other hand, when a quiz is given an hour, a day, a week, a month, or a term apart from the reading, where does comprehension end and retention begin? Does an adequate comprehender become a poor retainer?

Implications for instruction
1   In all probability comprehension is an holistic process rather than a series of skills to be presented to each learner in a given sequence. Teachers need to ascertain the strengths and weaknesses of students as they engage in this thinking process with varied materials in different situations. Learning should be directed towards integration of ideas.
2   If comprehension can be thought of as the difference between what

was known before the reading took place and what was learned during the reading – information gain, then we need to place some research activity on pragmatic means of measuring pre-knowledge. By pre-knowledge, I mean not only information possessed by the reader about a topic (or topics), but also knowledge about the cultural background, the linguistic background, the mental capabilities, as well as the feelings and attitudes of given readers. In daily teaching activities, instructors should attempt to learn as much as possible about each student's bank of knowledge in general; however, specific pre-knowledge should be tapped prior to the reading of a particular subject. Such 'tapping' will probably accomplish two ends: (a) improved reading performance, and (b) a clearer picture of actual comprehension of what was read.

3   In somewhat the same light, instructors should carefully consider the complexity of the material a student is to read as well as the 'distance' between the reader and the writer. Material far from the pre-knowledge bank of a given reader should probably not be introduced at all; if such material must be introduced instructors should help students build some pre-knowledge prior to engaging in the reading activity. Reading without some pre-knowledge will result in extremely limited or even zero comprehension.

4   In my opinion, there is no such entity as '*the* reading process'. Reading processes differ in relation to many factors, but particularly in regard to purpose. Instructors should assist their charges in developing suitable strategies for specific purposes. The more 'purpose' one sets for the reading, the greater the likelihood of increased comprehension. No one should be asked to read pages 22–67 and be prepared to discuss those pages tomorrow. Purposes should be set prior to reading; these will differ in terms of the nature of the learner, the nature of the material, the demands of the learner, the demands of the instructor and the demands of the curriculum. Purposes may also be differentiated – across the same material – for individual learners.

Students who are helped to read with purpose – to satisfy varying needs – can also be easily guided to establish their own purposes at the onset of any reading. Such purpose-setting on the part of the learner is assurance of improved comprehension. Perhaps a reason why some students perform miserably on standardized tests and even on some classroom quizzes is the nature of the task – to please the teacher, to ascertain achievement, to test weaknesses. Such external, mechanical purposes do not make for active, really purposeful reading.

5   Instructors should consider what aspect(s) of the reading-thinking process they want to tap when tests and examinations are organized. Undoubtedly the multiple-choice test is making different demands on the reader than the essay question. Two factors

need to be considered: (a) Which kind of questioning fits the nature of, and the purpose(s) of, the task best? and (b) What type of thinking is the test focusing on? Why?

Teachers may want to place differing weights on the results of different kinds of evaluation. In all probability an essay question which calls for high-level thought and organization, for many situations, is a more complex task than filling in the blanks or regurgitating content through answering a host of short-answer questions.

In the instructional situation, outside of formal measurement procedures, instructors will want to examine their own use of questioning in day-to-day teaching. Although many types of questions are needed and will be utilized in a classroom, efforts should be made to create questions which will call for synthesis, integration, organization, evaluation, creative utilization. Teachers will also want to evaluate the abilities of specific youngsters to cope with differing types of questions. Structured guidance in moving from regurgitation to digestion can only increase the student's repertoire and aid reading comprehension.

6 Although an important goal of education is to have students remember what they comprehend, instructors should keep in mind that there is a difference between retention and comprehension. A spurious conclusion following a student's poor performance on a recall test could be that he or she doesn't understand what was read. The student may have understood and not remembered – in a variety of ratios.

Instructors need to be certain that students do comprehend material when it is before them – open book – before making judgments about comprehension based on recall. Some students are helped in their battle to retain by structured guidance in moving from simple open-book tasks at which they succeed. Then, with further assistance, they may be ready to proceed to some of the tasks we have often taken for granted.

In conclusion
The task of the researcher who desires to come to grips with aspects of the complex concept called reading comprehension is bewildering and enormous. The task of the teacher is equally bewildering and enormous but also probably the most vital instructional job within the class setting. We all have much to learn. Perhaps some of the tentative implications for instruction stated earlier in this paper will be useful as instructional frameworks.

Comprehension is, indeed, an elusive concept!

References

CLELAND, D. L. (1968) 'A construct of comprehension' in M. A. Dawson (ed) *Developing Comprehension Including Critical Reading* Newark, Delaware: International Reading Association

GRAY, W. S. (1960) 'The major aspects of reading' in H. M. Robinson (ed) *Sequential Development of Reading Abilities* Supplementary Educational Monographs, No. 90. Chicago: University of Chicago Press

HUEY, E. B. (1968) (first published in 1908) *The Psychology and Pedagogy of Reading* Cambridge, Massachusetts: MIT Press

MILLER, G. A. (1976) 'Text comprehension skills and process models of text comprehension' in H. Singer and R. B. Ruddell (eds) *Theoretical Models and Processes of Reading* second edition. Newark, Delaware: International Reading Association

SIMONS, H. D. (1971) Reading comprehension: the need for a new perspective *Reading Research Quarterly* 6 (Spring) 338–63

SMITH, F. (1971) *Understanding Reading – A Psycholinguistic Analysis of Reading and Learning to Read* New York: Holt, Rinehart and Winston

THORNDIKE, E. L. (1971) Reading as reasoning: a study of mistakes in paragraph reading *Reading Research Quarterly* 6, 425–34. Reprinted from *Journal of Educational Psychology* 8 June 323–32

9 Assessing the readability of school texts

Colin Harrison

In selecting a book for a group, a teacher usually makes judgments about a whole series of factors, depending on the alternatives available. No doubt the subject matter in terms of story, information, or concepts introduced is the most important, but attention will probably also be given to how the book is written, how its content is organized, the book's legibility and the attractiveness of its format. While one accepts that the responsiveness of a specific potential reader will also be determined by that individual's own reading competence, interest in the subject, vocabulary knowledge etc., it is also clear that the text factors listed above are to some extent independent of the reader, and can be examined in a general manner in order to help decide about the possible value of a particular text. It is these factors that are generally referred to when one talks about the 'readability' of a book.

In normal conversation the terms *readability* and *readable* can have slightly perjorative overtones, suggesting that a book is perhaps interesting, or easy to read, but it is also not of the highest quality. It is possible that this connotation partly accounts for the reluctance of some teachers to accept the relevance of the concept of readability in their classroom practice. In fact the term *readability* is used in a much narrower sense in this paper. In attempting to predict the difficulty a reader is likely to have with a text, what we usually have in mind is what might more properly be called *comprehensibility* rather than readability. Broadly speaking, therefore, the term will be used to refer to those features of a printed text which make it easier or more difficult to read and understand.

The need for an objective method of estimating prose difficulty is related to the fact that it is not always possible for the teacher to establish in advance in a practical way whether or not a group of children can cope with a text. This would be no problem if as teachers we were always reliable judges of text difficulty. Unfortunately, however, a number of studies have suggested that while pooled teacher judgments are extremely reliable and consistent, the opinions of individuals may vary wildly in relation to particular books or passages. In a series of three small experiments carried out in inservice workshops on readability at Nottingham University, experienced teachers were asked to write down the age at which they thought 'the average child' could read and understand two printed passages. On each occasion within a group of twenty teachers a range of ages of about six to eight years on each passage was noted, with two or three estimates as low as nine or ten, and a few as high as sixteen or seventeen. When the scores were averaged out, however, a much clearer picture emerged. As Table 1 shows, the pooled scores of different groups of teachers are much closer to each other than were the estimates of individuals.

Table 1   Mean estimates made by three groups of teachers of the age at which 'the average child' could read two passages with understanding; Flesch formula readability levels given for comparison

	Passage A	Passage B
Group 1 (n = 20)	13.9	12.7
Group 2 (n = 21)	13.5	12.4
Group 3 (n = 20)	13.5	12.0
Overall mean (n = 61)	13.6	12.4
Reading level (obtained from Flesch formula)	13.95	12.32

The suggestion that in estimating text difficulty individual experts' judgments are often unreliable has been made by the greatest authority on this subject, Professor George Klare of Ohio. He has reported experiments (Klare 1963, 1975) with teachers, librarians and others which have given similar results to those given in Table 1. One would not want to infer from this, however, that anyone is suggesting that teachers are wholly incapable of choosing suitable material for their students to read. It is rather that in this important task there are certain measures available which can assist the individual teacher by offering an objective index of the prose difficulty of the passage. Like all tools constructed by educational researchers, readability formula results are not meant to displace the teacher, nor relieve him from the need to make judgments. Readability formulas offer, in exchange for some rather tedious arithmetic and word-counting, an objective estimate of text difficulty which it might be even more difficult to obtain by another method. This information can then be used as one factor in the decision about whether or not a book or passage is likely to cause problems for a particular class or group.

What is a readability formula?

In addition to information about the teachers' estimates of passage difficulty, Table 1 also gives the predicted difficulty level of the passages derived from one of the best-known readability formulas, that devised by Rudolf Flesch in 1948. We shall use his formula as an illustration of one of many which are available, but they are not all quite so highly regarded. It is worth noting that the Flesch formula scores on the two randomly chosen passages are both within six months of the ages obtained by pooling the subjective estimates of teachers.

His formula is as follows:

Reading ease score = $206.835 - (0.846 \times \text{NSYLL}) - (1.015 \times \text{WDS/SEN})$
NSYLL = average number of syllables per 100 words
WDS/SEN = average number of words per sentence
(The R. E. score is in fact a notional comprehension score out of 100. The US school grade is derived from a table, and in the UK this is converted to an age level by adding 5 to the grade score, since first grade starts at age six.)

The formula is typical of most of those used widely today. It was produced following a good deal of research into the factors which were associated with comprehension of prose passages. After analysing dozens of linguistic variables, Flesch found that two in particular seemed to correlate most highly with difficulty. These were the average number of syllables per word, and sentence length. Now of course it is the case that many long words are known to even beginning readers ('elephant' and 'aeroplane' are examples) and many adults would find it difficult to define 'palp' and 'khor', but in general the average number of syllables per word in a passage turns out to be a fairly good predictor of the overall level of vocabulary difficulty. Similarly, a long sentence need not be complex, but in practice measures of grammatical complexity, whether in terms of subordinate clauses or more intricate linguistic measures, have been found to correlate extremely highly with straightforward sentence length (see Bormuth 1966). There are in fact certain readability formulas which measure grammatical complexity using some syntactic variable such as clause structure, number of T-units per sentence, or frequency of propositional phrases. However, partly because measures of grammatical complexity are difficult to score reliably, and partly because such variables present the computer programmer with massive difficulties, the formulas included in the present study use sentence length as an estimate of grammatical complexity.

For estimating (or more correctly, predicting) vocabulary difficulty, most of the formulas use a measure of word length, such as the average number of syllables per word, or the average number of polysyllabic words per sentence. The exception to this is the formula of Dale and Chall. Their formula uses the percentage of words in a passage which are on a list of 3,000 familiar words as an indicator of vocabulary difficulty. The idea is that the greater the proportion of infrequently-used words, the more difficult the reader is likely to find the passage. This formula therefore neatly bypasses the problem caused in the other formulas by the fact that some long words are used frequently and many monosyllabic words are used very rarely.

The Dale-Chall formula has been proved in a number of cross-validation studies (reported by Klare 1963 and Chall 1958) to be one which is most accurate in predicting difficulty, but unfortunately it has one great drawback. This is that the formula is very tedious to work out. Each word in a sample passage needs to be checked against the 3,000-word list, and there are approximately thirty rules giving details of how suffixes, irregular verb forms, abbreviations and proper nouns are to be treated. Sue Davies, computing assistant at Nottingham University, has written a computer programme which works out the Dale-Chall formula score, and which can be readily adapted to cope with any other word list. The scope of her task can be estimated from the fact that it took over six months part-time effort to produce a working programme, whereas the programme which works out all the other formulas was written in two days by Graham Walker, who at the time was a trainee programmer at the Cripps Computing Centre. Their valuable efforts have not only assisted the 'Effective Use of Reading' project, but have led to the dissemination of a readability analysis package which is currently in use in six other universities.

The criteria for a readability formula's inclusion in the study were not simply related to ease of application, or convenience for computer programming, as the inclusion of the Dale-Chall formula demonstrates. A survey of the relevant literature in this country and the USA was undertaken, and formulas were included either because they had a good record in reliability and validity studies, or because they were already in fairly wide use in this country, irrespective of whether data on reliability or validity was available. The formulas reported on are the following: Mugford (1972), Flesch Reading Ease (1948), Flesch Grade (this is a transformation of the R.E. score which suggests a US school grade at which the average reader should be able to understand a passage), Fog (Gunning 1952), Smog (McLaughlin 1969), Smog-X (the Smog formula involves the teacher in making an approximation to a square root – this score uses the exact root in computing the score), Powers, Sumner and Kearl (1958) (this is a recalculation of the Flesch formula, and is most effective with junior-school passages), Farr, Jenkins and Patterson (1951) (this too is a reworking of the Flesch formula), Forcast (*sic,* Sticht 1973) (this is the formula devised for US Army research into literary problems; for ease of application it does not incorporate a sentence length variable), and Dale-Chall (1948).

The survey
Having offered some explanation of the notion of a readability formula, and some evidence to substantiate the claim that the information provided is of value, we now turn to the main point of the exercise, which was to apply various readability formulas to samples of texts from different school subjects and age groups. Thanks to the generous assistance and support of the Nottingham LEA advisory staff, all ten secondary schools in one county district (population 200,000) agreed to take part in the sampling exercise.

The headteachers of all these schools were visited, and it was made clear that the intention was not to make inter-school comparisons, but to gain information about the type of reading materials in use in different subjects, and to examine their difficulty levels. Rather than ask teachers in the schools what they normally used, it was decided simply to choose one week in the spring term, and to collect text samples for analysis based on what was actually in use in the classroom during that week. This method of data collection was chosen because it was less likely to tempt those cooperating to name books which were in the department's stock, but which were rarely used and read by the children.

In each school a single member of staff undertook to distribute to colleagues in English, Mathematics, Science and Social Studies departments a brief form which was to accompany each text sample. Staff who taught first-year and fourth-year groups were asked to supply at the end of the designated survey week copies of any books, worksheets or other printed materials which they had used in class.

The text samples were punched onto computer cards for analysis, together with details of subject, age group, type of material (i.e. textbook, reference book, worksheet, etc.) and whether the text was used in a supported or unsupported context. This final category was to differentiate between reading undertaken when the text was discussed with the teacher – or at least the teacher's support was available, and those occasions when the reader was working on his or her own with no direct support available. The length of text samples varied a good deal. The range was 102 to 810 words, with a mean of 399 words. The wide range was a necessary part of the research design. Usually in readability research a great deal of care has to be taken in establishing sampling reliability. For example, it is not very useful to announce that the reading level of a book is 10.5 years, if this has only been determined on the basis of a single hundred-word sample of text, when scores from other samples within the same book may differ from the first one obtained by three or four years either way. For this reason it was decided so far as possible to analyse the whole passage which the teacher had used. This may indeed have only been part of a chapter of one book, but it did at least represent what the child had been required to read. To this extent, therefore, the issue of sampling reliability within a text does not arise. We are not suggesting that each passage score represents that which would be obtained for the whole of the book from which it was taken, but that it does at least indicate the difficulty level of the sections read by those children during that week.

Not every school supplied samples of text for each subject and age group; no doubt this was partly due to organizational problems within the school, but it probably was also related to the absence of printed sources in the classroom in certain instances. As reported elsewhere (Lunzer *et al,* in preparation) the use of printed sources in some subjects is rather limited. Altogether 125 passages, with a total length of over 49,000 words were analysed.

Survey results

Table 2 below shows the number of text samples collected from each subject and age group, and the average reading level of the texts in each group as derived from the Flesch formula, together with the associated standard deviation for each group, which is a measure of how much variation in difficulty there was in the group. The term 'reading level' is used in preference to the more usual 'reading age' because the latter phrase is sometimes interpreted in unfortunate ways. A child who has a chronological age of eight and a 'reading age' (as derived from a standardized test) of ten is a very different reader from a fifteen-year-old with a 'reading age' of ten. The term 'reading level' is used to avoid this connotation; it should be taken to suggest the age at which those children whose reading competence is about average for their age should be able to cope with the passage.

Table 2 Flesch Formula grade scores for readability survey passages (Reading level = grade score + 5)

| | *First year passages* | | | *Fourth year passages* | | |
	N	Reading level	Standard deviation	N	Reading level	Standard deviation
English	17	12.4	1.2	23	12.9	1.4
Mathematics	5	11.3	0.6	15	12.7	1.7
Science	9	13.5	2.3	12	14.0	1.8
Social studies	22	13.0	2.3	22	14.1	2.2
Population means	53	12.73		71	13.60	

The results are given in terms of the Flesch formula grade scores since this formula is quite widely known, and it was found to be the second most consistent in the cross-validation study which will be referred to below. Dale-Chall formula scores were better in terms of correlations with teachers' judgments, but these were felt by the authors to be rather lower than the true reading levels, and need to be corrected using a conversion table (*vide* Klare 1963). A number of interest points emerge from these results.

Overall, texts used in English departments do not vary in terms of average difficulty level between year groups. It must be noted, however, that within every group there was a good deal of variation between texts. One would not want to suggest that English teachers are failing to give fourth-year students reading which will make a demand on the intellect. A number of interacting factors must also be considered. Firstly, readability measures are derived from analyses of normal prose, and their validity is doubtful when the text is essentially poetic. The fourth-year passages include, for completeness, extracts from Shakespeare's *Macbeth* and Eliot's *Journey of the Magi.* As it happens these both came out with a reading level score of about 12.5, but very few people would seriously suggest that this information is of much value. This is partly because the language patterns of poetry are not the same as those of prose, but also because in a sense it is irrelevant to ask whether the prose is readable or comprehensible in the way we might ask the same question of a novel or textbook. There are surely occasions when partial comprehension is not only accept-able but expected within the context of an English lesson. The fourth-year English passages also included a number of samples of modern novels, in which short sentences and racy dialogue might well produce a low readability score. Many first-year stories, however, are fairly demanding. A Leon Garfield Puffin for example, might well be expected to pose problems in terms of its prose complexity, and while its hero may be an adolescent, the book may be much more difficult to read than the John Wyndham novel encountered in the fourth-year CSE course. One would suggest that the implication for English teachers is not so much that the reading tasks of the fourth form are too easy, but that those given to first formers would appear to be only marginally easier than those given to fourth formers.

The levels of difficulty associated with mathematics textbooks and worksheets were low. Mathematics texts were also more even in difficulty than any others. One problem, however, that has been pointed out to us by mathematics teachers is that by training they are inclined to prefer terse and condensed prose to that which might be written by word-spinning humanities teachers. This could well produce low readability scores, but could still mask problems for readers unfamiliar with the subject. It is also the case that many of the sentences analysed in mathematics texts were brief instructions, rather than expository prose. This too might tend to lower the reading-level score. A further point is that, as with worksheets, instructions for a task ought to be in simpler prose than anything else a child reads. Normally comprehension is a building-up of meanings from the text, and partial understanding can be coped with. In the case of instructions this is not so, and any failure to comprehend is likely to leave the reader in a situation which can only be resolved by the teacher.

In both year groups, science and social studies (which includes history, geography and environmental studies) contain the most difficult prose, with first-year science standing out as particularly difficult. It is slightly disturbing to note that seven of the nine samples of first-year science prose were from teacher-produced worksheets. Some of these had prose which was as difficult as the standard O-level physics textbook. In a sense this is not surprising, since most textbooks are written by teachers, and scientists will tend to prefer a certain type of prose. Nevertheless, since the worksheet is essentially an instructional leaflet which should allow for individual and independent progress, a reading level two years above the pupil's average age does suggest that the children have to cope with difficulties associated with the way in which the text has been written, as well as those associated with the task itself and the scientific concepts involved.

The different patterns of integration of science subjects in each school at first- and fourth-year level made it impossible for comparisons to be drawn within the scientific disciplines, but one accepts that particularly in chemistry and biology the high number of specialist technical terms creates special difficulties for the reader. The different headings under which history, geography and social studies are taught in various schools also precluded differentiation by subject, although one must note that geology was a subject which seemed to have a particularly high number of unfamiliar and difficult words.

As has already been suggested, the difficulty level of a book is not the only determinant of how successfully it can be approached by a reader. The way in which it is used is also an important factor. We have already made the distinction between using a source in class, when problem words or passages can be discussed with the teacher, and using it in a situation such as for homework or for reference when no teacher support is directly available. American researchers have suggested that the reading level of books used in an unsupported context needs to be approximately two years lower than that of books used in a supported context. We controlled for this variable and found a slight negative correlation ($r = -0.07$) between passage difficulty and use in a supported context. In other words, the texts set by teachers to be read by children on their own turned out to be slightly *more* difficult than those used in class when help was available. This finding was related to the way in which science and social studies teachers used textbooks. As we learned on the LEA visits, the need felt by teachers to deal with practical work and give notes did not always allow time for reading in class, and therefore it tended to be related to homework. Often the task is not a reading homework as such, but one in which the student takes home the textbook for reference or note-making. It seems from our findings that the books which are the most difficult in the whole school to read and understand are in fact often given to children when there is no direct support available from the teacher. It seems clear that the implications of this should be considered carefully by our science and social studies colleagues.

Following the initial analysis of the data reported in Table 2, tests of statistical significance were applied but with little in terms of conclusive results. A two-way analysis of variance failed to show any significant differences between the prose samples in different age and subject groups, but this should not be interpreted as implying that the results are unreliable, or indeed in the general sense non-significant. As teachers we should perhaps be a little surprised to learn that the reading demands we make of first formers at secondary level are *not* significantly different from those related to CSE and O-level courses. An analysis of texts in terms of type (i.e. textbook, reference book, fiction or poetry, workcard or worksheet, and pamphlet or brochure) only revealed one significant finding, which was that reference books were harder to read than all the other types of text. This may surprise few people, but it reinforces the point made above concerning the need for alertness on the teacher's part if the most difficult reading tasks are undertaken in an unsupported context.

The cross-validation study

The secondary aim of the readability study has been to examine which of the many formulas currently available are potentially most valuable to the practising teacher. A cross-validation study was therefore planned, which would provide information about how closely each formula agreed with pooled subjective assessments of difficulty, and with actual comprehension scores as measured by the cloze technique.

A stratified random sample of forty passages was selected from the original set of 125 passages. Twenty-four of these were first-year and sixteen were fourth-year samples. In the event one first-year passage was dropped from the analysis because of an administrative error during cloze testing, which left twenty-three first-year and sixteen fourth-year passages. A group of twenty-four experienced teachers on an advanced diploma or M.Ed. course assessed each of the passages, and estimated its reading level. Since interest and motivation are vital in reading, the teachers were also asked to estimate on a four point scale whether the children at the age level they specified as appropriate would find the passage interesting or boring. It was also decided to ask children from a different school district from that in which the survey was undertaken to make similar judgments. The children (eighty-five first year and ninety fourth year) were asked to rate the passages which had originally been collected from their own year group, and were given a preliminary instruction to imagine they were a teacher choosing books for children.

The cloze-test passages were produced by deleting every tenth word in a passage, beginning after the fiftieth word. All ten possible versions of each passage were prepared. The children were asked to fill in each gap with the single word which they thought was most suitable, and the mean percentage of correctly replaced words was taken as an indication of how difficult the passage was to read and understand. As is common in large-scale cloze testing, only the exactly correct word was scored as correct but spelling errors were allowed.

Results of the cross-validation study
As Table 3 (page 00) shows, all the formulas correlated fairly highly with the teachers' assessments; none was worse than r = .60, and the highest correlations were with the Dale-Chall (.77), Flesch (.74), and Powers-Sumner-Kearl (.73) formulas.

It is clear that of the variables included in each readability formula, those related to vocabulary were the most important in predicting overall difficulty. As an illustration of this it may be noted that the count of syllables per word in a passage correlated .68 with the teacher ratings. By contrast, the average number of words per sentence correlated .33 with this criterion.

Table 3   Correlation of linguistic variables and readability formulas with criteria of pooled teacher judgments of passage difficulty
(based on thirty-nine passages assessed by twenty-four judges)

Letters/word	.53
Letters/sentence	.48
Words/sentence	.33
Syllables/word	.68
Dale-Chall Formula	.77
Flesch Reading Ease Formula	.74
Powers-Sumner-Kearl	.73
Smog (McLaughlin)	.71
Smog-X	.71
Flesch-Grade	.69
Farr-Jenkins-Patterson	.68
Fog (Gunning)	.68
Mugford	.68
Forcast (Sticht)	.61

In the study of teachers' and children's assessments of the interest level of passages the most consistent finding was that difficult passages were assessed as boring. This may seem predictable, but it may not be simply that children were reacting negatively to what they found difficult to understand. The responses indicated that, in general, when a passage was felt to be more suitable for an older age group, it was also felt that the children in that higher age group would find the material boring. In other words, the children were not asked to judge the interest level of the passage as if it were to be used with their own age group.

A further finding was that children consistently assessed instructions to do a task as very boring. This reinforces the point that if they are to be communicated successfully, instructions should be in simpler prose than anything else a child has to read. This insight is well known to writers of cookery books – it may not be so familiar to the overworked teacher struggling against the clock to complete ten worksheets.

One third of the passages assessed by children (ie. thirteen out of thirty-nine) showed a significant sex bias in terms of judgments of interest level. At both first- and fourth-year level, boys assessed English texts (whether narrative or language exercise) as rather boring; for girls, geographical texts particularly were graded as of low interest, but science and history were also marked down. In view of the interaction between reading comprehension and a reader's interest level (Shnayer 1969), this factor is one which teachers must consider carefully.

The results of the cloze tests (see Table 4 page 76) serve to remind us that while the technique gives us an interesting insight into the reader's response to a passage, unless the testing is on a fairly extensive scale the results may be unreliable or at best difficult to interpret. Groups of 100 first-year and fourth-year pupils were given the booklets of randomly ordered cloze passages. To score the completed tests took well in excess of 100 man hours. This expenditure of effort was necessary because the level of correct responses within one class can vary from 0 per cent to 100 per cent on two versions of the same passage (the average number of deletions per passage was approximately thirty-five). It seems clear that on the individual level, cloze gives us some idea how the reader is responding to the text, but to make generalizations about the overall difficulty level of the book for the whole class seems less than justifiable. Bormuth's (1967, 1968) suggested figures of 38 per cent and 44 per cent correct cloze items as a criterion of comprehension were based on the mean scores of one hundred subjects in each case. His 1968 study indicated at a standard deviation of 17 per cent was associated with the figure of 44 per cent, and this statistic has received very little attention from either teachers or researchers. This is a considerable range; in our own study the means of the most difficult and easiest passages were 25 per cent and 57 per cent respectively, and the standard deviations were usually about 10 per cent. One's confidence in cloze scores must be diminished if the area of uncertainty associated with individual results is almost as great as the range of mean scores found on a large-scale study.

Finally, some of the implications of the cross-validation study for using particular measures at classroom level must be examined.

Table 4 Intercorrelations of variables in cross–validation study
(all values of r given as positive)

First year passages (N = 23)

		1	2	3	4	5	6	7	8	9
1	T-Diff									
2	T-Int	39								
3	Cloze	51*	09							
4	C-Diff	86**	29	64**						
5	C-Int	55**	78**	10	31					
6	Wds/sen	11	10	16	24	15				
7	Sylls/wd	70**	50*	55**	78**	47*	18			
8	Mugford	69**	63**	44*	69**	63**	07	88**		
9	Flesch-Re	62*	44*	61**	64**	38	31	81**	81**	
10	Fog	38	26	51	34	23	76**	57**	57**	83**

Fourth year passages (N = 16)

		1	2	3	4	5	6	7	8	9
1	T-Diff									
2	T-Int	48								
3	Cloze	69**	35							
4	C-Diff	82**	46	50*						
5	C-Int	30	80**	48	20					
6	Wds/sen	74**	21	61*	37	16				
7	Sylls/wd	50*	29	32	61*	07	13			
8	Mugford	56*	21	35	64**	09	14	90**		
9	Flesch-Re	71*	33	51*	68**	12	37	86**	86**	
10	Fog	81**	36	57	67**	21	70**	75**	75**	94**

Among the formulas, with the exception of the Forcast formula, correlations with the criterion of pooled teacher judgment are above .68 for the set of forty passages. However, certain formulas correlated much more highly with teacher judgments at one year-group level than another. For example, as Table 4 demonstrates, Mugford's formula correlated r = .69 with first-year passages, and .56 with fourth-year texts. Conversely, the Fog index only correlated .38 with the first texts, but .81 with those from the fourth year. The reason for this is that Mugford's formula has a heavy weighting on the syllable count, and the Fog formula gives a greater weighting to the count of words per sentence. There are at least two ways these results can be interpreted:

1 Firstly, it could be that vocabulary is a more crucial determinant of readability at age twelve, and sentence length at age fifteen. The sample size in the present study, however, is not really large enough to warrant this conclusion on the basis of the data reported.
2 Alternatively, it could be that the vagaries of sampling have presented us with a subsample of fourth-year texts in which sentence length correlates unusually highly with judgments of reading difficulty. This is not a simple issue to resolve, but until an alternative interpretation is more strongly supported, one would tend to feel that a formula which is less sensitive to possible difference between the year groups might be best for general use, and this would suggest the use of Flesch formula. For ease of application in the classroom, the Fry graph could be used rather than the Flesch formula; in the pilot study carried out in 1974 (Harrison 1974) it was found that 80 per cent of Flesch scores were on the same grade level as those obtained using the Fry graph.

The Flesch grade scores have another advantage in that they give (when 5 is added) a 'reading level' for the passage which is reasonably close to that derived from pooled teacher judgments or pooled student judgments of difficulty. Some formulas, notably Gunning's Fox index, tend to give unrealistically high scores on difficult passages. Most utilization of readability formula results for dramatic or political purposes involves the Fog index, since it can suggest readability levels in excess of 25 on texts with rather long sentences. On our fourth-year passages, for example, while the teacher and student overall means were both 13.1, the Fog and Smog formulas both gave means in excess of 15.1 years, suggesting an average prediction of two years above the teachers' and students' judgments on every passage. Again this issue is a complex one, and not easy to resolve in terms of classroom practice. It seems clear that while readability formulas are effective in ranking materials in order of difficulty in a manner which correlates quite highly with both teacher and student judgment, the particular grade level given needs to be interpreted with care. Accepting these limitations, one may still suggest that formula scores give information which is of use to teachers and which cannot be obtained readily in any other manner, since individual teacher judgments and individual cloze-test scores can often be much more unreliable.

Conclusion

In concluding, one should stress what is *not* suggested. It is not suggested that readability formulas should be applied indiscriminately to everything a student is likely to read – apart from being totally unrealistic in terms of the time this would take, it would be inappropriate in some cases and potentially harmful in others.

It is not suggested that textbooks with a high readability score should be scrapped – in these times of economic restraint this would be folly. What one would suggest is that the results of this research, taken together with parallel findings from similar studies, give firm evidence that many students, perhaps even most students, learn less than they might otherwise do from school texts, because many texts present difficulties not just in terms of conceptual content, but because of the way in which they are written.

The implications for us as teachers are therefore:

1   We must be more alert to which of the books we use are likely to be causing extra problems; for example, we should not expect children to work effectively on their own in the library if the reference book we sent them to is harder than any other book in the school.
2   We should pay special attention to the difficulty level of books in the content areas when the student's intrinsic motivation to read is likely to be low, because it is precisely when motivation is low that high level of prose difficulty is likely to lead to non-comprehension.
3   We must look with particular care at textbooks, worksheets and workbooks which give instructions for a task. Very often these will relate to work which the student is to tackle on his or her own, and for which anything less than full comprehension will mean that no progress can be made. In our own study it was found that teachers tended to assume that this failure implied that the task itself was too difficult. It needs a high degree of professional skill to keep an eye on all the students in a class and to decide in particular cases whether a workcard is causing problems because of its conceptual content, or simply because of the way it is written. Nevertheless, at a time of increasing usage of individualized learning materials, it is a professional skill which we must foster.

Does readability level make a difference? The answer to this question has been answered for us in a number of carefully controlled studies conducted by George Klare in Ohio. He has shown that if you take two groups of readers who are equal in reading ability and give them exactly the same comprehension test, those given a more readable version of the test passage will learn and understand more. He prepared two versions of the test passage – the original one, and another which had been rewritten in simpler prose, and found significantly higher comprehension test scores were obtained by the group which was given the passage with a lower readability score.

Readability measures can, therefore, be of value not only to researchers, but to the classroom teacher. The Schools Council Effective Use of Reading project has found that in many cases teachers had low expectations about what use children could make of books in learning. For many, the reaction was to put their faith in their ability to purvey knowledge, rather than the child's capacity to learn for himself. Our team has come to feel strongly that children can be helped to use books much more effectively than they do at present, and although one should not overestimate their potential, measures of readability can be used to help in this important task.

References

BORMUTH, J. R. (1966) Readability: a new approach *Reading Research Quarterly 1*, 3

BORMUTH, J. R. (1967) Comparable cloze and multiple choice comprehension test scores *Journal of Reading* 10, 291-9

BORMUTH, J. R. (1968) Cloze test readability: criterion reference scores *Journal of Educational Measurement* 5, 189-96

CHALL, J. S. (1958) *Readability – an appraisal of Research and Application* Columbus, Ohio: Ohio State University

DALE, E. and CHALL, J. S. (1948) A formula for predicting readability *Educational Research Bulletin* 27, 11-20, 37-54

FARR, J. N., JENKINS, J. J. and PATTERSON, D. G. (1951) Simplification of the Flesch Reading Ease Formula *Journal of Applied Psychology* 35, 333-7

FLESCH, R. E. (1948) A new readability yardstick *Journal of Applied Psychology* 32, 221-33

GUNNING, R. (1952) *The Technique of Clear Writing* New York: McGraw Hill

HARRISON, C. (1974) *Readability and School* Schools Council project discussion document, University of Nottingham School of Education

KLARE, G. R. (1963) *The Measurement of Readability* Iowa State University Press

KLARE, G. R. (1975) Judging readability *Instructional Science* 5, 55-61

LUNZER, E. A. and GARDNER, W. K. (eds) (1977) *The Effective Use of Reading* Report of project carried out on behalf of the Schools Council, (in press)

McLAUGHLIN, G. H. (1969) Smog grading–a new readability formula *Journal of Reading* 22, 639-46

MUGFORD, L. (1972) A new way of predicting readability *Reading* 4, 2, 31-5

POWERS, R. D., SUMNER, W. A. and KEARL, B. E. (1958) A recalculation of four readability formulas *Journal of Educational Psychology* 49, 99-105

SHNAYER, S. W. (1969) 'Relationships between reading interest and reading comprehension' in J. A. Figurel (ed) *Reading and Realism* 1968 Proceedings, vol. 13, part 1. Newark, Delaware: International Reading Association

STICHT, T. G. (1973) Research toward the design, development and evaluation of a job-functional literacy program for the U.S. Army *Literacy Discussion* IV, 3, 339-69

10   Some influences of semantics on reading development

L. John Chapman

At a previous conference of this association David Crystal (1975) drew attention to the role that general linguistics plays in the study of reading. He pointed out its fundamental importance, stating that it 'inculcates a state of mind, provides a set of principles and, because of its coherent scientific framework, can inspire confidence when it comes to suggesting solutions to problems. He outlines three principles of significance for reading, the notion of language variety, the view of language as an integrated set of levels, and the idea of ordered stages of linguistic development.

In much the same way I would like to add a fourth to these – the ways in which a study of semantics might inform our understanding of reading. Semantics, whose study has presented such formidable problems in the past has begun, particularly so in the last ten years, to exhibit that same 'coherent scientific framework' that has characterized much of modern linguistics. (It is viewed by many, of course, as a branch of linguistics.) The insights provided by semantic studies will, in the future I'm sure, greatly influence the study of reading and help to solve some of its problems. The area of knowledge covered by semantics is vast and complex; however, it can be limited within a general linguistic framework.

The perspective adopted here is that provided by linguistics; semantics being regarded as a branch of that science. The boundaries can be restricted still further by singling out for comment one type of meaning for investigation. Leech (1974) gives a useful division of the different facets of meaning, showing seven basic types, as Figure 1 (page 82) shows.

Whilst meaning in terms of communication embraces all types of meaning, one type only is selected for consideration, that is *Conceptual meaning*, or *Sense*. This is not to say that the other types are not very important; it is purely a matter of reducing an enormous field of knowledge so that one facet can be analysed and its implications for reading examined. Conceptual meaning is also chosen for it is close, due to its logical, cognitive or dentative nature, to the study of reading comprehension.

Figure 1   Seven types of meaning
(After Leech, G. (1974) page 26)

1 Conceptual meaning (or sense)		Logical, cognitive or denotative content
Associative Meaning	2 Connotative meaning	What is communicated by virtue of what language refers to
	3 Stylistic meaning	What is communicated of the social circumstances of language use
	4 Affective meaning	What is communicated of the feelings and attitudes of the speaker/writer
	5 Reflected meaning	What is communicated through association with other sense of the same expression
	6 Collocative meaning	What is communicated through association with words which tend to occur in the environment of another word
	7 Thematic meaning	What is communicated by the way in which the message is organised in terms of order and emphasis

Components and contrasts of meaning

One way of looking at word meaning is by a process of 'breaking down the sense of a word into its minimal distinctive features'. For instance, the words man; woman; boy; girl, belong to the larger semantic field concerned with the human species. A simple two-dimensional diagram (Figure 2) illustrates how we can begin to analyse and to specify the *features* of the words within this semantic field.

These simple relationships can be represented in another way using the following type of notation for the features:

```
man:     + human + adult + male
woman:   + human + adult − male
boy:     + human − adult + male
girl:    + human − adult − male
```

Figure 2

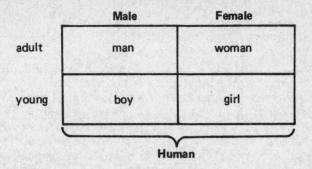

These are called componential definitions and can be used to show the interrelatedness of meanings within a semantic field by breaking down each concept into minimal components or features. Various types of opposition, which are not necessarily absolute, can be shown in this way by the differing logical consequences they have in sentences containing them. Further details of this type of analysis can be found in the reference to Leech cited above.

The child's acquisition of semantic fields

(To avoid misunderstanding, it is wise perhaps to recall that psychological studies have provided much data on concept development but, in this paper, the description and approach is that of semantics.)

If semantic fields can be analysed in this way, then it follows, by analogy to other developmental processes, that children may well acquire semantic fields by way of their components or features of meaning in an orderly fashion. The pace of this acquisition may well depend on the richness of the child's language environment. This being so then it is again probable that the distinctive features that are uncovered by such techniques as componential analysis will accrue during, and be dependent upon, language experience. Another way of putting this is to think of a conceptual field being in embryonic form only in the young child's awareness and gradually growing with linguistic experience by the addition of distinguishing features until the richness of a fully developed adult concept is reached. This growth of meaning could be by the accretion of the componential features, or markers, as they are sometimes called. The word could be 'in' the child's vocabulary, but be hollow or empty and mislead the teachers into belief that the child's usage is equivalent to her own.

Clark (1972) has already researched the early acquisition processes of semantic fields with children aged four to five-and-a-half years. Her findings were that:

1   children set up these semantic or conceptual fields automatically as
    they learn something of the meaning of relative words

2   there is a distinct order of acquisition based on the complexity of
    the structure of the field.

My own research (Chapman 1975) looked at the further development
of certain fields in school children aged five to eleven years. By using
'Happy Family' type games leading into judgment of the closeness of
meaning tasks, the research showed that there was a steady developmental growth from the early stages examined at five years towards the
adult model. This is not, of course, surprising. However, the
importance for the teacher is in the ways in which the componential
features are acquired – their order of acquisition, and the amount of
language exposure needed for the abstractions to be made and full
conceptual meanings to develop.

Three semantic fields were examined in the research – Kinship
terms, Colour names, and Pronouns. The latter – the Pronoun field
because of their semantico-syntactic significance – will be used as an
example. It could be argued that Pronouns are essentially syntactic and
not semantic and there is much to be said for this viewpoint as the field
is closely bounded and relatively unchanging, compared with some
Noun fields. However, the example was chosen here for it illustrates
the interplay between syntax and semantics in dynamic reading
situations.

Gleason (1969) provides a paradigm of the semantic field of
personal Pronouns. This gives some idea of the dimensions of the
field's organization and the componential features involved. From
their language use, children gradually acquire the features of the
pronouns:

1st person singular	I	Me	My	*Mine*
1st person plural	We	Us	Our	*Ours*
2nd person sing/plur	You	You	You	*Yours*
3rd person singular (M)	He	Him	His	*His*
3rd person singular (F)	She	Her	Her	*Hers*
Not used	It	It	Its	*Its*
3rd person plural	They	Them	Their	*Their*
Not used	Who	Whom	Whose	*Whose*

(After Gleason (1969), page 105)

A group of students (adults) were given a similar task to the children in
the experimental groups used and they arranged these pronouns in
three main clusters as follows:

The children and the adults were asked to put the pronouns, which were printed on small cards into piles so that those that were close in meaning were in the same piles. The grouping within the three main clusters contain the Pronouns judged as being closest in meaning:

Clustering by adult students:

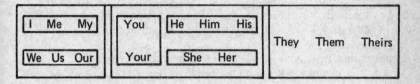

Compare this with the groupings of a class of 6–7 year old children:

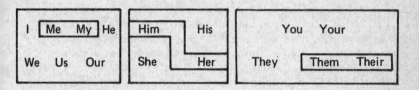

Another class of children aged 8 to 9 produced the following pattern:

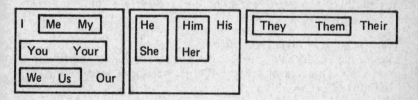

The elder group of children of 10–11 years clustered like this:

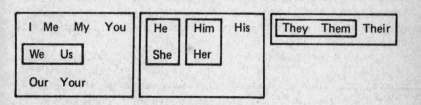

The grouping provided by the adults showed their appreciation of the organization of the field of Pronouns: they were able to put together as close in meaning those pronouns having most features in common and with close agreement to Gleason's theoretical model. The younger children however worked along another dimension that had priority at this developmental stage, grouping the male-female opposites as closest in meaning.

The main difference, however, among the children's clustering was in the strength of the groupings. The younger children's clusters in this and other fields was far less decisive and uncertain compared with the older children whose clusterings were tighter and stable.

Implications for teaching and classroom practice

Now to classroom realities and the implications for reading.

There are two direct classroom applications from semantic field development that I would like to bring to your notice. One is in productive writing, the other concerning pronouns in reading instruction. The first one is sketched lightly as it is the subject of a Workshop at this conference. This is the use of the basic notion of a semantic field in a remedial situation. Richard Binns, from St Mungo's Academy, Glasgow, who has organized the Workshop session, teaches secondary boys who are slow with written language. By using special techniques, he has managed to channel groups of basic associated words within semantic fields through editory procedures into continuous prose. This is with children experiencing difficulty. Richard Binns uses a left-hand/right-hand page editing technique to achieve this improvement. The pupil first records the development of a cluster of words, for example a group concerned with police and crime, on the left-hand side of a jotter. The associations are quickly derived, giving a drama in embryo:

> *Cluster given by twelve year old boy*
> Policeman, Constable, crash, Inspector, car, accident, detective, ambulance, fire, first aid, bus, traffic, news reporter, TV reporters, buildings, beat, drinking.

This field is then used to outline a plot with the action in picture sequences. These provide sentences which, after editing, are transformed to the right-hand page of the jotter into narrative form. The second application is concerned with one element in the development of fluent reading. In this the awareness of pronoun relationships might be seen almost as a prerequisite.

Various types of relationships exist amongst the words in a passage of prose. There are, for instance, the grammatical relations between parts of speech that help us to anticipate what is to come, for example, nouns and verbs, articles and nouns, adjectives and nouns, and many others. One that is not often made explicit to children is the process of anaphora, or the shortening or substituting for an expression, often by a pronoun, which is usually antecedent to it, and which has the same referent as the antecedent. (Bormuth *et al* 1970). The existence of this function with pronouns was utilized engagingly by Lewis Carroll, as the following verse from *Alice's Adventures in Wonderland* demonstrates:

> They told me you had been to her,
> And mentioned me to him,
> She gave me a good character
> But said I could not swim.

Here there are plenty of pronouns, but one of the reasons for the poem's puzzling quality is that there are no antecedents. The pronouns do not refer back to or replace any nouns. Two further illustrations provided by Mary Hoffman in the re-write of the Open University Course on Reading Development may help to clarify the point:

1 'After I had locked *George* in the shed, I began to feel sorry for *him*.' In this sentence *George* and *him* are related anaphorically – we understand that *him* stands for *George*. The cue for the reader is backward acting relying on his/her knowledge that George is '+ male' connecting this with a '+ male' pronoun in the correct case.

2 Another example uses three pairs of relations: 'From the time that *Burton* told *her* of *his* travels in *Arabia, she* longed to go *there*.'
     Even with so little context, the semantico-syntactic processes are:

Burton – his: + male, possibly + adult, so + male
                          pronoun, possessive
Her – she: relating pronoun to pronoun
Arabia – there.

There are, of course, other anaphoric structures and in their research Bormuth *et al* (1970) used fourteen types to test awareness of grammatical relations within and between sentences. Their examples demonstrate the importance of the process:

1 Joe may go. If *so,* we will . . .
2 He works in the cellar. It is cool *there.*
3 The man *who* lives next door makes . . .
4 John likes tennis. So *does* Bill.
5 The small boy came. *This* boy is . . .
6 The black horse belongs to Joe. *That* is his . . .
7 Several men went fishing. *Two* caught . . .

8   Joe, Bill and Mary went to the show. *All* enjoyed . . .
9   There are ripe and green apples. The *green* are mine.
10   Joe is sick. *So is* Bill.
11   Bill and Joe went shopping. *No one* bought . . .
12   Joe is stuck in the mud. *This* leaves us . . .
13   Those steel towers are Antennas. Those *objects* are . . .
14   Joe left the room. *He* had . . .

The more speedily a child anticipates these referrals back the more fluent the reading becomes. Preliminary trials with some materials using these pronoun relationships with beginning readers have shown that the process is also useful as a diagnostic aid to determine stages in the development of fluency.

Some early *pilot* research with individual readers using twelve passages from selected primers showed that those children who were regarded by their teachers as good readers (aged 6½–7½) could cope adequately in a cloze situation where the pronouns were deleted. The average and poor readers had much greater difficulty supplying the missing pronoun. The kinds of error made by an average reader (boy aged 7 years 5 months) concerned substitutions:

   her for she
   them for her
   you for me
   you for us
   him for our
   you for her (and other similar errors).

A poor reader (boy aged 7 years 5 months) substituted:

   I for he
   he for him
   he for she
   I for we
   he for we (twice)
   he for I (twice) etc.

In each case the pronouns were provided and had to be selected. The cloze passages were completed in normal class situations and were given by the children's own teacher. You will have spotted, of course, that in 'normal' reading situations other cues are present from graphemes, but to develop fluent reading through stumbling from individual word to individual word stage, needs greater basic development. Removing the grapheme cues to a distance revealed weakness.

You may suspect that the texts were very difficult and may be intrigued to know the twelve texts. They were as follows:

Example 1   from *Janet and John* Book 3
Example 2   from *Gay Way* Yellow Book
Example 3   from *Reading to Some Purpose* Book 1
Example 4   from *Reading to Some Purpose* Book 1
Example 5   from *Reading to Some Purpose* Book 1
Example 6   from *Reading to Some Purpose* Book 1
Example 7   from *Revised Beacon Study Reader*
Example 8   from *Revised Beacon Study Reader*
Example 9   from *Janet and John* Book 3
Example 10   from *Janet and John* Book 3
Example 11   from *Janet and John* Book 3
Example 12   from an article from *Reader's Digest*

Apart from example 12, they were all in use in schools.

It was seen during this work, and again I must emphasize its very preliminary nature, that the poor reader, defined as poor presumably because he had not yet achieved fluency, has great difficulty in coping with the anaphoric process of pronouns. The inability to utilize backward acting cues was noticed particularly. The weakness is very well demonstrated in a cloze-type exercise where the context should provide the cues necessary to supply the pronoun.

Marie Clay (1969) mentions that pronouns have high rates of self-correction (60 per cent, *cf* Nouns 20 per cent), which indicates that although often corrected, many errors are made with their usage in the first place. Those who do not correct their errors – the slower readers – will need instruction and practice.

It may be, of course, that the teaching of reading has not drawn attention to the process of forward and backward acting cues. As so often there are those children who will have little difficulty in transferring their ability to cope with relations in oral language situations to that of reading and who do not need instruction, but others will need to have each process taught and the presence of such elements made explicit.

This is only one very small but pertinent part of the many facets of semantics that can inform the reading process. There are many others like predication analysis to be developed as progress is made in our knowledge of the semantic structure of sentences and paragraphs which may well illuminate reading comprehension, especially those studies interrelating syntax and semantics which bring us so close to the dynamics involved in reading.

References
BORMUTH, J. R., MANNING, J., CARR, J. and PEARSON, D. (1970)

Children's comprehension of between – and within – sentences syntactic structures *Journal of Educational Psychology* 61, 5, 349-57

CHAPMAN, L. J. (1975) *An Investigation of a Structuring Model for the Acquisition of Semantic Structures by Children* Unpublished Ph.D. Thesis, University of Aston in Birmingham

CHAPMAN, L. J. and HOFFMAN, M. M. (1977) *Intermediate Skills* Block 1, Unit 4, Course PE231 Reading Development. The Open University

CLARK, E. V. (1972) On the child's acquisition of antonyms in two semantic fields *Journal of Verbal Learning and Verbal Behaviour* 2, 750-8

CLAY, M. M. (1969) Reading errors and self-correction behaviour *British Journal of Educational Psychology* 39, 47-56

CRYSTAL, D. (1975) 'Neglected linguistic principles in the study of reading' In D. Moyle (ed.) *Reading: What of the future?* Proceedings of the Eleventh Conference of the United Kingdom Reading Association. Ward Lock Educational

GLEASON, H. A. (1969) (Revised ed) *An Introduction to Descriptive Linguistics* Holt, Rinehart and Winston

LEECH, G. (1974) *Semantics* Penguin

11   Reading fluency in middle-school children

Anthony K. Pugh

Introduction

The stage at which a child no longer habitually reads aloud, and begins to read fluently to himself, is of considerable importance and interest. Although this stage has not received much attention from researchers, it is not only of concern for the child himself, but it is also of relevance to attempts to understand the route which the child must take in order to become an effective adult reader.

This route is not well understood since the tendency, so far as models of reading development are concerned, is to examine beginning readers and adult readers but to say little about the stages inbetween (see, for example, Mackworth (1972) for a review of models). There has for some time been interest in the inbetween stage from psycholinguists concerned with the growth of knowledge of structure, but Gibson (1972) considered that how the reader develops his knowledge of structures so that it is incorporated in his reading habits remains a mystery.

More recently Gibson and Levin (1975) suggest that the search for any single model of the adult reading process is unfruitful, and seem, moreover, to be out of sympathy with model making. Nevertheless, they suggest that there is a general principle – the principle of economy – which operates during adult reading. This principle, in some ways akin to the notion of cue reduction which Dearborn and Anderson (1952) considered of importance in reading development, indicates, for example, that the skilled adult reader ignores irrelevant information and processes the largest units compatible with his task.

A model proposed by Goodman (1968) also suggested that during reading development the units which are processed tend to become larger. However, this model is particularly interesting for the suggestions it makes about the mode in which information appears to be processed at three stages of reading development. It must be noted that Goodman takes care to suggest that his three stages should not be applied too rigidly and, in particular, that it should not be assumed that any person reads solely in a way appropriate to only one stage.

Emphasis in the three modes in this model has led to the three stages being designated the oral, the aural and the silent stages (Pugh 1975a). The aural stage is the inbetween stage referred to above, where the child does not yet possess the strategies available to the skilled adult reader, yet is no longer restricted by the need to read aloud. A number of studies at this aural stage have been carried out by this writer, jointly with Mary H. Neville of the University of Leeds, and the purpose of this paper is to review and discuss this research.

In the research we have been mainly concerned with 9–10 year old children in their first year at middle school. Three distinct but related lines of enquiry have been pursued. These are: an assessment of reading while listening as a means of developing reading fluency; a comparison of performance on cloze tests of reading, listening and restricted reading; and a study of children's performance and strategies when using silent reading to locate information.

Assessment of reading while listening

There is evidence that most reading is accompanied by some form of inner speech (Conrad 1972; Edfeldt 1959; Sokolov 1968; but see also Gibson and Levin 1975). The precise function of this sub-vocal activity in proficient readers is not entirely clear, but it seems certain that it is not merely a *sotto voce* verbatim reading of a text. Conrad suggests that it may be used as an aid to short-term memory processing. Whatever the function of inner speech in the reading of adults, however, there are grounds for thinking that at the aural stage there is justification in using a method to help the reader reconstruct the sound patterns of a text without the labour normally associated with this task. In other words, if the aural stage involves a 'listening in' to the text, then to read a text while at the same time hearing a recording of the same text may be helpful.

The theoretical basis for the approach is given more fully elsewhere (Neville and Pugh 1975a) and a review of empirical studies where reading while listening has been used is also available (Daly, Neville and Pugh 1975). Our own studies with middle school children (Neville and Pugh 1975b and forthcoming a) suggest that certain children of rather below average ability benefit from the approach considerably, whereas others do less well than their control subjects receiving conventional reading instruction. The mean improvement in reading ability as measured by a standardized cloze test of reading comprehension is found to be similar for both experimental and control groups but there is a greater variance within the post-test scores of the experimental group. Children appear to benefit as much when left to listen and read as they do when the teacher participates and there are, therefore, possible advantages of economy of teacher time.

One difficulty in assessing the effects of such a course arises from lack of tests of reading fluency. Indeed there is not much agreement on what is meant by fluency. Here we use it in the sense of being able to silently read a text as one might in listening to a story. This is different from the hesitating reading of beginning reading or the strategic application of various styles of reading which one might expect from the effective adult reader. Thus by our definition fluency relates to the aural stage. Other writers (for example Clark 1976) have used it in a less specific sense to mean any independent reading, whether aloud or silently.

Thus while it may be argued that cloze tests are not the most appropriate means of testing reading fluency, they have been used of necessity. More work needs to be done, however, to assess the effects of reading while listening on more realistic reading tasks. Also some account needs to be taken of long-term effects which may arise from possible increases in motivation, better attitudes to reading, or simply from the fact that, unlike most approaches to teaching reading, this approach appears to provide the learner with an actual experience akin to the desired behaviour rather than with segments of relevant behaviour.

The major questions are, therefore, not so much about the practicability of the method or its applications, for it has been found to be useful not only with middle school children but also with certain foreign students (Neville and Pugh 1975a; Pugh 1975b). Rather the questions relate to what precisely the method achieves and for how long it achieves it, to what exactly happens during reading while listening and to whether the processing which takes place is indeed close to the processing of fluent readers at the aural stage.

As indicated later, some data at present being analysed may help in discovering certain other characteristics of children who appear to benefit from listening while reading. An experiment already carried out (Neville 1975) casts some light on the processing involved. The purpose of the experiment was to determine the effect of changes of rate of an aural message on reading and on listening while reading. Subjects were 118 middle school children of normal reading ability. The subjects were divided into two groups. One group read three passages of equivalent reading difficulty (Neale 1966) while at the same time they listened to a recording of the passage. The apparent rate of speech in the recording was varied from passage to passage by retaining the original rate for one and by compressing or expanding the others (see Duker 1974). The second group listened, without a reading text. Scores on the comprehension test showed no difference for those who only listened whatever the rate of the recording, but for the reading while listening group the scores were higher the slower the rate of the text. There is some independent confirmation of these findings from Grant (1974), and it appears that there may be some difficulty for some middle school children in reading at a rate much in excess of normal listening rate.

This finding may help explain the plateau effect which puzzled early researchers (such as O'Brien 1921; West 1926) who were concerned with increasing speed of reading in children of a similar age to those studied here, but who found that progress was slight beyond a certain rate. Nevertheless, there does seem to be some evidence (Thames and Rossiter 1972) that with older subjects the rate of reading can be increased by using compressed speech as a pacer. However, the difficulty of obtaining meaningful measures of reading rate indicates caution in interpretation of these studies, and we feel that there may be dangers in using aural pacers beyond a certain stage because of differences which appear to exist between the processing involved in aural reading, and that used in silent reading.

Comparisons between performance on cloze tests of listening and reading

The studies described in the previous section have mainly had direct practical applications. However, some other work has been undertaken in order to investigate more closely the contrasts and similarities which exist between the processing employed by middle school children when taking cloze tests of reading, listening, and a restricted form of reading where the sequential presentation constraints of listening are similar in some respects.

The first study (Neville and Pugh 1974) was with sixty-six children aged 9–10 years. They were divided into groups and each group took one of two alternative forms of the GAP reading test (McLeod and Unwin 1970). A listening version of the test had been prepared and the subjects listened to the alternative form which they had not read, and attempted, on a specially devised answer sheet, to complete the gaps from the preceding context available to them as listeners. The purpose of the study was to compare children's performance on cloze tests in the two language modes with regard to incidence and type of error made. It was felt that the different constraints operating in the two modes would result in overall differences in error patterns. In fact, despite fairly detailed linguistic analysis of the errors, no clear pattern emerged, except that children obtained significantly lower scores in the listening mode and also made significantly more omissions. However, one could not be sure that this was not an artefact of the way the information was presented in this specific listening task.

This study was exploratory only, and some of the issues were examined more fully in a second study (Neville and Pugh in press). Here, in addition to the other tests, a test of restricted reading was also employed. This was in the form of a booklet and certain subjects had a booklet with one gap and the preceding context per page. This permitted a comparison to be made between cloze listening performance and performance on a restricted reading test where it was felt that the language restraints were similar. Also, fuller analysis was made, for it had been suspected from examination of the data from the earlier study that the range of ability among the subjects might be obscuring patterns in the error analysis.

In the second study, therefore, 130 subjects of the same age range as those studied before were given a cloze test of reading and a test of either cloze listening or restricted reading. The sample was then dichotomized about the median of the reading scores. Comparisons of scores for the group of poorer readers revealed no significant differences whatever the mode of presentation; for the better readers, however, there was a significant difference (p <.01) between the normal reading scores and either the listening or the restricted reading scores. However, the mean scores for restricted reading and for listening did not differ significantly with this group either.

Examination of incorrect responses suggested that poorer readers tended to make mistakes which were suitable only to preceding context on all tests, whereas the better readers did so more on the listening and restricted reading tests where only preceding context was available. It appears from these studies that there are differing styles of processing employed by children at this age, who are near the stage of transition from oral to silent reading.

Performance and strategies in information location

The third area in which the middle school children were studied was in their use of a book to locate information. The studies, which are reported elsewhere (Neville and Pugh 1975c; and forthcoming b), used a method devised for observing the silent reading behaviour of university undergraduates (Pugh 1974). It has also been used with sixth-formers (Pugh 1976a) and appears to have certain advantages over other approaches although it also has serious limitations with regard to analysing and processing the data (see Pugh 1976b for a review of approaches to observing and recording silent reading).

For these studies better readers, as defined by scores on standardized tests, were chosen. The task was to use a book to find answers to three questions on a sheet of paper which was given to the children before they opened the book. Their performance was then observed and recorded using closed-circuit television. Special apparatus permitted the observer to see both the book and the reflected image of the subject's face.

The recordings provided a useful source for discussion with the children's teachers who were surprised to note that the children did the task with little strategy, and less well than the teachers expected. After a year, a further study suggested that even when teachers paid specific attention to information location work, the extra attention appeared to have no effect on the performance of a similar group. It may be that a task of this kind is beyond the capacities of many children of this age, either because they lack the ability for the task analysis which is necessary or because their skill in silent reading is not yet adequately developed. On the other hand, it could be that the skills are capable of being taught at this age, but that very careful thought must be given to how to teach them. The evidence from correlating measures of performance on this task with scores on standardized reading tests suggest that the task is, to some extent, tapping different abilities from those needed in the standardized tests. The work with undergraduates and sixth-formers had also suggested this.

Conclusion and further research
These studies seem to suggest that at the age of 9–10 years children are at a stage where their reading differs from oral reading but where they still do not have the kind of abilities which the skilled silent reader possesses. The studies give some justification for the suggestion that there is an aural stage, which is particularly relevant in considering fluency in reading. However, much work remains to be done before one can talk with any certainty of the developmental stages of reading.

Some areas for further research have already been indicated, either directly or by implication in reviewing our studies. One disadvantage of the approach we adopted was that in the studies, children were treated as subjects for separate investigations, whereas it might be more useful to study several aspects of the same child. Consequently during the past school year, a group of forty first-year middle school children has been studied in some depth. Some of them have followed reading-while-listening materials, while the remainder have acted as their controls. Data has been collected using standardized tests, as well as the modified cloze tests and the information location task referred to in earlier sections. All the children have been interviewed and a scale to assess attitude to reading has been administered. It is hoped that when this data is analysed it will be possible to answer some questions arising from the studies reviewed here, as well as permitting clarification of the links between these distinct but related studies.

References
CLARK, M. M. (1976) *Young Fluent Readers* Heinemann Educational
CONRAD, R. (1972) 'Speech and reading' in J. F. Kavanagh and I. G. Mattingly (eds) *Language by Ear and by Eye* Cambridge, Mass: MIT Press
DALY, B. V., NEVILLE, H. and PUGH, A. K. (1975) *Reading while listening: An Annotated Bibliography of Materials and Research* University of Leeds Institute of Education
DEARBORN, W. F. and ANDERSON, I. H. (1952) *The Psychology of Teaching Reading* New York: Ronald Press
DUKER, S. (1974) *Time-compressed Speech – an Anthology and Bibliography in three volumes* Metuchen, New Jersey: Scarecrow Press

EDFELDT, A. W. (1959) *Silent Speech and Silent Reading* Stockholm: Almqvist and Witsell

GIBSON, E. J. (1972) 'Reading for some purpose' in J. F. Kavanagh and I. G. Mattingly (eds) *Language by Ear and by Eye* Cambridge, Mass: MIT Press

GIBSON, E. J. and LEVIN, H. (1975) *The Psychology of Reading* Cambridge, Mass: MIT Press

GOODMAN, K. S. (1968) *The Psycholinguistic Nature of the Reading Process* Detroit: Wayne State University Press

GRANT, R. (1974) When the speed of the tape deceives the eye *Times Educational Supplement* 3106, 6 December, p. 29

MACKWORTH, J. F. (1972) Some models of the reading process: learners and skilled readers *Reading Research Quarterly* 7, 701–33

McLEOD, J. and UNWIN, D. (1970) *Gap Reading Comprehension Test* Heinemann Educational

NEALE, M. D. (1966) (Second edition) *Neale Analysis of Reading Ability* Macmillan Education

NEVILLE, M. H. (1975) The effect of rate of an aural message on listening and on reading while listening *Educational Research* 18, 37–43

NEVILLE, M. H. and PUGH, A. K. (1974) Context in reading and listening: a comparison of children's errors in cloze tests *British Journal of Educational Psychology* 44, 224–32

NEVILLE, M. H. and PUGH, A. K. (1975a) An exploratory study of the application of time-compressed and time-expanded speech in the development of the English reading proficiency of foreign students *English Language Teaching Journal* 29, 320–9

NEVILLE, M. H. and PUGH, A. K. (1975b) 'An empirical study of the reading while listening method' In D. Moyle (ed) *Reading: What of the Future?* Ward Lock Educational

NEVILLE, M. H. and PUGH, A. K. (1975c) Reading ability and ability to use a book: a study of middle school children *Reading* 9, 23–31

NEVILLE, M. H. and PUGH, A. K. (in press) Context in reading and listening: variations in approach to cloze tasks *Reading Research Quarterly* 12, 1

NEVILLE, M. H. and PUGH, A. K. (forthcoming a) Reading while listening: the value of teacher involvement *English Language Teaching Journal*

NEVILLE, M. H. and PUGH, A. K. (forthcoming b) Ability to use a book: the effect of teaching *Reading*

O'BRIEN, J. A. (1921) *Silent Reading* New York: Macmillan

PUGH, A. K. (1974) *The Design and Evaluation of Reading Efficiency Courses* unpublished M. Phil. thesis. University of Leeds

PUGH, A. K. (1975a) The development of silent reading, in W. Latham (ed) *The Road to Effective Reading* Ward Lock Educational

PUGH, A. K. (1975b) *Approaches to developing effective adult reading*

Paper presented to the Fourth International Congress of the International Association for Applied Linguistics, Stuttgart University, August 1975. To be published in *The Modern English Journal* (in press)

PUGH, A. K. (1976a) Implications of problems of language testing for the validity of speed reading courses *System* 4, 1, 29–39

PUGH, A. K. (1976b) *Methods of Studying Silent Reading Behaviour* Paper for the Annual Conference of the British Educational Research Association, London, September, 1976

SOKOLOV, A. N. (1968) *Inner Speech and Thought* Moscow: Presvenshchenie Press (Trans. G. T. Onischenko, New York: Plenum Press, 1972)

THAMES, K. H. and ROSSITER, C. H. (1972) The effects of reading practice with compressed speech on reading rate and listening comprehension *Audio Visual Communication Review* 20, 35–42

WEST, M. (1926) *Bilingualism* (Bureau of Education, India. Occasional Report No. 13) Calcutta: Government of India, Central Publications Branch

12　An experimental pattern of inservice training for schoolteachers

Bruce A. Gillham

Existing course provision and the implementation of the Bullock Report

One of the major implications of the Bullock Committee's deliberations was that *the responsibility for and awareness of language and reading needs in the schools should be spread more widely beyond the territory of the English and Remedial specialists into the curriculum areas*. Early indications are that the work of Lunzer and Gardner for the Schools Council will reinforce the arguments in favour of such a development.

Laudable though this objective is there are good reasons why it will prove remarkably difficult to achieve. Ignorance of the substance and importance of the Bullock Report (DES 1975) should decrease as schools begin actively to develop their language policies but there are other problems which are just as serious and perhaps less easy to counter. The conservatism of the teaching profession is still one of its main characteristics and the failure of exciting Schools Council Projects to penetrate deeply despite the input of massive resources and expertise indicates just how difficult it is to overcome the comfortable feeling of being 'in control' of the traditional content. The economic climate of the 70s is claimed to be only a temporary brake although politicians vary considerably in their definition of 'temporary' – some extending it to a decade! Equally crucial to taking reading and language 'across the curriculum' is the provision of suitable courses and training materials and here the position is bleak indeed. Present provision for training in reading and language consists of highly specialist long courses leading to Diplomas in this aspect of professional work, for example the well-known course at Edge Hill has recently become even more specialist in its orientation by the initiation of a Master's Degree in Reading. The Open University, which has contributed to the development of expertise in the reading field in schools with its Post-Experience course 'Reading Development' as no other institution could hope to have done, has with its more recent development of the idea of a four half-credit 'Diploma in Reading', made a further substantial contribution in this area. However, even the

99

extremely popular 'Reading Development' course has only managed to reach something over 10,000 teachers since 1973, which represents only just over 2.5 per cent of the teaching force. The quality and scope of the general training provided at the initial level also continues to improve as the impact of the Bullock Report is felt in the training institutions. Nevertheless, there is one clearly neglected area – that is in the provision of short courses specifically designed to reach the non-reading specialist. Considerable work has been done by LEA advisory services and colleges which have made a variety of short courses available for teachers, but once again these have been attended mainly by those centrally concerned with the reading process and not those for whom it is a peripheral but necessary area of expertise.

There is clearly a real need for the creation of materials for inservice training which will achieve the necessary impact across the curriculum. What follows is an outline of a scheme which might result in the creation of such material.

An outline of the project
The project involves the production of modular course materials for teachers who are concerned with reading skills. The system is flexibly organized to allow the mapping of individual courses of varying length and complexity in response to a diagnosis of the wishes, needs and strengths of participants and the amount of time at their disposal.

The modular structure of the development emphasizes the relative independence of the units and ensures that the system is highly adaptable to individual needs. There are clear advantages to such course materials; firstly, they are flexible enough to reach teachers outside the mainstream of reading and language teaching; secondly, at a time when the cost effectiveness of long courses will inevitably be scrutinized carefully, patterns of inservice training are likely to change radically. Seen in this light the rapidity of impact and the numbers of teachers involved means that this pattern of inservice training has much to recommend it.

Three strong principles have underlain the development of the proposal:

1 Inservice training should be closely related to the real needs and constraints of practical teaching.
2 Such training should involve a significant proportion of self-instruction and self-evaluation. This is considered particularly important on grounds of efficiency and economy in the use of human resources and because it is difficult to envisage teachers who are adequately equipped to deal with mixed-ability groups and individual learning programmes in school unless their own training experiences have provided exemplars.

3   The training provided should be flexible and tailored to meet the specific needs of individuals.

Structure and planning

At least four organizations have been involved at some stage with the project. The United Kingdom Reading Association provided the committee from which the initial ideas were generated, and continues to provide personnel and moral support. The Council for Educational Technology helped in providing team members with a greater level of expertise in materials development and, in fact, the basic planning model for the project was developed jointly by members of the CET-sponsored CELP project and the Teacher Education Committee of UKRA. The Nuffield Foundation, by granting £1,500 towards the project, provided finance essential for the planning aspects of the work, and Newcastle-upon-Tyne Polytechnic, by providing space, staff time, internal facilities and a research assistantship, aided in the production arrangements. Two groups of personnel have responsibility for the work. The *Planning and Development Group* has eight members from a number of institutions of higher education and includes an LEA adviser and a practising schoolteacher; the function of this group has been to define the overall pattern, generate new ideas and to evaluate the materials which are produced. The materials are actually produced by a smaller *Implementation Team* who report periodically to the Planning and Development Group on their progress.

It is anticipated that a substantial number of packages will soon be available.

The operation of the course

The course involves the four components indicated in Figure 1 below.

Figure 1   The course components

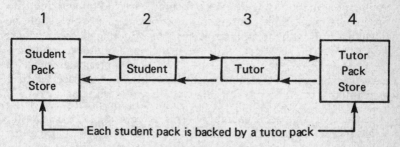

The *Student Pack Store* will contain a large number of independent or semi-independent packages each dealing with highly specific areas within the reading field. It is intended that in the interest of flexibility each package will be covered by at least three levels of comprehensiveness requiring six, four or two hours of study time respectively.

The *student* works independently on those packages which comprise his course and seeks help from the tutor when necessary. In addition he will occasionally be involved in seminar work relating to the packages he is engaged in working with.

The *Tutor Pack Store* contains the system Master Manual, Tutor Manuals for each student package and Back-up Materials for seminar work. Seminar work will usually be available when several students are working on the same package or series of packages and indeed they are considered necessary for social as well as academic reasons.

The tutor has clearly-defined responsibilities; for example, he will:

1 diagnose the wishes, needs and strengths of the incoming student
2 for short courses, map a route through the relevant course packages
3 for courses of Initial Training design the more substantial course route necessary to equip the student to function efficiently in the educational setting for which he is preparing
4 train the student to work within the system
5 help with the solution of problems specific to particular course packages
6 modify the selected route in response to any redefinition of wishes and needs which may occur during the course
7 organize seminars and other learning experiences as required
8 provide personal tutorials
9 generate new packages and modify existing packages in response to need and criticism.

An example of the course in operation
Student Dennis Doug presents himself and expresses *wishes* which packages A and E would satisfy. The tutor, in considering Mr Doug's application, identifies needs which would be served by working with packages C and D and a strength in package area F which could be linked usefully with the other packages. The tutor maps a course which puts the five packages into a promising sequence, perhaps F→C→E→D→A, and chooses the level of comprehensiveness for each package which the time constraints allow. In this case the time available is sixteen hours. Thus the student works with packages C, D and F at the two-hour level, package A at the four-hour level and package E at the six-hour level. This rather complex account is illustrated in Figure 2.

A strategy for development
The development of the teaching materials was based on a simple model developed by a small working group of UKRA teacher educators

Figure 2   The course in operation

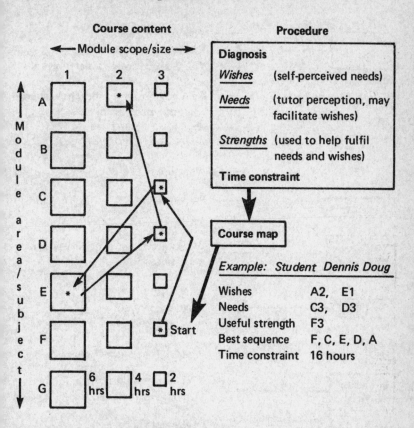

in conjunction with representatives of the Council for Educational Technology. Each package has been developed using ideas implicit in the model, although a too slavish adherence to it and a preoccupation with its persuasive sequentiality has been avoided. Rules are for 'the guidance of wise men and the obedience of fools' and it is easy for a model to stifle by overdirection. Originality and free thinking must be built in if such models are to be fully effective. The planning model is illustrated in Figure 3 on page 104.

The initial suggestions of the Planning and Development Group are acted upon and a package is produced by the Implementation Team. The series of stages through which it is anticipated the packages will then proceed are shown in Figure 4.

Summary and comment

What has been described in this paper is an attempt to suggest how

Figure 3   Materials development, a planning model

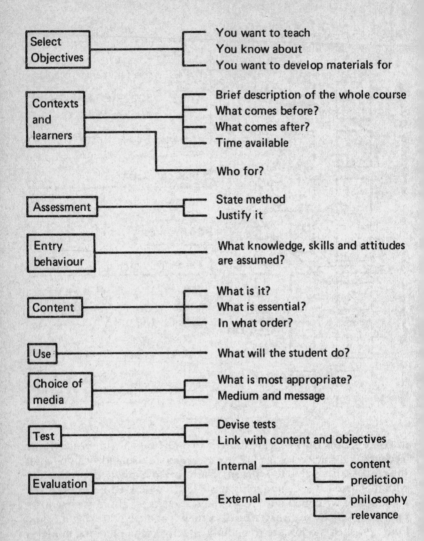

significant progress in literacy can be made without massive investment. The Bullock Committee were optimistic in claiming that much of what they wanted could be achieved without large-scale finance by the better utilization of existing resources. Whilst there is doubtless much to criticize in the multi-modular type of course, it does aim unflinchingly at a real area of educational need – the inadequate literacy skills of those teachers not centrally concerned with reading. In addition this development seeks by its flexibility and practical bias to draw teacher educators and teachers into a more fruitful dialogue.

Figure 4   Stages in the development of a package

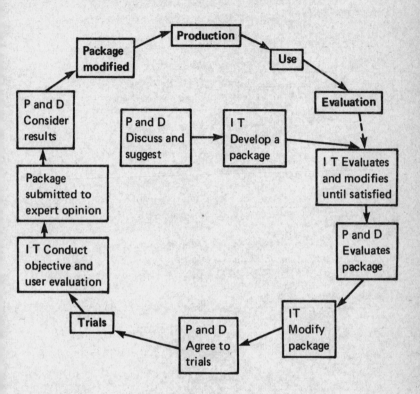

Reference
DES (1975) *A Language for Life* (Bullock Report) HMSO

Part 3

Reading and adult life

13 The adult reading curriculum

Wyn Barrow

In the present climate of interest in adult literacy and its attendant problems, there is a need to define and evaluate the level of functional literacy necessary for the adequate fulfilment of the day-to-day needs of adults in our society.

The US National Reading Centre has defined a functionally literate adult as one who 'has command of reading skills that permit him to go about his daily activities successfully, or to move about society normally, with comprehension of the usual printed expressions and messages he encounters'.

The study described here was an attempt to determine the nature of these 'usual printed expressions and messages' through an investigation of the reading habits of adults and school-leavers. In an effort to assess the social significance of various forms of reading matter, the opinions of school-leavers were sought as to the degree of importance and enjoyment placed on certain categories of reading material.

The purpose for reading, time spent on each reading occasion and, where possible, the readability level of the material involved, were all considered as important factors in the analysis to determine the degree of social necessity which should be attached to any given form of reading matter.

Survey of reading habits and opinions of school-leavers
When considering possible means of determining adult reading habits, the methods employed in various American surveys, including those employed by Murphy (1973), were studied. It was decided that, in view of the limited time available, neither postal surveys nor personal interviews would be practical. As the major part of the study was to be concerned with a survey to be conducted within the final year of a secondary school, it was felt that a small number of adult reading diaries would be a sufficient basis for the compilation of a questionnaire to be used with the children.

In all, fifty-six diaries were collected from DASE course members, their relatives, and teachers attending short inservice courses. These were then used in the compilation of a list of reading categories made up of all the reading material claimed to have been read. This list, containing sixty separate categories of reading material, formed the basis of a questionnaire to be administered to children in their final year of schooling.

It was hoped that this questionnaire would provide a means of assessing the opinions of school-leavers on the reading matter they would encounter in adult life. Ratings from essential to non-essential, and purely enjoyable to purely useful were used, as well as an opportunity to indicate the type of reading material the children had encountered during the previous twenty-four hours.

Instructions as to the completion of the questionnaire were entirely verbal, and the survey was administered in small group situations, with no attempt made to verify the accuracy of the information given regarding reading activities engaged in by the children.

Analysis of results

Much of the data collected could only be analysed in general terms. The opinions of the children regarding the importance and enjoyment value placed on each category of reading were assessed in quantitative terms, as was the number of categories read and the time spent in reading each type of material. It was found that some comparisons were possible between the results obtained from the adult reading diaries and those of the survey, but the limited sample size and the lack of verification of details must be borne in mind when considering the results.

Comparison of results with similar surveys

It was originally intended to make a direct comparison of results with those obtained by Murphy (1973) in the us National Survey of Adult Reading Activities. However, the categories used by Murphy were too broad to allow the sixty categories used in this survey to be compressed into his original thirteen categories.

Certain general findings from both surveys can, however, form the basis of the following comparison. All the material listed within the twelve most important reading activities as summarized from Murphy's conclusions are represented within either the list of reading material rated essential by the children, or the top 20 per cent of the list of material claimed to be most widely read by both children and adults. Approximately 75 per cent of these reading activities appear on both lists.

The average reading time shown from both the survey and the diaries is higher than that reported by Murphy, but this is possibly due to the small sample size and the biased nature of the sample from which the reading diaries were collected.

General findings from all diaries and survey results

Lack of specific information in some diaries and questionnaires meant that detailed analysis of *all* results proved impossible. The full results

110

were, however, used to compile ratings as to the importance and enjoyment value given to each category of reading material by school-leavers, and an index of importance was compiled from the adult diaries, based on the percentage of respondents claiming to have read material within each category. Comparison of the two lists appears to emphasize that the most essential reading material cannot be assessed on the amount of time spent reading any particular type of material.

Comparison of the index of importance from adult reading occasions and an index compiled from all the reading claimed by the children showed the first twelve items of both indices (i.e. the top 20 per cent) to have eight items in common, namely: newspapers, advertisements, popular magazines, street names, traffic direction signs, TV programme guides, words and sentences on TV, and novels and stories.

Ratings of material

Many of the items rated essential by the children also appear within the list of those assessed as purely useful and, although the rank order varies within each list, the first and last categories were identical on both lists.

Of the sixty categories, twenty-nine were rated essential, twenty-nine helpful, and two not essential. Enjoyment value was assessed by the children as follows: purely enjoyable, one item; useful/enjoyable, twenty-one items; and purely useful, thirty-eight items.

The following ten items were rated most essential:

Dosage instructions
Danger/warning signs
Emergency procedures
Traffic direction signs
Official forms (tax etc.)
Job application forms
Wage slips
Legal documents
First aid instructions
Highway code

Analysis according to reading time

Average reading time per adult amounted to 3 hours 57 minutes per day. Average reading time claimed by the children was 2 hours 36 minutes. The adults in the sample spent most time reading non-fiction material, and the children spent most time on popular magazines. Together with newspapers and novels and stories, these formed the basis of the material occupying most reading time per person. Most of the items included in the top 6 per cent of the index compiled from total reading time per category are not included in the material classed as essential. This points to a further emphasis of Murphy's (1973) comments as to the possibility of overlooking the importance of certain reading tasks because of the relatively short amount of time spent on them.

Purpose analysis
Of the fifty-six adult reading diaries obtained, only ten (approximately 18 per cent) gave details which allowed for any analysis on the basis of stated purpose. For the purpose of analysis the categories suggested by Merritt (1974) were used, together with Bruner's (1966) categories of needs, to form a role-needs matrix. In all, categories represented by the ten diaries covered all designated purposes and each area of human need.

Readability
Of the twenty-nine items rated essential, readability measures were only available for the following six:

Danger/warning signs	R.A. 16 plus
Emergency procedures	R.A. 15 plus
Tax forms etc.	R.A. 12.3–18.5
First aid instructions	R.A. 16 plus
Highway code	R.A. 9.6–14
Information leaflets (F.I.S. etc.)	R.A. 13.6–18.5

It would seem that any definition of functional literacy must take these reading levels into account. Even the grade eight reading level equivalent (approximately 13 years), considered by many as a target level for functional literacy programmes, would not be sufficiently high to allow for the necessary comprehension of many of the items rated essential by respondents in this survey.

Grouping of categories
When considering possible groupings of the original sixty categories for the purpose of analysis, it was felt that Murphy's (1973) groupings did not allow for much consideration of the types of skills needed by the reader.

Grouping according to type of media was felt to be useful in this respect, but would have meant very small groups, and would, perhaps, have been only marginally more useful than the original sixty categories.

It was therefore decided to use author-purpose as a basis for groupings as this was felt to bear a significant relationship to the type of media used, and is obviously related to the kind of response called for in the reader. As certain multi-media items (newspapers, magazines etc.) proved impossible to categorize in this way, a final grouping was arrived at on the basis of three general groups and six groups related to author-purpose as follows:

1 Newspapers
2 Magazines
3 Books
4 Materials intended to entertain
5 Materials intended to inform
6 Materials intended to persuade
7 Materials intended to elicit information
8 Materials intended to proscribe
9 Materials intended to prescribe

Rank order correlations based on both time and percentage of readers were calculated for each group. Although correlations within some groups were low, the overall correlation on all categories (.54 on percentage of readers and .57 on average time) would seem to suggest that the use of school-leavers in a survey of this type is reasonably feasible.

While the categories used in the survey do not allow for any significant comparison with similar research, many of the general findings would appear to supplement those drawn from wider samples.

Conclusions

1 *Evaluation of the reading curriculum of secondary schools*
However we define functional literacy, it must be recognized that the vocabulary and format of everyday reading tasks are fixed, and therefore children should learn to understand such vocabulary and format while they are still at school.

It would seem that many schools are, in fact, providing instruction in, and practice of, the skills necessary for the successful completion of adult reading tasks, but in such an isolated form that there can be no transfer to real-life situations. It is felt that where such skills are incorporated into the full reading curriculum, as a way of fulfilling particular and meaningful reading needs of the children, they have a much better chance of becoming incorporated into the regular reading strategies used by those children.

2 *Implications for future research*
It seems probable that there can never be an entirely satisfactory division of reading material to fulfil all purposes of analysis. The main problem stems from the fact that newspapers and magazines are multi-media in format. Where provision is made within a survey for respondents to include detailed information on the *parts* of newspap-

ers etc. read, and not only the type of magazine or book, but the exact title, then a matrix based on author-purpose and format of material could be compiled, which would provide a useful foundation for analysis of the types of skills needed.

Whatever type of analysis is used as the basis of a definition of functional literacy, it must be remembered that even an efficient definition must never be viewed as static, but must be constantly reviewed in the light of the changing needs of society.

References

BRUNER, J. S. (1966) *Toward a theory of instruction* Cambridge, Massachusetts: Harvard University Press

MERRITT, J. (1974) *What shall we teach?* Ward Lock Educational

MURPHY, R. T. (1973) *Adult Functional Reading Study. Project 1: Targeted Research and Development Reading Program Objective, sub-parts 1, 2 and 3. Project No. 0–9004* Princeton, New Jersey: Educational Testing Service

14 Curriculum development in adult literacy

Tom MacFarlane

During the year 1975-6, the Adult Literacy Resource Agency's Teaching Materials Sub-Panel (Rosie Eggar, Ruth Lesirge, Roy Grant, Tom MacFarlane, and Alan Tuckett) mounted two national conferences to encourage and explore the use of adult reading materials in adult literacy.

The objectives of the conferences were two-fold:

1 to 'train trainers' with a view to their mounting follow-up regional and local conferences in their own areas, and
2 to promote a willingness to look at real-life adult literacy tasks in such a way as to be able to use them in a meaningful sense with adults who have reading, writing and spelling problems.

The panel's conceptual planning was drawn from the following ideas:

1 The starting point of the learning processes in literacy should be the personal needs, interests, language and background knowledge of each student. 'No objectives without the learner' might be a summary slogan.
2 The closest possible replication of the complete adult reading and writing experience should be offered.

To develop these last two points briefly, the thinking on objectives is ground in the belief that 'selection of the material is the student's right and responsibility' (Mocker 1975) and that, in many senses, the literacy process is unlikely to develop without students being helped to undertake the responsibility for helping tutors to specify their objectives.

The second point draws on several areas which point to the same conclusion: the importance of purpose-skill integration concepts, as demonstrated in the OU (1973) course; the interactionist model of literacy skills posed by Bormuth (1973); and the philosophical concept of 'comprehensive entity' posed by Polanyi (1969).

115

These two very broad, and overlapping areas were drawn to the attention of course participants by the use of a pre-session briefing which tried to highlight the following:

1 The varied facets of literacy in adult life, based on Merritt's (1974) concept of 'roles and needs'. Here course members were asked to examine their own reading needs and interests.
2 A series of questions were posed to highlight the multi-facet of literacy skills – decoding, critical reading, skimming, etc, with two objectives in mind: firstly, to try and break down the still widely-held view that reading and spelling are decoding processes, and secondly, to highlight the fact that we all meet literacy problems.
3 A series of exercises were then offered to explore in greater depth the relatedness of skills, and their links with needs and interests.

From this whole exercise, this kind of inverse hierarchy was suggested:

1 Phonic and decoding skills are heavily dependent on prediction of word meaning.
2 Word meaning prediction is heavily dependent on surrounding passage meaning.
3 Passage meaning is heavily dependent on contextual factors and the reader's degree of involvement, background knowledge, as well as his actual reading skills.
4 Background knowledge, both in terms of language and interests are heavily dependent on personal and sociocultural factors.

Having discussed these issues, the course then went on to examine a specific literacy task chosen by a group on the basis of student needs as expressed in case studies.

This process involved the use of three packs: (a) literacy tasks, (b) reading skills (from prereading through to study skills), and (c) writing and spelling skills.

First it was important to define student-purpose, and then follow what the good reader and writer would do as he proceeded through to a completion stage, for example the completion of an application form.

Once this fairly massive task had been completed, a flow-diagram, or its equivalent, was prepared.

The group was then asked to consider how it would help a student to be aware of each stage in the real-life process, and to translate that into a programme which would be linked to follow-up skill work in reading and writing at the student's own level. Thus there was a conscious link with the concept of structure. We had merely tried to set that structure into a wider model, in the belief that its learning quality would be enhanced and not diminished.

To help focus the problem of the jump from the good reader and writer to the student, the following areas of questioning were offered:

1 What is student's purpose/reason for selecting task? (purpose setting; involve student's needs and interests)
2 Where is text (or texts) to be found? (access skills, and student awareness of)
3 What help does the student need in reading the text? (replication of adult reading experience)
4 What issues, problems, questions, discussion points are likely to be raised by the text(s) and student's reasons for needing to use it? (student helps evaluate usefulness of text – integrate all levels of the Barrett Taxonomy, at a discussion level, as appropriate to task and need)
5 What help does student need with written requirements? (give immediate help with, for example, form filling and letter writing)
6 What follow-up reading skills, relevant to student's ability level, can be extracted from the text and the discussion? (various word attack skills based on language of task)
7 What follow-up writing and spelling skills, relevant to student's ability level, can be extracted from the text?

Course members were allowed considerable freedom at this point, and the quality and intensity of the work clearly reflected that fact. Tasks chosen – in conjunction with case studies, included: job applications, DIY instructions, making a shopping list, buying a car, using mail-order catalogues, planning and booking holidays, writing letters of complaint, gardening, responding to letters, etc.

Completed assignments were summarized and duplicated, and the suggestions for work in the areas of questions six and seven made a useful exhibition on home-made resource possibilities.

In a paper of this length it is not possible to indicate in any meaningful way the excellence and depth of the work produced, and it is invidious to choose one example and ignore the rest. I want to run that risk by summarizing the work of the group at the Bingley College conference who worked on a woman student's very real need to master the literacy of shopping. Their summary is given in Figure 1 (page 00).

The group devised a wide variety of activities based on and around the reading and written requirements of the task, and their summary showed the width of their approach:

The group is convinced that help in writing skills, spelling and reading go hand-in-hand.
There is plenty of readily available material for use with a shopping theme.

Writing must be of primary importance for our student, and we would give a lot of time to developing this skill in conjunction with other activities.

The initial programme dealing with sight words on packets and cans and the development of a whole-word approach can be extended to reading sentences for meaning related to:

(a) instructions for the cooking and keeping of foodstuffs
(b) washing instructions on garment labels, washing powders and machines, etc.
(c) reading and applying recipes and cooking instructions
(d) inferential reading for economy shopping, price comparisons etc.

Figure 1
(Prepared by Doreen Mayor, Sylvia Singleton, Dave Buckley and Roy Grant)

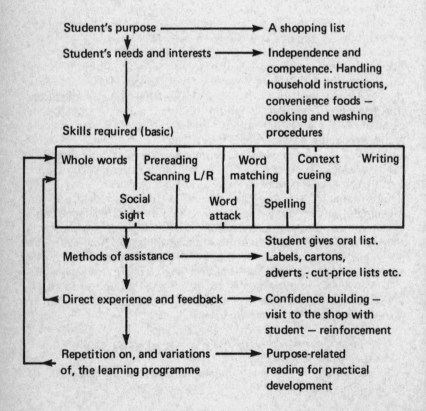

Two main problem areas appear to arise. First, the model offered is complex and open-ended. Those of us who launch this kind of enterprise are often very guilty of ignoring this fact. It would be easy to call at this point for greater published resources designed to help tutors undertake this kind of process. Unfortunately, the problem might then be that the real purposes of particular students would tend to be dovetailed to the published resource. The probability is that this is a training issue first, and a resources issue second. To that end, by the time this paper sees the light of day, the panel hope to have published a workbook for tutors to help them run this kind of approach with their student. It will also aim to place great emphasis on the importance of schemes enabling tutors and students to exchange the experiences in working through this kind of method. In a very real sense that ought in the long run to be the best response to the resource issue: packs of materials prepared by other tutors and students should become a growing resource for schemes to draw upon. At an adult literacy level this would be seen as an equivalent development to the experience-exchange techniques which have been advocated by Moyle in the ou course.

The second main area is in many ways of greater importance in terms of acceptance or rejection of this type of approach. We who are, broadly speaking, 'literate' tend to take for granted issues of motivation and purpose setting, and it may well be that we assume too easily that students will do the same.

It is true, in cases such as the lady instanced above with her urgent need to come to terms with shopping and literacy, that many students have a very real and urgent sense of purpose.

However, as many tutors know full well, there are many students with a very vague sense of purpose. The problem here, in my own experience, has been that tutors faced with this situation very understandably adopt a code-teaching approach in the hope that some purpose will emerge.

Whilst we have said nothing to detract from word-attack skills in these conferences – though we have at times been misunderstood on the point, we do believe as a panel that a greater emphasis in training is needed in helping tutors to help students to a growing awareness of the purposes of literacy as they relate to the student personally.

This personal relationship between literacy and the student seems to need re-emphasis. We who are 'literate' carry around with us semiconscious and unconscious attitudes towards literacy which are inherent in our culture: 'good' literature, moderate literature, and 'pulp' fiction; similarly, we tend to accept a newspaper hierarchy from *The Times* to *The Sun*!

It seems to me, rightly or wrongly, that these attitudes need further examination. The problem will be to steer a middle course between taking into adult literacy the older elitist concepts of 'literature' and falling into the opposite trap of patronizing students with notions of 'working class' culture which are, in some cases, downright sentimentalism. There is no substitute for a careful analysis of our perceptions of ourselves, our perceptions of others, their perceptions of themselves, and their perceptions of us. The first priority of literacy is where it has always been: that students shall feel safe enough to tell us what their purposes are.

The student who wrote this passage for his tutor clearly did:

> I have been asked to give you my opinion on free school dinners. I say that there is discrimination on the ones who need them. It is disgusting the humiliation which one has to go through to get your right. In some schools a child has a different colour ticket and table. In this day and age people should not have to go through it. The system is to help people on low income. But it's the old story – people look down on the needy. (Student: Newton-le-Willows College of Further Education, Merseyside)

References

BORMUTH, J. (1973-4) Reading literacy: its definition and assessment *Reading Research Quarterly* 9, 1, 7-66

MERRITT, J. (1974) *What shall we Teach?* Ward Lock Educational

MOCKER, D. (1975) Co-operative learning process: shared learning experience in teaching adults to read *Journal of Reading* 18, 6, 440-4

MOYLE, D. (1973) *The Reading Curriculum, Units 10 and 11* Open University Reading Development Course PE 261

POLANYI, M. (1969) *Knowing and Being* Routledge and Kegan Paul

15 Reading and the consumer

Alma Williams

Definition: what is a consumer?
We often equate a consumer with a shopper, as a housewife with a frilly apron and a self-belittling bird-brain ('I'm only a housewife, you know'). And the purchases a consumer/shopper makes are often understood to be the limited, repetitive repertoire of high-street commodities. But a consumer is not essentially female (in fact men spend more money on products than women, theirs being the expensive items for house, garden and garage – and men form the majority membership of consumers' associations). Nor do consumers confine themselves to goods. They *buy* goods, but they also *use* a multiplicity of services in repairs and maintenance, in insuring and banking, and in the vast field of social services. This is the commonly omitted area of definition: those social and welfare services which are often provided by the state or local authority and which we pay for indirectly through rates and taxation. So our definition is a wide one, embracing the consumer as user, patient, pupil, client, citizen and voter. And we also relate to the 'non-starters' among consumers – to those whose major consumer aim is a constant supply of pure, clean water, to those who have not enough to eat, to the Indian child in Maharashtra who defined a consumer as 'someone who gets enough to eat'.

A consumer of communications
Male or female, irrespective of age, income and origin, our user of goods and services is an inescapable consumer of communications. Much of this communication is written – information, instruction, labelling, advertising, admonition and prohibition, warning. Indeed, it has been claimed that 60 per cent of our information is still communicated by reading. Nor is this figure true merely of the relatively literate West: even in a developing country with literacy problems the abundance of communication is in writing, as is equally the superabundance of advertising. No wonder a young Moroccan worker participating in a UNESCO survey on the motivations for literacy gave his reason for learning to read: 'So I cannot be fooled and cannot be made to pay more than I should have to by law'.

Throughout the world there is this growing need for functional competence in dealing with consumer communications as their number, intensity and complexity increase, and as they pass over and beyond national frontiers. This paper is an introduction, tentative and suggestive, to the ways and means of seeking and achieving *functional competence*.

The dominance of print

Print which you have to read (or even pay someone in the market place to read for you) is the dominant '60 per cent' medium; but other media have their differing roles. In many countries – Fiji and the Philippines, for example – transistorized battery radio has brought a new dimension to communication, though still combining old cultures and traditions with new information and skills. In our country the importance of television and radio, both national and locally commercial, is as an interest-rouser, as an attraction through a personalized, possibly outrageous, story. Attraction, repetition, association are then backed up – in a growing multi-media system – by hoardings and posters, pamphlets and the press. And the last two can have at the will or whim of the consumer the consultative permanence of print.

The three categories of consumer communication

Who is responsible for producing consumer information in the United Kingdom? In this country large amounts are produced by government and semi-public organizations – indeed, our government is the biggest single advertiser at the moment. Some departments more than others communicate directly with the public, the DHSS, the DOE, the DPCP and the OFT, and the existence of the last two departments (both of them pretty recent) means that the UK is one of the few countries where there is a Minister and a Director respectively interpreting and simplifying new laws like the Consumer Credit Act, issuing specific leaflets and regular bulletins, preparing posters and syndicated tapes (in addition to the traditional non-stop issue of HMSO publications). Government also supports – along with industry – the independently-functioning British Standards Institution which produces many informative leaflets and educational materials, many not in the least technical. Its main concern is the operation of safety standards: getting the public to recognize, in modest little leaflets like 'What every Mum should know', the death-dealing potential of toys, prams, cots, fireguards. Government also supports the National Savings movement which concerns itself with budgeting and general financial management as well as with its more habitual (and less practicable) saving; it produces information for all age groups. With 'Money Sense in Society' and 'Making Money Sense' National Savings caters for the particular needs of schools, even designing specific CSE courses on banking.

The second group of information-providers consists of private and independent organizations, which even in an age of state intervention have an undisputed role. In the UK the major source of consumer information is the Consumers' Association which not only produces its subscription magazine *Which?* on comparative testing, but also books on more general subjects on sale in bookshops, and leaflets of the 'how to buy . . .' kind which are designed with Advice Centres in mind. The National Federation of Consumer Groups with its satellite local consumer groups produces consumer magazines usually dealing with local problems within a given community. In the widest consumer sense information is also available through a number of specialist charitable organizations such as Shelter, Age Concern, the Child Poverty Action Group, some of which actually publish educational materials (e.g. Shelter's housing kit, or the CVS's Joe and Jackie and the case of the shoddy shoes). And there is a vast output of an increasing number of environmental groups.

In the last three years there has been an interesting, and possibly uniquely British development, in that a 'consortium' has developed consisting of a government department (OFT), a semi-public body (BSI), an independent consumer association (CA) and an education authority (ILEA), which have got together to produce informative and educational materials for young people, firstly in 'Susie and the Supershopper' and secondly in 'Thinking about Shopping'. And still further development of joint activity are anticipated.

The third group of information is issued by commercial organizations such as banks and insurance companies (see the Save and Prosper Money Book, Co-ops, for example), by industrial concerns such as ICI, Dunlop, Lever Brothers, Procter and Gamble; by commercial publishers (E. J. Arnold and Tesco), and by trade organizations which produce fairly factual technical leaflets obviously on a non-comparative basis. And there is of course the whole flood of advertising which must not be idly dismissed as consisting completely of irrational blandishments and persuasions. Nor should we omit the press, which, particularly since the governmental abolition of the original Consumer Council, took over new social responsibilities; not seeking just to slam the outrageous, but providing straightforward guidance on nutrition, credit, finance in general, transport, holidays and personalized advice in the form of Action Desks and Action Lines. Since newspapers cater for particular target groups there is a variation in the 'readability' with the *Sun* and *Mirror* catering for reading ages of fourteen-plus.

The consumer's problems with communications
There is no doubt about the abundance, possibly superabundance, of written communications, supported by those in other media. But there is much debate about their adequacy:

1   Information can be physically hard to track down – *Which?* (July

1973) pointed out that only forty-two of eighty-eight main post offices had all the leaflets looked for, that only one of the Social Security offices out of sixty-one was able to provide all thirty-two leaflets (and seventeen were out of date).

2 Vital information can be non-existent: for example, most women running a one-parent family simply do not know that they could move home and get a building society mortgage with the Supplementary Benefits Commission acting as guarantor. The SBC handbook does not tell them.

3 The actual mechanics of printing can put the reader off: if you have to wander around looking for your glasses before you can read the small print; if there are too many words crammed in on a page; if your eye has to travel along long lines; if the lines and words are too close together; if paper and print conflict in colour; if you are allergic to capital letters or unfamiliar type, then you do not stand much chance of understanding in the first place or remembering in the second.

4 Officialdom which is too impersonal, pompous and lacking in the common touch, without humour and humanity, can make people react adversely.

5 Some leaflets and forms make people's minds close up, rejecting difficult words written in a cryptic, elliptic style, detesting their pretentious jargon, their grammar, their sentence length, their confusing use of double negatives, and their impersonality.

The producer's problems with communications

1 He has to lay out large amounts of money to provide and circulate information. This is often seemingly free – for example, the information and sometimes consequent visits from insurance salesmen which result from filling in little coupons in Sunday papers; or the glossy holiday brochures you send away for or pick up with such abandon at the travel agents. But the costs are redistributed among those comsumers who finally choose that particular insurance or holiday. They pay for the rejection of others. Public information on applying for a credit licence, or a rate rebate; warning you not to use your hosepipe during the drought, and telling you that a litre is bigger than a pint and a kilo bigger than a pound, is paid for by us all through general taxation.

2 Information is not a static product and has to be updated (often immediately after a budget) with expense and immediacy.

3 Even by using the whole range of mass-media communications, it is difficult to be certain of reaching everybody. We still have people bringing dogs into the country and saying they didn't know about rabies. The nationalized industries are vulnerable in that by statute they have to indicate price changes and calorific values in the press so that the public knows: protests follow in due course that people

didn't know, that the 'wrong' paper was chosen. And of course certain sections of the community – the elderly and the immigrant – are particularly vulnerable.

4 Information is often dull, especially official information, and is often passed over in favour of competing attractions.

5 People do not keep, or cannot find, information which is intended to be permanent, and they do not know about the significance of making copies of important letters and documents.

6 People are apathetic for a variety of reasons: they do not get round to doing things, and can penalize themselves for not conforming to dates. And they would rather get somebody else, like staff of Consumer Advice Centres, to make decisions for them.

7 The producer of information may well be trying to get people to do something they might not want to do, even if it can clearly be seen to be for their own good. There can be a conflict with people's rights to be left alone, for information often carries with it the burden of positive action, of decision-making.

What can be done to make things better?
Here is a presumptuous code for producers.

1 Since people vary in ability, it is important to define clearly the primary target audience and to issue information in accordance with their needs. There is too much excessively optimistic 'blanket coverage'.

2 It is important to monitor communications adequately. Without feedback there can be no improvement.

3 Alternatives to vast expanses of ponderous prose should be sought: flow charts, algorithmic diagrams, pictures, cartoons (like the *Evening Standard*'s twice-weekly 'Consumer Counsel').

4 Readability needs to be knowledgeably assessed before publication so that the following 'mistakes' do not happen:

the Highway Code needs a reading age of at least thirteen
the average packet of pastry mix of fourteen
an income tax form – fifteen
instructions on a bleach bottle about what to do if you get splashed – sixteen
a trade union application form and supplementary benefits – seventeen
the average HP agreement needs a reading age too high to be calculated.

Within the framework of the OU Diploma in Reading Development, we are investigating further the readability of common consumer communications.

5 We need a campaign for greater general simplicity of language and syntax, and clarity of presentation.

6   Even where language is apparently simple, misuse and ellipses can demean the content, making it ridiculous – 'Open here and run along under the edge', 'Shake well and turn over', or (of a step-ladder) 'ideal for those who dislike heights and the elderly'.

What is being done?
Informed consumer comments, in an economic situation where the consumer is having more say, are leading to improvements, even if this only means the incorporation of 'you' into a DHSS publication. The Civil Service is holding training sessions in communication; national organizations who need to communicate with the public are employing PR consultants – hopefully less remote – to work for them; certain branches of nationalized industries, for example some of the gas 'boards', are, at apprentice level and, more surprisingly, at middle-management level, teaching letter-writing; CA trains local-authority advice-centre staff in the art of communication, emphasizing what they call among themselves 'the marmalade rule' (i.e. the banning of any word longer than marmalade).

Public and personal pressures for greater simplicity, greater ease of availability, and indeed for more openness, are accelerating. One of the most interesting experiments to be watched over is currently being financed by the National Consumer Council. This is a 'Form Market' in Salford market which will help people apply for means-tested benefits. This is a follow-on to the work initiated by Chrissie Maher and the Impact Trust in Merseyside, who together were responsible for the publication with the City Council of a simple form. This form enabled people to apply for five benefits in one go – school meals, school uniform allowance, cash to keep children at school beyond sixteen, and rent and rate rebates. And the reading age of the form is seven-plus.

What's wrong with us educationally? What can we do about it?
The indictment against us as educationists and teachers is crystallized in the recent dropping of the idea for written examinations for learner drivers by the Minister of Transport. The reason? – so many people applying to take the test cannot read or write.

Obviously, then, there has to be an emphasis on better literacy, on basic skills which don't just include reading, writing and numeracy, but also ways of thinking. Edward de Bono is an advocate of courses in thinking, in priority ranking, in choosing, in decision-making. My Whichcraft is a practical manifestation of the adjacent philosophy of critical awareness. We would probably all of us accept that the relevance and reality of consumer studies can provide, world wide, a motivating force for establishing functional competence. That same UNESCO survey I mentioned in my first paragraph also reveals among those interviewed in Morroco the feeling that 'when one knows how to read one is master of one's own destiny'. How indeed do we teach our children to be masters of their own destiny?

16   The development of reading and writing abilities in adults

Hans U. Grundin

The development throughout the school years of various reading and writing skills was studied recently at the Linköping College of Education, Sweden. This project surveyed the development from grade 1 to grade 12, i.e. from the age of seven, when children start school in Sweden, to the age of nineteen. A summary of the results of this study is available in the proceedings of the 1975 UKRA Conference (Grundin 1976b).

One of the main objectives of reading and writing instruction in the comprehensive and upper-secondary schools is to help the students to develop abilities which enable them to cope successfully with the reading and writing situations they will meet in their adult life. It is, however, extremely difficult to judge from the performance of students still in school to what extent this goal has been reached. The school's normal evaluation of reading and writing abilities tells us very little about what kind of development we can expect after the students have left school. An attempt in our grades 1-12 study to establish whether the reading and writing skills of school-leavers are satisfactory according to teachers' judgments was, on the whole, a failure. The results of this inquiry (cf. Grundin 1975b and 1976a) were very interesting, but mainly because of the insights they gave into the difficulties involved in making judgments about what is satisfactory performance.

In order to find out more about the development of reading and writing abilities in adults, the study of students in grades 1-12 was followed up with a study of the corresponding skills of adults. The purpose of this study was twofold:

1   to assess various reading and writing abilities among adults in such a way that they can be compared with corresponding abilities among pupils in the upper grades of the comprehensive school (grades 7-9) and in the upper secondary school (grades 10-12)
2   to investigate the extent to which the reading and writing abilities of adults can be regarded as satisfactory in relation to their need of such abilities.

127

Since the study has to be limited in scope it was decided to concentrate on fairly young adults, namely twenty-five year olds and thirty-five year olds. A study of these two age groups should make it possible to reach some conclusions concerning how reading and writing skills develop during the fifteen to twenty year period after the end of formal schooling.

Design and subjects

The study was a survey collecting test and questionnaire data from random samples of Swedish-speaking adults born in 1940 (i.e. thirty-five years old in 1975) or in 1950 (i.e. twenty-five years old in 1975). The reading and writing tests used were the same as those used in grades 6-12 in the previous study (cf Grundin 1975a and 1975c and School Research Newsletter 1975/4), namely:

alphabet test (knowledge of the order of the letters in the Swedish alphabet)

copying test (ability to copy a given prose text by means of handwriting)

reading rate test (with multiple-choice questions interspersed in an easy prose text)

cloze test of reading comprehension

tests of 'practical' reading ability: (a) comprehension of insurance policy text; (b) comprehension of tables and instructions for their use; and (c) ability to understand and fill in forms

essay or free writing test (ability to express one's views on a given topic in writing), and

spelling test (ability to spell words dictated in sentence context).

The questionnaire comprised questions concerning:

general and vocational education and present occupation

parents' education and occupation

average amount of reading and writing per day – during leisure time and during working hours

self-evaluation of reading and writing ability in relation to perceived needs in one's occupation and in one's private life

subjective judgment of the importance of reading and writing abilities measured by the different tests.

The population of subjects for the study was defined as all Swedish-speaking inhabitants of Linköping community (a largely urban area with about 108,000 inhabitants) born in 1940 or 1950. People confined to institutions because of handicaps or illness were excluded. Lists of randomly selected adults meeting these criteria were obtained from the Swedish Central Bureau of Statistics. In all, 527 persons were invited to participate and were offered a small honorarium equalling £9.50 for attending a two-hour testing session. Slightly more than 70 per cent of those invited participated in the study.

We know very little about the 150 persons (30 per cent of the invited) who did not wish to participate. It seems reasonable to guess, though, that persons with low education and/or reading and writing abilities were more reluctant to participate than other categories. In other words, if the sample of persons included in the study is biased, it is probably biased through over-representation of persons with average or higher than average ability and level of education.

The sample of adults tested, less than 200 per age group, seems small compared to the entire Swedish population of twenty-five and thirty-five year olds (more than 100,000 per age group). The sample has, however, been drawn from the same community as the samples of students in the first part of the research programme. The results of comparisons between adults and students should therefore be fairly reliable.

General educational level of participating adults

The general educational level of the adults participating in the study has been expressed in number of years spent in school and in institutions of higher education. This number varies in our sample from seven years to fifteen-plus years, i.e. from seven-year elementary school to university studies at the doctoral level.

There is a marked difference between the two age groups in this respect. The average (median) level of general education is 11.7 years for the sample of twenty-five year olds but only 8.7 years for the thirty-five year olds. Nearly 40 per cent of the adults aged thirty-five have only seven or eight years of schooling, whereas the corresponding figure for the twenty-five year olds is less than 5 per cent. This difference is due to the introduction of compulsory nine-year schooling in Sweden in the early 1960s, a reform affecting those born in 1950 but not those born in 1940. The gradual increase during the 1960s in the recruitment to all sorts of higher education is reflected in the fact that 37 per cent of the twenty-five year olds as compared to just 16 per cent of the thirty-five year olds have at least one year of higher education.

This difference between the two age groups makes it necessary to take general educational level into consideration in all comparisons between groups of adults and between adults and students in grades 9-12. It must also be recognized that twenty-five year olds and thirty-five year olds with the same amount of schooling are not necessarily comparable subgroups with regard to their expected reading and writing ability. Many of the thirty-five year olds with nine years' schooling or less (and they constitute 61 per cent of their age group in our sample) probably could have benefited from more schooling than they have had. People who are in this sense undereducated can be expected to do better on reading and writing tests than people who, with the same amount of schooling, have been educated up to their full 'educational potential'.

At the other end of the scale of general education we find that the recruitment to higher education was much more selective among those born in 1940 than among those born in 1950. To the extent that this recruitment was based on academic ability rather than socioeconomic status, we should expect a higher average performance among thirty-five year olds with higher education than among twenty-five year olds at the same educational level.

These differences between the two age groups of adults included in the present study must be borne in mind when the test results are interpreted.

Overall comparisons between adults and students

Since the distributions of test scores are more or less skewed (i.e. the tests measure primarily the low and medium range of abilities), overall comparisons among groups of adults and students are based on the median scores for each subgroup. Knowing that the median level of education for the two age groups of adults is 11.7 and 8.7 years respectively, it should be of interest to see what grade levels (as computed from student data) the median performance levels of adults correspond to.

Table 1 (on page 131) shows the grade level equivalent of median test scores for the two age groups of adults. Values above 12.0 are put in parenthesis, since they are computed by means of extrapolation from the results for students in grades 9–12. The grade level equivalents in Figure 1 indicate, then, how the average twenty-five year old with 11.7 years of schooling and the average thirty-five year old with 8.7 years of schooling perform in relation to students in grades 6–12 actually in school. The general trend in the data is very clear: adults perform better on reading and writing tests than students with the corresponding amount of schooling. The difference is, however, particularly marked for the average thirty-five year old whose performance is close to grade 11 level although he has less than nine years of schooling. The average twenty-five year old with less than twelve years of schooling performs slightly above the median level for grade 12 students.

The mean grade level equivalent for all subtests is 12.1 for the average twenty-five year old as compared to 10.8 for the average thirty-five year old. The superior performance of the twenty-five year old is probably primarily due to his higher level of general education. It should be noted, though, that the difference between the two age groups in general educational level is three years of schooling, whereas

Table 1 Average performance levels (median values) for adults aged twenty-five and thirty-five expressed as grade level equivalents (computed from data for students in grades 6–12)

Test	Grade level equivalent of median test score		Difference between performance and ed. level*	
	Age 25	Age 35	Age 25	Age 35
Reading: Cloze	12.0	11.2	+0.3	+2.5
Reading: Rate	10.8	9.2	−0.9	+0.5
Reading: Ins. policy	(12.5)	11.5	+0.8	+2.8
Reading: Tables	(12.4)	11.2	+0.7	+2.5
Reading: Forms	(13.8)	(12.8)	+2.1	+4.1
Writing: Copying	10.6	8.8	−1.1	+0.1
Writing: Essay	(12.3)	11.5	+0.6	+2.8
Writing: Spelling	12.0	10.5	+0.3	+1.8
Average for all tests	12.1	10.8	+0.4	+2.1

* i.e. grade level equivalent minus 11.7 for twenty-five year olds and minus 8.7 for thirty-five year olds

the difference in reading and writing test performance only corresponds to about 1.3 years (when expressed in grade level equivalents). This seems to indicate that the thirty-five year olds, many of whom may be regarded as 'undereducated', have been able partly to compensate for their lack of formal education through some kind of informal education in the 'school of life'.

One may conclude, then, that the 'school of life' does play an important part in the development of adults' reading and writing abilities, particularly for those adults whose actual level of education is lower than their educational potential. But the 'school of life', although of great help to those who have not had sufficient formal education, does not seem to be an adequate substitute for formal education. The better educated twenty-five year old is, on the average, 1.3 grade level equivalents ahead of the thirty-five year old, which indicates that lack of formal education is only partially compensated for in adult life after school.

Development of the ability to cope with real-life tasks
Although the adults on the whole are doing better on our reading and writing tests than students at the corresponding level of schooling, they are not doing equally well on all subtests. On the two tests where rate of reading and writing is of particular importance, the reading rate and the copying tests, adults do not perform better than students. The

131

twenty-five year olds perform below their expected grade level on these two tests and the thirty-five year olds approximately at their expected grade level (*cf.* Figure 1 above).

On most of the remaining tests the twenty-five year olds perform at or above the expected level, while the thirty-five year olds perform much above the expected level. On one test, the reading test based on common, authentic forms, the average score for both adult groups is particularly high. This forms test calls for the performance of task which nearly all adults meet in real life. First-hand experience of filling in these and similar forms can be helpful in two ways in the testing situation: it provides training and feedback concerning success or failure, and it can increase the understanding of the importance of being able to cope with such tasks.

It is, however, also possible to interpret this finding in another way. Rather than concluding that adults do particularly well on tasks such as filling in authentic forms, one may conclude that teenage students do particularly badly on this kind of task. The main argument for this would be, of course, that students are usually poorly motivated for such tasks since they do not understand the importance of filling in forms correctly. That student performance is particularly poor on the forms test is also indicated by a finding in our survey of abilities in grades 1–12 (*cf.* Grundin 1975c). When teachers' expectations of student performance on various tests were compared to the students' actual performance, it was found that the average student performance usually equalled or even excelled the average teacher expectation. The forms test was, however, an exception, since student performance on that particular test was clearly below the average teacher expectation.

Having noted that adults do better than students on the forms test it is of interest to look at their performance from another viewpoint: to what extent have they mastered the task of filling in the forms correctly? A score of 0–5 points was given for each of the three forms in the test, depending on to what extent they were filled in correctly. Absolutely correct completion of all three forms gives a score of 15.

Of the total sample of 371 adults only forty-three, i.e. 12 per cent, reached the maximum score. A score of 13 or more, i.e. above 80 per cent of the score indicating complete mastery, was reached by 64 per cent of the entire sample, and by less than 50 per cent of the adults with low education (seven to nine years' schooling). Clearly, most adults did not show complete mastery of the task of filling in these simple, or only moderately complicated, forms, and a substantial minority made several mistakes.

The most difficult of the three forms in the forms test is one sent by the National Health Insurance Authorities to every person who has – or is believed to have – an income. The purpose of the form is to obtain information about personal income for the determination of the size of one's sickness benefit. This form was filled in correctly (5 points out of

5) by only 23 per cent of the 371 adults. Even among adults with higher education it was filled in correctly by somewhat less than one third of the sample. These figures compare favourably with those for students aged sixteen to nineteen (5 per cent in grade 9 and 17 per cent in grade 12), but they also indicate that many adults cannot cope successfully with the reading and writing tasks with which they are confronted in their everyday life.

I want to point out here that the findings discussed above – however alarming they might seem – do not necessarily imply that adults have less reading and writing abilities than they 'ought' to have. What has been observed is a mismatch between certain tasks which most adults are *expected* to master and the ability of many adults to cope with these tasks. Logically, the conclusion that the tasks 'ought' to be made less complicated is as valid as the conclusion that the abilities of adults 'ought' to be improved.

The problem of functional literacy
The discussion about the ability to fill in forms has brought us into the field of 'functional literacy'. The ability to cope successfully with various reading and writing tasks imposed upon us in our capacity as citizens, employees or employers, consumers etc. is an important ingredient in functional literacy regardless of how this concept is defined in more exact operational terms. However, in my opinion, functional literacy should not be narrowly defined in terms of what is practically and economically useful. In principle, a functionally literate person should be able to cope reasonably successfully with those reading and writing tasks that are important to him personally.

There is still no commonly accepted definition of functional literacy in Sweden. It has been argued (Grundin 1976a) that the ability level reached by the average pupil after six years of schooling can be regarded as a *minimum* criterion of functional literacy of our population. That is, literacy below grade 6 level will rarely be sufficient for adult life, and in many cases even an ability above that level may be totally insufficient in view of the needs of the individual.

Table 2 (on page 134) shows, for various tests, the percentage of adults with low, medium or high level of education who have not performed above grade 6 level (i.e. the median score for students at the end of the sixth school year, at the age of thirteen). The corresponding percentages for students in grades 9 and 11 have also been entered in the table. Among adults with nine years of schooling or less, about one fifth have not reached above grade 6 level in their performance on reading and writing tests. Approximately the same proportion of grade 9 students perform at or below grade 6 level.

It seems, then, that after nine years of schooling a substantial minority of something like 20 per cent of the population will not yet have reached functional literacy. And among those who leave school

Table 2 The percentage of persons in different categories of pupils and adults who have NOT performed above grade 6 level (=median performance at the end of grade 6)

Test	Pupils grade 9 (210)	Adults with low ed. level		Pupils grade 11 (224)	Adults with medium ed. level		Adults with high ed. level		Whole sample of adults	
		25 yrs (61)	35 yrs (109)		25 yrs (60)	35 yrs (42)	25 yrs (70)	35 yrs (29)	25 yrs (191)	35 yrs (180)
R: Cloze	23	19	22	10	2	4	0	0	7	14
R: Rate	21	20	37	8	4	9	3	1	9	24
R: Ins. pol.	24	20	21	10	1	9	0	0	7	14
R: Tables	27	11	19	10	4	4	2	2	5	13
R: Forms	17	3	5	4	0	0	0	0	2	3
W: Copying	14	22	23	4	1	2	1	0	8	14
W: Essay	32	20	14	14	3	3	1	0	8	10
W: Spelling	21	28	22	6	2	0	0	0	10	13

Note 1 Figures in parentheses in the column headings indicate number of subjects.
Note 2 Low educational level = 7–9 years schooling; medium educational level = 10–12 years of schooling; and high educational level = 13+ years of schooling and studies.

after nine years, at least 20 per cent remain at this comparatively low level of literacy. (To the extent that our sample is biased through inclusion of too many people with average or higher than average education, the true percentage can be expected to be even higher than 20 per cent.) The 'school of life' earlier referred to does not seem to remedy this lack of functional literacy, except perhaps when it comes to certain 'practical' tasks on which some training is provided in the everyday life of nearly all adults (*cf.* results on the forms test, Table 2).

Table 2 also gives the percentages of the entire samples of adults, aged twenty-five and thirty-five, who have not performed above grade 6 level. With the exception of the forms test, between 5 and 10 per cent of the twenty-five year olds have not performed above grade 6 level on the various tests, whereas the corresponding percentages for the thirty-five year olds range from 10 to 24 per cent. These results indicate that increased schooling can substantially reduce the proportion of persons who reach adulthood without being functionally literate.

The figures in Table 2 are only indicative of the magnitude of this effect of prolonged schooling, since more extensive surveys are needed before we can make highly reliable estimates. It seems, though, as if the prolongation of schooling which took place in Sweden during the late 1950s and the early 1960s may have reduced almost by a half the proportion of adults in an age group who have not reached the minimum level of ability needed for functional literacy.

The effects of increased schooling, which result in higher performance among twenty-five year olds (with an average educational level of 11.7 years) than among thirty-five year olds (with only 8.7 years) can, however, be confounded by a developmental effect. If there is a decline in reading and writing abilities, either for the whole age group or for certain subgroups, between the age of twenty-five and the age of thirty-five, such a decline would, of course, also lead to lower test scores for thirty-five year olds than for twenty-five year olds.

To what extent the difference in performance between twenty-five and thirty-five year olds is due to prolonged schooling and to what extent it is a result of a decline over time in the reading and writing ability of adults cannot be determined on the basis of the data discussed here. There are some indications, though, that there may be no decline – and even increase – in the abilities of average and above average readers, whereas the abilities of those who leave school as poor readers may actually decline somewhat before they reach the age of thirty-five years.

Are adults satisfied with their skills?
To try and determine whether the skills of various groups of adults are satisfactory in any general sense, for example from the point of view of society, seems an almost impossible task, and this has not been

attempted in the present study. We have, however, asked the participating adults whether they personally find their reading and writing abilities sufficient:

1 for the tasks with which they are confronted in their work
2 for the activities in which they actually engage in their leisure time, and
3 for the activities in which they would like to engage in their leisure time.

For the whole of six questions (three for reading and three for writing ability) the percentage of adults who said they were not satisfied with their abilities varied from 9 to 24. There is a significant correlation between satisfaction with one's skills and performance on tests of these skills, but the coefficients are typically low: between 0.2 and 0.3. That is, the poor readers/writers regard their skills as insufficient somewhat more often than the average or above average readers/writers, but low ability does not preclude satisfaction with one's ability, and, conversely, even an ability well above average may be experienced as insufficient.

Very little, unfortunately, is known about the criteria upon which these self-evaluations are based, but it is nevertheless worth underlining that nearly one adult out of four in our sample (23 per cent) finds his reading or writing abilities insufficient in view of the tasks met with at work. And nearly one adult out of three (32 per cent) finds his reading or writing abilities insufficient for the activities he would like to engage in during his leisure time.

Summary

The data collected in this study of Swedish adults' reading and writing abilities will be analysed and discussed in much greater detail in the final report. The conclusions presented here should therefore be regarded as preliminary. Some general trends in the results seem, however, quite clear.

The basic reading and writing skills of many adults can be expected to improve between the time they leave school and the time they reach the age of thirty-five. This improvement, largely a result of informal education – the 'school of life' – can partly compensate for insufficient schooling during adolescence. But prolonged schooling during adolescence apparently leads to even greater improvement in reading and writing ability.

A substantial minority of adults do not reach the minimum level of reading and writing ability which is considered necessary for functional literacy. However, the proportion of an age group which does not reach functional literacy seems to be reduced – perhaps halved – through increased schooling. Those who leave school with abilities which are insufficient for coping with the reading and writing tasks of adult life run a great risk of remaining at that low level of ability – or even suffer a decline in ability.

And, finally, more than 30 per cent of the adults studied have found their reading or writing abilities insufficient for at least some of the tasks they undertake – or would like to undertake if they could trust their ability.

References

GRUNDIN, H. U. (1975a) 'The development of reading, writing and other communication skills during the comprehensive and upper secondary school years . . .' in W. Latham (ed) *The Road to Effective Reading* Ward Lock Educational

GRUNDIN, H. U. (1975b) 'Judgment in the evaluation of reading ability' in E. Hunter (ed) *Reading Education: A UKRA Periodical* Summer, pp. 20–6

GRUNDIN, H. U. (1975c) *Läs- och skrivförmågans utveckling genom skolåren* (The development of reading and writing ability throughout the school years.) In Swedish with a summary in English. In the National Board of Education series 'Utbildningsforskning' 20, Stockholm: Liber Läromedel

GRUNDIN, H. U. (1976a) 'Evaluating competence in functional reading' in J. E. Merritt (ed) *New Horizons in Reading* Proceedings of the Fifth IRA World Congress on Reading, Vienna, Austria, August 1974. Newark, Delaware: International Reading Association

GRUNDIN, H. U. (1976b) 'The reading and writing abilities of Swedish pupils: a survey of the development from grade 1 to grade 12' in A. Cashdan (ed) *The Content of Reading* Ward Lock Educational

School Research Newsletter 1975:4. Current project: Survey of certain reading, writing and other communication skills among adults (the *Vuxenläsk* project). Stockholm: National Board of Education (mimeographed)

17   The organization of provision for adult literacy

Robert J. Kedney

Perhaps one of the most remarkable phenomena of recent years has been the recognition and response to the newly identified problem of adult illiteracy. The deeply-felt need to provide tuition in the basic educational skills that are becoming so increasingly critical in our complex society has led to a radical model of provision that may provide a testing ground for new thinking. The apparent rejection of experiences gained in schools, remedial centres and colleges may be based on myth or reality, the endeavours to develop new responses untainted by a history of supposed failure have yet to stand the test of time. In any event the high level of involvement of teachers, both as volunteers and as part-time, paid tutors would seem to be providing direct links and experience in the teaching-learning situation. Less evident is the sharing of thoughts and experience in the more abstract areas of project design, organization and management, yet it would seem to be here that the radical changes are most clearly developing.

It is often assumed that adult literacy provision is a phenomenon of the last two years, rising like a phoenix on the wings of the carefully preparatory work of the BBC in canvassing local authorities prior to the production of *On the Move*. Its origins, however, are as long and venerable as those of adult education itself, though the post-war period is often cloaked with shadows of anonymity in order to protect the students. To a greater or lesser degree the patterns of key decisions in any project are governed by the situations in which they are made and are influenced by the history of the situations and that of allied models of practice. It is perhaps, therefore, not surprising that the evolutionary growth identified below in Table 1 drew its guidelines from adult and further education in the administrative area and remedial education in the classroom.

The response in the 1970s can thus be seen as an outgrowth from both the long-established pattern of activity in the local authority field and the innovatory approaches developed by the voluntary organizations in the late 1960s.

The trend in modern thinking away from simplistic models of instruction to the identification of the complex interactions of tutor,

Table 1 Origins of literacy projects (from Kedney 1976)

Date	Ad Ed Insts	Tech Colls	Private schemes	Prisons	Borstals	Others
Pre 1945	(Bethnal Green 1920 +)	—	—	(Pentonville 1842)	(Hollesley Bay 1939)	—
	(Lansbury ILEA 1898)			(Maidstone 1930s)		
	2			2	1	
1945-9	—	—	—	4	—	—
1950-4	8	2	1	2	1	—
1955-9	5	1	—	1	1	—
1960-4	8	3	1	3	9	4
1965-9	40	14	5	10	11	7
1970	6	6	1	7	1	—
1971	10	5	2	7	2	3
1972	19	6	2	10	4	1
1973	10	9	1	1	—	2
1974	10	5	4	1	—	1
(1970-74 totals)	55	31	10	26	7	7
No date	11	4	—	27	11	—
Sub Totals	129	55	17	75	41	18

student, subject and environment in recent years has served to reveal the significance of many factors other than the teacher's diction or adoption of 'the' teaching method (McMullen 1969). The shift in role of the teacher-tutor from the didactic pattern to that of manager-designer and participant in teaching-learning situations is well documented and has an increasingly less hollow ring as staff become sensitive to the range of options open in so many areas of decision-making and the students in turn become involved in defining their own needs and directing their own learning.

In a field where so many of the traditional constraints are being questioned the concept of management becomes yet more critical. It can be argued that many of the major decisions are taken deliberately or by default, before the tutor and student ever meet and that the range of choices open to both are either extensive or closed within the first five minutes. In a well-designed and managed project it should be no part of a student's or a tutor's task to struggle manfully with unnecessary constraints imposed by an unthinking system. This paper endeavours to identify examples of major areas of decision-making and some of the range of options that are open. In so doing it only samples a limited field and raises but some of the choices. The implications for practice in the teaching-learning situation are explicitly stated in some instances but only implied in others, the reader is invited to expand on both areas of decision and implication, for personal experiences often readily supply positive and negative examples of decision-making.

As yet no research into the design and management of literacy projects and the implications for teaching-learning has been undertaken, and the field is dependent on personal experience and anecdote. This is perhaps not surprising as it is still in its infancy as an area of serious educational concern and practices are still evolving. Indeed it is only a year since the major national initiatives were underway – a short period when compared with the history of the majority of the school and college systems of provision. The field would seem to be providing a clear model·of Williams' (1972) 'management of imperfection', for as he points out, 'the reality of managing is that decisions have frequently to be taken on a basis of incomplete data, inadequate resources and inconsistent co-operation'. Both the tutor and the student are asked to manage in a context where a range of fundamental decisions have already been taken that effectively provide a foundation for their actions.

The following examples are drawn from five areas, namely, decisions relating to organizational design, staffing, students, teaching and institutionalization, and are limited to one or two areas within each.

Organizational decisions
In most forms of educational provision the basic administrative unit is regarded as being the class, whether it is taught as a whole through lockstep teaching, through subgroupings or through individualized programmes. In adult literacy the debates as to the relative merits of groups and 1:1 teaching situations would seem to be lessening as organizers pay at least lip-service to the virtues of both and claim to develop projects based on the strengths of each. The development of reading groups where volunteer tutors and their students meet and work in the company of other pairs and the use of volunteers in group situations under the guidance of a paid tutor are serving to blur the edges. A pattern of progression that moves the acutely embarrassed and emotional student gently through an evolving range of social situations as his literacy skills and confidence are enhanced has been proposed. How far such an idealized model is supported by the realities of practice on a satisfactory scale remains to be seen.

Both home-based and group teaching situations would seem to have identifiable strengths and weaknesses that can be matched to the needs of the student and the resources of the schemes, both in turn having implications for tutor and student. As has already been suggested that would not seem to be the only possible alternative.

Some schemes have related group tuition with a paid tutor to a

Figure 1 Literacy projects: some variants (from Kedney 1975)

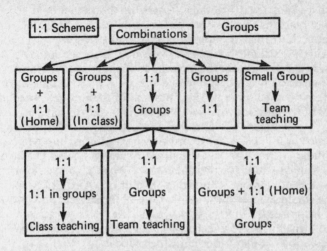

second supporting session during the same week at home with a volunteer tutor working on material set during the group session. Others have developed team-teaching situations as enrolments have grown by retaining staff and students in a single large flexible unit thus maximizing the availability of the range of resources – both human and physical – that are available. It is not difficult to envisage that with planned growth a range of options can be developed in any scheme that can move from a simplistic model to a complex variety of opportunities that endeavour to match needs effectively to teaching opportunities.

The development and adoption of any such scheme should have as its baseline the needs of the students rather than administrative expediency if it is to meet the range of objectives identified by project organizers recently (Kedney 1975). The overall concern expressed for the growth of literacy skills and the development of social competence and confidence places high demands on the design and selection of teaching environments. We have as yet to see the development of the clearly skills based approach that is inherent in the learning laboratory approach that has evolved in the USA where, through the use of self-programming following an initial diagnostic period, students can call in at any time and follow their own individual reading programme. Whilst economics may be the limiting factor at present, the philosophical dilemma produced by the deliberate minimization of staff-student contact as contrasted with the existing heavy emphasis on human relationships in this country may produce discussion of a more fundamental issue than the relative merits of 1:1 home-based or group teaching situations.

Organizational decisions are clearly not limited to the choice of teaching contexts; one has only to consider the influence of decisions about the utilization of time in terms of the frequency of meetings, length of individual meetings, length of the course and terms and holiday patterns to recognize the freedom that is available to make decisions that radically impinge upon teaching. The contrast between a little often in school and the two hours once a week approach of many adult literacy projects or the open-ended commitment to course length of the latter contrasted with the normal fixed period adult and further education course serve to identify some of the options. Similarly the choice of teaching location would seem to range from launderettes and public houses to public libraries and colleges of education and the influence of the image of the institution in terms of anonymity, social acceptability, prestige, accessibility or simply availability at chosen times would seem to warrant as careful a consideration as the choice of room and equipment within that institution. Also linked to such a choice would seem to be the aspirations of the student and tutor, for in some instances the links with the public library or vocational training would logically link to a technical college where literacy could lead to participation in other forms of further education.

Staffing

Staffing, like many other areas of decision-making, would seem to have largely been approached in an *ad hoc* manner, often simply as a reaction to growth as it took place and now bears no relationship to such planned patterns as those implemented for a new school. The generalist role, as a jack-of-all-trades, adopted by tutors and organizers, would seem largely to be a response to a failure to discriminate specialist functions rather than a deliberate policy. Should industrial techniques such as job analysis be applied to the needs of the situation as well as the practices it is likely that an extensive range of specialist staffing activities could quickly be identified. If such tasks could then be identified as roles, for example receptionist, secretary, clerk, interviewer, diagnostician, audiovisual technician, graphics technician, action researcher, writer, counsellor, tutor-trainer, recruiter, it may be possible, through part-time and full-time, voluntary and paid staffing, to match such roles to individuals. This approach not only indicates areas of responsibility and their relationship to individuals, but also provides reference and referral points for advice and removes from the individual tutor the necessity, though perhaps not the opportunity, of being all things to all men.

The development of such an approach and the subsequent adoption of clearly-defined job descriptions, be they for specialist staff with delineated functions or a deliberate choice of generalist staff who are allocated a number of functions, represents the first cycle of staff development. The present piecemeal model of appointing staff to undefined posts, of offering broad and shallow induction training programmes of some six to eight evening meetings and then to place staff, with a greater or lesser degree of continuous support, into the teaching situation would seem to beg a series of questions. No training programme can undo the problems that can be created at the point of staff selection, nor can it effectively relate to the needs of a specific situation, unless it, and the training group, are carefully tailored to fit such a situation. Off-the-job training cannot be an exercise undertaken in splendid isolation if it is meant to be designed to be effective; its place in the cycle of staff development has to be identified and decisions taken accordingly.

Figure 2   A staff development programme

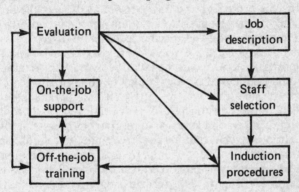

The centrality of decision-making in the area of staffing in such a labour-intensive activity would seem self-evident and has been highlighted on both sides of the Atlantic. In Vera Southgate-Booth's (1973) view, 'teacher training, both initial and inservice, is a crucial issue and is probably the most important factor affecting the reading ability and general language development of children, students, and the whole adult population'. Pagano (1970), in laying similar stress on staff development, observed that because there are few persons in any community who have had experience in teaching the economically and socially deprived adult, all teachers entering adult basic education should be given an intensive preservice training course for this endeavour. Clearly such training should be related to the process of management and decision-making on which any project is based and drawn from a clear definition of staff roles (see Ast's (1970) model in the context of the learning laboratory), and an ongoing definition of needs as part of a staff development policy.

Students
To many projects that appear to have adopted an open-door policy,

143

the introduction of decision-making with regard to students would appear to be an anathema, yet, in adopting a stance of first-come-first-served and then matching students to tutors, teaching locations and materials, such projects are inevitably in a process of selection. If the currently projected numbers of illiterate adults are accepted, and there would seem to be good reason for questioning such guesstimates, it is clear that the most successful projects are only attracting a tiny minority to tuition. At present, concern would seem largely to be for indiscriminate recruitment for the sake of growth, the only common factor being someone's belief that an individual needs tuition, the only commonly excluded categories being mentally handicapped adults and immigrants with little or no spoken English.

Given an in-depth review of the limited resources and skills available for any project, and even a cursory analysis of the needs of the community, it may be possible to identify potential priority areas. The tailoring of provision and specific recruitment drives would then seem a viable alternative as a positive decision to the current pattern of highly generalized recruitment, the latter being perhaps retained as a deliberate and considered option. It may be then in an area of high unemployment and a demand for entry to training that some special effort could be focused on the hard-core unemployed, or alternatively, in a time of early redundancy and retirement or unemployment amongst school-leavers, that drives are made to recruit specific age-bands. Similarly, in areas with large immigrant populations both coloured and white, for example Ukranians, Poles, Hungarians, and with provision for English as a foreign language tuition that adult literacy programmes could be placed alongside as a priority activity. Decisions to recruit amongst such specific groups have clear implications for staffing, teaching materials, time and locations. The needs of the young mother with children at school are clearly different from the unemployed sixteen year old or the self-employed immigrant, but they are identifiable and can in turn be related to decisions made elsewhere.

Aspects of teaching

The teaching-learning process does not, and cannot, begin in a vacuum, and the early stages involve a range of rapidly taken decisions that may or may not be revised later. It is inevitable that attitudes, opinions and expectations are formed from the very first point of contact, be it through newspaper articles, a television programme, a poster or a chance remark, and that they sharpen and strengthen as involvement deepens. That such a process is common to both tutor and taught is sometimes lost in the early concern for self-identification and establishment, in a new and strange environment.

The early and critical diagnostic stages would seem to be approached in a variety of ways by different literacy projects, in part due to their differing designs and staffing patterns (Livingstone 1974;

144

Allan 1974). The contrast between the informal interview, with or without formal testing, with the full-time organizer of a volunteer-based project, and the completion of an interview schedule from which matching with a volunteer tutor, a teaching location, times and teaching materials are selected with the approaches utilized in group situations where the diagnostician is also the tutor, are sometimes very marked. It would be too easy to highlight the strengths and weaknesses of such situations; what would perhaps be more important would be the identification of the needs of the situation and the means by which they are met. Criticism of existing tests (MacFarlane 1976) and their uses may be justified, but what are needed are viable alternatives.

It has been proposed that book-boxes outlive tutors and certainly a heavy investment in teaching materials would seem to be a major area of decision-making that will influence teaching practices for many years. The adoption of reading schemes in primary schools, or history or mathematics texts in secondary schools, illustrate the often all-pervading influence of such materials with trained teachers. It would not, perhaps, be too unfair to project the supply of teaching materials for a student as a more powerful guide than any training programme. Whilst it is easy to preach that such resources should be made widely available, that careful selection of parts based on a knowledge of need and content and adaptation or the design of new materials should be practised where a scheme is based on a two-hourly meeting for staff who may or may not be adequately skilled and motivated to undertake such professional tasks, it would seem to be making wholly unreasonable demands.

A third aspect of teaching that would seem to have to be effectively initiated before tutor and student meet would be that of designing and recording an evaluative system. It would seem necessary to decide what needs to be known, when and how it is to be discovered, measured and recorded before the process gets underway. The overtones of testing with imprecise and inappropriate instruments often provide an adequate smokescreen for avoidance of the central issues arising from a concern for quality and efficiency. It would seem reasonable for a student to expect a professional attitude from providers, for a meaningful diagnosis and agreement as to needs, and some indications as to any success that is achieved. Here again a decision to prevaricate would seem to be a decision that is deliberately taken in the face of a series of complex issues. How far any literacy project can provide initial basic information about its students, other than the details contained in any register, and how far it can indicate progress and future directions with some degree of precision may provide a useful yardstick of its worth.

Institutional approaches
Whilst the potential influence of the nature of the establishment that

houses a literacy project has already been hinted at, it need not follow that the providing agency is also the home – many examples exist of technical colleges acquiring a motley collection of annexes. The relaxation of house rules described by Margaret Ben-Tovim (1974) in such areas as staff-student ratios, fees, enrolment procedures and term lengths has largely, though not wholly, been achieved within overall economic contraints.

What is perhaps more fundamental is the degree of integration or separate identity adopted by a literacy scheme in both economic and practical terms; whether it is preferable to earmark a small but specific sum in revenue estimates, or to remain within a larger overall heading and risk gaining or losing finance through open access, would seem a delicate choice. Similarly, how far tuition should be identified and practised as a discrete entity, a separate project housed away from other areas of post-school education, or how far it should be integrated and be accessible and give access to other forms of provision, would seem again to be dependent on local factors. Guidance, it would seem, can be drawn from the nature of recruitment patterns, of students' purposes, of the ethos of other establishments and what can be defined of the attitudes of significant decision-makers; in any event such decisions as are taken would need also to take account of the options and the strengths and weaknesses of the position taken up.

An analysis of the two national surveys of literacy projects (Kedney 1974) indicate that some 57 per cent of projects were based on adult education centres, a further 14.6 per cent in further education colleges and of the remaining 28.4 per cent, the majority (18 per cent) were in penal establishments. Of the remainder, 4.8 per cent were voluntary schemes, and colleges of education, universities and school psychological services largely account for the other part. The financial and administrative context of adult literacy provision would largely seem to be that of the local education authority, and the diversity of practices developed across the country would suggest that the range of possible options are considerable, interpretation being a matter for local decisions.

It is difficult to envisage any other area of educational development where the fundamental ground rules are so flexible as to provide such extensive opportunities for creative management as those that currently exist in adult literacy provision. The challenge to project designers, be they organizers or tutors, is at one and the same time daunting and exciting. The examples discussed above serve to illustrate but some of the range of options in some of the areas of decision-making that are open to planners. However, as time passes and organizational practices settle into patterns, what may be regarded as the *rigor mortis* of bureaucracy sets in. Patterns of activity begin increasingly to interlock and become interdependent on the practices of others as staff and students develop expectations and habits that are subsequently difficult to change.

If a literacy project deliberately builds into its approach an expectation and acceptance of innovation, a basically questioning approach to its own actions and suppositions and a willingness to experiment and evaluate, it may be possible to extend the period of flexibility. Researchers have as yet to question how far guiding philosophies are drawn from overt, deliberate planning or from an unconscious and perhaps unquestioning acceptance of current practices. Similarly, any relationship, or lack thereof, of theoretical models and paper plans to reality has, as yet, to be explored.

This paper opened with the proposition that adult literacy projects are characterized by their potential flexibility in so many areas of key decision-making and consequently that the management of projects can largely predetermine the practices of tutors and students. The case studies provided in such publications as *The Adult Illiterate in the Community* (Kedney 1975) or the *Literacy Symposium in Adult Education* (Kedney 1975) provide examples of the diversity of current practices. It is perhaps not too difficult to envisage sharply contrasting situations where on the one hand planned decisions based on needs and resources provide the basis for teaching and learning and on the other tutors and students endeavour to resolve issues arising from *ad hoc* situations and chance. A stitch in time may indeed save nine.

References

ALLAN, G. (1974) 'Assessment and diagnosis of adult illiterates' in M. Ben-Tovim and R. J. Kedney (eds) *Aspects of Adult Illiteracy* Merseyside Institute of Adult Education

AST, R. (1970) 'Recruitment and training of professional staff for adult basic education learning centre' in W. S. Griffiths and A. Hayes (eds) *Adult Basic Education: The State of the Art* Chicago: University of Chicago Press

BEN-TOVIM, M. (1974) 'Structures of adult literacy provision' in M. Ben-Tovim and R. J. Kedney (eds) *Aspects of Adult Illiteracy* Merseyside Institute of Adult Education

KEDNEY, R. J. (1975) 'The design of literacy projects: some variants' in R. J. Kedney (ed) *The Adult Illiterate in the Community* Bolton College of Education (Technical)

KEDNEY, R. J. (1976) Educational objectives in adult literacy provision *Studies in Adult Education* 8, 1, 3. National Institute of Adult Education

LIVINGSTON, A. J. (1974) 'A class for adult illiterates' in T. W. Pascoe (ed) *Aspects of Adult Illiteracy* National Association for Remedial Education

MACFARLANE, T. (1976) You teach what you test, OK? *Adult Literacy Resources Agency Newsletter 6* Adult Literacy Resource Agency

MCMULLEN, I. (1969) 'The identity of a teacher' in W. Taylor (ed) *Towards a Policy for the Education of Teachers* Butterworth

PAGANO, J. (1970) 'Teachers in adult basic education programmes' in J. Pagano (ed) *Strategies for Adult Basic Education* Newark, Delaware: International Reading Association

SOUTHGATE-BOOTH, V. (1973) 'Training the teachers of reading in England and Wales' in M. Clark and A. Milne (eds) *Reading and Related Skills* Ward Lock Educational

WILLIAMS, M. (1972) *Performance Appraisal in Management* Heinemann

18　Girls and alienation: implications for the reading teacher

Susanne M. Shafer

In the diocesan newsletter, Dr Donald Coggan, the Archbishop of Canterbury, wrote (*The Times,* 12 July 1976):

> We must recognize the fact that we are a multiracial society and shall continue to be so. Many of our immigrants are now second-generation immigrants. It is no good saying: 'Send them all home.' They are here to stay.

With Dr Coggan's reminder clearly before us, I should like to sketch in the conditions of life that face so many minority girls in Britain, conditions which their teachers must take into account as the curriculum is developed. If the school is to serve these girls well, that curriculum, including the reading curriculum, must be addressed to the challenges that minority, or immigrant, girls encounter in their daily life and in the long run as well.

Today's growing girl in the USA and the UK finds herself not only in a world that is changing significantly but also in cultural milieus where the role expectations for women are broadening. For minority women, these changes create an even greater juxtaposition of the female traditions in their respective subcultures and the part women are beginning to play in each dominant culture. Their growing daughters, even more than they themselves, encounter cultural dissonance, which is further confounded by the so-called double jeopardy of racism and sexism still awaiting American and British minority girls as they move into adulthood. Both countries have a distinct history of discriminating against women and those of Black, Asian, or Indian origins. Mexican-Americans are a racial mixture and have also been relegated to a virtual caste status in many American communities.

Immigrants in the United Kingdom
In the United Kingdom West Indians and East Asians, in addition to the Irish, represent the largest immigrant groups entering the country. As with Blacks and Chicanos in the United States of America, they in no way resemble each other culturally, but they are subjected to

similar forms of discrimination. Still considered inferior because of their colour and colonial origins (Allen 1971), West Indians and East Asians hold the poorest paying jobs, those the society considers least desirable. West Indians speak English but often a dialect of Creole considerably at variance with standard English. Whether Pakistani or Indian, East Asians may speak English, although it is often not their first language and they and their children may not speak a standard dialect of English. Immigrants occupy the poorest housing in many British cities. By January 1972 immigrant children represented 3.3 per cent of all pupils in maintained primary and secondary schools. Of these '. . . 36.4 per cent came from the West Indies, 20.1 per cent from India, 10.9 per cent from Pakistan. . . .' (Whitaker's Almanack 1974). Special compensatory educational measures to aid these children are only in the early stages of application, perhaps because each group, East Asians and West Indians, are implicitly viewed as members of separate, inferior castes (Abbott 1971). The intensity of the recent parliamentary debate of the Race Relations Bill substantiates the prevalence of this social attitude in Britain (*The Times,* 10 July 1976).

Cultural dissonance and immigrant girls
Under these social conditions, immigrant girls in the United Kingdom find themselves subject to several forms of cultural dissonance which serve to interfere in the educational process into which they are routed by the authorities. The term cultural dissonance draws attention to the juxtaposition of disparate cultural expectations for an individual growing up as a member of a minority group. Cultural dissonance is exemplified by the socialization of girls in West Indian and East Asian families in Great Britain and Black and Chicano families in the United States. What role expectations are conveyed to girls in these communities? What career aspirations are fostered? What view of self can one conjecture develops?

West Indians
The West Indians' life style in England reflects cultural patterns brought from the Caribbean. There the male verifies his masculinity by having women bear his offspring, even if poverty precludes a European-style marriage. The 70 per cent rate of illegitimacy in Jamaica is accepted as a normal phenomenon (Krausz 1971). Once in Britain, the male can exhibit his manliness in few new ways. He does not acquire much education since he seldom has access to grammar schools or the prestigious public schools. He is in effect barred from most well-paying or esteemed jobs. He continues to exercise his interest in procreation through a rather open, common-law approach to marriage. In other words, the West Indian society, whether in the Caribbean or in England, does not demand formalized, lifelong marriages.

150

For the West Indian woman living in London or some other urban area, the implications of these marital patterns, a 'bastardization of several cultures' (Rawlings 1973a), create economic uncertainty and stress. Close to 50 per cent of West Indian women are on their own (Avent 1973). Many have small children, whom they raise without the benefit of a permanent spouse or an extended family. The family's economic and, of course, psychological wellbeing falls to the mother. Often employed outside the home, she places her children with a childminder, a neighbourhood West Indian woman who earns a living overseeing groups of these children during the workday (Rose 1969).

For the girl being socialized in these surroundings, several distinct role expectations emerge. She sees her future heterosexual relations as warm; at the same time her liaisons with males are not likely to be permanent. She knows motherhood lies on the road ahead. Like her own mother, she anticipates joining the labour force in a relatively unskilled capacity. 'Typical employment for West Indian women would be catering, transport and laundering ... (Rawlings 1973b). Since the girl expects to have to handle her roles of wife, mother, and breadwinner simultaneously, she may begin to view her status as an adult as equal to that of the adult male, at least in the local West Indian community. Here she may develop a real sense of personal warmth.

East Asians

The young girl growing up in Britain's East Asian community encounters quite a different set of experiences. She is encouraged to do well in her schoolwork, although from early on she knows that her schooling will probably not go beyond the years of compulsory attendance. While she may even attain some vocational skill, she will make use of that skill only until an early marriage. If she is employed anywhere after she leaves school, she will work side by side with other East Asian females. Since most East Asian families in England are among the poor, mothers may work outside the home, albeit in low-paying jobs, to supplement the family's income. Young girls are expected to help at home, where the extended family may be considerably smaller than it was in its pre-emigration days outside of Britain. For girls, marriage continues to be arranged in rather traditional ways. Since that process requires that the girl has had carefully screened heterosexual contacts in adolescence, East Asian parents closely supervise their teenage daughters (Hiro 1973). In contrast to West Indian customs, their marriages tend to be formalized and far more stable. These cultural patterns surely imprint themselves on the growing girl and leave her with fairly clear role expectations. Unless she rejects her cultural background, she will acquiesce to an arranged marriage. She will bear and raise her husband's children. She may eventually work outside the home but probably only in a place where other East Asian women work. For the outside world she will appear to accept a status inferior to that of the male. Female inferiority, one may recall, is a rather uncontested maxim of Islam; Indian cultures vary more in the status assigned to males and females, respectively.

Work/career
Naturally, school performance and, more particularly, career aspirations are affected by the role expectations of West Indian and East Asian girls living in England. West Indian girls anticipate entry into the labour market, but find anything but low-paying jobs or opportunity for later advancement highly unlikely to come their way. They also anticipate that their life will be divided between a job, a male, and children yet to be borne. To aspire to a career either generated through vocational or professional preparation or on-the-job advancement appears out of tune with these role expectations.

Similarly, an East Asian girl in England sees herself working only briefly after her school years in a place approved by her parents. If not actually employed, the girl is at home, perhaps to care for young brothers or sisters while her mother is at work. Again, the thought of a career enters the mind of only those few girls from upper-class East Asian families living in Britain. For neither the East Asian or the West Indian girl does British post-secondary education necessarily arouse much interest.

Status of women in British society
How do these expectations compare with those of other girls in Britain? In general girls in England find access to apprenticeships far more limited than do boys. They experience such forms of sexism in education as:

1   Single sex schools, although boys' schools are more prestigious and preferred by male teachers
2   counsellors who steer girls into the humanities in the sixth form, thereby eliminating these students' future access to subjects that require a mathematics or science background, and
3   reduced exposure even in comprehensive schools to science and industrial arts classes.

Even for non-immigrant females in the British labour force wage scales and employment opportunities favour males. So do aspects of the law and the National Health Service. Women, too, still experience discrimination, although in recent years parliamentary actions have ameliorated obvious forms and in general have served to raise the level of awareness of at least some Britons in regard to sexism extant in the society. For young girls growing up among the working class of that society, role expectations largely consist of being a schoolgirl to age sixteen, then a clerk, shopgirl, or unskilled factory worker for a few years, and finally a wife and young mother with no job outside the home. Even for those who remain in school through part or all of the sixth form, the role expectations may be nearly identical: 'One-third of all married women are at work (in Britain), yet girls of sixteen persist in a romantic expectation of marriage at the age of twenty and no further employment (Avent 1974).

Some girls, of course, avail themselves of post-secondary education, including higher education and preparation for a profession. Still, access for females to corresponding educational programmes has so far been more difficult than for males. The Open University's popularity with women attests to that roadblock and also to the changing aspirations of a considerable number of women in England. At least 40 per cent of the enrollees at the Open University are female, and a sizeable number of these hold clerical positions, occupations traditionally considered appropriate even for the brightest of female achievers in school (McIntosh 1976). British women may be more aware of the increased rate of female participation in the labour force, which today stands at 42 per cent (Central Statistical Office 1972). Young women, too, tend to remain in the labour force even after marriage, and childbearing has been limited through family planning, which receives government support. Britain's birthrate has been declining and now stands at 13.9 (United Nations 1975).

Whatever cultural dissonance exists for immigrant, or minority, women in England, that phenomenon is not wholly absent from the lives of women here in general. While females still find themselves subject to sexism in the labour market and in the educational system, minority women encounter racism as well. In view of the increasing awareness that the society must move to reduce racism and sexism, the education of girls, including particularly West Indian and East Asian ones, may be altered so as better to prepare them to share more equitably in British life and society.

Education of minority girls
On the basis of their role expectations and the current status of their families in the dominant culture, one may draw certain implications for the education, including reading education, of minority girls in the United Kingdom. The cultural dissonance they experience may induce a more passive, accepting behaviour on their part which will make their efforts to reduce racism and sexism rather unlikely. If an assumption of equality of opportunity undergirds the society's value system, educational arrangements must be such as to facilitate minority girls' preparation to live in the dominant culture, or even, if they so wish, to assimilate themselves in the mainstream as they attain the independence concomitant with adulthood. What education practices recommend themselves under these circumstances?

153

Regardless of whether minority girls live in Great Britain or the United States, a crucial part of their education must focus on the continuous expansion of their language competency. In the case of East Asians in England (and Mexican-Americans in the United States), such a concern requires the inclusion of bilingual education in the curriculum. English may have to be taught as a second language to enable the students to break out of the restrictions imposed on them by their limited command of English. Derrick (1966) writes:

> . . . Immigrant pupils come from different societies where the pattern of living and of what is socially acceptable differs in many respects from the British pattern. . . . Adjustment to the new milieu is made the more difficult by the language problem. . . . One hears of some pupils who after even a year or more at school in Britain have hardly opened their mouths or uttered one word of English.

To enhance a minority pupil's self-confidence as well as preparation for effective participation in the larger society implies continuous expansion of his or her language competence (Valtin 1975). For minority girls, versatility in English becomes crucial if they are to be free to select and succeed in the occupation of their choice and in due time to aid their future families to reduce the aversive impact of racism and poverty.

Once language competence expands, these girls presumably will meet with increased success in learning to read well. That skill appears particularly useful as a means of expanding minority girls' self-confidence and knowledge to make decisions about personal and occupational goals. Through encounters with a variety of characters in literature, a woman's possible roles may be considered and personal sights may be raised. In the literature of history, accounts are found of how men *and* women have altered their world, however limiting or restrictive that world may have been. Always to be able to read for information frees that reader from ignorance and from debilitating uncertainty.

To help minority girls to accept themselves and their families, in spite of the racism, sexism, and poverty to which society subjects them, may mean that the teachers of reading take a look at the work of Sylvia Ashton-Warner. In her work with Maori children in a New Zealand primary school, Sylvia Ashton-Warner developed the concept of the 'key vocabulary'. She encouraged her beginning pupils to tell her stories – of family, their environment, or their imagination. She recorded what they said and then read the stories over with them. An acceptance of the Maori culture was fundamental. The child had to feel that the stories of his people were as suitable to be put into print and to be read as stories drawn from the dominant culture.

A similar procedure where necessary geared to older, more mature West Indian or East Asian girls might encourage these to record the riches as well as the stresses of their families' traditions and current modes of life. In turn, these writings may become the reading materials for these girls and their non-immigrant classmates. They may even form the beginnings of a literature of immigrant women in Britain. In the United States the literature produced by Black women today is a powerful vehicle for expressing the many levels of feeling in a world too often fraught for them with racism, sexism and poverty. Encouraging immigrant girls in England to deal with their heritage in writing, and then reading, at least for some may reduce the cultural dissonance they have experienced and hence avoid alienation.

A third means of assisting minority girls to cope in the future is for schools to aid them to gain an understanding of the cultures around them. Again, reading skills mean access to the books, magazines and newspapers that are the source of much contemporary information about one's environment. The literature of her or her family's country of origin may provide support for self-understanding for immigrant girls. Shaping one's cultural matrix in adulthood is measurably eased if, for example, a West Indian girl fathoms that the vestiges of a matriarchy she notices among her people is attributable to the slavery origins of her ancestors. Should she wish to reject the female role attendant to a matriarchy, she very likely can do so in Britain without restraint from the dominant society whose changing culture in regard to marriage and family she must also understand. An East Asian girl needs to contrast the role of women circumscribed by the family, kinship, and caste systems of her parents' culture with practices prevalent among the British, her new fellow-countrymen.

Other basic educational requirements include:

1 health education including sex education and eventually family planning
2 family life studies to develop insight into male–female relations, parent–child relations, and home management
3 history to meet women who asserted themselves to make significant contributions to the world
4 political education to grasp the citizen's role in the political process and to adjudge the growing political militancy of minorities, and
5 preliminary career preparation to expand occupational knowledge and to test occupational interests and potential.

To achieve these ends, schools must seek to make each minority girl an efficient reader in each of these spheres. She must be given access to reading materials as widely ranging as the above topics. She will want to be helped to read these for full understanding and also to consult them alone during personal reading.

Once equipped with reading skills and knowledge useful in the society and aware of the cultural dissonance that may be present in her life space, the maturing West Indian or East Asian girl in the United Kingdom, one hopes, will develop sufficient self-confidence to decide on her future life style. That the choice is up to each girl is basic to the perception of life in a multiracial society. Julius K. Nyerere's theme in *Education for Self-reliance* (Nyerere 1968) holds true:

> The education provided must . . . encourage the development in each citizen of three things: an enquiring mind; an ability to learn from what others do, and reject or adapt it to his own needs; and a basic confidence in his own position as a free and equal member of the society, who values others and is valued by them for what he does and not for what he obtains.

References

ABBOTT, S. (ed) (1971) *The Prevention of Racial Discrimination in Britain* Oxford University Press

ALLEN, S. (1971) *New Minorities, Old Conflicts* New York: Random House

AVENT, C. (1973) Senior Careers Adviser, Inner London Education Authority (personal communication)

AVENT, C. (1974) *Practical Approaches to Careers Education* Hobson Press

CENTRAL STATISTICAL OFFICE (1972) *Social Trends* 3, 71 HMSO

COGGAN, D. (1976) *The Times* (12 July)

DERRICK, J. (1966) *Teaching English to Immigrants* Longman

HIRO, D. (1973) (revised edition) *Black British, White British* Monthly Review Press

KRAUSZ, E. (1971) *Ethnic Minorities in Britain* MacGibbon and Kee

MCINTOSH, N. (1976) Open University, Milton Keynes, Buckinghamshire (personal communication)

NYERERE, J. K. (1968) Education for Self-Reliance. Reproduced in UJAMAA: Essays on Socialism Oxford University Press. Reprinted in I. Lister (1974) *Deschooling* Cambridge University Press

RAWLINGS, M. (1973a) Vice-Principal, Paddington College of Further Education, London (personal communication)

RAWLINGS, M. (1973b) *The Education, Training and Employment of Women and Girls* Inner London Education Authority

ROSE, E. J. B. (1969) *Colour and Citizenship* Oxford University Press

UNITED NATIONS (1975) *Statistical Year Book 1974* 83

VALTIN, R. (1975) Analyse von Sprachforderungsprogrammen im Bereich der Eingangsstufe *Gutachten fur den Bildungsrat* Stuttgart: Ernst Klett Verlag, 71–95

WHITAKER'S ALMANACK (1974) *Whitaker's Almanack 1974* 1043

Part 4

Attitudes and response to reading

19 Nursery teachers' behaviour: some implications for beginning reading

Asher Cashdan

Most human beings enjoy thinking and talking about themselves. We take a great interest in our relationships, our experiences and our own behaviour, often discussing these at length with relations, friends or colleagues. Yet we can be amazingly unaware of ourselves, in particular of our own habitual behaviour. The Bullock Committee (DES 1975) reviewed observational studies showing how much of secondary-school lesson times are occupied by teacher talk. Typically, pupils have very little opportunity for sustained verbal interaction. Few teachers, however, would recognize this phenomenon as occurring in their own classrooms – as when 95 per cent of interviewees describe themselves as above-average drivers! Alan Cohen (in this volume) has reviewed this area well, so it need not be dwelt upon in this paper. One particularly relevant study will suffice. Southgate and Lewis (1973) reported an observational study in infant schools. They found that, in perfectly normal classrooms, six year olds spent only about half their lesson time 'on task' during their reading and language periods and also that very little of this time was devoted to the use of the standard reading scheme. Neither of these findings would have been predicted by the average teacher, who might expect children to spend nearly all of their lesson time on task and that a high proportion of this time would be spent with the reading scheme.

The point is in no sense that teachers are incompetent or stupid. Hospital patients often report that 'the doctor did not tell me what was wrong', even in controlled studies where the diagnosis was specifically communicated to a set percentage of patients! It is indeed very difficult to monitor one's own experiences and behaviour, particularly under conditions of overwork or stress. But if curriculum development and innovation are to be possible, they have to be carried out against a background of self-knowledge. In other words, the teacher has to have considerable insight into her own behaviour and that of the children she teaches, as both baseline and yardstick for new departures.

Curriculum change is not, of course, sought for its own sake. It is pursued mainly as a result of dissatisfaction with present achievements. The reading attainment of many children, particularly those in the inner-city areas, is indeed unsatisfactory. To help them, I would argue, we need not only new approaches based on self-knowledge, but those founded also on an adequate psychology of learning.

Contemporary psychologists such as Piaget and Hunt (see Hunt 1969) seem to me to offer the most fruitful approach. They see virtually all children as intrinsically motivated learners who need no driving or encouragement to acquire knowledge and skills. What happens to many of them is that their environment fails to prepare them adequately for the demands of school and the school experience itself may easily make things worse. In this light, the task of early schooling is to reinforce the child's intrinsic motivation, to help him see how effective he can be – and, if his motivation is really damaged, to help restore the child's natural desire to learn.

'Teaching styles in nursery education'

At the Open University, Dr Janet Philps and myself, with two other colleagues, are currently involved in an observational study in the nursery school. We are looking at the behaviour of both teachers and children in ten fairly typical Outer London Borough nursery schools. The study involves twenty-five teachers and their groups of children, though for more detailed study we are looking at about two hundred children (i.e. eight children per teacher). Over the four-term fieldwork period, each classroom is being visited for two or three weeks and regular samples taken of the verbal and non-verbal behaviour of teachers and children.

We have two main purposes. First, the collection of a data base. Here, we want to find out how teachers behave, how far there are discernible teacher styles – ways in which different teachers resemble each other. We want to see also, at least in an initial way, if children play and learn differently according to the predominant style of their teacher. Obviously, the mere existence of a systematic body of knowledge such as we hope to collect and publish will give teachers a great deal to think about and, hopefully, will suggest useful modifications and developments. However, as a second facet of our research, we have spent just over a term working with half the teachers in our research group on a set of 'intervention' strategies for use especially with children who are in need of motivational and intellectual encouragement, in the normal classroom situation.

The data collection in our project uses four main techniques. In the *teacher-focused observations*, continuous records are taken by an observer in the classroom for regular three-minute periods. Recording is by a pencil-and-paper method, where much of the teacher talk is taken down verbatim, but where names of children addressed and speaking, the teacher's other activities and qualitative aspects of what is happening in the classroom are noted in specially designed brief codes. Although the focus is on the teachers, the system is designed to

160

take account of the other participants in interactions which go on, including particularly the behaviour of the children.

In the *child-focused observations*, the behaviour of the eight selected children in each teacher's group is also sampled and recorded, paying particular attention to the child's levels of activity, the materials he uses, his involvement and the complexity of his activity. Thirdly, in specially set up *one-to-one sessions*, we have been tape-recording conversations between individual children and their teachers, using specially designed play materials (a toy zoo and a model house). This technique, though slightly artificial in its organization, will, we hope, help us to get a much more detailed picture of the way in which the teacher talks to children in her class as well as of her habitual teaching 'style'. We are of course able to relate such behaviour to the general observations mentioned above.

Finally, we have used Kelly's (1955) personal construct system to construct repertory grids with each teacher, using the children in her class. This enables us to build up a picture of how the teacher sees each of the children in her class, the concepts she uses and how she rates the children on them. This means that when, as we have done, we select the eight children for detailed observation, we are able to constitute these groups in a balanced way from those boys and girls whom the *teacher* sees as functioning well or poorly, not on the basis of externally administered 'tests'.

After the first two terms of our study, we introduced the second aspect of our approach. This was to set up an 'intervention' programme, working experimentally with twelve of the teachers in our research group, thus providing for both an experimental and a control group. Drawing very heavily on the techniques described by Marion Blank (1973) in her work with children in the New York area, we have been trying to help teachers to re-motivate children by working in short, individual sessions, and fitting the 'demands' they make to each boy or girl's current level and capabilities. We have some half-dozen main principles. They include:

1 using a good range of cognitive demands
2 the sequential development of a single theme
3 the appropriate selection and use of materials
4 verifying the child's response
5 using appropriate child activity
6 pacing the session, so that an appropriate level of success and failure is achieved at each stage
7 following up the child's response.

Numbers 1 and 7 contain perhaps the most crucial principles. To achieve success for the child, the teacher must learn, from lists which are supplied, from discussion of 'lessons' both before and afterwards and from occasional examination of audio- and video-tape records, how to make demands on the child which are neither too low nor too high and, additionally, how to simplify, or 'follow up' inadequate responses.

This is, of course, only a brief, outline description of both the research techniques and the intervention work, but it should suffice to indicate the kind of work we have been doing and its rationale.

The results of the study

Data collection in the study will be completed by the end of 1976. It will then take some months to analyse the material and begin to prepare it for publication. Meanwhile, we hope to continue to work with some of the teachers who have been involved in the experimental project and to extend this work. At this stage, therefore, there are no findings to report. But our own pilot study (Philps and Cashdan 1975) together with our intuitive feelings so far, tend to confirm the observations in the introduction to this paper. Many teachers do not seem to hold sustained conversations with the children in their groups, certainly not on a one-to-one basis. Furthermore, sustained conversation when it does occur, whether in group or individual work, is surprisingly often weighted towards those children whom the teacher sees as functioning well already. Obviously, many teachers find it difficult to persevere with just those children they know to need help most. We suspect also that many teachers classify children, even at the ages of three and four, in a fairly static way. For example, they see them as 'mature' or 'immature', rather than as developing and changing.

Our study includes both an immediate follow-up, a few weeks after the experimental teaching was undertaken, and a longer-term follow-up a few months later. It will be interesting to see how far teachers are able to modify their styles and whether the results of any such modifications can be traced in our records of the children's behaviour, even though this latter has not been our main focus. Most important, no curriculum change is of value unless by the time the project has been carried through, the teachers are genuinely convinced of the worthwhileness of the ideas that have been developed. We are therefore extremely sensitive to the discussion and investigation of the acceptability of the ideas we have been working out with the teachers.

Some implications

A study of the kind I have been describing is worthwhile if it increases the effectiveness and the satisfaction of both teachers and pupils in the nursery school. But its true use must lie in the possibilities it helps to open up in the consolidation and further development of the child's learning at later stages. I should like to pick out four main areas.

First, I think we need further study of the well-functioning child. Our research is predicted on the assumption that successful children are not just the genetically well-endowed, or those from 'good' families, but that all children can learn effectively at school, provided they can see that it is a meaningful place, where success is within their grasp. Such children, we believe, become 'self-running'. That is, they learn to relate to the teacher, not as passive recipients of handed-out information, but to use her as a resource for learning, whose value they know for themselves. We need to investigate these hypotheses; to explore how far children who have learnt to work productively with the teacher do acquire and retain this independence. Clearly, much will depend not only on how well the job has been done in the nursery school, but on how far its philosophy integrates with that of the first, middle and later school periods.

Then, we are all too conscious that our work is but a start. If the experimental programme seems promising, then we need implementation studies to take it further and fill it out. We need to ask how far what goes on in the reading lesson in the infant and later stages, sets up a meaningful relationship between child and teacher in which demands are set correctly and appropriate 'follow-ups' used. Essentially, the argument is that many children become 'remedial' cases because they have not seen the purpose or the relevance of the school's demands; in turn, this may be due to the school's failure to work from where the child is.

Thirdly, what is needed is not a once-and-for-all research study, but a constant interaction between the teacher's practice and its selfconscious evaluation. Teachers need to be constantly monitoring their own behaviour, checking on the response they get and trying again. A research study is not an expensive way of starting off such a process, but its continuance depends on how far such a project succeeds in building up an awareness and a commitment on the part of teachers, so that (as happened in one of our schools) they decide themselves to incorporate part of what has been done in the study into their everyday practice, often in ways not foreseen by the researchers.

Finally, a point that has not been discussed in this paper, but which we have been aware of throughout the nursery study, is that children relate to a number of other adults as well as to their teachers. We need to ask questions, therefore, about the demands and expectations made of children by nursery nurses and other assistants, by friends and relatives whom they encounter regularly and, above all, by their parents. Mothers (and fathers, too, as often as is possible) need to be involved in what happens in school. This involvement includes not only enlisting the parent in helping the child to see the purpose, the use and benefits of schooling, but also getting their help in the formulation of educational policy. For literacy, and indeed the whole of schooling, depends in the end on the felt needs of both the parents and the children we are involved in educating.

References

BLANK, M. (1973) *Teaching Learning in the Preschool: A Dialogue Approach* Columbus, Ohio: Charles Merrill

DES (1975) *A Language for Life* (Bullock Report) HMSO

HUNT, J. McV, (1969) *The Challenge of Incompetence and Poverty* Urbana: University of Illinois Press

KELLY, G. A. (1955) *The Psychology of Personal Constructs* New York: Norton

PHILPS, J. and CASHDAN, A. (1975) Nursery teachers' classroom behaviour in the light of their constructs of pupils: an exploratory study *Biennial Conference of the International Society for the Study of Behavioural Development* Guildford, Surrey

SOUTHGATE, V. and LEWIS, C. Y. (1973) How important is the infant reading scheme? *Reading* 7, 2, 4-13

Footnote: The research reported in this paper is financed by a grant from the SSRC.

20 Teachers' perceptions of their pupils' reading ability

Helen Arnold

In trying to define teachers' perceptions of their pupils' ability and progress in reading, I must emphasize that I am only offering my own perceptions of the teachers, gleaned from contact with a small sample during our research project *Extending Beginning Reading*. This project is examining the stage of reading development reached by 'average' readers of seven to nine years, and the classroom practices relevant to their reading during these years. As we have just finished a year of intensive observations in the schools, I have little to offer yet in the way of statistical findings. The reality of the classroom is evident when you are in it, but difficult to pin down in retrospect. We hope to emerge with well-authenticated analyses – at the present moment of time I apologize for my subjective and anecdotal information. All that I say, however, is based on direct observation during the past three years.

I submit that there are three main factors which shape teachers' perceptions of their pupils' reading behaviour. These are:

1 The teacher's *own concept* of what the reading process constitutes. Although she works within the framework structured by the headteacher (often very loosely), and is given reading materials, she is usually free, in English schools, to use the materials and initiate the instruction in any way she sees fit. Therefore she will base her own emphases on teaching reading on these initial concepts, and her expectations of her pupils will depend on how far they measure up to her own model of reading.

2 Through experience the teacher will have built up *general expectations* of children's reading at certain stages of development, but her perception of the child as a reader often depends to a great extent on her assessment of the child's ability and attitudes *in general,* for example on her beliefs about age and sex differences. She will, for instance, probably expect a child from a 'good' home to be a good reader.

3 Achievement in reading will be assessed *directly* in various ways, and the teacher will obviously use the results of these assessments to form her perceptions of reading progress. The type of measures

165

used for formal assessment – often involving those elements in reading which are most easily measurable – will be influential in forming her attitudes.

I propose now to look at these three factors in more detail. Since the project is limited to the first two years of junior schooling, and to average readers within these two years, I can form no general conclusions. Since, however, I believe this to be a crucial stage in reading development, I make no apology for this limited focus.

The teacher's model of reading

It seems that primary teachers see reading mainly as the mastery of initial decoding skills. They look for certain specific signposts to gauge achievement, for example the mastery of key-words (sight-words), the ability to 'sound out' words (phonic attack), and the successful completion of a reading scheme. The word most often used by teachers to signify mastery of reading is 'fluency'. This is seldom defined, but appears to mean the ability to read a given passage orally 'with expression'.

Teaching of reading is often understood as giving instruction and practice in phonic rules. This preoccupation with initial skills is understandable for three reasons:

1 Junior teachers have rarely been trained in teaching extended reading skills. When they realize – often with some alarm – that they need to teach reading as such, they look backward to the infant years, where there is a recognizable existing structure, rather than forward to the model of the skilled reader.
2 It is easier to test achievement in the initial skills than to assess the outcome of 'reading in use'.
3 The dependence of most schools on formal reading schemes implies over-reliance on such schemes by teachers.

Thus they tend to see reading as a hierarchy of subskills which can (even should) be mastered sequentially. The results of our measures with individual 'average' readers tend to refute this hierarchy. All levels of language are used simultaneously (phono-graphemic, syntactic and semantic) in order to crack the code. Children will work through their strengths; the sequential model of reading does not allow for this.

As far as teaching is concerned, therefore, the teacher will generally follow an accepted pattern which chops up the process of reading into discrete compartments. Sessions are devoted to reading 'instruction' based on phonic rules and progression through the basic scheme; there are other lessons in 'vocabulary', 'spelling' and 'comprehension', usually taking the form of written exercises. Her perception of children as readers will be formed from her impressions of their achievement in these separate skills. For example, 'imagination' is quoted by teachers as occurring or not occurring, in connection with creative writing. Imagination is rarely associated with reading. A child can be 'good at reading' but 'poor at comprehension'. 'Vocabulary' is a skill learnt from exercises bearing little relationship to words in use. The compartmentalization of knowledge is already well under way.

When we look at the teacher's perception of the child as reader, it seems to be based on two polarities – the first, at one extreme, on a generalized view. Because she knows that reading is part of language, her perceptions of the child's overall language ability will affect her impressions of his reading potential. It is perhaps inevitable that the child who is conscientious, pleasant and willing to try, will convince the teacher that he is going to be a better reader than the sullen uncooperative pupil. Most teachers in primary schools are females – perhaps that is why they perceive girls more favourably than boys. Certainly the only finding which showed statistical significance when a large group of 250 teachers were asked to estimate the reading ages of their pupils was an overestimation of girls and an underestimation of boys compared with actual scores on a Schonell word-recognition test. Another interesting finding is that children from a low socioeconomic background often score just as highly on the Crichton Vocabulary scale as those from a 'privileged' home background. But teachers do not expect this. It is not the place to go into the self-fulfilling prophecy, but it seems very relevant here.

The importance placed by teachers on this general, intuitive judgment relates to the type and quantity of objective measurement which occurs – my third factor. Assessment of reading progress is frequently carried out so informally and spasmodically that it is almost non-existent, and there is little attempt to link goals with outcomes. Standardized word-recognition tests are often administered annually by the headteacher, usually at the behest of the LEA rather than for the information of the class teacher. Sometimes a teacher never sees the results. When she does have a reading age available, it is usually derived from a word-recognition test administered at the beginning of the school year, when the teacher first becomes acquainted with her new class. The result of this one test is therefore likely to influence her initial approach to her pupils and her grouping of the class. On this result a child is likely to be classed as a good, average or poor reader throughout the year, regardless of the serious limitations of a norm-based word-recognition test. This will happen simply because there will be no other valid measure of progress administered during the rest of the year. Indeed, because a Reading Quotient appears to bear some affinity to an IQ, results may be taken as a sign of innate reading ability or disability rather than a limited measure of achievement at a particular stage of development.

There appears to be very little ongoing record-keeping in the primary school; the only written check on progress is confined to the slip of paper kept in the child's reader, usually merely recording the page reached at the last oral reading session. Teachers say that they *know* without writing things down because of their frequent contacts with individual children. These, as shown from our observation schedules, are often limited to 2–3 minutes a day with some children. There are few cumulative records, even in classrooms where team-teaching requires shared responsibility. Backward readers, according to the normal pattern of events, are withdrawn daily for remedial tuition, but there is only incidental verbal discussion of individual progress between the remedial and class teacher.

From where, then, does the teacher gain her knowledge, always confidently expressed, of her children's reading progress, if not from formal assessment or written records? It is based on the component of the teaching which all teachers hold sacrosanct through the early years of schooling – the practice of 'hearing children read'. Responses to questionnaires showed us how much effort and time go into this practice. The overwhelming majority of first- and second-year junior teachers say that they hear backward readers every day, average readers two or three times a week, and good readers once a week. This is obviously the most direct method of assessing reading skill – but again it is only oral reading which is involved – the tip of the iceberg, a very different activity from silent reading and one which is likely to hold a child back on word-by-word decoding. The answer given to the query, 'Do you systematically work through a book for instructional purposes with an individual child?' is invariably 'Always', rather than 'Frequently; Sometimes; Never'. Such reading is usually from the reading scheme. The text is therefore unlikely to be of intrinsic interest. The activity is not used diagnostically or for instruction, and is often interrupted by multitudinous requests from other children. There is rarely any attempt to probe comprehension. Although the ritual could be made meaningful (for example, by analysing the miscues made), it is usually left as a ritual, but one on which the teacher bases all her perceptions of a child's reading progress.

Because each aspect of reading tends therefore to be taught in self-contained units, assessment of progress is presumably similarly divided. As the perception of skill is based on oral reading, intermediate or higher-order skills are either neglected or taught through formal exercises in English workbooks. The outcomes from reading are always writing, thus enclosing the activity in a circle of decoding reproduction. No wonder that most children interviewed thought that the purpose of reading was 'to learn to write' or 'to help us to spell'. The many other ways of assessing successful understanding – for example, making up plays, following recipes, carrying out experiments from written instructions – are almost never utilized.

Reading and writing become end-stopped activities. Where discussion of a text occurs it is usually at the literal level of finding out facts and reproducing them. Open-ended questions are always in the affective domain. Questions in the cognitive domain allow only the retrieval of information from the text, so relevance to the child's own experience or judgment is minimal.

I suggest therefore that teachers' perceptions of their pupils' reading are often based on intuitive generalized judgments at one extreme and assessment which concentrates on a narrow spectrum of the whole skill at the other. The corollary of this is that once a child appears to have mastered the discrete skills, he is left to fend for himself in his development of reading as a tool.

Comments made by teachers on their average pupils concentrate on certain dimensions, examples of which I quote because of their typicality.

With regard to reading ability
'Reads fluently but carelessly.'
'Knows phonic rules and can build up well.'
'Still needs practice in fluency.'
'Is now putting expression into his reading.'
'Reading still needs mechanical improvement and also her comprehension.'
'Attained a high degree of fluency.'
'Reads well and with expression.'

With regard to understanding and the use of reading
'Written work is not reflective of her reading fluency but obviously of the level of comprehension.'
'Enjoys comprehension and usually presents an accurate piece of work.'
'Copes reasonably well with comprehension and English exercises.'

With regard to attitudes
'Willing polite hard worker.'
'Bright but lazy.'
'Anxious to please.'

The reader who matches up to the teacher's ideal model will be a pleasant, cooperative girl from a 'good' home background, who exhibits her skill through fluent oral reading. She will be able to extract factual information from a given text and to write her information down neatly. She will be happy to pursue a set reading scheme systematically, use phonic attack successfully, but not necessarily prediction skills.

Is this enough?

21 Teachers' perception and children's reading in secondary schools

Terry Dolan

The theme of this conference, the notion that the teacher and the researcher are often out of step, is particularly applicable when one examines research into reading in the secondary school. It is as if teacher and researcher are looking at one another from opposite ends of a telescope. One regards the other as being a person of considerable magnitude concentrating on only one section of a wide panorama, whilst the other views the first as a person of lesser magnitude set as a distinctive small piece in a distant and complex scene. Depending on whether the reader is researcher or teacher, he may identify with the view from one or other end of the telescope. And perception from either end is distorted and the view out of proportion. One cause of this misperception is that certain assumptions about the teacher are made by the researcher, and vice versa. The researcher, for example, assumes that his topic of research is one of crucial importance for his customer, the teacher. On the other hand, the teacher may rate the problem under investigation as being much less important than others which he could name, and these problems may be deemed much more pressing and immediate.

The publication of the Bullock Report (DES 1975) drew to the attention of all secondary teachers their responsibility for developing the language of children in their classes. This recommendation came as a bombshell to those who had previously regarded this responsibility as belonging to the province of others in the school, notably in the English department. At the same time, the report stressed that the problem of the slow learner or poor reading child was no more serious than that of leading the average and above-average reader to read critically and strategically.

The Schools Council Effective Use of Reading Project set out to examine the reading demands made by teachers together with responses made by pupils in the final year of primary and first and fourth years of secondary schooling. Information from previous research was slight and, to the knowledge of the project team, there had been no extensive empirically-based investigations in the United Kingdom. The excellent publications emanating from the Writing

Across the Curriculum Projects provided useful reference, and the comments of insightful observers such as Barnes *et al* (1969) were valuable. Unfortunately, results of the survey carried out by members of the Bullock Committee were not available to the project in 1973 when investigations began. The team, therefore, had to start by consulting teachers over a wide range of schools and subject specializations, and by carrying out a careful observational study of classroom practice.

One vital assumption made by the project team from the outset was that teachers have high regard for what children may learn from reading. Another was that this expectation would prove in many cases to be unrealistic. This paper is a brief report of our findings in relation to how teachers regard reading, and how classroom practice reflects the beliefs which teachers profess.

Evidence was gained from three sources: answers given by secondary teachers to questions in the course of interviews and discussion during formal visits to schools in LEAS across the country; replies to a fairly open questionnaire completed by 130 teachers from across the subject range in project secondary schools; and from a carefully conducted observational survey of the incidence and context of reading and writing in project primary and secondary schools. One of the objectives in executing the observational study was to assess how teachers actually set about improving reading ability and another was to record the exact amount and type of reading and writing involved in lessons.

The following three questions were put through questionnaires and during interviews:

1 *What and how much reading is involved in your subject?*
Predictably, the amount of reading involved in lessons varied from subject to subject and from year group to year group, with considerable differences in the quantity and type of reading assigned to children. However, emerging from the many responses, a few generalizations may be drawn. Secondary teachers questioned by the team feel by and large that reading often plays an important part in their lessons, but are reluctant to rely on it as the chief vehicle for learning. It would appear that the main reason for this hesitancy is that many teachers consider that children in the lower years of the secondary school are not very skilled as readers. A sizeable vein of reading runs through many subjects, such as English and humanities, whereas teachers of science and mathematics report that they do not consider that reading is a very reliable way to introduce their subjects. Some teachers drew attention to the fact that syllabuses are often so content-packed that they are compelled to 'feed' children with information rather than let them discover, perhaps through reading, under their own steam and at their own pace. Numerous teachers stressed the transactional nature of the

171

reading they set children, claiming that the chief purpose of reading is to allow pupils to 'do something' rather than to read 'merely for the sake of reading'. At the same time, a commonly-expressed point of view was that one of the least effective ways for children to acquire vital information is through reading alone.

2 *Are you always able to find suitable reading material, and, if not, where do you feel the present situation is inadequate?*
In general, teachers reported that it is not always easy to find suitable reading material and very rare to find a single textbook which fills the needs of a course. A frequent complaint referred to the impossibility of finding a suitable course book to cater for the range of ability levels in mixed-ability·group situations. English teachers in particular commented on the poverty of reading material with adult themes and problems, presented in a simple but appealing format. Too often the only suitably readable books are those written for junior children, and secondary children are reluctant to tackle such books with enthusiasm. It is interesting to note that there was wide disagreement among teachers about the content of some books, even when teachers from within the same subject area were talking about the same book. Some felt that explanations and descriptions are too wordy and long-winded, whilst others considered the very same text to be terse, cryptic and confusing. The most general complaint is of a lack of funds to purchase sufficient supplies of up-to-date material.

3 *Do you feel that there are any special problems connected with the reading specific to your subject and, if so, what are they?*
The most general problem referred to the specialist terminology and vocabulary which children need to acquire. It was generally felt that there is too little provision for a build-up of technical terminology over the lower years in the secondary school – 'too technical too soon'. Leading children to grasp and acquire the vocabulary of a subject is further complicated if children have a preferred meaning of a word derived from its more common everyday usage, or when the same word has different meanings depending on the subject – for example, solution, scale and trace.

Teachers seem willing to try to teach techniques peculiar to their own subject, such as finding map references, the use of foreign language dictionaries, reference keys and new symbols. However, many claimed that proficiency in studying their subject depends to an extent on abilities and skills of another subject. Another stumbling block referred to is the feeling reported by many secondary teachers that they are untrained to teach children to read and write. Literacy skills are regarded as largely the responsibility of the English department and it is felt unreasonable to expect a subject teacher to cope with a massive syllabus at the same time as trying to develop tool skills in the basic subjects. Many teachers were irritated by having to spend time correcting 'English' errors and one mathematician seemed to put his finger on a commonly-held point of view – 'in the eyes of children, mathematics is concerned with numbers. When there is a lot of reading involved the children complain that words are English and English is not mathematics!'

Several teachers from across the subject range mentioned that, be it through lack of interest, motivation or ability, many children seem able to cope with reading at a decoding level but are quite unable to comprehend beyond a literal level. Teachers, in general, confessed that they do not really know what to do about this situation. The strategy of one mathematician seemed widespread. He felt ill-equipped to assist children who 'read' but did not 'understand' and his answer was to orally represent the mathematics from the text in a simpler non-wordy manner. By his own admission he was dodging the fundamental issue: in bypassing the need to deal with texts he was only delaying the need to tackle the problem, and, incidentally, encouraging the children to avoid it as well.

The above questions were answered before the publication of the Bullock Report in 1975. Since the report has been available to teachers, there has been an increased awareness of the difficulty in extending children's reading in the secondary school. Particularly, there has been considerable discussion of reading in the context of learning and language across the curriculum. Stauffer (1960) and Walker (1974) have outlined techniques for extending and developing higher reading ability, whilst others such as Herber (1969) and Aukermann (1972) have discussed reading development within content areas. The response by secondary teachers in general has been guarded to suggestions that reading ought to be timetabled as such (Walker 1974) and that the activities which both Stauffer and Walker have outlined lend themselves to adaptation to specific subjects. Most teachers who have considered the recommended techniques have found them interesting but insufficiently developed for immediate implementation into the subject areas of secondary-school curricula. Besides, many teachers consulted by members of the project team have drawn upon the support of the Bullock Committee's recommendation that advanced reading is best developed in context rather than in specially timetabled lessons. Before launching into relatively unexplored territory using relatively untried techniques, they feel that they would like to see evidence of the efficacy of the techniques on the one hand, and the feasibility of their use in content areas on the other. Some, perhaps more cynically, have resisted Walker's suggestion that time be allocated on the secondary timetable for concentrating on the extension of reading ability; after all, they argue, if the techniques genuinely improve advanced reading ability, then this ability should be available through the process of transfer whenever and wherever children need to use it. And if this is the case, then there is no real need for 'non-English' teachers to be directly involved, space on the timetable being given to the activities from the 'English' allocation. Of course, this is to miss the point and to underestimate the scope and application of the reading activities. The project team firmly believe that such reading activities as described by Stauffer and Walker should be regarded as means of increasing knowledge of the subject being studied rather than merely as ways of improving reading comprehension.

In summary, it would appear that secondary teachers questioned in our surveys value reading as an important vehicle for learning and use it to an extent in their lessons. However, they are well aware of the danger of relying on reading as the sole source of information to children. There is a certain dissatisfaction felt over children's ability to apply their reading, especially younger pupils in the secondary school. Teachers appear to be sensitive to this situation and adjust lesson content and structure to deal with it. There is a widespread feeling of lack of expertise in the teaching of effective reading, but a general belief that reading is best extended and developed in the context of subject lessons.

In a first effort to obtain some idea of estimates of the amount of reading in various lessons, teachers in two large comprehensive schools were asked to monitor their lessons and log over a period of one week the average amount of reading undertaken by children in lessons, as well as estimates of the longest average amount of continuous reading. Results are shown in Table 1 (below) where it can be seen that the teachers estimated that children read an

Table 1 Estimates of the amount of reading in lessons

		Lesson units	Average duration of reading in all lessons	Average duration of reading in lessons which involved reading	Average length of longest continuous period of reading
English	*1st year*	24	12	26	10
	4th year	23	11	14	7
Maths	*1st year*	17	13	13	1
	4th year	15	4	7	1
Social studies	*1st year*	20	11	21	5
	4th year	16	4	17	15

(*Note*: Lesson units indicate the total number of periods – single period = 1 unit: double period = 2 units.)

appreciable amount in lessons and that much of this reading was continuous. The rest of this paper will be given to reporting the actual amount of reading recorded during observation in secondary schools, together with the contexts in which reading and other language activities occurred.

Lesson activities were recorded using a behaviour inventory devised by the project team and briefly described to the UKRA Annual Conference in 1974 (Dolan 1975). A fuller account of the inventory will be presented in the project's final report, to be published in 1977. Very briefly, the inventory allows observation of a single child at a time through time-sampled recordings at minute intervals of specified classroom activities of the pupil and teacher. A more detailed record of the type of reading and writing observed plus an estimate of the length of reading and writing minute-by-minute is also noted.

Recording took place in project primary and secondary schools and was undertaken by members of the project team and by specially trained experienced teachers on advanced courses at the university. Children in primary schools were monitored over the entire school day, whilst those in secondary schools were seen in lessons from the timetable in four main subject areas – English, mathematics, science and social studies.

It may be useful at this stage to digress a little to present a brief summary of the primary-school survey. A daily average of 33.4 minutes of reading was recorded over the period of observation. Well over one-third of this reading was of library books during either set reading periods or when children read for pleasure between lesson activities. The rest of the reading was reading for an expressed purpose, with half taking place in other 'English' sessions and the rest being distributed over such lessons as mathematics and social studies (topics, projects, history, geography, etc.). Continuous reading, that is non-stop reading for the whole minute or thereabouts, was only seen in any substantial amount during reading sessions (and, interestingly enough, during music and hymn singing – material being read at singing pace!). Only one-tenth of all other reading observed was continuous. Now, it could be reasonably argued that such advanced reading ability as detecting the main points in a passage and making inferences from information presented over a passage can only be developed through continuous reading. If this is the case, one could conclude that although there is reading in the context of lessons in project primary schools, by far the greatest amount of such reading takes place when children are reading privately to suit their own purposes rather than to complete an assigned learning task.

Table 2 (page 176) shows the overall percentage of time spent by teachers on the activities noted on the observation inventory. The figures give some indication of the overall pattern of activities in the lessons but ought not to be taken to represent 'typical' lessons. There

Table 2   Percentage of TEACHER time spent on various activities

	Administration	Supervising	Informing	Discussing	Individual tuition	Reading	Writing	
English	15	23	16	21	11	13	5	
Maths	11	5	11	8	54	6	4	
Science	15	12	21	14	37	4	3	
Social studies	12	12	21	16	39	3	4	S1
All lessons	13	13	17	15	35	7	4	
English	14	16	11	22	19	19	2	
Maths	13	14	17	15	35	2	8	
Science	13	9	37	14	23	2	8	S4
Social studies	18	17	23	17	13	8	3	
All lessons	15	14	23	17	22	7	5	

S1 = First year secondary: S4 = Fourth year secondary.
(*Note*: Percentages relate to the entire period of observation and to the incidence of recordings – it is quite possible for a teacher to be doing two things at the same time, for example reading and informing. As a result the percentages are not exclusive and their sum in any one cell may exceed 100.)

are some interesting patterns in the lessons overall, with the 'individual tuition' of children which predominates in first-form lessons giving way to 'informing' in fourth-form sessions. English lessons did not follow the general pattern in either first or fourth years, with teachers engaging in much more discussion and less individual tuition than their 'non-English' colleagues.

Table 3 (page 177) shows the overall pattern of percentages of lesson time spent by the children on the inventory activities. The predominant activity in all except mathematics lessons is 'listening'. There is little difference between the amounts of 'reading' noted in first- as opposed to fourth-year lessons in any subject area, but children read much more in English than they do in other lessons. It is interesting to note the increase in the amount of writing which children have to do by the time they reach the fourth year. The upper section of Table 4 (page

Table 3 Percentage of CHILD time spent on various activities

	Administration	Waiting attention	Not involved	Listening	Observing	Practical	Discussion (with teacher)	Discussion (with child)	Deliberating	Writing	Reading	Calculating
English	6	11	38	2	3	2	6	1	13	22	0	
Maths	12	10	16	3	13	3	10	6	5	10	13	
Science	9	8	26	7	23	4	9	1	11	9	1	
Social studies	10	13	26	4	18	5	6	1	9	15	0	
All lessons	9	10	26	4	14	4	8	3	9	14	4	
English	3	14	42	5	0	3	5	1	13	29	0	
Maths	8	17	18	7	5	3	10	6	11	8	23	
Science	5	10	31	8	11	4	7	2	20	10	3	
Social studies	8	11	24	3	9	4	8	1	21	16	0	
All lessons	6	13	29	6	7	3	8	2	17	15	6	

178) shows the type of writing completed in the course of lessons observed. There is little change in the pattern between first- and fourth-year mathematics lessons, but in other subjects there are some interesting contrasts. About one quarter of writing in English lessons is 'reference' writing and, although the actual amount of writing does not increase between year groups, children spend more time copying and writing personal accounts and less time answering questions. In science lessons there is a marked increase in the time spent writing by older children, with less 'answering' and 'personal writing' and more 'copying' – (note taking). The pattern also changes in social studies lessons, with more 'reference' and 'personal' work but less 'copying' – (note making).

Table 4   Percentage of types of writing and reading material

	English		Maths		Science		Social studies	
	S1	S4	S1	S4	S1	S4	S1	S4
Writing								
Copying	8	16	50	60	46	56	33	13
Reference	22	27	0	0	0	19	3	17
Personal	34	44	0	5	29	8	37	45
Answering	36	13	50	35	25	17	27	26
Reading								
Textbook	66	71	37	59	30	13	34	42
Reference book	5	16	0	0	7	1	25	7
Library book	1	5	0	0	0	1	3	0
Exercise book	15	5	12	23	14	43	16	10
Blackboard	12	1	4	18	22	25	13	6
Other (work-cards etc.)	0	3	47	1	27	18	9	36

The lower half of Table 4 indicates the material actually read in lessons. Children were observed reading textbooks in all subject areas, particularly English, but it has to be pointed out that the category 'textbook' might include sets of books read by the class which if read privately by individuals might have been categorized 'library'. Reference books were not read much except in first-year social studies and fourth-year English lessons. Workcards were used widely in first-year mathematics lessons but their usage dropped off dramatically by the fourth year. Many of the changes indicated above can be accounted for by the type of class arrangement predominating in the two year groups, with much more mixed-ability grouping across the curriculum in first-year forms.

Table 5   Time spent on LANGUAGE activities in secondary school lessons

(averaged out in terms of a forty-minute lesson)

	English		Maths		Science		Social studies	
	S1	S4	S1	S4	S1	S4	S1	S4
Listening	15	17	6	7	10	12	10	10
Reading	9	12	4	3	4	4	6	6
Writing	5	5	2	4	4	8	4	8
Discussion (child)	2	2	4	4	4	3	2	3
Discussion (teacher)	1	1	1	1	2	2	2	2
Percentage of lesson	80	95	42	47	60	72	60	72

Table 5 (above) focuses on 'language' activities recorded on the inventory with a summary presented in the form of the average amount of each activity expressed in terms of forty-minute lessons in the four subject areas. Language activities account for the greater proportion of time in most areas, particularly in English with 95 per cent of fourth-year lessons comprised of one or other aspect of language. The exception to the general pattern is in the case of mathematics, where less than half of lesson activities are language orientated. But it may be felt that calculating is a form of verbal mediation. The patterns are remarkably similar in science and social studies lessons. The most noticeable overall feature from the table is the large proportion of 'listening', particularly in English sessions. It is interesting to return to Table 1 in which it can be seen that teachers may be overestimating the amount of reading which children complete.

Table 6 (page 180) indicates the extent of continuous reading recorded. (*Note:* The method of recording the amount of reading observed in any and every minute is to record estimates of the total reading observed on a 1 to 4 scale. Type 1 reading signifies a total of between 1-15 seconds reading in the minute; type 2 is a total of 16-30 seconds; type 3 is 31-45 seconds; and type 4 is from 45 seconds to the full minute.) If one amalgamates type 1 and type 2 reading, that is total reading in the minute amounting to less than half a minute, some startling features emerge. Continuous reading in any appreciable amount occurs only in fourth-year English lessons, all other subjects having recorded at least 80 per cent of reading in short fragmentary bursts. Again, returning to Table 1, it can be seen that most teachers greatly overestimated the continuous reading in their lessons. Mathematicians, however, were quite accurate.

Taken as a whole, the survey produced results which will confirm much of what teachers might have predicted: reading is undertaken to an extent in most subject areas, especially in English; usually this

Table 6   Patterns of continuity in reading given as a percentage of the overall reading time recorded in lessons

		Type 1	Type 2	Type 3	Type 4
English	S1	53	27	10	10
	S4	34	25	14	27
Maths	S1	70	22	8	0
	S4	72	24	4	0
Science	S1	75	21	3	1
	S4	57	36	4	3
Social studies	S1	60	28	8	3
	S4	44	42	9	5

Total reading during the time-sampled minute:
   type 1   1 to 15 seconds
      2   16 to 30 seconds
      3   31 to 45 seconds
      4   46 to 60 seconds

reading is carried out to complete a task set in class; and, as suggested in the questionnaires, reading is rarely the sole or main vehicle for learning in lessons other than English. Although there was no observed increase in reading across the two year groups, there was a marked increase in children's writing as they reached the upper school. Again this was predictable. What was somewhat unexpected was the pattern present in the continuous reading data.

Earlier in this paper, it was reported that reading in project primary schools has a sizeable 'reading for pleasure' component. Such reading is comparatively rare in secondary lessons and, as can be seen in Table 4, there is little reading of library books in class. The primary-school survey revealed little continuous reading outside library-book reading sessions, and there is some indication that this pattern also applies at secondary level.

One of the most common complaints from teachers who have talked to the project team is that few children who can read are able successfully to apply their reading. From the survey, one might infer that reading is generally not regarded as a well-developed learning skill in secondary-school children, and is not to be trusted as a reliable information-gaining activity, particularly in the case of first-year pupils. It may be that teachers feel that learning by reading is desirable and would welcome classes full of children able to readily comprehend information from printed sources. At the moment, however, it seems that very many teachers support an observation made by a history teacher on a questionnaire: the pace at which one needs to proceed in order to cover a syllabus is hectic enough already, and too large a reliance on learning through reading may lead to time-consuming sessions which themselves may need to be repeated if children's performance has not been successful.

A popularly-held belief is that teachers set 'reading for learning' for homework. John Coles's study of homework (in this volume) has not shown this to be so. Children do read for homework, but it is not the case that they are set lengthy tracts to comprehend.

This researcher, from his end of the telescope, sees some anomalous situations when looking at reading in the secondary school. Teachers claim that advanced reading is best developed in context. And it is certainly the case that most secondary-school reading is of this type. However, the type of reading which predominates is not that which one anticipates will lead to the development and extension of the reading ability sought after and needed for private study. A more perplexing situation is seen when focusing on teachers of reading, particularly those engaged in activities designed to lead children to acquire higher-order reading strategies. When, one asks, will children need to use advanced reading and where will they have the opportunity to practise their reading prowess in secondary education?

References

AUKERMANN, R. C. (1972) *Reading in the Secondary School Classroom* McGraw Hill

BARNES, D., BRITTON, J., ROSEN, H. and the LATE (1969) *Language, the Learner and the School* Penguin

DES (1975) *A Language for Life* (Bullock Report) HMSO

DOLAN, T. (1975) 'The incidence and context of reading in primary and secondary schools' in D. Moyle (ed) *Reading: What of the Future?* Ward Lock Educational

HERBER, H. (1969) *Reading in the Content Areas* New York: Syracuse University Press

STAUFFER, R. G. (1960) *Teaching Reading as a Thinking Process* Delaware Press

WALKER, C. (1974) *Reading Development and Extension* Ward Lock Educational

22   Intervening in the teacher-learner dialogue

David A. Pendleton

The appropriate paradigm

It is my contention that for many years teacher training was, and to some extent still is, bedevilled by at least two counter-productive forces. The first is the 'Education or Training?' controversy with the mistaken belief that training is a low-level activity. The second is a relatively profound lack of adequate paradigms to describe and account for classroom activity, or, more precisely, to describe and account for the minutiae of the interactions which take place between a teacher and a learner. Since the late 1960s, however, teacher training has begun to overcome these forces, prompted by the advent of microteaching (Allen and Ryan 1969).

We are now, therefore, in a happier position, but it is incumbent upon those of us engaged in teacher training to create, adopt and develop models of the activities of teachers and learners which do not create illusions and which do facilitate action and research. Mystical notions such as intuition will not do: they are pessimistic, indefensible and irrelevant. It is, however, easy to understand how such notions arise. Spontaneous activity can, sometimes, be strangely appropriate, and it would be hard to say that any conscious decision-making was undertaken in order to arrive at the action. What we require is an understanding of a teacher's actions which accounts for the spontaneous as well as the deliberate; which suggests that improvement can occur and that the ability to teach can be learned. Such an understanding will provide a basis for optimism and hope in the student-teacher or the experienced teacher who wishes to improve. A similar understanding of a learner's actions is at least as necessary.

Skilled activity

The model we seek is a skills model. Skilled activity is organized, goal-directed, well rehearsed and largely spontaneous, but – most important of all – it is increasingly adaptive. It usually operates, however, at a level of unawareness. Take, for example, the skilled car driver. He is able to operate his vehicle smoothly and adapt to changing conditions. He is able to react spontaneously as well as to deliberate over the more deeply problematic situation. What is more, he is able to do all of this whilst listening to the radio or carrying on an involved conversation. One would find it hard to imagine that this same individual was once the hesitant, jerky, easily distracted learner-driver. The route to skilled activity has been marked by a change from hesitancy to smoothness and from absolute concentration on every movement to the relative lack of awareness of individual actions characteristic of the expert. The problem comes, however, when the skilled performer has to teach the skill to a naive individual, for, as we have just argued, the passage to skilled performance has left him unaware of individual actions and it is extremely difficult to raise that awareness to an adequate level for teaching, let alone to raise awareness of the decision-making which produced the actions.

Clearly, skills involve several components which can be summarized as:

1 perception of the situation which is accompanied by
2 an extrapolation of the relevant cues and
3 a processing of the information with reference to
4 learned judgments which give rise to
5 decisions for action and
6 the actions themselves.

All of these factors are, of course, subject to:

7 feedback which is more or less available and, therefore, more or less effective in maintaining adaptive behaviour.

Schematically the cycle may be represented, as in Figure 1 below.

Figure 1 The skill cycle

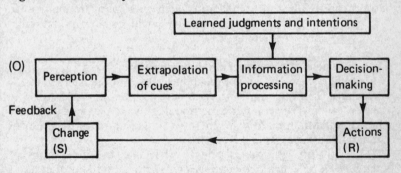

It is easy to identify this as a stimulus – organism – response model which has been elaborated to become more cognitive. The problem is to devise training programmes which actually affect the organism part.

Microteaching aims to produce sufficient feedback about performance to alter teaching behaviour temporarily. It is also relatively simple to modify a teacher's intentions, but if the change in the skilled teaching cycle is to be maintained then the perception, information-processing, decision-making and judgments must change too.

We know that skilled performers have altered perceptions in the area of their skill. They not only have more dimensions of judgment available to them but a greater range of distinctions along each dimension. They can notice subtly different changes and it is the subtlety of the change they can notice which suggests they have become *sensitive:* perceptually sensitive and unrelated, ostensibly, to emotions. What is more, skilled performers have a greater range of actions available to them; that is, they have become *flexible*. Without the increased sensitivity to the stimulus situation, however, the flexible behaviour cannot operate adaptively on anything more than a crude, almost random basis. Equally, it is the sensitivity of perception which facilitates 'fine tuning' in the area of learned judgments, information-processing and decision-making. It is just in this area of sensitivity, therefore, that it is crucial for the teacher trainer to operate, albeit the most difficult area in which to operate.

The teacher acts on the basis of his/her selective perception of the teaching situation, having processed the data and made decisions. Changes in the behaviour of the teacher, therefore, suggest changes in the decision-making and changes in the perception of the situation. It is essential to the topic in hand that we realize that this is also true of the learner: *viz,* changes in the behaviour of the learner suggest changes in the learner's decision-making and perception of the situation. Thus, if the teacher can be sensitive to minute changes in the learner's behaviour he/she can accumulate the right kind of data from which to hypothesize the perception on which it was based. The teacher can also deal with smaller problems preventing the emergence of larger ones. This kind of sensitivity could be seen as the most important aspect of teaching skill.

The assessment of perceptual and judgmental sensitivity
I should like to outline an approach based on George Kelly's (1955) Repertory Grid technique which I have been adapting for use in teacher training. The computer methodology was developed by Laurie Thomas and Mildred Shaw (1976), also of the Centre for the Study of Human Learning at Brunel University.

The repertory grid helps one to articulate the dimensions of judgment along which one perceives any kind of stimulus material. I have found it helpful to use brief extracts from a videotape of children with reading difficulties reading aloud to a teacher. Student teachers watch each extract, which lasts between ten and thirty seconds. Their own repertory grid is then elicited. The procedure takes the following form:

1   Groups of students watch the twelve extracts of video, called 'elements'.
2   The students are asked to consider the first three elements and to decide upon any reason whereby any two elements would be considered, by them, to be more alike than a third.
3   Each is asked to state the similarity as briefly as possible and then the difference.
4   This has created for each student a dimension of judgment, a 'construct', which is then applied to all nine remaining elements. The constructs can be applied to all the elements in turn with a $\sqrt{}$, X or 'not-applicable' scoring system (i.e. a three-point scale). Clearly a five-point scale or 'n'-point scale may be used as appropriate.
5   After the first construct has been created and ratings made the next three elements are presented to suggest another construct and so on, until one has built up a relatively complex matrix of judgments and decisions about each element, and, usually, until the students have exhausted their supply of constructs (approximately 12–16). The particularly helpful point here is that the relatively complex matrix has been made up from relatively simple operations and elementary decisions.
6   The grid is analysed.

Figure 2   An example of a section of a grid

Constructs	Elements	Extract 1	Extract 2	Extract 3	Extract 4	Extract 5	Extract 6	Extract 7	Extract 8	Extract 9	Extract 10	Extract 11	Extract 12
(similarity .../... difference) 1 Children speaking / silence		√	x	√	√	x	√	x	x	√	√	√	x
2 Teacher active / Teacher passive		x	√	N/A	x	√	x	√	x	x	x	√	√
——— etc. ———													

The computer programme devised by Thomas and Shaw (1976) restructures the grid so as to show areas in which differentiation is high and areas in which it is low. The degree of statistical differentiation is an indicator of what I have called sensitivity.

Essentially, the programme ignores the words used to articulate the constructs and simply analyses the scores in the matrix. The constructs are analysed by comparing each row of scores with each other row of

Figure 3   Raw grid

	1	2	3	4	5	6	7	8	9	10	11	12
1	1	3	1	3	1	1	3	3	3	2	2	2
2	1	3	3	1	1	3	1	1	1	3	3	2
3	3	3	1	3	3	3	3	1	1	1	1	3
4	3	3	1	3	3	3	1	1	1	1	1	3
5	3	3	1	3	3	1	1	1	1	1	1	3
6	2	2	3	3	3	3	1	3	1	1	3	3
7	2	3	2	1	1	1	2	2	2	2	2	2
8	3	2	1	3	3	3	1	1	1	2	1	3
9	1	1	3	1	1	1	3	3	3	3	3	1
10	1	3	3	3	1	3	1	1	1	1	3	1
11	1	1	3	1	1	1	3	3	3	3	3	1
12	1	3	3	1	1	1	3	1	3	3	3	3
13	3	1	3	1	1	3	1	1	1	1	3	1
14	1	2	1	2	2	3	3	3	1	1	3	1
15	2	1	3	1	1	3	1	3	1	3	3	2
16	3	3	3	1	3	3	1	1	1	1	1	1

Figure 4   Re-sorted grid showing areas of insensitivity

	10	9	7	8	11	3	6	2	4	5	1	12
16	1	1	1	1	1	3	3	3	1	3	3	1
1	2	1	1	1	2	3	3	1	1	3	3	2
13	1	1	1	1	3	3	3	1	1	1	3	1
10	1	1	1	1	3	3	3	3	3	1	1	1
2	3	1	1	1	3	3	3	3	1	1	1	2
15	3	1	1	3	3	3	3	1	1	1	2	2
5	3	3	3	3	3	3	3	1	1	1	1	1
11	3	3	3	3	3	3	1	1	1	1	1	1
9	3	3	3	3	3	3	1	1	1	1	1	1
4	3	3	3	3	3	3	1	1	1	1	1	1
3	3	3	1	3	3	3	1	1	1	1	1	1
8	2	3	3	3	3	3	1	2	1	1	1	1
12	3	3	3	1	3	3	1	3	1	1	1	3
7	2	2	2	2	2	2	1	3	1	1	2	2
6	3	3	3	1	1	1	1	2	1	1	2	1
14	3	3	1	1	1	3	1	2	2	2	3	3

scores, and the reverse of each other row of scores (since the constructs are bipolar). A construct-matching score matrix is compiled, the constructs reordered so as to place those which are most alike next to each other, and draws out a hierarchy of relationships between the constructs. The elements are analysed in a similar way by working with the columns of scores. The final operation which is the most helpful to the teacher trainer, is a recompilation of the grid elicited from each student but now both constructs and elements are reordered so as to place similar scores next to each other wherever possible. This reveals large areas in the perceptuo-cognitive space of each student in which there is a relative lack of sensitivity.

The amount of space in the re-sorted grid occupied by these large conglomerates of identical scores is inversely proportional to the sensitivity of the student, since the more sensitive the student, the more subtle the differences noticed and thus the more unique each element is seen to be. The degree of similarity of the constructs, similarly, is a measure of the extent to which the judgments are different from each other. The more the judgments are different and the more judgments, the more changes in the stimulus situation can, potentially, be handled.

The merits of such an approach
Clearly it is advantageous to be able to monitor teachers' or student-teachers' sensitivity. The next stage is to take the individuals back to the undifferentiated areas and create differentiation by allowing another individual (not necessarily the tutor) for whom that area is well differentiated to share constructs and, if possible, to point to the specific cues on the video which are being missed. This will be the activity we shall begin to explore in the workshop which follows.

The main advantage is that this technique begins where the learner is and creates change from that point. A subsidiary advantage is that groups of students can tutor each other. Microteaching can then be introduced to map the perceptuo-cognitive (organism) change onto an altered behavioural repertoire.

The use of tools
Microteaching becomes more than just an adjunct to other things in such an approach. Any technique which allows a record of behaviour to be produced can become an excellent change-creating agency if it is used conversationally, with the individual whose behaviour has been recorded, as a mnemonic to raise awareness of the information-processing and decision-making which underpinned the behaviour. The mistake, which is often made, is to offer the behavioural feedback and suggestions for change *in vacuo*. The use of such feedback devices can be maximized by talking the student back through the behaviours in which he/she engaged and pointing out behavioural changes in

teacher or learner, however small. Again, the behavioural changes indicate changes in decision-making, and the subject of the feedback can be tutored to analyse the implications of the change, both in terms of its effect and the process which led to it.

A word of warning

Anyone who has attempted to improve, in another individual, skills which are already evident to some extent, will know that students tend to get worse before they get better. The skill paradigm, suggested above, will account for this. The moment feedback is offered in an unusual way the relative lack of awareness, characteristic of the smooth, skilled performer, is destroyed. Raising awareness is a necessary prerequisite to an examination of what is taking place and to eventual change, but it does reintroduce the hesitancy and jerkiness which has, in the past, been eliminated. At this stage the student will want to retreat to the strategies he/she has used all along, in order to re-establish the old level of performance. The role of the tutor becomes, at this point, that of the supportive counsellor until reintegration and a new spontaneity have been achieved.

Conclusions

Teacher training, initial or inservice, whether it be for the teacher of reading or for the teacher of anything else, is not to be seen as the poor relation of teacher education. Until recently we have acted as if it were so, but, with the advent of techniques of skill analysis and training in the perceptuo-cognitive sensitivity, which is the foundation of adaptive teaching, teacher training can develop its own rigorous and respectable methodologies. Without such training, intervention in the teacher-learner dialogue will be, at best, crude and, at worst, maladaptive, since the very subtle cues, on the basis of which the teacher hypothesizes understanding or lack of it in the child, may be missed.

References

ALLEN, D. and RYAN, K. (1969) *Microteaching* Reading Massachusetts: Addison-Wesley

AUGSTEIN, E. S. HARRI- and THOMAS, L. F. (1975) *Towards a theory of learning conversation and a paradigm for conversational research* BPS Annual Conference, Technical Report 92, Centre for the Study of Human Learning, Brunel University

BROWN, G. A. (1975) Teaching and microteaching: models, rationale and programme *Education for Teaching* 98, 71–9

KELLY, G. A. (1955) *The Psychology of Personal Constructs, Volumes 1 and 2* New York: Norton

THOMAS, L. F. (1976) *Towards achieving personal meaning* (chapters 2, 4 and 10) in press

THOMAS, L. F. and AUGSTEIN, E. S. HARRI- (1972) An experimental approach to the study of reading as a learning skill *Research in Education* 8

THOMAS, L. F. and SHAW, M. L. G. (1976) *Focus: A manual for the Focus computer programme* Centre for the Study of Human Learning, Brunel University

23 Children's reading for homework: teacher prediction and pupil claim

John Cole

In the time allowed it is not possible to go fully into the methodology of our project's survey of 'Children's reading for homework'. An outline of the size, scope and occasion of the survey should provide sufficient backing for our deliberations here. Before I go any further, however, I would remind you that the 'results' that we shall discuss are the results of a 'survey' only. What we have canvassed are the opinions of teachers about what they think will happen in the homework they have set, and the claims (or admissions) of the children concerning what they say they have done. While such outright cynicism as 'All, all are liars' is probably as foolish as an unquestioning belief of whatever information is given, nonetheless the results must be regarded with the healthy, proper and scholarly scepticism which so frequently helps to enliven the duller passages of academic dispute and disagreement.

The survey

In ten secondary schools of varying types, some first- and fourth-year teachers and some of their pupils were asked to complete questionnaire forms relating to homeworks set and done during the week of 6–13 October, 1975 – both dates inclusive. The decision to make enquiry of first- and fourth-year groups only was taken to conform with the wider pattern of the team's researches which both by brief and practicality were confined to these years in the secondary school. Similar considerations governed the choice of the subject areas in which we were interested; namely, English, mathematics, 'science' and 'social studies'. With the benefit of hindsight I am slightly unhappy about the crude categorization of 'science' and the all-embracing blanket of 'social studies' which included 'subjects' – history, geography, RE – and such modish hybrids as 'integrated studies' and 'the humanities'.

The intended maximum possible questionnaire commitment for each school was as follows:

First year: 1 teacher of English + 12 pupils (from one group) × 2 questionnaires

1 teacher of mathematics + 12 pupils (from one group) × 2 questionnaires
1 teacher of science + 12 pupils (from one group) × 2 questionnaires
1 teacher of social studies + 12 pupils (from one group) × 2 questionnaires

The above pattern to be exactly replicated in the fourth year.

It was not a requirement of the survey that either each teacher or each pupil concerned should necessarily complete two questionnaires during the week. The need to adhere most particularly to 'normal' homework practice was strongly argued, and if this meant that despite the requirements of a more or less official homework timetable only one, rather than two, homeworks were normally set, then this pattern should not be altered. It was assumed that those teachers who never, in any circumstances, set any homework would not volunteer to take part in the survey.

In fact, then, each questionnaire completed by teachers and children related to one single homework. It must be stressed that the selection of the twelve or so pupils from each group who were to complete questionnaires was left in the hands of the teachers. They were asked to choose twelve pupils from the survey class of average or above-average ability. The notion was adopted that the lower limit of 'average' might be taken to mean that the pupil might reasonably expect at the very worst an eventual grade 4 in CSE in that subject. Teachers were also asked to ensure as far as possible that forty-eight *different* children from each age group should be involved. If a child had been selected by, say, his maths teacher to complete questionnaires for the week, then no other teacher should ask the same child to cooperate. An examination of the initials on the returned questionnaires shows that this constraint was generally, but not universally accepted. There was, too, nothing 'magic' in the number twelve. Since ten, or approximately 33.3 per cent of any one group was felt to be a reasonably satisfactory number, 'twelve' was suggested to allow for absentees, lost questionnaire forms, and other hazards to be encountered in the field.

If, in each school, with one exception where homework was only set in the fourth year, the predetermined pattern had been exactly adhered to, the maximum possible response would have been a return of 1,824 questionnaires from pupils and 160 from teachers. In fact, 1,186 questionnaires were eventually returned and analysed; of these 1,092 had been completed by children and 94 by teachers. It is considered that this response is entirely satisfactory since the notion of two homeworks per week per subject may exist in the timetabler's mind, but not perhaps in the practice of teachers, many of whom claim that one 'long' homework is always more worthwhile than two 'short' ones. Additionally, one homework per week was the norm in several cases.

The 1,186 questionnaires analysed were distributed among the groups as set out in Table 1 below.

Table 1

Subject	Year	Teachers	Boys	Girls	All pupils
English	1	15	89	89	178
	4	8	49	66	115
Maths	1	12	54	78	132
	4	15	80	96	176
Science	1	9	48	52	100
	4	11	71	45	116
Social Studies	1	8	41	51	92
	4	16	78	105	183
Totals		94	510	582	1092

The week of questionnaire completion was backed up in the following month in all the schools by one afternoon of interviews, when in each school the intention was to interview sixteen children chosen at random from the original sample. In the discussion which follows the most important comparison will be made between the results of teachers and pupil questionnaires, since no formal interview with teachers formed a part of the whole study.

The main reason for this survey into reading for homework is not hard to find: if the results of the project's observations of the incidence and context of reading in the classroom (Dolan 1975) tended to show that not much reading goes on in class, and that which does occur is generally of brief duration and of an intermittent and fragmentary type, then we wished to pre-empt the probable reply: 'Ah, yes . . . but they all do lots of lengthy and sustained reading for homework.'

It must be briefly noted here that another cause of this research was the very paucity of any evidence on homework at all. A diligent search produced a mere sprinkling of references to work in which the comment on homework was either brief, passing, of remote date, from another angle, or a survey into habits of homework in another country.

Results

That there is some kind of reading for homework expected by most teachers and claimed by nearly all children is scarcely surprising since the working definition of 'reading' given to respondents was 'looking at written or printed words'. It was intended to provoke the answer 'Yes' to the question, 'Did the set homework involve any reading at all?', since an earlier pilot study had shown that both teachers and children tended to reply 'No' if they considered that the homework about which they were being asked had not been a reading homework. In our intention to claim recognition for the fact that some kind of reading must go on in nearly all homework of whatever type we were extraordinarily successful since, under our gentle duress, 97 per cent of teachers and 96 per cent of all children claimed that the homework in question had involved some reading. A science teacher who sent his class out into their fathers' gardens 'to look for worm casts' could legitimately claim, as could his charges, that the homework had involved no reading at all.

The teacher's task in completing his questionnaire was more difficult than that of his charges since he had to attempt to estimate how long the whole homework would take an 'average' child, how long that child would spend reading, and the likely length of his 'longest continuous read'. The pupil had only to recall what he had done, to guess, to estimate or to boast. Accordingly, the measure of agreement in some of the broader findings of the survey is very striking. Across the board, the teacher and pupil means for length of homework (1), length of time spent reading (2), and longest continuous time spent reading (3) are as follows:

	Teacher	Pupil	
(1)	38.93 mins	43.7 mins	A.H.T.
(2)	13.9 mins	14.0 mins	A.R.T.
(3)	6.2 mins	7.8 mins	L.C.R.

This agreement can be further pursued if we look at the percentage of teacher and pupil responses which predict various minimum lengths of time on each of the three variables noted above. 61 per cent of all teachers estimate that the whole homework task should take thirty minutes or less, which 57 per cent of pupils claim that it actually did. Similarly 70 per cent of teachers estimate, and 76 per cent of pupils claim, that the length of time spent in reading for homework would be (or was) fifteen minutes or less. Finally, 74 per cent of teachers and 69 per cent of pupils expect and claim the longest continuous read to be of no more than five minutes' duration.

Both teacher and pupil questionnaires were further analysed using the computer programme 3 DRAX 9 (Youngman 1975). An important benefit of this analysis is that it is possible to present the results on all variables arranged by subject and by age group. With pupils, but not with teachers, it was felt appropriate to look at the separate returns of boys and girls, to see if the general assumption that girls are more conscientious than boys is born out by the claims of the girls and the admissions of the boys. The results broadly, but not entirely, support such a view, since the mean time claimed for all homework by the girls is 45.03 minutes while the figure for the boys is 39.64 minutes. On the other hand, first-year boys' claims produced a higher mean for all homework time than did those of the girls in both maths and science, though by the fourth year and girls had either caught up with, or overtaken, the boys in the mean length of time claimed for those homework subjects:

		Year 1	Year 4
Maths	Boys	27.16	32.28
	Girls	20.98	32.23
Science	Boys	33.22	34.14
	Girls	24.25	67.11*

*The cell number for girls fourth-year science (45) is very small, and in the sample, one homework at an all-girls school is notably eccentric. The teacher in this case estimated that the whole task would take ninety minutes, while the girls' claims ranged from 80–180 minutes (a notably extended time).

Earlier it was noted that nearly all homeworks in the survey involved some reading. It is therefore interesting to examine the quantity and kind of that reading, the purposes for which it was undertaken, the materials used, and its outcomes, if they can in any way be measured. Accordingly the results of the survey will now be set out under those headings. While it is both helpful and illuminating to set teacher-prediction and pupil-claim side-by-side and, normally, to talk in terms of percentages, this cannot always be done, since, when the data is divided into eight different cells (by subject and by age group) the teachers' numbers in each cell are far too low to permit any meaningful use of the term 'percentage'. Therefore, in this discussion of results the actual number of teacher responses is used, but the replies of pupils are given as percentages.

A comparison of first- and fourth-year results shows that homeworks tend, predictably enough, to lengthen as time goes on. It seems that teachers of English and social studies in both first and fourth years expect to get a greater length of time for their homeworks than do teachers of maths and science. There is much interest in speculation

Table 2 Percentage of homeworks of thirty minutes or less

| | (a) First year | | (b) Fourth year | |
	Pupil %	Teacher	Pupil %	Teacher
English	58	9/15	31	1/8
Maths	85	12/12	65	12/15
Science	82	7/7	68	8/11
Social studies	62	5/8	23	3/16

about the inferences that can be drawn from this. Perhaps it is further evidence of that adolescent disenchantment with the sciences that is so often complained of by educationalists whose cosmic thoughts receive wide publicity, but have little global influence.

Table 3 Percentage of reading time for homework of ten minutes or less

| | (a) First year | | (b) Fourth year | |
	Pupil %	Teacher	Pupil %	Teacher
English	54	5/15	45	2/8
Maths	97	11/12	79	13/15
Science	80	7/9	68	5/11
Social studies	54	1/8	34	1/16

These figures emphasize the trend noted in the results for all homework time. As will be expected, less reading takes place in maths and science than in the other areas. Another trend is also, perhaps, discernible. In English and social studies the teachers' predictions of the time that the children will spend reading are a consistent overestimation of the actual time claimed. In fourth-year English, for example, while nearly half the children say that their reading took less than ten minutes, three-quarters of all the teachers expect it will take longer. In 'social studies' the comparison is even more striking. One third of the fourth-year pupils admit to a reading time of ten minutes or less, but fifteen out of the sixteen teachers in the cell predict that it will take longer.

It is fair to infer from these figures that there are few grounds here to support the view that large numbers of children read for long and extended periods when engaged in homework tasks. Indeed, the percentage figure of all fourth-year children claiming a reading time of more than half-an-hour is as follows:

English 4;   Maths 1;   Science 11;   Social studies 11.

If the amount of reading that is done for homework is limited, what of its kind and quality? Figures in answer to certain survey questions reveal at least a part of the picture. Both teachers and children were asked to say whether most of the reading in the homework would compel them, or did involve them in: (a) reading continuously; (b) reading in frequent short intervals, or (c) reading only occasionally. There is much room for debate about the precise meaning of each of (a), (b) and (c) above, but the general imputation is clear. If (a) is the salient answer, then the reading demands of homework are certainly extensive. If either (b) or (c) are most prominent, then claims that reading is more than a means to an end in most homework are harder to substantiate. The results are as follows: across the board 24 per cent of all children claim that most of their reading time was spent in continuous reading (a); 45 per cent say that they read 'in frequent short intervals' (b); 31 per cent say that they read 'only occasionally' (c). The teacher figures for the same categories are: (a) 12 per cent; (b) 51 per cent; (c) 37 per cent.

While twice as many children claim continuous reading than their teachers would expect, it is nonetheless striking that the salient reading type, both for teachers and pupils is 'reading in frequent short intervals'. It is even more notable, perhaps, that 88 per cent of teachers and 76 per cent of pupils acknowledge, by implication at least, that there is something fragmented about the quality and kind of most of the reading that is done for homework.

To support the view that children's reading for homework is more frequently a secondary than a primary task, consider the figures in the survey which relate to teachers' and pupils' estimates of their 'longest continuous read'. It is perhaps most instructive to give the figures here for pupil-claim and teacher-prediction of a 'longest continuous reading' time of five minutes or less, by subject and by age group.

Table 4   Percentage of children whose longest read was five minutes or less

	(a) First year		(b) Fourth year	
	Pupil%	Teacher	Pupil%	Teacher
English	56	8/15	53	5/8
Maths	98	12/12	88	14/15
Science	83	9/9	76	8/11
Social studies	50	4/8	43	10/16

Any notion that sustained silent reading is a frequent feature of our children's reading for homework cannot be supported here in the face of these figures. If we look for a moment at the numbers of children who claimed in their questionnaire responses that they really settled down to a good, long read – i.e. those children claiming a longest continuous read of more than half-an-hour – the percentage figures are very low. In English the figures are 5 per cent and 6 per cent in years one and four respectively. In maths there are, not surprisingly, no claimants. In science, 1 per cent and 2 per cent claim a longest continuous read of more than thirty minutes, while in social studies the figures are 1 per cent and 4 per cent.

A brief glance at the salient reading purposes predicted by teachers and claimed or guessed by children is instructive here (Table 5). From the list of eleven reading purposes on the questionnaire form, both teachers and children could claim that any or all of them, in whatever combination, were part of the reading purpose for that particular homework. In broad terms the two blanket purposes (not mutually exclusive of 'to do questions' and 'to find answers' stand out as predominant. To 'read for pleasure' is arguably not merely a purpose of reading, but also an outcome. Nonetheless in English, where perhaps the notion for reading for its own sake can be an enjoyable activity ought to be prominent, the numbers of children claiming 'pleasure' for their purposes are disappointingly low when it is remembered that some who claim the purpose that they expect the teacher to like may well share some of Uriah Heep's character deficiency: 21 per cent of first-year and 11 per cent of fourth-year pupils claim reading for pleasure in English; $^6/_{15}$ first-year English teachers and $^1/_8$ fourth-year expect or hope that 'pleasure' will be part of the reading purpose of their charges in their English homeworks.

Detailed discussion of reading purposes is not possible here, and there are reservations about the quality of the data revealed in this part of the survey. Nonetheless, the scatter of reading purposes acknowledged by pupils across the different subject areas tends to support the general view that reading in homework is nearly always an essential prerequisite of some task or other but that it is very seldom the *raison d'être* of the homework itself. This comes as no surprise to any of us who are aware of the low status given by children to any reading task set for homework. There are not many secondary teachers of any experience who have not overheard scathing and pejorative reference in the conversation of babes and sucklings to homeworks that are 'only reading'.

A general examination of the kinds of reading matter used by the children for their homework during the week of the survey reveals a similar pattern of the use of different reading materials to that shown by the project team's observations in the classroom.

Table 5 Percentages of responses for each reading purpose; teachers and pupils compared by subject and age groups across the whole survey

Purpose	English Teacher 1	4	Pupil 1	4	Mathematics Teacher 1	4	Pupil 1	4	Science Teacher 1	4	Pupil 1	4	Social Studies Teacher 1	4	Pupil 1	4
Test preparation	7	0	6	8	8	0	9	7	0	9	8	9	13	13	3	15
Revision	7	13	7	4	33	33	9	26	0	27	8	10	0	13	2	14
To do questions	27	38	14	32	83	93	81	83	56	64	32	42	63	38	26	21
To find answers	20	38	16	27	67	20	39	46	44	36	44	40	75	44	50	42
To prepare for lesson	40	50	24	24	0	7	8	8	22	0	19	14	38	25	29	18
To make notes	7	13	4	15	0	0	3	3	56	55	13	27	25	38	22	38
To check work	20	13	44	26	8	0	12	15	22	0	30	16	0	0	23	13
To do corrections	13	0	7	9	0	0	3	2	11	0	2	3	0	0	2	2
Read for pleasure	40	13	21	11	0	7	3	2	0	27	2	3	13	0	0	3
To follow up lesson	40	38	24	20	50	40	13	17	78	45	32	34	38	50	18	24
Other	20	25	8	9	8	0	1	1	0	9	3	1	25	13	3	3
Number	15	8	239	178	12	15	183	260	9	11	143	193	8	16	157	270

1 = 1st year pupils; 4 = 4th year pupils

Table 6 Percentages of different reading materials observed in classroom use

	English					Maths					Sciences					Social studies				
	T	R	L	E	W	T	R	L	E	W	T	R	L	E	W	T	R	L	E	W
Year 1	38	6	8	46	26	50	—	—	30	36	12	26	4	56	6	13	46	1	24	48
Year 4	60	2	10	28	21	59	—	—	20	24	71	1	—	23	35	51	19	3	28	32

Key   T – Textbook
R – Reference book
L – Library book
E – Exercise book
W – Worksheet/card

Some explanation of the legend and method of categorization is necessary. The reading material was not categorized by the respondents, but by a member of the research team working from the information on the returned questionnaire forms. Different categories presented different difficulties in different areas. It is not hard to categorize a textbook in, say, maths, but how, for example, would a fourth-year girl's use of *Wuthering Heights* be classified? If, from the information on the respondents' questionnaire, the teacher's questionnaire and the replies of others in the same group, it was clear that *Wuthering Heights* was being studied as a set text, then it would be classified as a textbook. Anxious English teachers can therefore breathe again. The survey revealed no evidence that the collected works of Ronald Ridout are still being widely studied. Dictionaries and encyclopedias were always coded as reference books, even if the source was very probably a library. A book, which might be a textbook in fact, but which was being used by only one or two in the same group, would normally be coded as a reference book, particularly if the homework book task, described by the child, clearly indicated such an assignation. A library book was generally, but not always, a work of fiction, or a factual work, unique to not more than one or two individuals within the group, that neither by function nor design could be readily coded as 'reference'. The categories of exercise books and worksheets presented very little difficulty.

Some general points can at once be made: in all subject areas there was a more extensive use of textbooks in the fourth year than there was in the first, though the higher figure in mathematics does not appear to be particularly notable. More surprising than this perhaps is the apparent decline in the way of reference books between the first and the fourth years. In science and in social studies this fall-off cannot be explained by the increasing reluctance of the adolescent to consult a dictionary; rather it is, perhaps, indicative of the firmer and more single direction taken by larger groups as examinations approach. It was noticeable, too, that worksheets tended to be found in clumps. In one school or department, one might gain the impression that the worksheet had not yet been invented; in another, the abolition of the book seemed already to have taken place. A disturbing implication of this latter situation was that many children might only rarely in the course of a school year become acquainted with 'extended print material'. The 'tyranny of the worksheet' has in some cases replaced the tedium of the standard course book or class reader, and it is alarming that much of the reading matter presented to some children is in tabloid form, and confined to one or two sides.

Most unfortunate of all, to me – an ardent advocate and supporter of school libraries – was the comparatively little use made of library books by children both in home and class. It must of course be emphasized that class work and homework, by the very nature of the activity, inhibit the use of purely recreational materials, but it is nonetheless alarming that library sources do not appear to be more widely used. It is worth remarking here that such use of library material as we found during the survey tended, like the use of the worksheet, to be found in small identifiable groups. It should also be stressed that the 46 percentage use of reference books in first-year social studies very probably includes material whose source was the school library.

If this survey has cast some acceptable light on the amount and quality of reading that goes on for homework; if we now know more (just a little more) about children's reading purposes (as judged by them), and if we can claim some validity for the picture of reading materials here revealed, then it would be most improper of me not to admit our inability to offer much of weight on the matter of the outcome of the children's reading. Even though the questionnaire forms were in the schools for two full weeks, the very force of circumstance compelled their completion before the full outcome of the homework could be known. It was not felt to be practical or desirable to attempt to test 'reading gain' after the completion of a homework task, and, in any case, who can say, save in the most meaningless general terms, what the *outcome* of one simple homework should or could be? Nonetheless, most teachers, in most subject areas, felt that all or most children had 'satisfactorily' completed the homework task. The figures are:

	1st year	4th year
English	13/15	8/8
Maths	11/12	12/15
Science	8/9	10/11
Social studies	6/8	16/16

While one might find this almost unanimous avowal gratifying, it would clearly be erroneous to infer from this that all is well with our children's homework. How satisfactory is 'satisfactory' and by what standards is a state of 'satisfactoriness' established?

One area of the survey, concerned with the outcome of homework, revealed what was at first sight a striking discrepancy between the allegations of the pupil and the claims made by their teachers. Was the homework *discussed* by teachers and pupils either beforehand or afterwards? On the questionnaire form the teachers were asked to note whether or not they had discussed the homework with the class before it was set and/or after its completion. The pupils too were to record whether or not they had discussed the homework with their teachers before attempting it, or after its completion. The returns on this variable are notable for the consistently higher figures returned by the teachers for discussion of the task either beforehand or afterwards, as Table 7 shows.

Table 7 Percentages of children discussing homework before or after completion

First year

Discuss before	Pupil %	Teacher	Discuss after	Pupil %	Teacher
English	65	13/15	English	28	7/15
Maths	27	6/12	Maths	8	6/12
Science	37	7/9	Science	19	7/9
Social Studies	55	7/8	Social Studies	18	4/8

Fourth Year

Discuss before	Pupil %	Teacher	Discuss after	Pupil %	Teacher
English	43	6/8	English	23	5/8
Maths	30	8/15	Maths	16	9/15
Science	30	6/11	Science	19	9/11
Social Studies	45	14/16	Social Studies	18	13/16

The discrepancies are striking, but there is no real cause for alarm since later questioning established the intentional veracity of both parties. Broadly, a child will not claim to have *discussed* his homework with a teacher unless he (the child) has actually said something. On the other hand, teachers quite rightly take discussion to mean 'talked about with the class' and they would not always regard a pupil's silence or the lack of actual verbal response from most of the class as indicating a lack of discussion. Very few, if any, homeworks in the summary were set or completed without some kind of dialogue between teachers and taught. I merely draw attention to this point to show how important it is to avoid a glib or facile interpretation of what appear to be incontrovertible figures.

In conclusion, it is necessary to bear in mind the very real physical limitations of this research. Even though it is probably fair to assume the goodwill and best intentions of the vast majority of all respondents, it is nonetheless equally fair to draw attention to the fact that *estimates*, both of length of time spent on homework, of length of time spent reading, and of the length of the longest continuous reading time, are most certainly crude. That this is true is shown most clearly by the pupils' responses to questions which really required an increasingly greater measure of refinement: yet this is what happened – the estimate of total homework time produced in all sixty-five different responses; the estimate of total reading time produced just thirty-two, while that measure calling for an estimate of the longest continuous period spent reading generated a mere twenty-five different replies. It is further argued, that if these estimates are crude, then they are also likely to be gross – after all, most people like to create a favourable impression – and that therefore the mean results here represent a consistent overestimate of the amount of reading that takes place in homework. A notion propounded above must again be emphasized: reading is secondary to homework itself. Generally and chiefly it appears that the main function of reading in homework is to enable the child to carry out some other task. Teachers do not expect, nor do children claim, that the bulk of reading that is done for homework is 'reading for learning'. It is for doing in order to do something else. When children, but not teachers, were asked to categorize the type of homework they had done, the responses were as follows:

> Writing 48 per cent
> Calculation or thinking 31 per cent
> Reading 17 per cent
> Other 4 per cent

It is only surprising that the figure for reading (17 per cent) is so very high,

References

DOLAN, T. (1975) 'The incidence and context of reading in primary and secondary schools' in D. Moyle (ed) *Reading: What of the Future?* Ward Lock Educational

YOUNGMAN, M. B. (1975) *Programmed Methods for Multivariable Data* University of Nottingham

Part 5

Assessment and evaluation

24 Reading measurement and evaluation: some current concerns and promising developments

Peter D. Pumfrey

Introduction

It has been suggested that the appreciation of the theoretical and practical value of any new scientific technique passes through five stages. In the first no one, other than its inventors, is particularly interested. Indeed, workers in allied fields may be hostile. During the second stage the technique begins to gain support on the basis of its promise. Stage three is characterized by extensive and even indiscriminate use by those working in the field, often irrespective of whether or not they are competent to assess its value. The reaction that occurs in the fourth stage leads to a disillusionment with the technique without the critical examination logically demanded in such circumstances. The fifth stage occurs when both the strengths and weaknesses of the technique are acknowledged and it is applied appropriately.

History

The use of reading tests based on conventional test theory is an example of such a technique (Magnusson 1967). Currently the value of standardized reading tests is being called into question. Other approaches are being suggested as alternatives. There is a danger that the reaction is fuelled by emotion based on unwarranted expectations. Basic psychological research concerned with the nature of human abilities led, during the last century, to the development of techniques by which mental abilities could be assessed. Indeed, one of the earliest tests of man's higher cognitive powers was virtually a test of reading comprehension. It was devised by Ebbinghaus in 1879 and called the Completion Test. Its purpose was to assess the subject's ability to complete sentences of the following type:

One ( ) ( ) eagle ( ) with the ( ) birds . . . etc.

Ebbinghaus described this test as a 'simple, easily applied device for testing those intellectual activities that are fundamentally important and significant both in school and in life.' The technique has been developed extensively and there are numerous sophisticated variants of it represented in currently available reading tests (Pumfrey 1976).

Certain assumptions concerning the nature and distribution of mental abilities underpinned the testing movement. The first was that inter-individual differences in cognitive abilities existed and that in many instances the distribution of these differences approximated the 'normal law of error'. The 'normal law' was originally developed in relation to the theory of probabilities in games of chance and had been used by Gauss to describe errors in observations. Adolph Quetelet (1796-1874) ascertained that certain anthropometric measurements were distributed in approximate agreement with the bell-shaped probability curve. Galton used Quetelet's findings to convert the frequency of occurrence of genius into indices of the degree of genius. In this way application of the normal law of error entered into the quantification of mental ability (Linden and Linden 1968). Thus research workers in various European countries contributed concepts and techniques essential to the development of a technology of mental measurement that enabled abilities to be identified and inter-individual differences assessed. The initiative in relation to the assessment of reading attainments and the associated theory and practice of test construction moved to the USA. It is largely due to the extensive work of American researchers over the last seventy-five years that most major advances have been made in this area.

Although resources were not as readily available in Great Britain, some notable contributions have been and are being made. Pioneers included the first officially appointed educational psychologist, the late Sir Cyril Burt, and Professors Ballard and Thomson. Their contributions have led to many initiatives.

Current British contributions
The Scottish Office of Education, the Godfrey Thomson Unit for Academic Assessment and the Moray House College of Education have recently produced an excellent series of reading tests known as the Edinburgh Reading Tests. The Scottish Council for Research in Education has this month published a new standardization of the Burt Graded Word Reading Test. The National Foundation for Educational Research in England and Wales is active in the development of test theory and construction and in the dissemination of reading test information. Early in 1976 they were commissioned by the Department of Education and Science to provide reading tests as an interim step in response to the call in the Bullock Report (DES 1975) to make a national survey of the reading standards of primary-school children. Both the Schools Council and the Social Science Research Council have supported projects involving the development of reading tests. The Department of Education and Science is currently supporting the construction of the British Intelligence Scale under the direction of Dr C. D. Elliott at the University of Manchester. This is probably the most

sophisticated psychometric instrument yet devised (Elliott 1975). It is pleasing to note that one of the sub-scales is a reading test and that this, together with the other sub-scales, is currently being standardized on a nationally representative sample of children. The scale uses a novel method of item analysis and scaling known as Rasch technique, after its originator. It is based on a probabilistic method of scaling having considerable advantages over conventional test theory. In its basic form, the scale relates to the chances of success when individuals deal with items. It is claimed that the Rasch model makes possible the construction of scales which might allow 'individual progress to be objectively monitored over a long period of time without recourse to norms unless this is desired' (Elliott 1976). It seems likely that the technique may form the basis of the system of monitoring that will eventually be adopted in this country.

The method has been utilized in the USA in the Woodcock Reading Mastery Tests (Woodcock 1973). The tests can provide the same type of information as that obtained from an informal reading inventory, but having also the advantages of a standardized presentation, more precise measurement and being keyed to grade levels.

In 1974 the Department of Education and Science announced the establishment of an 'Assessment of Performance Unit' (hereafter APU) in a White Paper *Educational Disadvantages and the Educational Needs of Immigrants*. The unit's terms of reference are 'to promote the development of methods of assessing and monitoring the achievement of children at school, and to seek to identify the incidence of underachievement'. A Consultative Committee has been set up under the chairmanship of Professor Barry Supple. Its membership was announced in February 1976 and includes representatives of local authorities and of educational associations, the NFER, plus representatives of both employers and unions, and parents. The committee's function is not to control the APU but to discuss its work and make suggestions for its programme.

Insofar as the development and use of reading tests is concerned, the publication of the Bullock Report is likely to have considerable long-term effects. Within the broader context of the learning and teaching of English in our schools, the report makes many recommendations that, if implemented, will improve the uses made of reading tests within our schools. The five chapters dealing respectively with 'Standards of reading', 'Monitoring', 'Screening, diagnosis and recording' are ones that are particularly important insofar as testing is concerned.

The preceding catalogue of activity suggests that the importance of measurement and testing in the teaching of reading is being increasingly recognized in this country. There is, however, a different tide which cannot be ignored.

The *zeitgeist*, the fashions of thought and feeling current in our society, affect us all. Discrimination between individuals is not as acceptable a notion as it once was. Men and women are equal in the sight of God and of the ballot box, and must be treated equally under recent legislation. Discrimination on the basis of sex or race is deemed undesirable. Labelling individuals is seen to have certain adverse consequences that are to be avoided. Teachers' expectations amplify differential performances by their pupils, and the professional validity of such expectations is also questioned. In schools, streaming or setting is often seen as suspect. There is a backwash from this spirit of the times which can be detected in a rejection of the use of tests that discriminate between individuals. It is interesting, however, that the book by Jencks and his colleagues (1975) on *Inequality* could not have been written without the evidence of both inter- and intra-individual and group differences operationally defined by scores on a wide variety of tests. In passing one cannot help but note the tremendous popular concern that discriminations be made in one of the most important aspects of our life where excellence in performance is recognized as desirable and is striven for, albeit vicariously. The reference is, of course, to sport. Football League Championships are decided by fractions of goal averages, gold medals are won by margins of 100ths of a second. 'We are the champions' – 'and by *this* much' is a cry for both discrimination and standards. One way of improving performance is by studying and analysing excellence and encouraging its emulation. In reading, Clark's recently published work with young fluent readers follows an analogous path (Clark 1976). As she says, '. . . it is crucial to explore the parents' perceptions of education and the support and experiences they provide, by measures far more sensitive and penetrating . . .'.

Is diagnosis possible?

Not infrequently, both lecturers and, in their turn, reporters, overstate a case for effect. The headline 'Tests no guide to reading' appeared in a professional periodical over a summary of a conference held in Birmingham on 'New approaches to reading'. An infant-school headmistress who has written a book on the teaching of reading was reported as saying, 'There is no such thing as diagnostic testing in the teaching of reading'. Her argument was that since we do not understand how children learn to read, we cannot diagnose weaknesses or learn how to remedy them. She pointed to the fact that some good readers scored no more or less than poor readers on certain tests. It was surprising to find this followed by her statement that the greatest handicap to reading was poor concentration which, it was reported, did not show up in the tests. In other words, after claiming diagnosis was not possible, one was made. This was followed by a prescription for alleviating children's lack of concentration. We were given an intuitive diagnosis of the cause of children's difficulties in learning to read and a prescription based on that diagnosis. To find both of these following immediately after a rejection of the possibility of diagnosis and prescription using reading tests, gives reason for doubting the validity of the headmistress's initial assertion and the logic of her own analysis.

At the level of teacher politics one finds an executive member of the National Union of Teachers warning of the danger of turning schools into 'nightmare test factories'. In the same address the speaker is reported as saying, 'We do not want to divert even more public money into the blind alley of producing even finer and more sophisticated tests of ability.' Yet he also recognized the need to reassure parents on the objectives and aims of our schools, including the prime duty of our schools to demonstrate their ability to help children to change and to learn. The need to monitor certain standards as the Bullock Report recommends was also conceded. However this was followed by the statement that this did not make a case for developing 'so-called' (note the pejorative implication!) 'highly sophisticated tests to be applied indiscriminately'.

If any educationist is using tests indiscriminately, the criticism might more appositely be placed on the individual who decides to use a particular test rather than on the test itself. Using a stop-watch to hammer in a nail hardly justifies criticism of the watch's ineffectiveness as a hammer.

One welcomes informed criticism of any educational practice. Argument is essential to advance. It is, however, disconcerting to see stage four in the evaluation of the testing movement receiving from its opponents such impoverished criticism. Indeed, to find the critical acumen that has led to advances in both the theory and practice of testing, one is driven to those who are knowledgeable. Whilst some teachers are in their ranks, it is a pity that there are not more.

Perhaps my paranoia is showing. I would not argue that all forms and levels of discrimination are equally valuable. My plea is that we must be discriminating in our consideration of discrimination.

The calling of all residential placements 'community homes' is an example in which the ostensive lack of discrimination must be offset by someone somewhere knowing which unit is most likely to meet the needs of which children that are to be sent to it. Whether the confusion created is offset by alleviating adverse effects of labelling is unknown. Similarly, in the teaching of reading we must know which approaches best suit which children at a given stage of reading development. We need to be able to identify aptitude × instruction interaction for individuals and, if possible, for groups. We must discriminate.

One can argue that there is nothing more rational in attempting to analyse the reading process than a consideration of its emotional aspects (Pumfrey and Elliott 1970; Elliott and Pumfrey 1972). In contrast, there are few things in education more emotional than meetings between exponents of contrasting interpretations of the reading process. Indeed, one of the strengths of the Bullock Report was that it attempted, albeit uneasily, to integrate the approaches of those who viewed reading as a hierarchy of acquired skills with those who emphasized the inter-relationship with all the other learnings the child experiences.

A recent example of the reaction produced by evidence that does or does not fit our preconceptions is the international response to the findings reported by Dr Bennett of the University of Lancaster in *Teaching Styles and Pupil Progress* (Bennett 1976). Indeed the reverberations of this controversy can be felt at this conference.

The measurement of the emotional aspects of the child's reading development are less well advanced than that of cognitive areas. A study of Lawrence's work on the self-concept of children experiencing reading failure and of criticisms of such studies reveal the weakness of measures based on self-reports (Lawrence 1973; Coles 1976). This is not to deny the importance of subjective perception and the techniques such as repertory grid and semantic differential that are increasingly being used. In terms of the five stages in the development of a technology referred to earlier, measurement of the affective dimensions of reading development is still only at the second stage.

Key concepts

1 Reading
The essence of reading is the ability to understand, through the medium of a text, the knowledge, thoughts and feelings of another mind. It is primarily a matter of comprehension.

The reading process is also a developmental one, becoming progressively more complex as the reader matures and learns to use different skills as the situation demands. In this one is aware that reading is but a facet of the child's general intellectual development, albeit one that both contributes to and is nourished by that development. Comparison of the reading behaviours of the child learning to read with those of the competent reader and the adult illiterate involved in the Adult Literacy Project makes this point. Thus decoding print to sound may, for some children, have value in the early stages of learning to read but is a redundant skill in the competent reader. The limitations in the child's thought processes, his inability to appreciate others' points of view inevitably restrict his ability to understand a text even if he is able to decode it to sound. Hence the hypothetical hierarchical structure of reading comprehension skills indicates that ability to cope with one level is a necessary but not sufficient condition to cope with a more complex level of comprehension. Literal comprehension might be expected to precede inferential comprehension (Pidgeon 1976). However, an important Australian investigation into the hierarchical structure of both listening and

210

reading comprehension skills suggests that though there is evidence of hierarchies in each, they are not of a simple class-inclusion variety (Clark 1972; 1973).

The ability to read facilitates both intellectual and social development. To argue that modern technological innovations have made reading obsolescent is to misconceive the nature of both cognitive development and reading development. The emotional and social consequences of failing to learn to read are costly both to the individual and to society. Talking to any individual who has not learned to read, whether he is still attending school or not, will soon reveal the personal costs of this failure. Learning to read leads to the ability of reading to learn. In Bruner's terminology, the skill acts as an amplifier of human abilities. In our Western industrialized society, to be unable to read is to be seriously and progressively disadvantaged.

Professor John Merritt, as reported in the TES, made the following point at a UKRA conference held in Leicester last year: 'People sometimes talk as if a reading age of nine were an indication of functional literacy, but we should regard fourteen or fifteen as the realistic minimum.' The report continued: 'He quoted estimates of reading ages of fourteen for an article in *The Sun* and seventeen for the claims section of a Department of Health and Social Security Family Income Supplement Form. . . . By these criteria the real number of functional illiterates in this country is vastly greater than the one-million figure usually quoted.'

The quotation is given to make a point. Namely, illiteracy is a relative concept. One operational definition of functional literacy given four years ago by a government official was 'the ability to write one's name rather than merely putting a cross'. In contrast and an extreme hypothetical example, even if all our five year old pupils could read accurately and understand a leader in *The Times*, some would do so more rapidly, more accurately and with more understanding than others. Those children who were the least competent might be said to have a 'reading problem', to be 'backward', to need 'special help'. It can be argued that in the same way that there are limits to the speed at which man on this planet can run 100 metres, there are also limits to the functioning of those mental abilities that process information and are manifest in reading behaviour. To note a possible danger in continuously raising expectations is not to deny the even greater one if we fail to minimize the unnecessary failure in reading that can be identified.

2 Reading tests

There are many misconceptions current among the teaching profession concerning the nature of psychological tests in general and reading tests in particular. For many, testing is an annoying and unnecessary erosion of valuable teaching time. Others see testing as essential to effective teaching. The majority of teachers find tests of some value, but have reservations. These reservations often arise from erroneous and limited ideas of what a reading test is, from justifiable anxieties concerning the particular instruments and from a lack of training in the uses and limitations of reading tests (Pumfrey 1974).

A reading test is a means of obtaining information that will help teachers, inspectors, psychologists, administrators, education-committee members, parents and pupils to answer questions and make decisions more adequately than would be possible without the test results. The five key characteristics of the formal reading test are:

1 it provides public data
2 the test is so devised that information for a particular purpose is obtained efficiently
3 the results obtained are valid; in other words, the test measures what it is intended to measure
4 the results are reliable and provide a consistent means of assessing whatever aspect of reading behaviour is being tested, and
5 the information obtained leads to more efficient teaching.

We are aware of the complexity of the reading process. No single reading test yet devised is able to provide information on all the aspects of reading in which the teacher is likely to be interested. Some tests measure more than one aspect; for example, the Edinburgh Reading Tests Stage 2 provides measures of six reading skills. Many tests, however, measure only one aspect. The most popular reading tests in use in Britain today are of this type. The Schonell Graded Word Reading Test R1 and the Burt (rearranged) Word Reading Test are used respectively in 72.5 per cent and 34.3 per cent of the sample of 936 primary and middle schools that provided evidence for the Bullock Committee. Frequently these tests are expected to provide more information than their authors designed them to elicit. As well as providing normative information on the child's reading age and the amount of progress since the last administration of the test, some teachers expect to obtain diagnostic information that will identify the types of difficulties a pupil has with particular types of words. In practice the absence of a sufficient number of words of a given type makes it impossible to carry out a reliable diagnosis.

There is a wide variety of reading tests suitable for various purposes at all ages from the prereading to university level. Although the appreciation of the range available is not as great or as extensive as might be, the UKRA has attempted to improve this situation in two of its recent publications (Turner and Moyle 1972; Pumfrey 1976).

The Bullock Report recommends that standardized reading tests '. . . should ideally have been developed and evaluated within the last ten years' (page 249). Table 1 (on page 213) is an adaptation of information given in that report. It shows the popularity of different reading tests in a sample of 936 primary and middle schools. The dates of publication of the tests have been added. Two points merit comment. Firstly, if a ban was placed on all reading tests more than ten years old, much of the testing of reading currently done would have to stop. Secondly, many schools are using sets of norms established in different years. Are these schools wasting the time they spend on using these tests?

Table 1   Popularity and age of reading tests in primary and middle schools

Name of test	Rank order of popularity	% of schools using test	Year when constructed and when revised or renormed
Schonell Graded Word Reading Test R1	1	72.5	1942; 1972; 1974
Burt (rearranged) Word Reading Test	2	34.3	1938; 1954*; 1974**
Holborn Reading Scale	3	27.2	1948
Schonell Silent Reading Test A	4	24.8	1942
Schonell Silent Reading Test B	5	23.9	1942
Standard Test of Reading Skill	6	17.7	1958
Neale Analysis of Reading Ability	7	16.6	1958
N.F.E.R. Reading Test AD	8	15.0	1954
Southgate Group Reading Test 1	9	6.7	1959
Young Group Reading Test	10	6.1	1968
Southgate Group Reading Test 2	11	4.5	1962
Vernon Graded Word Reading Test	12	3.6	1938
Word Recognition Test	13	1.5	1970
Various other reading tests		17.3	
No reading tests used		7.4	

Adapted from the Bullock Report (DES 1975, Table 39, page 381)
*Data collected in this year but not published until 1967
**Data published in this year but not published until 1976

The Bullock Committee's point derives from the ever-changing nature of both spoken and written language. Words become obsolete, neologisms proliferate and only the fittest survive. Phrases can become archaic, divorced from the language experience of the child on which his reading skills will be developed. To be valid, the content of reading tests must reflect these changes. The recent rearrangement of word difficulty of the two most popular tests shown in Table 1 shows the need for such revisions (Shearer and Apps 1975; SCRE 1976).

Further, reading standards change over time. The extensively documented and discussed increase in the reading attainments of successive groups of eleven year old pupils tested on the same sentence completion test of reading comprehension between 1948 and 1961 is one example at the national level. If the same test had not been used, it would have been difficult to have assessed the extent of the changes. The subsequent finding in 1971 that standards of reading had apparently not continued to improve would also not be open to discussion, and the Bullock Committee might never have been set up (Start and Wells 1972; Burke and Lewis 1975).

It can be perfectly valid to use tests that are more than ten years old as long as the data they provide is helpful to the school. A school may have the records of pupils over many years. This helps the staff become aware of fluctuations in the reading standards in their own school. Additionally one must accept that because of the slowness of biological evolutionary processes, the nature of the cognitive abilities underpinning reading is unlikely to change rapidly. Examination of a variety of word frequency lists shows that the twelve most commonly used words have not changed for a very long period. The pupils' ability to recognize these words is a legitimate index of one aspect of a school's reading programme. The number of pupils able to do this at given age level in successive years does give an indication of whether a school is or is not maintaining standards in this aspect of reading. The influx of a large number of non-English speaking children is likely to reduce this and other indices of reading attainments in the short term at the very least.

Inner London Education Authority Local Survey 1968–71
The population of the ILEA is atypical, being skewed towards a preponderance of lower income groups. The proportion of immigrants at the time of the survey was 17 per cent. Between 1968 and 1971 the mean standardized scores of the same children at 8+ and 11+ on the same test of reading comprehension moved from 94.6 to 94.9. These scores are markedly below the national average. Yet the stability of mean score for this one group over a three-year period obscures an important fact. During those three years, the proportion of poor readers in the semi-skilled and unskilled groups increased from 17.9 per cent to 25.9 per cent for the former and from 22 per cent to 28 per cent for the latter (DES 1975). Any complacency induced by the stable mean scores for the total group is dispelled by the progressive decline in the relative reading attainment of children from the lower socioeconomic groups. It is possible to have stable standards or even rising standards *and* an increasing proportion of illiterates. But only if there exists a testing programme and an efficient record-keeping system can such important trends be identified and action taken.

The appreciation of similarities and differences is a process on which our survival both as individuals and as a species exists. The naked eye notes many similarities and differences in our physical, social, emotional and intellectual environments. A microscope allows more precise observation, clearer description and enhanced conceptualizations. Teachers perceive both inter- and intra-individual differences in children's reading attainments. Reading tests enable one to make, and encourage one to make, more precise observations, replicable and communicable descriptions leading to an enhanced understanding of the phenomenon under consideration.

Children's reading behaviour is both the inspiration and the cemetery of any theory of reading. Reading tests are tools that help practitioners evaluate and subsequently either develop – or bury – the suggestions of theorists. Good technology drives out bad theory.

There are two major types of reading tests. That most widely known is the normative objective reading test. The items making up such an instrument are deliberately selected so that they optimize individual differences in test scores on the particular aspect of reading being measured. It follows that items passed by all or by no pupils are of no value in normative test construction since they tell one nothing about inter-individual differences within the group. Items which discriminate between children on the ability being tested are selected on both psychological and psychometric grounds. The result is an instrument that enables the user to make valid inter-individual comparisons with a known degree of reliability. Provided that the test has been standard-ized on a suitable sample of children, it is then possible to compare the attainment of an individual or group to whom the test is subsequently administered, to the original sample. If standardization is carried out on a nationally representative group, the attainments of an individual, a class, a school or an LEA can be compared to the national norms.

It would be possible to coach or allow practice on the test. This would increase the pupils' raw scores and reading ages, giving the impression of a higher standard of reading than was in fact the case. The avoidance of the extensive learnings that normally underpin success on the specially chosen items of a standardized reading test completely invalidates any normative interpretation. To coach or allow pupils to practise normative test items is to abdicate profes-sionalism. In this context it is surprising to find in the manuals to both the 1938 and the 1976 revisions of the Burt Graded Word Reading Test the following comment. If the child being tested '. . . is clearly unable to pronounce a word and seems dissatisfied and desirous of help, help may be given; such a word should of course be counted wrong. In any case the test should never be turned into a lesson on how to pronounce difficult words' (SCRE 1976, page 4). By 1976 such an instruction should have been modified.

Normative tests have come under considerable criticism because they do not provide direct guidance as to what should be taught to a child. For a number of years increasing attention has been paid to testing that is objectives based. A more common name is content criterion-referenced testing. Unlike the standardized test where a pupil's score is compared to those of other pupils as the basis of interpretation, criterion-referenced test results are interpretable in terms of explicitly stated objectives that are operationally defined. The notion behind this approach is no more than a sophisticated extension of the grade system to allow for individual differences in a flexible manner. The tests are sometimes referred to as mastery tests. An example taken from a practice common in schools illustrates the idea. If a teacher is using a graded reading scheme, a child who has read one book and wishes to continue to the next is typically asked two questions. The first is, 'What was the story about?' The second, 'Will you read these words please?'. This refers to the out-of-context list frequently found at the back of the book. If the child shows an understanding of the text and is able to read correctly all, or nearly all, of the out-of-context words that comprise the book's content, the child proceeds to the next graded reader with the teacher's blessing. If the child does not meet the criteria of understanding and word recognition, he will not proceed to more difficult work but will be directed to something at a level in keeping with his instructional needs.

This aspect of testing reading leads logically to the use of checklists of skills that the child should master (Dean and Nichols 1974).

The great strength of this approach is that there are a clearly defined number of quite specific objectives that the child is expected to master. The teacher can set to work teaching the skills to the children. In contrast to the normative test, failure to encourage the children to master the content criterion-referenced tests is a dereliction of one's professional responsibilities. The content criterion-referenced test tells one what must be taught and learned.

In such tests the teacher is not concerned with individual differences between pupils in their mastery of a given reading skill. From one point of view, all children should score full marks on the criterion test. A whole new industry is being built up to produce content criterion-referenced reading tests. The following extract from one firm's catalogue (Instructional Objective Exchange 1976) indicates the line taken:

> . . . educators are becoming increasingly disenchanted with standardized tests as a measure of educational performance. Standardized testing is giving way to criterion-referenced (objectives-based) testing. Unlike the typical standardized test in which a student's score must be compared to the scores of other students in order to be interpretable, criterion-referenced tests results are interpretable in terms of explicitly stated objectives.

One of the most advanced of these systems is the Prescriptive Reading Inventory. This is designed to allow the diagnostic teaching of reading based on ninety clearly defined objectives. The analysis of the results is linked to the prescription of suitable reading activities likely to help the pupil develop the skills he has not yet mastered. At present the system is keyed to more than thirty-two reading schemes (Pumfrey 1976). Its scope and promise are extensive. One awaits with interest research reports on the reading progress of children with whom it has been used.

Test profiles

Increasing use is being made of diagnostic reading tests that provide information on different aspects of the reading attainments of an individual. Frequently the results obtained are presented in the form of a profile of intra-individual differences. The initial and intuitive approach to interpreting a profile is by a visual identification of areas of apparent strength and weakness. The purpose is usually to decide in which subskills of the reading process the child needs help, and how to use relative strengths to minimize or rectify weaknesses.

In the case of a normative diagnostic test such as intuitive interpretation ignores several important points. Looking at the profile one may consider the pupil's score on one subtest to be higher than that on another. Before starting a pupil on a course of remedial teaching, one would wish to be reasonably certain that a further administration of the test would result in a similar profile. Other considerations than the visual pattern therefore matter. The following questions must be asked. Firstly, how reliable is each of the subtests? Secondly, to what extent are the subtests intercorrelated? This information is vital because the lower the reliabilities of the subtests, the higher is the standard error of measurement of the differences between subtest scores. Unreliable subtests can only give unreliable profiles and unreliable differences between them. Additionally, the correlations between subtests affect the interpretation of the differences between the subtests. The more highly correlated the subtests, the less likely are any differences between subtest scores to recur (Pumfrey; in press). The position is well summarized by the following extract from an article on the interpretation of multiple measurements (Cooley 1971):

> One very serious shortcoming of such within-profile contrasts, especially within the achievement area, is the unreliability of difference scores. This unreliability is partly the result of the high correlations among the traits measured by the battery. Some publishers attempt to 'solve' this problem by not reporting these correlations! . . . To provide a battery that measures a set of highly related traits and then to encourage educators to make interpretations regarding trait differences for students without even reporting the typical correlations among these traits is certainly an irresponsible practice.

The simplicity of the visual presentation of a normative profile of reading skills is deceptive. Expertise in the interpretation of a reading profile requires considerable study, practice and application. It demands an awareness of mental measurement concepts, of test theory. Devising a remedial programme requires further qualities. Experience of various methods and materials, an appreciation of their respective efficacies in helping children acquire or develop skills, and a theory of development which includes reading are essential corollaries to the efficient use of a normative diagnostic reading test.

Fortunately a number of teachers are aware of the complexities of profile interpretation. There is evidence that the approach using normative intra-individual tests is a promising albeit complex one (Naylor 1973).

The content criterion-referenced approach differs from the normative, largely because items are not selected to maximize individual differences. Having drawn up an analysis of the reading process, the skills to be learned by the child are taught. The major dangers that can occur from working to such a scheme of operationally defined objectives arise from the fact that there is, even in a criterion-referenced test, a measure of individual differences. Often the number of items in a content criterion-referenced test is small, and hence not very reliable though this cannot be assessed as with a normative test. The validity is usually face validity only and the aspects of reading measured are highly intercorrelated. The psychometrics and theory of mastery tests are still in a rudimentary stage. Their major contribution to improving the teaching of reading is because their use involves analysing the reading process, defining observable and measurable objectives for the children and teaching the mastery of these objectives. The hierarchy of skills on which certain content criterion-referenced reading tests are based is often suspect.

Of the two approaches, the content criterion-referenced measurement approach will have more immediate appeal to the teacher because it tells her what to teach. The normative is probably of more interest to the research worker.

Perhaps the most interesting developments in diagnostic reading tests attempt to combine both normative and criterion-referenced approaches. It has been said that today's norm, that is, the average reading attainment of a group, becomes tomorrow's criterion to be achieved by all. Such an aspiration should be treated with caution as was noted earlier. Landing on the moon without the technology of NASA would be easier than achieving the initial aspirations of the 'Right to Read' Programme.

In terms of its theoretical development content criterion-referenced profile analysis is at a rudimentary level, but has some promise.

Early identification of potential reading failure

This area is one of great conceptual and practical complexity. The early identification of educationally 'at risk' children was the concern of a recent international symposium organized by the Priorsfield Project for the Study of Learning Disabilities in Children last year under the aegis of the University of Birmingham School of Education. The resultant publication is essential reading for any educationist concerned with both the identification of groups of children likely to require positive discrimination and the assessment of the particular child's individual requirements (Wedell and Raybould 1976). The account deals with conceptual problems, psychometric approaches and schemes currently in operation. Indeed, a number of contributors to that symposium are taking part in the programme for Topic 2 on 'Measurement in reading and the evaluation of progress' running at this conference.

Research findings have helped greatly in establishing which factors within the child and his environment are predictive of potential failure. Thus, on the basis of the National Child Development Study, Davie is able to say '. . . the need for special educational help will be six times higher for children in Social Class 5 than in Social Class 1 . . .'. Yet the power of social class as a predictor cannot be used in explanation of the differences which emerge because, 'It is a crude reflection or measure of a large number of factors, some of them genetic and some environmental . . .'. Despite the validity of social class as a predictor of later need of help, the predictions are based on groups of children and not on individuals.

In terms of individual children, the chances are about 3 to 1 against any individual child aged seven years in Social Class 5 needing such help (Davie 1976). (Of course some critics argue that the NCDS is like Hamlet without the Prince, as no measures of intelligence were included in the test battery.) Despite this, the point is made that using such an approach to identify children likely to need help will result in the identification of a large number of children who will prove to have been mistakenly identified. Such pupils are referred to as 'false positives'. This will be paralleled by the failure to identify a considerable number of children who will later meet difficulties.

These problems arise in part as a consequence of the unreliability of difference scores between correlated variables referred to in the comment on the need for caution in profile interpretation. The major point is the tentative nature of an identification procedure for an individual based on a survey of a group. If any survey is carried out and we identify a number of cases requiring help in reading, we can expect a considerable number of those cases to disappear when retested. This is because we have capitalized on unusual combinations of errors of measurement. Cases have been identified with plus errors on one test and negative errors on the other. Such individual cases will not hold up if looked at more closely. One of the consequences of such a screening or identification procedure is that a number of apparently miraculous improvements will occur. These are likely to be attributed to whatever approach has been used and thus lead to entirely unjustifiable claims concerning the efficacy of the identification procedure and the treatment. One way of minimizing such undesirable consequences is to develop increasingly valid tests.

Some LEAs use identification procedures that do not involve the use of normative tests. Thus at the end of the child's infant-school education teachers may be asked to nominate those pupils who have not progressed beyond a given level in the graded reading scheme used in the school. As it is well established that early progress in reading is positively related to later progress, the idea of identifying poor readers and providing such help as they require is an appealing one. The simplicity of the scheme also appeals to teachers who are able to say with some confidence which pupils are failing to reach an objective criteria. One authority organized a screening procedure that resulted in a profile of information on criterion measures plus the teachers' recommendations concerning which individual children needed help in reading. Because promotion to the junior school occurred in September, the system resulted in a dramatic over-referral of summer-term-born slow-learning pupils. The absence of a normative test with monthly age allowances led to autumn-term-born children and summer-term-born children being compared on their reading attainments in an absolute sense in July. For children of a given ability, those born in the autumn term were both older than the summer-term-born pupils and had experienced a longer period of infant education. Their reading attainments were understandably superior to those of the younger pupils in an absolute sense but who would argue that this justified giving special help mainly to the summer-born children? Had the date of transfer been amended to January, then the autumn-term-born pupils would have been over-recommended (Pumfrey 1975). It seems plausible that the need for special help with reading is evenly distributed in that approximately a third of the yearly groups requiring this help should come from each of the three school terms in which their date of birth fell. Only a standardized test with monthly age allowances could identify children whose difficulties were relatively equivalent.

This cautionary point is made so that those looking at identification procedures will realize that the content criterion-referenced tests have at least one major weakness.

A further danger is that in identifying children 'at risk' one has established a self-fulfilling prophecy. The pupils may respond to the teacher's expectations and exhibit the anticipated difficulties in learning to read.

Normative tests have an important role in the early identification of children likely to find difficulty in learning to read. Research findings give valid indications concerning the host of variables that are predictive of later success or failure in reading. The teacher's responsibility is to be aware of these predictors and to endeavour to find ways of defeating them. If she is successful then our understanding of and control over the reading process will have been enhanced. But without reading tests, the skills, understandings and insights of the most effective teacher cannot be made public and used to advance our professional expertise (Askov *et al* 1972; Bilka 1972).

Accountability

The concept of accountability is one with which the teaching profession is likely to become increasingly familiar. Its frequent use in discussions concerning the running of our schools has important implications for teachers of reading in particular (DES 1975). The concept has been brought to public and professional attention for three major reasons. The first is related to financial pressures. Six years ago it was estimated that one school-leaver in thirty was only semi-literate and there is no evidence that the situation has improved. With Britain now spending 6 per cent of its gross national product on education compared with 2 per cent during the 1930s, with class sizes much smaller and with teachers trained for a longer period, questions are raised concerning the efficiency of the system. Leader writers in reputable papers argue that, 'It is a crime to allow a child to finish school unable to read and write adequately'. The implication is that teachers are responsible in large measure for a failure to increase standards of reading. Secondly, as a consequence of certain of the Bullock Committee's recommendations, some LEAS are considering introducing a monitoring system in addition to whatever scheme is introduced by the Department of Education and Science. Thirdly, research studies such as that carried out by Bennett at the University of Lancaster and the apparently less well controlled 'action-research' at the William Tyndale Junior School in London have encouraged the unproductive progressive/formal argument to be re-examined in the light of the most profound prejudices.

There are dangers that need to be recognized in the deceptive and, to some, appealing simplicity of adopting the type of accountability systems currently dominant in educational thinking in the USA. The major characteristics of such systems are:

1 they have a small set of specific goals
2 these goals are operationally defined
3 reinforcement is provided to encourage achievement of the goals, and
4 pupil performance on output measures such as reading attainments are maximized and little concern is paid to side-effects. Clegg has

221

referred to the dangers in a trenchant article 'Battery fed and factory tested' (Clegg 1975).

Such a model is typical of the 'commodity' concept of education for which sociologists sometimes criticize psychologists. An early application of such a system occurred in Britain during the last century when in the Revised Code of 1862, the Education Department established the system of 'payment by results'. The aims of elementary education were clearly understood, namely that children should learn to read, write and do arithmetic. The Revised Code specified the standards to be reached after each year of education. Thus a child completing his first year in Standard 1 was expected to be able to read 'a short paragraph from a book used in the school not confined to words of one syllable' (Pidgeon 1972). The test was a criterion-referenced one, albeit rather crude and open to subjectivity in its administration. Inter-individual differences were not the focus of concern; absolute standards in the basic subjects (and others) were. Pupils were examined by a visiting inspector and then passed on to the next standard. Successful pupils earned a grant for the school. No child could be presented more than once at the same grade. The system was both mechanical and rigid. It led to a neglect of the pupils least likely to produce money for the school by passing the examinations. It is argued that the same system operates today in directing a greater proportion of a school's resources to those pupils likely to achieve examination successes (Jencks *et al* 1975). The advocate of the system, Lowe, defended it by the argument: 'If it is not cheap, it shall be efficient; if it is not efficient, it shall be cheap'. The system operated for thirty-five years until it was disposed of in the Code of 1897. In the demonology of teachers' folklore, the memory lingers on. It is the profession's emotional equivalent to the means test of the 1920s. The echoes of Lowe's cry that can once more be heard in the corridors of political power must be dealt with constructively and not by Luddite-like reaction.

A more sophisticated example of the same idea is manifest in what the Americans call 'Educational Performance Contracting'. Commercial firms have undertaken responsibility for the instruction of pupils in the basic subjects, the arrangement being that payment would only be made if the pupils reached predetermined levels of attainment in reading and number in a prescribed period. The vital role of the tests of reading used to determine whether the children had made sufficient progress to justify payment to the firm will be readily appreciated. The US Department of Health, Education and Welfare has carried out one of the most rigorous evaluations of the effectiveness of Educational Performance Contracting systems. The conclusions reached are pertinent to the functions that reading tests will play in accountability.

In terms of children's developing abilities, the performance contracts did not produce dramatic gains on standardized reading attainment tests, but in most instances gains were made. One consequence of the investigation was to focus on the many technical problems associated with the use of gain scores on standardized achievement tests. Standardized reading test scores have some attractive features as indices of educational output, but they can be misused. The central problem is that such tests were not designed to assess the effects of short-term instruction in reading. They were mainly intended as predictive instruments. Thus, given a pupil's standardized reading test score at a given age it is possible to predict with a given degree of probability his likely future relative performance in reading. Hence the importance of normative tests in the early identification of children likely to experience difficulties in reading at a later stages. The tests were not designed to distinguish between the effects of 'good' teaching as distinct from other variables influencing reading attainments such as those associated with socioeconomic and cultural variables touched on in the previous section.

One aspect of this problem is that the skills a performance contracting programme may seek to teach can be different from those tested by available normative reading tests. If this is the case, such tests are not adequate. Where a programme concentrates on a narrow set of reading skills such as those concerned with word attack on the assumption that this will enable the student to master more general reading comprehension skills, one might have reservations about a standardized reading test providing valid information concerning the effectiveness of the teaching.

Again, one might object to the programme's objectives if they are too narrow, but even if the objectives are not so restricted, no standardized reading test is likely to match a given programme's particular content. It has been suggested that this problem can be overcome by drawing selectively from the items in a standardized test so as to match the programme's content. Such a procedure completely vitiates the one great strength of such tests, namely the existence of norms.

As touched on earlier, much academic attention has been given to the conceptual and practical difficulties involved in interpreting change in scores on normative reading tests. An article published in *Psychological Bulletin* and entitled 'How we should measure "change" or should we?' deals with this complex problem (Cronbach and Furby 1970).

If standardized norm-referenced reading tests are suspect for the evaluation of performance contracting projects, are 'mastery' or content criterion-referenced tests more appropriate? The step seems an obvious one. However, it is easier said than done. In the American studies of performance contracting the construction and use of such tests was attempted. The official report concluded that no one had anticipated the difficulties involved. 'Much more work needs to be done on criterion-referenced tests before their results can be interpreted meaningfully' (Carpenter and Hall 1971). The system of performance contracting indicates that those responsible for passing judgment on the efficacy of a reading programme whether it is of a class, a school, an LEA or a nation, must become involved in both selecting and devising instruments that are capable of measuring programme effectiveness.

Without doubt performance contracting develops a marked emphasis on the individual pupil and his reading attainments as an index of the programme's efficiency. It facilitates the introduction of radical changes in teaching by encouraging learning system contractors to contribute to the education of pupils. A danger is that the teacher of reading may not make her voice heard because the profession's knowledge and understanding of the technicalities of mental measurement in this country is relatively undeveloped. Equally, our interest in all aspects of development should ensure that the notion of a simplistic view of accountability should be questioned. We may be teachers of reading, but before that we are teachers of children (Elliott 1976).

Conclusion

Testing, measurement and quantification do not necessarily lead to precision, to unambiguous communication, to objectivity and understanding. Figures often function as a smokescreen. The Ulsterman who said he was 100 per cent behind the anti-terrorist campaign and then, as if suddenly aware of the ravages of inflation, amended his statement by adding, 'To tell the truth, I'm 200 per cent behind it', is an example. The young apprentice engineer described how he had to work accurately to a ten-thousandth of an inch. When asked how many of these units there were in an inch, after a period of struggle he replied 'millions'.

There are occasions when the use of basic concepts in mental measurement that are essential to the effective use of reading tests are either unfamiliar to or misunderstood by teachers. What are the relationships between raw scores, ranks, percentiles and standard scores of various types? What exactly do we mean by the various types of validity and reliability and how are they related? What is the standard error of a reading test score? Do such esoteric ideas merely confuse simple issues? Or does such knowledge help one deal with other questions such as the following:

How can we interpret reading test profiles?
What is the best way to identify both groups and individual children likely to experience difficulties in reading?

In what ways should accountability be conceptualized and operationally defined?

The profession is becoming increasingly conscious of the important role that testing plays in the efficient teaching of reading and is keen to improve its ability to use reading tests effectively (Pumfrey; in press). In this respect the literacy of our pupils is to some degree dependent on the numeracy of their teachers. Let us as a profession move as quickly as possible to that fifth stage in the development of reading test technology when both the strengths and weaknesses are acknowledged and it is applied to the benefit of all.

References
ASKOV, W., OTTO, W. and SMITH, R. (1972) 'Assessment of the De Hirsch predictive index tests of reading failure' in R. C. Aukerman (ed) *Some Persistent Questions on Beginning Reading* Newark, Delaware: International Reading Association
BENNETT, N. (1976) *Teaching Styles and Pupil Progress* Open Books
BILKA, L. P. (1972) 'An evaluation of the predictive value of certain readiness measures' in R. C. Aukerman (ed) *Some Persistent Questions on Beginning Reading* Newark, Delaware: International Reading Association
BURKE, E. and LEWIS, D. G. (1975) Standards of reading: a critical review of some recent studies *Educational Research* 17, 3, 163-74
CARPENTER, P. and HALL, G. R. (1971) *Case Studies in Educational Performance Contracting: Conclusions and Implications* Santa Monica: Rand
CLARK, M. L. (1972) *Hierarchical Structure of Comprehension Skills*, volume 1: *Theoretical models and related research on the definition and measurement of reading and listening comprehension* Hawthorn: Australian Council for Education Research
CLARK, M. L. (1973) *Hierarchical Structure of Comprehension Skills*, volume 2: *Factorial and 'smallest space analysis' of primary reading and listening test correlations: an empirical study of grade 7 children's performance* Hawthorn: Australian Council for Educational Research
CLARK, M. M. (1976) *Young Fluent Readers: What Can They Teach Us?* Heinemann Educational
CLEGG, A. (1975) Battery fed and factory tested *Times Educational Supplement* 11 July
COLES, C. M. (1976) *A replication and extension of Lawrence's work on the effects of counselling on retarded readers* unpublished M.Sc. thesis. University of Manchester Department of Education
COOLEY, W. W. (1971) 'Techniques for considering multiple measurements' in R. L. Thorndike (ed) *Educational Measurement*

(second edition) Washington, D.C: American Council on Education

CRONBACH, L. J. and FURBY, L. (1970) How we should measure 'change' – or should we? *Psychological Bulletin* 74, 68-80

DAVIE, R. (1976) 'Children at increased educational risk: some results and some reservations' in K. Wedell and E. C. Raybould (eds) *The Early Identification of Educationally 'At Risk' Children* Educational Review Occasional Publications, No. 6, Edgbaston, University of Birmingham, School of Education

DEAN, J. and NICHOLS, R. (1974) *Framework for reading* Evans Brothers

DES (1974) *Educational Disadvantage and the Educational Needs of Immigrants* HMSO

DES (1975) *A Language for Life* (Bullock Report) HMSO

ELLIOTT, C. D. (1975) British Intelligence Scale takes shape *Education* 145, 17, 460-1

ELLIOTT, C. D. (1976) 'The measurement of development' in V. Varma and P. Williams (eds) *Piaget: Psychology and Education* Hodder and Stoughton

ELLIOTT, C. D. and PUMFREY, P. D. (1972) The effects of non-directive group play-therapy on some maladjusted boys *Educational Research* 14, 2, 157-61

ELLIOTT, J. (1976) Preparing teachers for classroom accountability *Journal of the National Association of Teachers in Further and Higher Education* 100, 49-71

INSTRUCTIONAL OBJECTIVES EXCHANGE (1976) *Catalogue: Select your own objectives-based materials for curriculum design and evaluation* Los Angeles: Instructional Objectives Exchange

JENCKS, C., SMITH, M., ACLAND, H., BANE, M. J., COHEN, D., GINTIS, H., HEYNS, B. and MICHAELSON, S. (1975) *Inequality* Peregrine

LAWRENCE, D. (1973) *Improved Reading Through Counselling* Ward Lock Educational

LINDEN, K. W. and LINDEN, J. D. (1968) *Modern mental measurement: a historical perspective* Guidance monograph series. Series III Testing. Boston: Houghton Mifflin

MAGNUSSON, D. (1967) *Test theory* Palo Alto: Addison-Wesley

NAYLOR, J. G. (1973) *Some psycholinguistic disabilities of poor readers, their diagnosis and remediation* unpublished M.Ed. thesis, University of Manchester Department of Education

PIDGEON, D. A. (1972) *British Primary Schools Today: Evaluation of Achievement* Macmillan Education

PIDGEON, D. (1976) Logical steps in the process of learning to read *Educational Research* 18, 3, 174-81

PUMFREY, P. D. (1974) Promoting more sophisticated use of reading tests: a national survey *Reading* 8, 1, 5-13

PUMFREY, P. D. (1975) Season of birth, special educational treatment and selection procedures within an LEA *Research in Education* 14, 55-76

PUMFREY, P. D. (1976) *Reading: tests and assessment techniques* UKRA Monograph Series. Hodder and Stoughton Educational

PUMFREY, P. D. (in press) *Measuring Reading Abilities: Concepts, Sources and Applications* Hodder and Stoughton Educational

PUMFREY, P. D. and ELLIOTT, C. D. (1970) Play-therapy, social adjustment and reading attainment *Educational Research* 12, 3, 183-93

SCOTTISH COUNCIL FOR RESEARCH IN EDUCATION (1976) *Manual for the Burt Reading Test* (1974 revision) Scottish Council Research in Education Publication No. 66. Hodder and Stoughton Educational

SHEARER, E. and APPS, R. (1975) A re-standardization of the Burt-Vernon and Schonell graded word reading tests *Educational Research* 18, 1, 67-73

START, K. B. and WELLS, B. K. (1972) *The Trend of Reading Standards* NFER

TURNER, J. and MOYLE, D. (1972) *The Assessment of Reading Skills* United Kingdom Reading Association Bibliography, No. 2

WEDELL, K. and RAYBOULD, E. C. (eds) (1976) *The Early Identification of Educationally 'At Risk' Children* Educational Review Occasional Publications, No. 6, Edgbaston, University of Birmingham School of Education

WOODCOCK, R. W. (1973) *Woodcock Reading Mastery Tests Manual* Circle Pines: American Guidance Service

25   Screening and early identification of children with problems

Christopher P. Marshall and Sheila Wolfendale

Introduction and background

In recent years there have been an increasing number of attempts to identify children's difficulties as early as possible, especially in terms of the basic skills of literacy, with a view to matching children and curriculum content. If any such attempt is to be relevant and make a valuable and valid contribution to the practice of teaching, it should incorporate principles of child development with the requirements of school-based learning. It is proposed to examine a number of the issues concerned with the early identification of children with problems before introducing descriptions of two procedures currently being developed in this country.

1   The concept of early identification

The psychologist J. McV. Hunt has outlined the views of those who maintain that environmental effects begin so early that it is feasible and justifiable to introduce enriching stimuli and appropriate education from birth, if possible (Hunt 1969). According to this view, early-appearing learning habits and individual ways of learning can be identified and used as the basis for learning programmes. Similarly, he maintains that developmental delays can be identified and revealed for preventive and remedial purposes, and for special education.

There is accumulating evidence of long-lasting effects of alleged deprivation, in terms of educational progress and social adjustment, and the term 'disadvantaged' has been used to describe those children who are said to lack certain opportunities and amenities from birth (DES 1967; Davie, Butler and Goldstein 1972).

In principle, therefore, identification could be from birth, although early identification in terms of our state provision of education usually refers to the infant-school stage.

2   The nature of the problems to be identified

The developer of any measuring instrument is free to select and employ any theoretical rationale. For example, the Aston Index (Newton 1974) accepts and uses the concept of specific developmental dyslexia, as does the American Slingerland Test (Slingerland 1970). The Thackray Reading Readiness Profiles centre around the requisites and criteria for learning to read. In the USA various screening devices abound for the identification of 'learning disabilities', so that training programmes employing a similar rationale can be used for children revealed on the screening as having some specific learning disability.

3 Forms of early identification

The distinction has to be made between individual assessment of children, which is time-consuming and expensive, and screening of large numbers of children, measuring them all against specified criteria, in order to reveal those children whose development and progress are causing concern.

Therefore screening cannot be an in-depth procedure, and in order to be optimally useful any form of mass early identification must possess certain characteristics and requisites. These are briefly enumerated as follows:

(a) There must be an adequate theoretical rationale – the compiler of a screening instrument is dependent upon the evidence available at any one time that backs up or refutes current theory. Thus he must ensure that the times selected reflect consistently the theoretical rationale he has decided to employ.

(b) Reliability and validity – the reader is referred to texts on educational measurement to ascertain the various ways in which reliability and validity can be established (for example, Cronbach 1970).

(c) The data should be related to the goals and processes of the school.

(d) The collected data should be readily available within the school.

(e) The measure must be short and easy to score if it is to be used by busy teachers on large numbers of children.

(f) It has to be sensitive enough to distinguish between groups of slow-learning children, and those children whose progress in school does not cause concern. This implies the existence of a cut-off point, where scores lower than a certain number define those children and their problems, i.e. those who may be 'at risk' in the learning situation (see DES 1975, 17.2 for discussion on the 'at risk' concept).

4 The purpose of early identification screening

The aim of revealing children with problems is to be able to translate the information from the measure used into action, whether it be preventive, remedial or compensatory. Generally the intention is to intervene positively – intervention in this context has been defined as 'a conscious and purposeful set of actions intended to change or influence the anticipated course of development' (see Sigel, in Anderson 1973).

The form of action, therefore, can vary. Some familiar examples will suffice to make the point: a language programme for use with groups; a perceptual-motor training programme for individual use; reading readiness material; a carefully planned and consistent approach for children with particular emotional and social difficulties.

Information revealed on a screening instrument should not have to call for drastic measures, should not need to disrupt school routine and should not make heavy demands on teachers' time. It is hoped by compilers of early identification procedures that some teaching methods and curriculum content can be geared to the needs of children in general, and to children with learning problems in particular.

There now follow details of two procedures currently being used or investigated in a number of local education authorities in England.

A description of a recently devised procedure for the identification of learning and behaviour difficulties in 6+ year old children using teachers' observations and a criterion-referenced objective measure of children's abilities

In September 1973 a three-year project began involving two University of Durham lecturers and a local education authority in the North-East of England, which was to devise a satisfactory procedure to identify children in their penultimate term of infant schooling who were educationally or behaviourally 'at risk'. (See Marshall and Gilliland 1976, for a fuller discussion of the background and rationale of the procedure.)

It was decided to develop two forms of assessment: teachers would be asked to complete a questionnaire and children would be required to answer a variety of questions covering different skills known to be associated particularly with reading and number development. The purpose of the procedure was to identify those children aged 6½–7½ years who were experiencing such extreme difficulties that they might need to be educated in a special school, and also those children who were most likely to be in need of some extra help or attention within the normal junior school.

All teachers of the selected age group were asked to 'rate' children on a four-point scale – equivalent to a categorization of above average, average, below average, extremely poor – on basically two sets of questions. The first set consisting of eight questions related to special educational needs and also asked the teacher's opinion of the child's 'academic' performance in the classroom in a number of areas; for example:

(a) Do you consider that as a result of educational or mental backwardness the child would benefit from attendance at a special school *now* or within the *next two years?*

(b) Consider the vocabulary and comprehension in reading of the child.

If the child's reading is above average	... Code 1
If the child's reading is about average	... Code 2
If well below average (makes frequent recognition errors, lacks fluency and comprehension) ...	... Code 3
If the child is a non-reader (recognizes only a few isolated words, no fluency and little evidence of comprehension)	... Code 4

The second set was an attempt to assess significant behavioural characteristics of the child. This set which was finally agreed also consisted of eight questions, for example:

(c) Consider the verbal and physical aggression which the child displays.

If the child hardly ever behaves aggressively towards peers or adults	... Code 1
If the child occasionally behaves defiantly, attempts to dominate others	... Code 2
If the child is quite frequently disobedient, destructive and teases and fights others	... Code 3
If the child is very frequently disruptive, destructive, pushes, bites, kicks	... Code 4

Each child within the selected sample was, therefore, rated on each of the sixteen questions and the judgments were recorded on a matrix-type grid for twenty children at a time. This facilitated an easy, visual, cross-comparison for a total class of children, highlighting any child who was seen to be vulnerable in any area, or an immediate inspection of the results for any one item.

The questionnaire items were selected so as to reflect certain key behaviours and aspects of learning which relate to a child's overall functioning in school and which can readily be commented upon by a class teacher.

The *children's tasks* were, in every case, of the pencil and paper type, but all the instructions were given orally. Care was taken to ensure that as far as possible every child understood the nature of the task before proceeding with the scorable items. Since the project began three administrations of a children's test have been given. The current version is somewhat different from the original, although most of the subtest tasks have remained the same even though some are now in a modified form. The final version to be recommended to the local education authority in question will most probably consist of eight different tasks: five associated specifically with reading and associated skills (visual discrimination, aural discrimination, visual sequencing, spelling and the identification of orally presented words, i.e. reading); two assessing numerical skills (number identification and counting, simple number concepts); one tapping visual and motor areas of functioning and related to basic learning skills (copying geometric designs). These were selected on the basis of many previous researches as likely to reflect areas of weakness in children experiencing learning difficulties.

This test differs from most previous attainment-type measures in that the rationale for including any item was that it should have a failure rate of between approximately 6 per cent and 15 per cent of a normal school population of 6½-7½ year olds. Thus most children succeed at most items and only the weakest children are likely to get low scores – occasional failures due to carelessness or inexperience at test-taking can be ignored. In this way a fine grading of the less successful children can be achieved and it is possible to make decisions concerning follow-up and the allocation of resources in a rational manner.

The test can be administered after a relatively brief familiarization with the manual of instructions and there is a simple objective-scoring system whereby each item scores either one or nought. Although the children's test has not been devised so as to give significant and detailed diagnostic information, it does provide, through its eight subtests, some guide as to the possible areas of weakness which may benefit from further follow-up and investigation. Although the research effort so far has centred upon the development of the teacher questionnaire and the screening test, the intention is not that a one-off 'application' of the procedure is all that is required to identify all children who are likely to be in need of special help. It is anticipated that it will form part of an overall plan which might well commence when a child first starts school and continue, possibly, through to the time that he leaves.

The theoretical rationale for the procedure, therefore, centres around two concepts:

1 that at age seven information should be gathered from both the teacher and the child himself, and
2 that a test which is criterion-referenced (i.e. referring to a fixed standard of achievement, in this case the level at which at least 85 per cent of the population will be successful) is more appropriate for mass screening purposes than a norm-referenced measure (which has a wide spread of item-difficulty and grades all children from the least to the most successful).

The items were selected as being consistent with this rationale and relevant and related to the likely success of a seven year old child at the basic school subjects.

Attempts have been and are currently being made to monitor the likely effectiveness of such a procedure in terms of its reliability and validity. A test-retest coefficient of 0.79 was obtained using the earliest version of the test and with modifications this is believed to have been increased. During the first two years a published reading test (Word Recognition Test, Carver 1970) was administered alongside the screening test and correlation coefficients of 0.82 have been calculated between the two tests. There is reasonable evidence, therefore, on the early version at least, that the screening test will prove to be adequately reliable and valid in comparison with existing group tests for seven year olds.

The procedure has been devised so that the score on the two methods of assessment can be combined to produce, say, an index of priority or an overall score, below which children can be considered to be in need of additional educational assessment, help or resources. If it is found that certain items are of greater importance than others, then the scores on these items can be weighted accordingly and thus make a more significant contribution to the total score. In the same way, adjustments can be made to the 'test' element of the score to make an allowance for the factor of age. It is anticipated, therefore, that the procedure will be sufficiently sensitive to discriminate both between the fairly small groups of children who are failing completely in school and also between the larger group of children whose problems are somewhat less severe. It is hoped to identify very small groups of children whose overall scores are satisfactory but who have specific difficulties as indicated by the total failure of any one subtest collection of items.

Three years have been spent in developing the above procedure, during which time several amendments have been made – maybe more will follow. Since the authors were working in a university setting it proved impossible to integrate the procedure within a total plan of identification for the local education authority concerned. Thus specific inservice work by way of preparation before the administration of the procedure as well as in terms of adequate follow-up has so far been rather limited. It is appreciated, however, that if early identification is to serve any purpose at all it must lead to positive action, involving both the sensible deployment of the limited resources and also more effective intervention by a child's class teacher.

A consideration of issues and implications arising from the Croydon Screening Procedures

A screening of all infant-school children in the London Borough of Croydon was introduced in 1972, as part of a primary schools screening 'package', the purpose of which was to identify and to help children revealed as having difficulties in learning to read.

A brief description of the system may suffice to give the background and context. More extensive descriptions appear in the Bullock Report (DES 1975, chapter 17, annex B, example 1) and in Wolfendale

(1976a). The theory and practice are discussed in the latter reference. The stages of the screening are as follows:

1 A nineteen-item observational profile on children's development (the checklist) is completed by class teachers on all children towards the end of their first term in school. It is administered again, in the last term of the infant school, as a further screen to identify children still having learning difficulties in general, and specifically with learning to read, and to try to pinpoint the reasons for lack of progress. The four areas of the checklist are: speech and communication; perceptual/motor; emotional/social; response to learning. We included the four items of this last section, in an attempt to tie up developmental features with readiness and adjustment to the requirements and situation of school.

Thus the items of the checklist are in the context of developmental norms, whilst also being geared towards the requirements of the school. It is intended to be a combined norm and criterion-referenced measure. The items, too, reflect current research evidence as to the requisites for the acquisition of reading skills.

2 In the last term at infant school, the Neale Analysis of Reading Ability is carried out on all children. Only the first two pages are adminstered, children who read these successfully being classed as out of risk.

3 All children are given the Young Group Reading Test during the first term of their second year at junior school.

4 The Neale Analysis of Reading Ability is administered to children, in their last term at junior school, who are still having reading problems. Some schools have enough staff and time to screen all children on this reading test, to add to the information going through to secondary school.

Each child's school record card contains the screening results, which are also sent to the Borough's computer centre, and to a teachers' centre. Names are not used, each child being allocated an identification number.

In each junior, infant, and junior and mixed infant school a scale post of responsibility has been allocated for the administration and direction of screening and/or reading and language development. These teachers were prepared and briefed at preliminary inservice training sessions on the rationale behind the checklist and subsequent stages, the overall aims, the administration of the tests, and checklist completion. Videotape film was used.

One year after the full implementation of the screening, the two psychologists who had compiled the checklist published a *Guidelines for Teachers* (Bryans and Wolfendale 1973), the structure of which follows the developmental pattern of the Croydon Checklist, and the

234

purpose of which is to enable the teacher to provide any child revealed on the checklist to be in need of help in any one or more areas with the appropriate exercises and activities.

This LEA scheme came into being in a local and national context of concern about children failing to make progress with basic skills of literacy, and the numbers of pupils leaving school illiterate or semi-literate.

Concern, too, has been expressed about the limited or short-term success of traditional remedial approaches (see the Bullock Report DES 1975 chapter 18, paras. 10, 11, 12). Explicit in the move towards forms of early identification screening is the notion of some kind of ensuing action or intervention, as has been mentioned in the introduction to this chapter.

The conclusions and recommendations made by the Bullock Committee about screening and diagnosis of reading difficulties cover those areas in which they would like to see LEAS investing money, personnel and time: for example, 'Early detection of educational failure is of the greatest importance and there should be a far more systematic procedure for the prevention and treatment of learning difficulties' (recommendation 195, page 537). Also, 'The outcome of the observation procedure should be a detailed profile of each child's strengths and weaknesses, and this should be used to plan an appropriate learning programme. This record should accompany the child when he transfers to a different school' (recommendation 198, page 537).

The Report also sounds a cautionary note (recommendation 199, page 537):

In our view there is no advantage in mass testing and centrally stored data unless the outcome is individualized help directed precisely at the children who need it. As a general principle we prefer that systematized observation should be followed by selective diagnostic testing of those pupils about whom detailed and specific information is required.

Reading failure is also put in a wider context of school-based learning thus: 'The screening procedure should be seen as only the first stage in a continuous process of diagnosis, used by the teacher to design appropriate learning experiences' (recommendation 203, page 538).

If results from such early identification lead to the design of 'appropriate learning experiences' it then follows that the success and value of any 'new' or 'special' approach should be monitored and evaluated. Here the collaboration of the teacher and the educational psychologist could well be fruitful (Wolfendale 1976b) and psychologists are already appraising the extent to which traditional clinical practice of differential assessment and diagnosis of children's problems is useful, within an educational framework.

A screening instrument like the Croydon Checklist, which is a teacher-based observation profile, does put a lot of onus upon the teacher in terms of his/her knowledge of child development, nature of the teaching experience, skill in interpreting information and translating it into action, where necessary. In recognition of this, there has been a considerable emphasis on the inservice teacher training programme in Croydon as an integral part of the screening procedures. Some series have been recapitulatory, others have explored concepts and kinds of intervention, others have led to small groups working in specific areas, and other have been concerned with diagnostic testing of reading, and diagnostic interpretations from the reading tests used in the screening, particularly the Neale Analysis of Reading Ability.

Some schools are using their screening results to reappraise their approaches to teaching reading, and to their provision of remedial reading. In some cases a changed school policy to the teaching of reading and communication skills has resulted.

It is said that these are the days of accountability in education. This is a many-edged coin. As far as a swing towards early identification of problems and learning difficulties is concerned, it represents an attempt to ensure that educationalists are not culpable of allowing any child to slip through the net with those inevitable consequences of recurring and irreversible failure. The development and optimization of human potential may be the central aspiration to which we in education are accountable.

References

ANDERSON, S. B. (1973) 'Educational compensation and evaluation – a critique' in J. C. Stanley *Compensatory Education for Children aged 2 to 8* Johns Hopkins University Press

BRYANS, T. and WOLFENDALE, S. (1973) *Guidelines for Teachers, No. 1* from the Reading and Language Development Centre, Cotelands, Croydon

CARVER, C. (1970) *Word Recognition Test/Manuel* and *Record Form* Hodder and Stoughton

CRONBACH, L. J. (1970) (third edition) *The Essentials of Psychological Testing* Harper

DAVIE, R., BUTLER, N. and GOLDSTEIN, H. (1972) *From Birth to Seven – Second Report of the National Child Development Study* Longman and National Children's Bureau

DES (1967) *Children and their Primary Schools* Volume 1 (Plowden Report) HMSO

DES (1975) *A Language for Life* (Bullock Report) HMSO

EVANS, R. and FERGUSON, N. (1974) Screening school entrants *Journal of the Association of Educational Psychologists* 3, 6, 2-9

HUNT, J. McV. (1969) *The Challenge of Incompetence and Poverty – papers on the role of early education* University of Illinois

MARSHALL, C. P. and GILLILAND, J. (1976) *A screening procedure for the early identification of children in need of help* Occasional Papers of the Division of Educational and Child Psychology of the British Psychological Society, 9, 392-400

NEWTON, M. (1974) *The Aston Index* Department of Applied Psychology, University of Aston, Birmingham

SLINGERLAND, B. H. (1970) *Screening Tests for Identifying Children with Specific Language Disability* Cambridge, Mass: Educators Publishing Service

THACKRAY, D. and L. (1974) *Reading Readiness Profiles* University of London Press

WOLFENDALE, S. (1976a) 'Screening and early identification of reading and learning difficulties – a description of the Croydon Screening Procedures' in K. Wedell and E. Raybould (eds) *The Early Identification of Educationally 'At Risk' Children* Educational Review Occasional Publications, No. 6 104-18

WOLFENDALE, S. (1976b) The effects of a short language intervention programme with infants *Reading* 10, 2, 11-20

26 Providing reading tests for different purposes

Fergus McBride

The Bullock Report (DES 1975) refers to the question of testing pupils in reading in at least three contexts:

1 as a means of monitoring national standards of reading ability
2 as a means of screening, i.e. identifying pupils who are experiencing difficulties in learning to read (17.13)
3 as a means of diagnosing and detecting the difficulties children have in learning to read (17.15).

The Committee, in general, commended the use of tests for these purposes – with important provisos regarding the limitations of certain types of test and the importance of the professional skill of the teacher in making use of the information gained from the testing.

The Committee were in no doubt as to the importance of the monitoring of national standards of reading and 'by the most sophisticated methods possible' (3.2). They were less certain regarding the use of tests for screening, but with regard to diagnosis by the teacher they recommended that new tests should be devised for this purpose. The Committee rightly emphasized the importance of teachers possessing a high degree of professional skill: This emphasis should lead to an effort to provide highly-skilled professionals with the most useful instruments and materials possible rather than, as the Report appears to suggest, a minimizing of the importance of test materials. The provision of such instruments is also a useful means of arousing the interest of teachers in reading problems and of disseminating fresh insights to teachers in service. The 'backwash effect' of tests is not always bad. The more skilled and professionally competent the teacher becomes, the more she will need adequate materials to diagnose and remedy weaknesses, to discover and stimulate strengths in her pupils' reading abilities, attitudes and habits.

However, this Report recognizes the fact that tests are used for differing functions. It also draws attention to the wide gap existing between what is desirable and what obtains in respect of the limitations of existing tests and the extent and nature of the uses to which they are put. The Report has the characteristics of a Bible for the development of teaching of reading – and one of those characteristics is the general nature of its recommendations for the provision of test materials for different purposes.

If we are to 'fill out (the Report's) imperfections with our thoughts' we will have to:

1 determine the different functions for which tests are needed and the different characteristics required in tests of different types
2 examine existing tests as to their adequacy to perform those functions
3 commission the production of new tests on traditional lines where these have been shown to be valid and useful
4 experiment with new types of testing.

From the beginning of this century the development of techniques for testing reading stemmed from and was based upon the concepts of workers in the field of mental measurement, such as Terman, Thorndike and Thurstone in the US and Burt and Thompson in the UK. Since their concern was mainly with measurement for purposes of selection and screening, they applied rigorous statistical constraints to the process of test construction. So much so that, I believe, the statistical tail came to wag the dog and often the prestige of a test was determined more by the complexity of its statistical appendix than by the nature of its reading content or the usefulness of its results to the teacher.

This insistence upon rigorous statistical constraints, however necessary, has had two unfavourable effects:

1 Many teachers are deterred from using tests because of the complexity of the statistical procedures involved in scoring and obtaining numerical results from the tests.
2 Test constructors have to exclude from tests many dimensions of reading ability which cannot be assessed with the degree of accuracy which will meet the widely accepted statistical criteria.

As a result of these factors, I believe, we have recently had quite significant innovations in the assessment field, for example the informal reading inventory, and even revolt in some quarters, for example the 'educative' and 'criterion referenced' test movement summarized by R. P. Carver (1972). According to this author the 'edumetric' test focuses attention upon individual gains in ability to carry out essential reading tasks. He contrasts this with what he alleges to be a concentration upon 'between individual differences' by 'psychometric' test makers.

This movement to emphasize the importance of the validity of test content is to be welcomed, but I believe Carver creates an artificial and exaggerated contrast between two types of tests which is not typical of existing materials.

It is easy to see how the corpus of statistical constraints surrounding tests grows. The teacher may wish to find out whether the child can recognize single words without the support of context. She may first point to some words on the page. She may count the number of words each child recognizes – this is the first step towards standardized reading ages, which are only an extension and necessary refinement of her counting. Later she may print the words on a card to avoid pointing to the page. Which words will she choose? She may use criteria concerned with the phonemic regularity or meaning of the words, but counting soon enters into the procedure, for example to decide which words most children experience difficulty with – the first step towards item analysis, and so on. The fact was that mathematical expertise was available whilst insights as to the processes involved in reading were less definitive, so statistical sophistication proceeded apace whilst the content side of tests made much less headway.

The way ahead now would be not to condemn the statistical expertise built up over years by test makers, but to make this expertise the servant and not the master. That is, to determine the function of test first and the use to be made of results from it, and then to draw upon the statistical techniques available to make the test a more effective tool to perform that function.

In the case of tests for national or local surveys we are interested in means and variability and in this case test reliability may be less important than sampling error. In the case of the headteacher who wishes to survey an age group of pupils – and I see nothing wrong with this practice – we need both reliability of norms and high test reliability, for he is interested in obtaining reliable individual assessments as well as a reliable estimate of the standard of reading in the school. In the case of diagnostic tests, norms may not be required, but some form of item analysis only. We need a description or inventory of the characteristics of tests to be used for different purposes.

It would be wrong to think, however, that nothing much has to be done on the statistical side of testing. The theoretical knowledge is available, but this is not always applied and certainly not always reported systematically.

Recently a headteacher administered two tests, the Schonell Silent Reading Test B (R4) and the Daniels and Diack Test of Reading Experience (Test 12) to seventy-three pupils aged 11.4 to 12.3. The mean reading age given by the Schonell test was 12.3, whilst that given by the Daniels and Diack test was 11.7 – a difference of eight months (9 to 11 points in terms of Standardized Reading Scores). When one considers the similarity of these tests in respect of item form, one feels that the discrepancy would be explained by the norms sampling procedures. The correlation between the two sets of reading ages was 0.82 ±.02. This may appear promising for some purposes but the headteacher was interested in obtaining a reliable assessment of the individual pupils, and the fact that the differences in individual pupils' reading ages on the two tests exceeded eleven months in approximately one third of cases caused him to reject the use of these tests for his purpose. (This degree of discrepancy is approximately what we would expect statistically if we work out the standard error based upon the test intercorrelation given). This sort of inconsistency in means could be eliminated to some extent by calibrating existing tests of a similar nature against one another. The differences in the scores of individual children on different tests may be due to differences in the nature of the tests but the provision of intercorrelation data would enable users to anticipate the extent of the differences in individual scores.

In the process of the statistical validation of the *Edinburgh Reading Tests* Stage 3 (ERT 3) this tests was given along with the NFER Reading Comprehension Test, DE (NF.DE) to 250 pupils in the 10.0–12.6 age range. Both tests are new and occupy similar lengths of time. Both attempt to sample reading skills of a higher order consistent with the reading activities of pupils of this age.

The scores of this sample of pupils on the whole ERT 3 and on the various subtests were very similar in respect of means and standard deviations to those of the pupils in the sample used in obtaining the norms. This would indicate that the sample was representative.

The mean scores of a large subsample (n = 119) of these pupils on each test were:

	Mean Score	S.D.	S.R.S.*
ERT 3	83.84	32.73	99
NF.DE.	24.85	10.44	100

(*Standardized Reading Score. See Lewis (1972) pages 93–6.)

Scores at one sample standard deviation above and below the means were as follows:

	+ 1 S.D.	− 1 S.D.
ERT 3	112	85
NF.DE.	110	88

The intercorrelation between scores on the two tests was .90 ±.02 (and this is probably an underestimate because of some degree of inaccuracy in the transferring of scores by pupils for computer marking). Taking this low estimate of intercorrelation of .90 yields a standard error of 6.45, which means that the chances are two in three that an individual's scores on the two tests will not differ by more than 6.45. However, if the intercorrelation is as high as 0.95 this figure would be reduced to approximately 4.5.

The ERT 3 has five separate subtests designed to sample the following types of reading tasks:

A Reading for facts
B Comprehension of sequences
C Retention of main ideas
D Comprehension of points of view
E Vocabulary

The intercorrelation of subtests scores for this sample were very similar to those reported in the manual.

The NF.DE is not subdivided into subtests to sample different types of reading but in the provisional manual questions scattered throughout the test are grouped into categories as follows:

1 Global Understanding   9 questions
2 Detail   22 questions
3 Inference   11 questions
4 Vocabulary   8 questions

                         Total   50

The intercorrelation between these subtests of NF.DE were comparable to those between the ERT 3 thus showing the subtests to be sufficiently different in nature to provide useful profiles of pupils' performances. Unfortunately, the NF.DE provides no easy means for the tester to obtain these separate scores and the numbers of items falling into categories 1, 3 and 4 are very small indeed.

This field study of these two tests provides encouragement by indicating:

1 that the norms are compatible; hence surveys based on either test will be comparable
2 that there is a high level of correlation between scores on the two tests; hence the individual scores on the two tests can be expected to deviate by minimal amounts
3 that it is possible to construct subtests of different types of reading adequate to reveal some of the pupil's strengths and weaknesses which will be helpful in teaching.

References

BARNARD, E. L. (1974) *Reading Comprehension Test DE* (Test 179) NFER

CARVER, R. P. (1972) Reading tests in 1970 versus 1980: Psychometric versus edumetric *The Reading Teacher* 26, 3, 299–302

DANIELS, J. C. and DIACK, H. (1958) Graded Test of Reading Experience (Test 12) in *The Standard Reading Tests* Chatto and Windus

DES (1975) *A Language for Life* (Bullock Report) HMSO

EDINBURGH READING TESTS (1973) *Stage 3* and *Manual* Hodder and Stoughton

LEWIS, (1972) *Statistical Methods in Education* University of London Press

LORD, F. M. (1959) Test norms and sampling theory *Journal of Experimental Education* 27, June

SCHONELL, F. J. (1955) *Silent Reading Test B (Test R4)* and *Manual (Reading and Spelling Test)* Oliver and Boyd

27   The development of cloze tests

Peter Davies and Denis Vincent

The work reported in the following pages was intended to explore the possibility of producing comprehension tests which would indicate the level of material appropriate for readers at varying levels of attainment. Opinions appear to be divided on the extent to which readability tests and cloze procedure measure the same aspects of prose difficulty, and the extent to which readability formulae measure a cause of prose difficulty, or simply a symptom or correlate. Most formulae concentrate upon two aspects of prose: syntactic complexity (indicated by sentence length), and vocabulary (indicated by length of words, number of syllables or the frequency with which words occur in the language). The question appears to be: do these two characteristics themselves constitute the intrinsic cause of difficulty or are they merely an indirect consequence of an author's efforts to express more or less difficult ideas in his writing? It was decided that before any firm decisions could be reached about the way in which readability measures and cloze procedure might be further developed for use in schools more information was required on these subjects.

First, therefore, a study was carried out to discover how far the difficulty of cloze tests could be predicted from the readability of the passages upon which they were based. This was followed by a study intended to identify determinants of the difficulty of questions (items) in cloze tests which were unrelated to the overall readability of the passage in which they occurred, and finally a study was executed which sought to test the extent to which readability measured factors which in themselves caused prose passages to vary in difficulty. While the research was regarded primarily as a test-development programme it was accepted throughout that an important byproduct might be a set of guidelines and techniques to aid teachers in producing their own test materials.

The first study involved the production of sixteen prose passages of approximately 100 words in length, which were designed to reflect sixteen points on Fry's Readability Graph (Fry 1968). This particular measure was chosen because it had been validated over both the primary and secondary age range (Fry 1968, 1969), was more convenient to use than more sophisticated formulae and was free of the spurious precision characteristic of other formulae. All three are attributes which favour its classroom use. Fry's chart requires the calculation of the average number of syllables and sentences per 100 words, and the chart is used by cross-tabulating the two counts, to place a text on a curve of reading ages or grades between seven years and adult level. Care was taken, particularly in the early passages, to draw the bulk of the vocabulary from words found in *Words Your Children Use* (Edwards and Gibbon 1973) and *Key Words to Literacy* (McNally and Murray 1968) so there could be no question about the general appropriateness of the language of the test passages.

The passages were then converted into cloze tests by randomly deleting five words which performed a syntactic function ('structure' words), and five which performed a semantic one ('content' words). Where inspection suggested that for some commonsense reason the word would be impossible to guess, another word was chosen. The tests were printed in order of readability in two booklets each containing eight of the tests. The tests were attempted by complete first-, second-, third- or fourth-year groups in eleven primary schools. As a result data from 164 first-year, 236 second-year, 199 third-year and 118 fourth-year children was obtained. Marking keys were devised which allowed close synonyms of a deleted word to be marked correct. The acceptance of synonyms represents a departure from the usual practice in experimental cloze testing. For ordinary classroom purposes it was thought that the use of alternative words would be an activity that teachers would want to monitor and study for themselves. The difficulty of each passage was expressed by the mean percentage of children answering each item correctly, and the correlations between their means and the two Fry dimensions were found.

For each of the first three-year groups the correlation between the test difficulty and number of syllables per 100 words was -0.7 and the correlation between test difficulty and number of sentences per 100 words was 0.8. In the case of the fourth-year sample these values were -0.6 and 0.6 respectively. From this it was taken that some relationships betweeen cloze and readability appeared to exist, and that further investigations into the nature of this relationship would be worthwhile. In particular it was necessary to identify influences other than readability which affected cloze-test difficulty.

It was clear from a cursory examination of the results that many individual items tended not to follow the trend of readability and difficulty: easier passages sometimes contained relatively hard items while hard passages contained relatively easier items. If a test was eventually to be produced which predicted a reader's 'level' it would be necessary to eliminate or control this apparent tendency for cloze tests to reflect influences over difficulty related not to their readability but to the types of words deleted.

Accordingly a rationale for word deletion was sought which could provide some control over the balance of hard and easy items in any one test, or series of test passages (A and B). This was done by preparing ten versions of two of the original passages. In each version a different set of words was deleted. In the first version deletion started at the first word, in version two deletion started at the second word, and so on, until in the tenth version deletion of every tenth word commenced at the tenth word in the passage. Single versions of each passage were then attempted by complete year groups of fourth-year junior pupils in a sample of seven schools. The ten versions of the two sets were administered so that a random sample of pupils attempted each version. When the tests were marked, only answers which gave the exact original word were marked correct. The main hypothesis was that, as each of the ten versions were based on the same passage, the versions themselves would not vary in difficulty.

The difficulty of each version was expressed as the mean percentage of pupils answering each question correctly. As Table 1 (below) shows, these averages varied across versions, particularly in the case of passage A which lent itself to distinctly easier and harder versions. In both cases the intercorrelations between versions were statistically significant.

Table 1 **Mean percentages of children answering each cloze item correctly in ten different versions of passages A and B**

| Passage A | | | | Passage B | | | |
Version	n	$\overline{X}$	S.D.	Version	n	$\overline{X}$	S.D.
A1	70	61%	26	B1	70	48%	31
A2	69	44	24	B2	69	42	29
A3	68	56	26	B3	69	48	29
A4	70	67	21	B4	70	59	22
A5	70	38	28	B5	72	56	23
A6	70	42	27	B6	67	43	31
A7	65	40	30	B7	64	48	29
A8	66	55	25	B8	67	44	25
A9	64	58	26	B9	64	50	28
A10	63	60	24	B10	62	49	13
Total	675	52	28	Total	674*	49	27

*This discrepancy in numbers was due to a printing error in one of the scripts.

These differences demonstrated a need to devise some kind of hierarchy of cloze-item difficulty.

A major study by Bormuth (1968) had identified a number of effective criteria for predicting cloze-item difficulty; however, it was felt that many of these would be too complex or time-consuming to be applied by teachers endeavouring to devise their own cloze tests.

Three characteristics of cloze items were therefore chosen for further investigation:

1   the frequency of the words, as indicated by their inclusion in, or absence from, McNally and Murray's *Keywords to Literacy* list (1968)
2   the grammatical function of the words
3   the strength or quality of the processes which appeared to cue each word.

The first two criteria are simple and objective but are also somewhat crude and static. The third is more sophisticated and requires the test-producer to attend to the dynamic aspects of cloze procedure. After some thought and discussion and close re-examination of answers to some of the tests used in the previous study the following classification scheme was drawn up:

Category 1   *Syntactical constraints*
Word is cued almost exclusively by syntactical rules. Context and meaning not really relevant. Reader must use knowledge of syntax.

Category 2   *Common language patterns*
Word is cued by its customary usage in particular phrase or pattern of language. Reader must use familiarity with style and usage.

Category 3   *Explicit context*
Word is cued by its use, or use of close synonym or transformation elsewhere in the passage in such a way as to leave little doubt as to its appropriateness. Reader must manipulate information already given in the passage.

Category 4   *Implicit context*
Word is cued indirectly from the context of the passage. All necessary information is available in the passage, but it must be accessed by inferential processes rather than simple identification.

Category 5   *Circumstantial context*
Word is not cued from any specific source in the passage, nevertheless its meaning is still loosely implied from the whole context. Reader must supplement any information obtained from passage with some degree of general knowledge and reading experience.

Category 6   *No cues available*
Word not cued, even remotely, by matter in the passage and

reader will require specialized or particular prior knowledge to answer correctly.

It would be misleading to pretend the allocation of words to these cue categories was entirely objective; it became clear, for example, that categories 4 and 5 were not discrete, and an element of subjective judgment is probably present in all the categories. Nevertheless, it proved practical to classify all the words in the two passages in this way. It was also strongly felt that a scheme such as this might well form the foundation for a diagnostic technique which could be developed and refined subsequently. This scheme is offered for the information of

Table 2 Difficulty of cloze-test items (as percentages of pupils answering an item correctly) grouped by parts of speech and 'Keywords to Literacy'

Passage A

Parts of speech	Keywords		Non-Keywords	
	n	$\overline{X}$	n	$\overline{X}$
Nouns	6	51	22	41
Verbs	3	40	11	22
Adjectives	1	(52)*	13	35
Prepositions	12	61	7	34
Pronouns	3	61	—	—
Conjunctions	3	56	—	—
Articles	19	79	—	—
Total	47	64	53	35

Passage B

Parts of speech	Keywords		Non-Keywords	
	n	$\overline{X}$	n	$\overline{X}$
Nouns	—	—	31	43
Verbs	2	55	11	26
Adjectives	3	34	5	45
Prepositions	12	53	2	55
Pronouns	8	39	—	—
Conjunctions	1	(28)*	—	—
Articles	20	69	—	—
Adverbs	—	—	3	21
Total	46	56	52	39

*Two items were omitted from the analysis.

anyone wishing to experiment along similar lines. It should, however, be appreciated that it is far from satisfactory for a number of reasons, and it is to be hoped that, in the course of further research, schemes with much greater validity will be evolved.

All three ways of grouping cloze items appeared to have some capacity for explaining differences in the difficulty of items. Keywords were generally easier than words outside the list, and some parts of speech proved to be generally easier or harder than others.

The system of classification of words by their cues appeared in practice to provide an ordering very close to that hypothesized; only the reversal in the difficulty of categories 2 and 3 items really violated the expected sequence.

Table 3 Difficulty of cloze-test items (as percentage of pupils answering items correctly) grouped by cue categories

Cue category	n	$\overline{X}$	S.D.	n	$\overline{X}$	S.D.
1	37	73	15	35	56	24
2	9	41	17	20	49	20
3	10	55	21	17	50	21
4	17	40	20	6	30	12
5	16	29	15	14	32	10
6	11	22	9	6	25	11

The possibility that imbalance in the number of words in harder or easier categories accounted for the deviations of individual versions from the overall level of difficulty was then investigated. This was done by inspecting the correlation between numbers of words in certain categories and the mean difficulty of versions. Variations in numbers of words in nearly all the categories examined were significantly associated with variations in the difficulty versions of passage A, but these relationships were negligable in the case of passage B. In fact variation in difficulty between versions of passage B was much less in the first place, so there was less chance of obtaining high correlations in any case.

The original finding that readability and difficulty of cloze-test passages were correlated had been established only for the case of cloze-test passages of different readability. Further, these passages had all been written by one writer who was unavoidably aware of the experimental purpose to which they were to be put.

The next study sought to discover (a) how far cloze tests based on passages of the same readability would prove to be of equal difficulty, and (b) whether readability and cloze difficulty would be related when test passages were produced 'blind' by authors working independently with no preconceptions of how relatively easy or difficult their passages were expected to be. To this end a number of volunteers were asked to write a passage of 100 words in length. The writers were instructed to select 70 per cent of the words they used from the 'Keywords' list, to ensure the vocabulary of the material was roughly typical of children's everyday reading material. They were further asked to use a set number of sentences and syllables so their final product would meet a specified level of readability.

Five passages at each of eight levels of readability on the Fry chart were obtained. These levels were chosen to provide one set of 'easier' and one set of 'harder' passages for each of the four junior-school year groups. At the same time the authors were not informed of the purpose to which the passages were to be put. Thus there was no possibility that either equality or difference in difficulty between any of the passages could be attributed to contrivance on the part of their authors.

Words were then deleted from each passage according to the cue-based category, as follows:

(a) one category 1 word
(b) one category 2 word
(c) two nouns and two verbs not on the Keywords list, meeting the requirements for category 3 words
(d) one noun and one verb, not on the Keywords list, meeting the requirements for category 4 words.

This scheme was designed to provide new easier items in order to permit less able readers to make some attempt at the tests, while the bulk of the items would provide tasks of intermediate difficulty. Keywords were excluded in order to avoid making the tasks too easy. By confining words in (c) and (d) to nouns and verbs, a further element of uniformity between tests was introduced. Despite the meritable element of subjectivity in categorizing words it was thought the use of this scheme had attained a degree of inter-passage comparability greater than that resulting from sheerly random deletions.

The experiment was so designed that no differences between performance on test passages would arise from practice effects or fatigue. It was thus necessary to ensure that (i) all five passages at any one level of Fry readability were attempted equally often in first, second, third, fourth and fifth place and (ii) that as the sets of tests would have to be attempted over two test sessions, so the 'harder' and 'easier' sets would be completed equally often in both sessions.

A sample of over 1,000 junior-school children, consisting of complete year groups in twenty junior schools, was obtained. The children attempted one of the five sets of 'easier' or 'harder' test passages, allocated at random, in a first session, and the remaining set of five passages in a second session – usually the following day. For practical reasons all children in a school attempted easier or harder passages first.

The marking scheme allowed synonyms of the original word to be scored as correct. As Table 4 (below) shows, passages of equal readability did not prove to be of equal difficulty. Within all eight sets were variations larger than could be attributed only to chance fluctuations. Further, as Table 5 (below) shows, for the third- and

Table 4   Variation amongst cloze passage mean scores

Year group	Means for the 'easier' passages					Means for the 'harder' passages				
	A	B	C	D	E	A	B	C	D	E
First	3.09	3.71	3.08	2.08	1.90	3.15	2.88	2.81	2.59	2.22
Second	4.09	3.72	4.34	3.98	3.68	3.68	3.22	3.72	2.80	4.52
Third	2.34	3.78	3.65	3.90	2.91	4.19	3.94	4.12	3.24	3.15
Fourth	5.43	3.97	3.62	3.14	4.20	3.74	4.57	5.18	4.07	4.39

Table 5   Differences between the means of the first passage attempted in a session and four subsequent passage means

	First session			Second session		
	Passage means			Passage means		
Year	1st	2nd-5th	Differences	1st	2nd-5th	Differences
1	2.98	2.69	0.28**	2.88	2.71	0.17*
2	3.97	3.73	0.24*	3.92	3.74	0.18
3	3.68	3.52	0.16	3.63	3.47	0.16
4	4.27	4.22	0.05	4.40	4.19	0.21**

(*Significant at .05)
(**Significant at .001)

Table 6   Differences between the set of easy passages and the hard passages

	Year			
Set	1st	2nd	3rd	4th
Easy passages	2.77	3.96	3.31	4.07
Hard passages	2.73	3.59	3.73	4.39
Differences	0.04	0.41**	0.42**	0.32**

(**Significant at .001.)

fourth-year pupils the supposedly 'harder' passages were in practice significantly easier. Finally, it appeared that a decline in performance occurred after the first passage.

The results suggest that a re-interpretation of the first study is required. The correlation originally obtained could clearly not be confidently attributed only to the different readability of the passages. The results do not of course invalidate readability measures as predictors of textual difficulty, but they do support the view that sentence length and number of syllables are only a symptom of such difficulty, not a cause.

The tendency for the 'easier' third and fourth year passage to prove more difficult in fact is not easy to explain. However, one possibility may be that the specification of sentences and syllable numbers at this level had a distorting effect on the style of prose, not so marked in passages produced at easier levels on the Fry chart. Another possibility is that involvement in a new and different reading activity may have caused children to be especially careful and attentive with the earliest passages, but becoming bored or fatigued after a while as the later passages had to be done.

The item-deletion scheme unfortunately failed to fulfil its promise, either because the various categories managed to include items of a greater range of difficulty than the results of the preceding study had suggested, or in application it was insufficiently reliable or objective to give predictable results. Again this is an area for much more basic research.

The work which has been carried out to date on these cloze tests, and the attempt to relate cloze-test performance with measured complexity of prose, has raised more questions than it has answered about the relationship between these two indicators – cloze and readability. The degree to which deletion of words distorts the measurable readability of a passage is unknown, as is the extent of the effects of practice on performance in the tests. Little is known, also, of the relationship between actual linguistic complexity and the two *indicators* of it which readability formulae most frequently employ – sentence length and word length. Bormuth (1966) studied many aspects of actual complexity, including the frequency of occurrence of particular parts of speech, and the 'depth' of words and sentences (i.e. the amount of language processing required to produce them, assuming a sequential, 'left-to-right' ordering to the production of a sentence). It was found that sentence and word length correlate so highly with more complex measures that they were sufficiently sensitive indicators of difficulty. In both the reception of language (reading and listening) and in its performance (speaking and writing), it is obvious however that length of utterance is occasionally an inadequate indicator of complexity. Young children, for example, can produce inordinately long or repetitive expressions through an inability to control punctuation or phrasing. Some areas of subject matter will be more difficult to assimilate than others whatever their 'measurable' complexity might be. Motivation and the degree of abstraction in the text may easily overlay 'measured' aspects of prose.

The general background to the research discussed earlier mentioned the hope that a byproduct of the enterprise might be a set of guidelines by which teachers might construct test materials of their own. The implications of this aspect of the work are significant. The manual to the tests which the NFER will publish will include a copy of the Fry Graph and details of its use. In view of the scarcity of assessment materials at adult level for example, the potential of these processes (readability measurement and cloze procedure) to initiate a much broader-based assessment at all levels of educational practice is great indeed.

A set of eight of the original sixteen test passages are now available from the NFER in experimental form. These *Reading Level Tests* have been subjected to all routine statistical processes to ensure each item included provides an efficient measure of performance and discriminates between readers of different levels of performance. In addition, a more sophisticated statistical analysis of the test items has been carried out. This has shown that the test is largely homogeneous and measures a single dimension of performance, rather than a number of discrete skills.

As so much technical groundwork had been conducted with these test passages and the results had proved to be so satisfactory, the decision to make them more widely available in an interim form appeared to be justified – unresolved problems of readability notwithstanding. The future development and use of the tests will depend to some extent on the experience of users of the experimental versions. It may well be found, for example, that they prove an effective practical means of matching readers with books of appropriate readability – in spite of, or because of, the contrived nature of the relationship between their readability and their difficulty.

Their diagnostic use has also yet to be explored. There is a dearth of useful diagnostic materials for any aspects of reading beyond the word-recognition stage. Conventional comprehension tests have not as a rule proved to be outstanding aids to diagnosis. Cloze tests have yet to be tried in this way, and work needs to be done on the identification of the strategies and style of thinking used by readers in guessing cloze words. In particular, efforts should be made to devise 'cloze miscues inventories' along the lines of the existing studies of oral miscues. If it does prove possible to identify consistent difference or difficulties in performance of cloze tasks, this may well have implications for diagnosis of problems in prose reading generally.

Much information is to be obtained from looking closely at the reading strategies adopted by pupils, revealed in 'right answers' (i.e.

which appear in the marking key), 'alternative answers' (i.e. ones which teachers may consider equally acceptable to those in the marking key) and 'wrong' answers. Work on miscues in oral reading has provided an interesting starting point for an appreciation of errors in children's reading and writing performance and much useful information can be obtained from studying a child's errors in reading. This technique is already being used in many diagnostic tests of phonics and word attack, but less frequently in tests employing language units greater than individual words.

Current psycholinguistic models of reading suggest a dynamic process involving a basic left-to-right orientation but imposing on it a system of backward-acting and forward-acting 'searches' for useful guides and meaning based on visual information, phonics, knowledge of word usage and aspects of a more general language experience. Failure to operate any aspect of this model would result in confrontation with the gap in a cloze passage with no recourse to the context other than instincts about which words can follow others in English. Categories 1 and 2 from the experimental classification would tend to be involved in this. Other wrong answers may reveal a weakness in employing pronouns correctly, perhaps through an inability to infer from the implicit context of what is said in the passage. With very young readers, non-standard or non-native English speakers, other miscues may isolate errors in number agreement (for example, we *was* going), tense marking (for example, we went to the shop. When we *go* there it was shut), or knowledge of grammatical class (He *the* there).

It should be clear that these tests are not designed to replace existing reading tests, where teachers require a reliable and easily obtained score. The cloze test will, of course, yield scores of this kind. The initial intention was, however, that cloze tests should be part of a much broader concept of assessment of children's reading, involving different levels of performance on passages of known complexity as well as enabling teachers to define children's reading strategies more accurately.

Beyond these validation stages further considerations about the applicability of the tests becomes somewhat speculative. It may be that use of the tests will enable us to answer questions of the sort: 'Are some children, reading ability aside, better suited than others to the performance of the closure task?' Does the teacher's experience accord with the theory that cloze procedure favours introspective convergent thinkers? More importantly, we might ask whether, using the test individually and discussing a child's performance on the test with him, it can offer the teacher new opportunities for extending a child's understanding of what is expected of him in reading.

References

BORMUTH, J. (1966) Readability: a new approach *Reading Research Quarterly* Spring

BORMUTH, J. (1968) Cloze Test Readability: criterion-referenced scores *Journal of Educational Measurement* 5, 189–96

EDWARDS, P. A. and GIBBON, V. (1973) *Words Your Children Use* Burke

FRY, E. B. (1968) A readability formula that saves time *Journal of Reading* 2, 513–6

FRY, E. B. (1969) The readability graph validated at primary levels *The Reading Teacher* 6, 534–8

MCNALLY, J. and MURRAY, W. (1968) *Key words to literacy and the Teaching of Reading* Schoolmaster Publishing Company

28   Structured informal assessment

Rene Boote

In its recommendations for raising standards the Bullock Report reminds teachers of their responsibility for recording children's reading progress and diagnosing reading needs. Such informal assessment is the subject of an investigation by a small group of teachers in the Stockport area, set up in 1976 under my direction as Research Associate with the Open University. The materials we produced will be available for inclusion in the revised OU course on Reading Development.

By informal assessment I mean the kind of monitoring that can be carried out by the teacher as part of her daily routine, using materials available in the school. 'Informal' is not, therefore, to be equated with a casual unsystematic approach. In order that results and methods may be evaluated it is necessary that assessment procedures should be structured.

Informal assessment is intended to supplement standardized testing; to give teachers, and children too, an insight into that 'wider range of attainments' which the Bullock Report envisages. The exact nature of these attainments is not specified. The skills discussed in the chapter on 'Screening, diagnosis and recording' are mainly those of decoding and the lower levels of comprehension. We need to consider what other reading skills children of different ages and abilities should possess, and how we as teachers can monitor these skills.

In seeking answers to these questions we examined eight published checklists of reading skills, and collated them with each other and with paragraphs from the Bullock Report. The result was a long and cumbersome catalogue, too unwieldy for direct use in the classroom, but valuable perhaps for reference purposes. A teacher could select from it a shorter checklist of skills and subskills suitable for her own children.

In any event, checklists must be approached with caution; they seem to function better in theory than in practice. The Bullock Report states: 'Opinions are divided on the respective merits of simple and detailed checklists.' The one was attractively easy to use but had the defect of being a relatively blunt instrument; the other was a very precise instrument, but too time-consuming.

The teachers working on this project would add that unless there is precise agreement about what constitutes a satisfactory level of achievement on each item of the checklist, confusion and even mistrust may result. Furthermore, teachers are naturally unwilling to spend valuable time on work from which the child – as opposed to the teacher – learns virtually nothing.

A third objection to checklists lies in the nature of reading skills themselves. Some questions implicit in the checklist have a straightforward *yes* or *no* answer. For example, can a child distinguish between words and letters, or has he not yet attained that concept? For other skills, however, and in particular for comprehension, there is no absolute criterion of achievement. All that can be said is that on a particular occasion the reader comprehended a specific test in a certain way. Such considerations have led us to analyse the nature of skilled reading and its relationship with the so-called 'reading skills'. This work is currently in progress.

What further guidance has Bullock to offer on informal assessment? And what methods of assessment and recording do practising teachers find useful in the normal busy classroom?

Most of the teachers approached said they keep a record of what children read, usually a library list and a note of the page numbers for children who are on a reading scheme. A few teachers scribble notes continuously as an individual child reads aloud, and later analyse these notes as a guide to providing remedial work for those children who are having difficulty – usually with certain phonic combinations.

The Bullock Report commends this activity of error analysis as providing 'a continuous window into the reading process'. After commenting on teachers' extensive use of 'the process of hearing children read', it goes on to deplore the fact that few teachers regard it as 'an essential part of the diagnostic process'.

Again, we would go further, and say that hearing children read can provide evidence not only about what supplementary phonic exercises they may need, but also about their reading strategies and comprehension, the suitability of a text for a particular reader, and his responsiveness to it. In brief, a session devoted to hearing a child read can profitably share many features with the *Informal Reading Inventory* devised by Johnson and Kress (1965). We have reason to prefer this development of current practice to the 'series of graded paragraphs' proposed by Johnson and Kress. The response elicited by such a test does not necessarily reflect the subject's normal reading behaviour.

Similarly we have found that Strang's group reading inventory on survey and access skills does not entirely fulfil our requirements. Strang (1969) assesses the performance of a group of children on a particular geography book. In our opinion the ability to answer questions in a test of this kind is no guarantee that the skills displayed will ever be put to practical use. Thus a correct answer to the question:

'In what part of the book can you find the meaning of a word you might not know?' gives no indication of whether the reader ever takes the trouble to use the glossary, even though he knows its purpose.

This hiatus between test performance and private practice is matched by a failure on the part of many children to transfer learning from one situation to another, a failure to move from the instructional exercises to the real situations for which they were designed.

In sum all the evidence leads to two inescapable conclusions:

1 *Skills are learned best when learned on the job* (i.e. as the need to acquire them arises).
2 *Skills are tested best when on the job* (i.e. where they *will* be used if actively acquired).

Of course, we claim no originality for these conclusions; what needs emphasizing, however, is that they are rarely interpreted with a full appreciation of what they imply.

How then do we propose to assess reading skills? It is our belief that methods of evaluation are inseparable from goals. If skills are to be tested 'on the job', it follows that reading goals are best expressed in terms of reading behaviour. More simply, the teacher must ask herself: 'What should this child be able to do in this reading task?'

I return now to Strang's inventory on the use of books. In this investigation I have been using it as a basis for generating questions to be asked by the teachers when children are in the act of selecting books from the reference library for a real project. The resulting questionnaire has several advantages:

1 It may be used for teaching as well as for testing. If children fail to refer to an aspect of the book which seems important the teacher can draw their attention to it.
2 The children can be allowed into the secret of what the teacher is looking for. They can use the questionnaire to remind themsleves of what they can do, and to help each other.
3 It can be used with a *group* of children to make a general assessment of their ability to find what they want; or as a more rigorous *individual* test.
4 It is not specific to any set of materials.
5 It can be adapted or extended as its effectiveness is evaluated.

For the teacher, then, it is seen as a flexible, adaptable instrument for teaching while testing; and one that can be used with groups as well as with individuals, regardless of the materials to hand.

The need for *structure* in informal assessment procedures is evident. If a general pattern can be established for tests, the amount of paperwork is reduced. There is also less need for the teacher to develop tests related to specific materials.

The questionnaire, then, is a suitable form of assessment for certain reading skills. However, it needs to be supplemented by other evaluation techniques.

One such technique is currently being examined by members of the Manchester Council of UKRA, where particular interest is centred on the interaction that takes place when a child reads aloud to the teacher. We need to know what he does when he reaches a difficult word, how the teacher tries to help him, and whether he is able to respond successfully.

This form of assessment would appear to have advantages similar to those listed for the survey skills questionnaire. In the case of interaction analysis, however, the procedure reveals how much responsibility a child is capable of taking for solving his own reading problems, provided always the teacher is prepared to delegate such responsibility.

In this brief review of our findings to date on structured informal assessment, I have suggested ways in which we can respond to the Bullock Report's recommendations that teachers should assess the reading progress and reading needs of their children.

The basic principles our working party has formulated can be stated simply:

1 Choose the reading skills appropriate to the children's development.
2 Define specific reading goals in terms of behavioural objectives.
3 Construct procedures which will assess the children's performance in real situations with real materials.

None of these principles is as easy to put into practice as it is to state in theory. The effective production of informal assessment procedures requires a sound understanding of reading skills, practical knowledge of how children learn, and a willingness constantly to evaluate and revise material in the light of experience.

We do not ourselves expect to produce a set of finalized tests. The most we hope for is to provide a pattern of testing which individual teachers may adapt to their own pattern of teaching. We believe that informal assessment is most successful when those who are to use it have been involved in the design and production of its materials. *And logically this must include the children themselves.*

References

DES (1975) *A Language for Life* (Bullock Report) HMSO
JOHNSON, M. S. and KRESS, R. A. (1965) *Informal Reading Inventory* Newark, Delaware: International Reading Association

STRANG, R. (1969) 'Informal Reading Inventories' in *Diagnostic Teaching of Reading* (pp. 192-204) McGraw Hill

Appendix
Informal Reading Inventory Questionnaire

Access and survey skills

1 What is this book about?
   Refers to title, contents, index, preface, illustrations, blurb.

2 What other features of the book might be helpful to you in deciding whether to use this book?
   Refers to author, qualifications, edition, series or publisher, text-sampling.

3 What are you trying to find out?
   States general purposes, specific purposes.

4 Can you show me how to find out whether this book will help you to answer your questions?
   Locates information efficiently, uses headings, sub-headings. Skims to assess suitability. Rejects unsuitable book.

5 Show me where to find other books on this subject.
   Locates appropriate section of library. Uses card index. Uses encyclopedias.

6 Where else might you find information on this subject?
   Mentions magazines or journals, leaflets, letters to authorities, interviews, visits, audio-visual aids.

Part 6

Aspects of remedial reading

29 Dyslexia or specific reading retardation? A psychological critique

Christopher H. Singleton

When a child experiences inordinate difficulty in learning to read or write and no obvious cause is apparent, it has become fashionable in some quarters to label the child 'dyslexic' and assume that his difficulties are of a constitutional nature. However, amongst educationists and educational psychologists the prevalent attitude regarding the value of this type of diagnosis is one of extreme scepticism. There appear to be four main reasons for this. Firstly, there is a strong tradition in British education, originated largely by Burt (1937) and Schonell (1942), that backwardness in reading should properly be regarded not as a specific disability resulting from inborn cerebral malfunctioning, but, rather, as part of a wider syndrome of educational difficulty with many causes, most of which are thought to derive from unfavourable factors in the child's home background. Secondly, dyslexia is seen by many to be a medical, rather than an educational or psychological problem, because of its purported associations with neurological dysfunction and because members of the medical profession have consistently been most prominent in debates on the disorder. Thirdly, since the first observation of the syndrome at the end of the last century, the concept of dyslexia has constantly been plagued with controversies, the lack of resolution of which has only served to reinforce the misgivings of educationists and psychologists on the matter. Finally, while the label 'dyslexic' may possibly enable some children to get help when they might otherwise have been overlooked, it does not have any specific remedial implications at the present time. The teacher must still assess each child's individual difficulties in reading, writing or spelling, and prescribe treatment in terms of conventional remedial instruction. Knowing that a child has been diagnosed as 'dyslexic' does not make this task any easier.

In recent years an alternative concept – that of 'specific reading retardation' which was first discussed by Schonell in the 1930s – has been reintroduced into the dispute, and Rutter and Yule and other co-workers of the Institute of Psychiatry in London have adduced much empirical evidence in support of this concept whilst at the same time making trenchant denunciation of the concept of dyslexia (Rutter and Yule 1975). The purpose of this paper is to outline the central issues in the controversy and to make some suggestions which might help to resolve it.

Definitions

Two independent Government committees chaired, respectively, by Professor Jack Tizard and Sir Alan Bullock, have observed that the concept of dyslexia is not susceptible to unambiguous definition (DES 1972; 1975). Adams (1969) discussed many definitions of dyslexia at length without being able to reach any satisfactory conclusions, and Keeney and Keeney (1968) revealed that a five-member, doctoral-level research group concluded after two days of deliberation that they could not frame a worthwhile definition of dyslexia. A major problem is that definitions of dyslexia commonly embody highly questionable aetiological assumptions. For example, the definition most frequently encountered in the literature is that devised by the Research Group on Developmental Dyslexia of the World Federation of Neurology, under the chairmanship of Macdonald Critchley, in 1968 (Critchley 1970):

> Specific developmental dyslexia: A disorder manifested by difficulty in learning to read despite conventional instruction, adequate intelligence, and socio-cultural opportunity. It is dependent upon fundamental cognitive disabilities which are frequently of constitutional origin.

The inadequacy of this type of definition has frequently been exposed (Reid 1969; Rutter and Yule 1975): not only does it make nonsense of the idea of a developmental condition (because it rules out children of below-average intelligence or from disadvantaged backgrounds) but also one cannot help but question the meaning of every essential component it contains (what, for example, is 'conventional instruction'?).

By contrast, specific reading retardation can be precisely defined and embodies no aetiological assumptions. It is based on the old idea of a reading achievement ratio (reading age divided by the mental age multiplied by 100) but makes allowance for the 'regression effect' which arises whenever the correlation between measures (such as mental age and reading age) is less than perfect. Children of substantially above-average intelligence will tend to have reading scores of lower value than their intelligence scores, while children of well below-average intelligence will tend to have reading scores rather higher than the value of their intelligence scores. In the middle of the intelligence range, the reading scores and intelligence scores will tend to be roughly the same. The reality of this effect has been clearly demonstrated by Yule *et al* (1974), and it is apparent that if it is ignored, the result is an overestimate of the number of under-achieving readers amongst children of high IQ and a corresponding underestimate of the number of under-achieving readers amongst children of low IQ. The technique of regression analysis (Fransella and Gerver 1965; Yule 1967) means that given the value of the correlation between reading score and IQ it is possible to calculate the predicted value of reading attainment for any specified IQ.

Employing regression analysis with data derived from the Isle of Wight studies of nine and ten year old children (Rutter, Tizard and Whitmore 1970) and from a study of 1,634 ten year old children in London (Berger, Yule and Rutter 1975), Yule *et al* (1974) predicted that 2.28 per cent of children should fall into the category 'specific reading retardation'. This category was defined in terms of a reading score (in this case the Neale Analysis of Reading Ability was used) at least two standard errors below that predicted by age and intelligence. (For these groups this meant reading accuracy and reading com-prehension scores between two and two-and-a-half years below prediction.) In fact, the actual percentages of children falling into this category ranged from 3.09 to 9.26, this being significantly more than expected in all groups except one. Thus serious underachievement in reading would appear to be much more common than would be expected from the assumption of a normal distribution of reading retardation. This discovery, which has been referred to as the 'hump' on the lower end on the curve (Rutter and Yule 1975), implies that there is a group of children with severe retardation in reading which is not simply that lower end of a normal continuum.

Hence we may compare a precise definition of specific reading retardation which permits reliable assessment of incidence, with a variety of highly imprecise definitions of specific developmental dyslexia which have led to widely differing and speculative estimates ranging up to about 25 per cent of the population (Critchley 1970; Klasen 1972). Estimates of this type tend to be extrapolations based upon studies of clinic cases of severe reading disability rather than upon epidemiological studies.

However, it may be argued that a precise definition should be the goal and not the starting-point of a scientific inquiry. Advocates of dyslexia would claim that they are gradually moving towards a better definition of the phenomenon; opponents might suggest that their time could be better spent in trying to find effective remedial techniques to apply to the already-definable phenomenon of specific reading retardation.

Diagnosis of dyslexia
Specific reading retardation is, of course, not 'diagnosed' (in the accepted sense of the term); rather, it is assessed by means of appropriate psychological tests and statistical techniques. The World

Federation of Neurology definition of specific developmental dyslexia gives the impression that it, too, is assessed, firstly by means of an appropriate reading test and then by eliminating other potential (but non-dyslexic) causes of the reading difficulty. Although seemingly incongruous, dyslexia is sometimes assessed in this way, but naturally a dyslexic group thus constituted is something of an elite: poor, unintelligent, disadvantaged, or inadequately taught dyslexics don't exist in this scheme of things. More commonly, however, dyslexia is diagnosed on the basis of a variety of 'symptoms' or 'positive signs' of the disorder (see Singleton (1975) for a more detailed discussion of this).

Unfortunately, no one sign or group of signs may be regarded as definitive, and any sign or signs might appear in a non-dyslexic retarded reader or even in the occasional proficient reader and speller. Signs can also be of a transistory nature or inconsistent in their appearance. Thus dyslexia might be called a 'variable syndrome', the main characteristic of which is the clustering or coincidence of several signs together. Newton (1971), for example, lists some twenty positive signs of dyslexia which include perceptual, motor and language difficulties, anomalies of development (such as late speech or mixed-handedness), disordered spelling, lack of concentration, hyperactivity, low tolerance of frustration, accident proneness, and even 'seems "odd" – different from other children'. However, this list is accompanied by comments that the symptoms might only include *some* of the aforementioned behaviour patterns, and that *some* children with these behaviour patterns learn to read quite normally. No definition of any of the behaviour patterns is given, so parents or teachers (for whom this pamphlet is intended) must rely upon their own subjective judgment as to how numerous and how serious these signs need to be for any child to be labelled 'dyslexic'.

Miles (1974) suggests we think of dyslexia as a 'family' of difficulties. Whilst this may be regarded as medically respectable in some quarters, the point at which the cluster of signs is large enough to enable a positive diagnosis to be made is somewhat arbitrary, and, in any case, authorities disagree as to the relative importance to be assigned to different signs. The notion of a 'variable syndrome' also makes nonsense of the idea of dyslexia being a *specific* condition.

Some workers (for example, Miles 1974) try to combine the discrepancy criterion, which is inherent in the concept of specific reading retardation (i.e. a discrepancy between IQ and reading attainment), with the use of 'positive signs' to diagnose dyslexia. For example, confusion of left and right or of the letters 'b' and 'd' in a child of below-average intelligence would not be taken by Miles to be indicative of dyslexia, while the same symptoms in a bright child of only average educational attainment for his age, would be suggestive of dyslexia. There are two separate problems with this type of diagnosis.

The first problem is: how is intelligence to be assessed? Schiffman (1962) has shown that children with reading difficulties frequently obtain low scores on group tests of intelligence, scores which reflect their degree of reading disability rather than their intellectual potential. Thus the use of group tests is highly questionable. However, individual intelligence scales have also been criticized, particularly the verbal subtests of such scales. On the WISC, for example, the typical profile of the poor reader is substantially below average on information, arithmetic, digit span, and coding subtests, and (in some studies) below average on the vocabulary subtest also (Klasen 1972; Naidoo 1972). Miles advocates omitting these subtests when testing a child for the purposes of establishing a discrepancy, and obviously this would have the effect of increasing the number of children diagnosed as dyslexic, since subjects are only tested using those subtests of the WISC on which they might be expected to do well.

The second problem concerns the value of positive signs as diagnostic tools for discriminating dyslexic from non-dyslexic backward readers. That children with severe reading difficulties as a group generally display a variety of psychological, neurological, and developmental anomalies is not in dispute (Rutter, Tizard and Whitmore 1970). However, virtually all of these anomalies are cited as 'positive signs' of dyslexia by one 'authority' or another (see Critchley 1970; Miles 1974; Newton 1971). The proliferation of increasingly lengthy lists of positive signs of dyslexia can only serve to exacerbate this problem, since it has the effect of making the 'variable syndrome' even more variable and consequently less useful. What is surely required is a narrowing of the concept until it can sensibly delineate a truly specific condition with definite remedial implications, not a progressive widening until it becomes synonymous with 'reading difficulty' (the sense with which the term is now frequently used in the USA).

Ravenette (1968; 1971) has made the point that the presentation of specific developmental dyslexia is like a theme with variations where the theme is never formally stated, but has to be deduced from the context in which it appears. Recognition of the condition is consequently a rather private and personal matter, and it is not surprising that the concept has found little favour outside the medical profession where judgments of 'opinion' are accepted as commonplace.

The characteristics of children with specific reading retardation
Davis and Cashdan (1963) noted that there is little point in distinguishing children with specific reading retardation from the general group of backward readers unless the two groups are also distinguishable on criteria other than reading scores. In particular, the distinction needs to be meaningful in terms of matters such as

aetiology, prognosis, and educational treatment. In the Isle of Wight studies a distinction was drawn between specific reading retardation and general reading backwardness, the latter group being defined in terms of reading attainment at least twenty-eight months below *chronological* age level. A number of characteristic differences were found between these two groups (Rutter and Yule 1975). In the retarded group up to about one third were found to exhibit a variety of motor abnormalities (constructional difficulties, clumsiness, etc.), but a significantly greater proportion of the backward group exhibited these abnormalities, the figures being well over 50 per cent in some cases. Neurological disorder was also found to be significantly more common in the backward group

By contrast, both groups had roughly the same proportions of children with family histories of reading difficulties or of speech delay. Also, both groups had similar proportion of children who had exhibited delays in speech and language (about one third of children), although poor language complexity was found to be more frequent in the general reading backwardness group. Mainly on the basis of these differences, Rutter and Yule argue that the two categories can be meaningfully differentiated. General reading backwardness is associated with a variety of neurological and developmental abnormalities (including delays and defects in speech and language development), whilst (it is suggested) specific reading retardation is predominantly associated just with delays and defects in speech and language development. The authors comment: 'Reading retardation was associated to a *marked degree only* with abnormalities of speech and language development' (page 189; my italics). In another paper, Yule (1975) states unequivocally: 'We had to conclude that there were indeed qualitative differences between reading backwardness and specific retardation' (page 14). Examination of the figures shows that the appropriateness of the terms 'marked degree' and 'only' to be debatable, and the point at which *quantitative* differences between two groups may be interpreted as indicating an underlying *qualitative* difference between two conditions is open to dispute.

It must be admitted that there were two other important differences between the groups: a high incidence of boys in the specific reading retardation group, and relatively poorer prognosis of that group on measures of reading and spelling, but better prognosis of that group on arithmetic and mathematics (Yule 1973). However, it is not absolutely necessary to posit a special qualitatively different syndrome to account for these findings.

It is widely recognized that boys are more psychologically vulnerable than girls and are consequently much more likely to exhibit learning difficulties, personality and behaviour problems, stuttering and speech difficulties, and delinquency (Maccoby and Jacklin 1975). It is conceivable that since the reading backwardness group had a mean

IQ well below average, their reading difficulties stem largely from intellectual shortcomings, while the children in the specific reading retardation group (who were of roughly average intelligence) got into that group through high vunerability to stress or to other adverse influences. If that were the case one would naturally expect many more boys than girls in the latter group, and one would also expect these boys to be more likely to display maladjustment in their reaction to this educational failure and consequently to make less improvement in reading. Moreover, during adolescence boys tend to develop a superiority, on average, over girls in arithmetic and other mathematical tasks (Maccoby and Jacklin 1975), so it is not surprising that the predominantly male group have a better prognosis in this area at age fourteen-and-a-half years (the age at which they were retested).

My purpose here is not to discredit the concept of specific reading retardation, but to question the claim that sufficient differences have been established between that category and the category of general reading backwardness to enable the former to be pronounced a valid educational and/or medical concept at the present time. To return to the point made earlier, the distinction between the two groups also needs to be meaningful in terms of educational treatment, a task which yet remains (although the findings on prognosis indicate that the reading retarded child cannot be expected to make up ground *merely because* he is of average or above-average intelligence). In this respect, the concepts of dyslexia and specific reading retardation are both in the same boat: they both require demonstration of educational value sufficient to justify the diagnostic effort required.

Aetiology

Most authorities would agree that the concept of a constitutional condition is the *raison d'être* of dyslexia, although there is disagreement as to the relative importance of such potential aetiological factors as brain damage (whether clear-cut or 'minimal'), heredity, defective lateralization, or developmental delay (see Singleton (1976) for discussion). Controlled studies of backward, retarded, and 'dyslexic' readers have revealed a *diversity* rather than a clustering of disabilities within all these groups, suggesting multiple aetiology (Clark 1970; Naidoo 1972; Rutter *et al* 1970). Such studies have failed to delineate a pattern of developmental anomalies which might warrant the postulation of a single special syndrome and the name 'dyslexia'.

The evidence on specific reading retardation indicates that it is probably multi-factorially determined and may be due to failure in the normal maturation of certain specific functions of the cerebral cortex, *or* some neurological damage, *or* a lack of suitable environmental stimulation *or* a combination of all three (Rutter and Yule 1975). These factors also seem to interact with school influences, personality, and family background, as there is a strong association between reading retardation on the one hand, and on the other, large family size, high teacher turnover in schools, and poor concentration, restlessness and impulsiveness in the child (Rutter and Yule 1973). However, the issue of the 'specific' association of reading retardation with abnormalities of speech and language development (discussed in the previous section) is a crucial one, as Rutter and Yule (1975) have chosen to assign special aetiological importance to this association: 'It appears that language impairment (due to either some biological factor or environmental privation) renders the child at risk and that whether he actually shows reading retardation will depend also on his personality characteristics, the nature of his home environment and the quality of his schooling.' (page 193)

The relatively high incidence of reading and spelling difficulties and speech delay amongst the families of dyslexic children has been put forward by the advocates of dyslexia as one of the principle reasons for believing the condition to be an hereditary one (Critchley 1970; Miles 1974; Naidoo 1972), despite the fact that there are obvious non-hereditary explanations which could possibly account for this. Moreover, Critchley (1970) has confessed: 'We owe to genetics the most cogent single argument in support of the conception of a constitutional specific type of dyslexia' (page 89). It is therefore difficult to argue that specific reading retardation is merely an alternative term for dyslexia, for to do so would mean abandoning one of the major pieces of evidence commonly adduced for the constitutional basis of the disorder, since children with specific reading retardation were found to be no more likely to come from families with a history of such problems than were children with general reading backwardness (Rutter and Yule 1975).

Furthermore, specific reading retardation was found to be more than twice as common in London compared with the Isle of Wight (Berger, Yule and Rutter 1975) and the evidence strongly suggests environmental, rather than genetic causes for this difference. A relatively high proportion of London families experience marital discord and disruption, many of the parents show mental disorder and antisocial behaviour, families often live in poor social circumstances, and London schools are more often characterized by a high rate of turnover in staff and pupils (Rutter *et al* 1975). These findings reinforce the conclusion that specific reading retardation cannot be equated with dyslexia so long as the latter is defined in constitutional terms.

Some suggestions for the direction of future research
To date, neither dyslexia nor specific reading retardation have been shown to be educationally useful concepts in terms of practical implications for remedial teaching. With both there is a real danger that attention may be diverted away from less able children who are

backward in reading because of the assumption that children of below-average intelligence can only be expected to read at a low level (Miles (1967) for example, makes this assumption). Of course, this is a social as well as an educational problem, and it is a matter of opinion whether priorities lie in trying to raise all children in normal schools to a level of reading performance which is adequate for living and working in our society, or, rather, in trying to ensure that bright children are not academically handicapped by possessing only average reading skills.

The conviction of some sort of constitutional disability remains strong amongst neurologists and some other researchers. Critchley (1970) asserts that 'neurologists believe that within the community of poor readers there exists a hard core of cases where the origins of the learning defect are inborn and independent of any intellectual shortcomings which may happen to co-exist' (page 102). Neither the concept of specific reading retardation nor any concept of dyslexia in which the discrepancy criterion is an inherent feature, can help to shed much light on this central problem, since such concepts are not independent of the factor of intelligence.

Typically, researchers have approached this problem in a very diffuse way, trying to note all the myriad features of the very poor reader in the reading clinic, rather than trying to pin down the fundamental deficit in a scientifically controlled manner. How then, ought research on this matter of a constitutional disorder to proceed? The approach of generating increasingly extensive diagnostic batteries for 'dyslexic-type difficulties' is arguably not an ideal research strategy, since this has the effect of widening rather than narrowing the concept of dyslexia, making the task of relating symptoms to specific remedial treatment even more difficult. Whilst any diagnostic test can be of potential value to the teacher, there is little point in conducting an elaborate screening procedure unless you have appropriate facilities and techniques for treating those found to be at risk; at the present time such facilities and techniques do not exist, apart from the normal educational provision which the child will receive anyway.

The approach of exploring the ramifications of vague hypothetical constructs such as 'cerebral dominance' would appear to be equally fruitless in the search for a clear underlying pattern in dyslexia. Not only is the concept of cerebral dominance just as contentious and confused as that of dyslexia (in which case one is led from one scientific quagmire into another), but also there is the real problem of what significance, exactly, should be attached to the supposed manifestations of failure to establish dominance (for example, inconsistent lateral preferences, confusion over left and right, etc.). To accommodate the further problem that the vast majority of ill-lateralized children learn to read quite normally (Zangwill 1962), vague qualifying factors such as stress or minimal brain damage tend to be introduced, despite the fact that these only serve to make the 'variable syndrome' yet more variable.

To be of educational value, the concept of dyslexia must be *narrowed down* to refer to some *fundamental deficit* which is empirically and experimentally substantiated and has clear implications for remedial teaching. Thus the sensible alternative for research is the examination of reasonable hypotheses which can yield clear predictions that are testable by experimentation. Some examples of hypotheses regarding the fundamental deficit in dyslexia which meet this criterion are: inability to retain complex information over time (Miles and Wheeler 1974), lack of visual, egocentric frame of reference (Richardson 1974), inability to grasp sequential relationships (Vernon 1971), and inappropriate saccadic eye movements in reading (Dossetor and Papaioannou 1976; Rubino and Minden 1973; Zangwill and Blakemore 1972). (Note that these hypotheses are framed in terms of *performance deficits*.) In such research it is important to compare 'dyslexics' not only with normal readers but also with the range of backward and retarded readers in order to establish that the distinction is a valid one. Most studies make only the former comparison, which by itself is not very helpful. It is also necessary to discover whether there are some children who exhibit the particular 'fundamental deficit' under experimental scrutiny who are nevertheless able to read satisfactorily, and, if such children do exist, what the reasons are for their apparent immunity. Finally, to be educationally worthwhile, any hypothesis about reading difficulty, whether constitutionally based or not, must pass the test of being relatable in some meaningful way to teaching (in the widest sense), and this should surely be the ultimate goal of most scientific research on this subject.

References

ADAMS, R. B. (1969) Dyslexia: a discussion of its definition *Journal of Learning Disabilities* 2, 616–33

BERGER, M., YULE, W. and RUTTER, M. (1975) Attainment and adjustment in two geographical areas: II – The prevalence of specific reading retardation *British Journal of Psychiatry* 126, 510–9

BURT, C. (1937) *The backward child* University of London Press

CLARK, M. M. (1970) *Reading difficulties in schools* Penguin

CRITCHLEY, M. (1970) *The dyslexic child* Heinemann

DAVIS, R. D. and CASHDAN, A. (1963) Specific dyslexia *British Journal of Educational Psychology*, 33, 80–2

DES (1972) *Children with Specific Reading Difficulties* (Report of the Advisory Committee on Handicapped Children under the Chairmanship of Professor Jack Tizard) HMSO

DES (1975) *A Language for Life* (Bullock Report) HMSO

DOSSETOR, D. R. and PAPAIOANNOU, J. (1976) Dyslexia and eye

movements *Language and Speech* 18, 312–7
FRANSELLA, F. and GERVER, D. (1965) Multiple regression equations for predicting reading age from chronological age and WISC verbal IQ *British Journal of Educational Psychology* 35, 86–9
KEENEY, A. H. and V. T. (1968) *Dyslexia: Diagnosis and Treatment of Reading Disorders* New York: C. V. Mosby
KLASEN, E. (1972) *The Syndrome of Specific Dyslexia* Medical and Technical Publishing Company
MACCOBY, E. E. and JACKLIN, C. N. (1975) *The psychology of sex differences* Oxford University Press
MILES, T. R. (1967) 'In defence of the concept of dyslexia' in J. Downing and A. L. Brown (eds) *The Second International Reading Symposium* Cassell
MILES, T. R. (1974) *The Dyslexic Child* Priory Press
MILES, T. R. and WHEELER, T. J. (1974) Towards a new theory of dyslexia *Dyslexia Review* 11, 9–11
NAIDOO, S. (1972) *Specific Dyslexia* Pitman
NEWTON, M. (1971) *Dyslexia: a guide for teachers and parents* University of Aston, Birmingham
RAVENETTE, A. T. (1968) *Dimensions of Reading Difficulties* Pergamon Press
RAVENETTE, A. T. (1971) The concept of 'dyslexia': some reservations *Acta Paedopsychiatrica* 38, 105–10
REID, J. F. (1969) Dyslexia: a problem of communication *Educational Research* 10, 126–33
RICHARDSON, G. (1974) The Cartesian frame of reference: a structure unifying the description of dyslexia *Journal of Psycholinguistic Research* 3, 15–63
RUBINO, C. A. and MINDEN, H. T. (1973) An analysis of eye-movements in children with a reading disability *Cortex* 9, 217–20
RUTTER M., TIZARD, J. and WHITMORE, K. (eds) (1970) *Education, Health and Behaviour* Longman
RUTTER, M. and YULE, W. (1973) 'Specific reading retardation' In L. Mann and D. Sabatino (eds) *The First Review of Special Education* New York: Grune and Stratton
RUTTER, M. and YULE, W. (1975) The concept of specific reading retardation *Journal of Child Psychology and Psychiatry* 16, 181–97
RUTTER, M., YULE, B., QUINTON, D., ROWLANDS, O., YULE W. and BERGER, M. (1975) Attainment and adjustment in two geographical areas: III – Some factors accounting for area differences *British Journal of Psychiatry* 126, 520–33
SCHIFFMAN, G. (1962) 'Dyslexia as an educational phenomenon: its recognition and treatment' in J. Money (ed) *Reading Disability* Baltimore: Johns Hopkins Press
SCHONELL, F. J. (1942) *Backwardness in the basic subjects* Oliver and Boyd

273

SINGLETON, C. H. (1975) The myth of specific developmental dyslexia: I – History, incidence and diagnosis of the syndrome *Remedial Education* 10, 109–13

SINGLETON, C. H. (1976) The myth of specific developmental dyslexia: II – Aetiology *Remedial Education* 11, 13–17

VERNON, M. D. (1971) *Reading and its Difficulties* Cambridge University Press

YULE, W. (1967) Predicting reading ages on Neale's analysis of reading ability *British Journal of Educational Psychology* 37, 252–5

YULE, W. (1973) Differential prognosis of reading backwardness and specific reading retardation *British Journal of Educational Psychology* 43, 244–8

YULE, W. (1975) 'Dyslexia' or 'Specific reading retardation'? Labels do matter! *Dyslexia Review* 13, 11–15

YULE, W., RUTTER, M., BERGER, M. and THOMPSON, J. (1974) Over- and under-achievement in reading: distribution in the general population *British Journal of Educational Psychology* 44, 1–12

ZANGWILL, O. L. (1962) 'Dyslexia in relation to cerebral dominance' in J. Money (ed) *Reading Disability* Baltimore: Johns Hopkins Press

ZANGWILL, O. L. and BLAKEMORE, C. (1972) Dyslexia: reversal of eye-movements during reading *Neuropsychologia* 10, 371–3

30 Attitudes to reading failure

James M. Ewing

Introduction

The field of attitudes to reading has received less attention in general than other aspects of reading, such as reading skills, reading materials, standards of performance etc. Consequently, the topic of attitudes to reading failure has attracted even less attention. There are, in fact, very few references in modern texts and journals to the study of attitudes to reading failure and the articles which do appear originate mainly in America.

The investigation described here is primarily aimed at documenting the views and attitude held by three categories of person to reading failure: the pupils, their teachers and their parents.

The method of assessing these views is informal and involves a structured interview for the pupils and questionnaires for teachers and parents. While the findings of the investigation described here support some of the widely-held impressions about reading failure, they indicate at least one area, i.e. of pupil anxiety, where teachers' views of the pupils may well be out of touch with reality.

According to Pumfrey (1976) there are three main sources of information about attitudes to reading: informal observation, standardized tests and criterion-referenced tests. Of the tests of attitudes to reading which Pumfrey mentions only three are British, *viz* Dunham Attitude to Reading Scale, Georgiades Attitude to Reading Scale, and Williams Attitude to Reading Scale. They are all adequately described in an earlier article by Pumfrey and Dixon (1970). None of these is commerically available. Each is a standardized test of attitudes to be used with children in the eight to ten year age range, but none is specifically about reading problems.

It is widely held that attitudes to reading and reading attainment are closely related. Therefore using an attitude test with children who have serious reading difficulties might expect to produce predominantly 'low' attitude scores, on standardized tests. Although that information itself is useful and valuable, the present investigation is aimed at documenting some self-expressed views about reading using fairly open-minded techniques.

Design of the investigation

Having decided to use, for this largely unexplored area, fresh questionnaires and schedules rather than standardized or criterion-referenced tests, four schedules were prepared:

Form A Structured interview guide (pupil interview)
Form B Teacher questionnaire (individual pupil)
Form C Teacher questionnaire (reading failure)
Form D Parent questionnaire (separate forms for parents of primary and secondary children)

Form A   Pupil form

The pupil form was constructed to assess the views of pupils about their own difficulties with reading, how these difficulties were helped, the day-to-day problems of not being able to read well, and some idea of the need to read well after leaving school. A reading achievement test (Schonell Word Recognition Test) was administered along with the interview.

Form B   Teacher questionnaire (individual pupil)

An attempt was made to document any relationship between the teacher's view of the child, and the child's own view of reading failure. The teachers were therefore asked to comment on each of their pupils in the sample on a variety of factors ranging from pupil independence and classroom behaviour to the amount of help each required in class. The teachers were also asked to assess the standard of performance of each sample pupil.

Form C   Teacher questionnaire (reading failure)

The teacher's form about the general topic of reading failure covers views on the influence of poor readers on the rest of the class, and how best these problems may be tackled. This form also asked for candid opinions about how well informed teachers thought they were about the nature of reading difficulties, and their own views on how the school organization should tackle reading failure.

Form D   Parent questionnaire

The parents' form asks parents to identify reading difficulties and to judge whether their own child may have such difficulties. Frank views about the causes and handling of reading problems are then requested together with the parents' views on their own role in helping to overcome these difficulties.

The narrow age range of tests and questionnaires in the area of attitude to reading, evidenced in Pumfrey's documentation, was borne in mind. This investigation set out to construct questionnaires and interview schedules which could be used over an age range of eight to fifteen years. The only exception was the parents' questionnaire where separate forms were found necessary for parents of primary-school and secondary-school pupils.

Student involvement

The administration of the interviews and the issue of the questionnaires was carried out by a number of university graduates undergoing a one-year training course at Dundee College of Education. Each had just completed a term's course in individual pupil assessment where practice in administering intelligence tests and reading tests had been given.

The sample

One major difficulty in the investigation was to identify a sample of pupils who could be defined as experiencing reading failure, particularly across a wide age range.

In the first instance, therefore, the schools involved were asked to select the children judged to be 'very backward in reading' or to 'have serious difficulties with reading'.

Each pupil was given a reading test as part of the interview and this served as a check on the degree of each child's backwardness.

The sample consisted of 118 pupils from below eight years to over sixteen years of age. The distribution of pupils over that age range is shown in Table 1.

Table 1

Age distribution of sample

Age	Number
Under 8 years	1
8 – 9	7
9 – 10	20
10 – 11	12
11 – 12	13
12 – 13	19
13 – 14	27
14 – 15	11
15 – 16	7
Over 16	1
Total sample	118

The reading standard of each of these pupils was measured using the Schonell Word Recognition Test and the distribution of the reading ages is given in Table 2.

Table 2

Reading ages of sample

Reading age	Number
Below 6 years	2
6 – 7	10
7 – 8	36
8 – 9	49
9 – 10	13
10 – 11	5
11 – 12	3
Total sample	118

As would be expected, the bulk of the reading ages are below nine years. Perhaps a little surprisingly, rather few are below the seven year level. This finding may reinforce the widely-held view among reading teachers that children with reading difficulties appear to 'stick' at about the seven to eight year reading level. This view still seems true as far as mean reading age is concerned, for a sample ranging from <8 to >16 years of age, as Figure 1 shows.

Figure 1

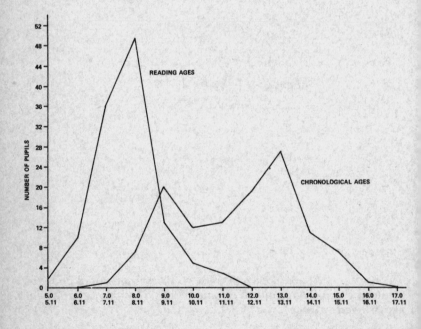

278

The distribution of the amount of backwardness in reading across the age range of the sample (Figure 2, below) follows a clear-cut pattern. The trend is probably an expected one: that older children with reading difficulties show an even greater gap between chronological age and reading age than younger children. This is expected, perhaps, on the basis of a 'constant ratio' between chronological age and reading age.

Figure 2

AMOUNT OF BACKWARDNESS BY CHRONOLOGICAL AGE

AMOUNT OF BACKWARDNESS IN MONTHS

CHRONOLOGICAL AGE IN YEARS AND MONTHS (Yrs/mths)	0 to 11 months	12 to 23 months	24 to 35 months	36 to 47 months	48 to 59 months	60 to 71 months	72 to 83 months	84 to 95 months
BELOW 8 0		1						
8 0 to 8 11	2	3	2	1				
9 0 to 9 11	1	11	5	3				
10 0 to 10 11	1	2	6	2				
11 0 to 11 11		1	3	8	1	1		
12 0 to 12 11		1	4	4	7	2	1	
13 0 to 13 11		1	1	1	6	14	4	
14 0 to 14 11					1	6	3	1
15 0 to 15 11						1	3	2
16 0 to 16 11							1	

The implications of this trend, however, are fundamental to the current philosophy of remedial education. Perhaps, the question is raised as to whether remedial education is really working! The older children become, the more backward they seem to be! It is certainly true that positive remedial work is set against this background and makes the task of those teachers at secondary level rather different from those at primary-school level. For instance, the bulk of the secondary pupils in the sample show over five years' reading retardation.

Each school clearly has different standards by which 'serious reading difficulties' are established, and the distribution in Figure 2 (page 279) shows that some of the pupils are not seriously retarded in reading. By applying a 'cut-off' of a minimum backwardness of twelve months for all children under ten, of two years for all children between ten and twelve years of age, of three years for all children between twelve and fourteen years of age and five years for all children over fifteen years of age, the sample would be reduced by fifteen (indicated by the broad line in Figure 2). Because these children have been defined by the school as having 'serious reading difficulty' it seems correct to keep them in the sample.

Results of the investigation
It was considered important to document how pupils, identified by the school as having serious reading difficulties, actually perceived their own standard of reading. Two of the questions asked therefore were:

1   Do you think you are a good reader?
2   Do you find any difficulties with your reading at school?

It can be argued, and often is, that pupil self-concepts might well reflect the views of teachers or parents of their reading ability. It is interesting to note therefore that in answer to question 1, 58 per cent of the sample categorized themselves as not being good readers and in reply to question 2, 66 per cent of the sample admitted to having reading difficulties in school. More strikingly, however, 42 per cent of the sample described themselves as being good readers, while 34 per cent stated that they had no undue reading difficulties.

Self-judgments such as these may well be a reflection of what poor readers feel they ought to say. If this is true, it may indicate that a poor reader's self-image is a result of what his teacher, his parent, his peers or his siblings think and possibly say. His expressed opinion, however, especially to an external interviewer, might well reflect an ideal self-image far removed from 'reality' as seen by the teacher, or even the same pupil in the classroom. Nevertheless, the intriguing question remains: are there, as the figures seem to indicate, some pupils, categorized by the teacher as backward readers, who genuinely see themselves as having no difficulties?

In view of the different possible interpretations of pupils' responses to these questions, it seems obvious that a future investigation would have to probe much more deeply.

A core difficulty, in this area, therefore, is that of assessing validity of pupil response. This is further exemplified below.

Perceived reading difficulties after leaving school

A further question asked was: Do you think you will find reading easy or difficult after you leave school? Only 30 per cent of the sample answered that they thought they would have difficulties. It is hard to assess from these results just how realistic poor readers are capable of being about their own difficulties. There is a clear indication that their view of the present time is different from their view of a few years ahead.

It could be argued that children generally are unable to view realistically their situation a few years ahead, and this might be particularly true of poor readers. This is an important consideration for remedial teachers, especially at the secondary-school level.

The responses, however, may well indicate a more fundamental feature of 'reality' as perceived both by the pupils and by their peers and elders, of how appropriate are school instruction and progress therein, to living and functioning outside school. It was not within the scope of this investigation to probe much further into this area, apart from asking pupils' views of the place of reading after school days. This important area of how meaningful school experiences are to the poor pupil after he has left school remains largely unexplored here.

Post-school reading requirements

The percepts of poor readers of post-school reading requirements were assessed by asking the questions indicated:

(a)   Do you think people read as much when they have left school as when they were still at school?

The results of question (a) are given in Figure 3 (page 282) and clearly indicate that most of the sample consider less reading to be done after leaving school than at school. This is probably an indication that these pupils perceive reading to be school-oriented and possibly instruction-oriented. It would be very useful to know just how much less reading these pupils think is involved in post-school life. It would also be interesting to have an objective measure of how much reading activity actually takes place both within school and after school. Just how realistic the views of the sample as shown in Figure 3 are might then become clearer.

(b)   Do you think people need to be able to read at work?
(c)   Do you think people need to be able to read at home?

In response to question (b), 90 per cent of the sample, and in response to question (c), 82 per cent of the sample thought that people need to read at work and at home. Without ignoring the expected majorities, one interesting aspect of these figures is that some of the sample felt that people did not need to be able to read for work or at home. A corollary of this would again be an objective measure of how many people actually do not read at work or at home. It certainly is a widely-held belief amongst educators that everyone needs to be able to read, yet some 18 per cent of poor readers in this sample see no need for it at home. There may be a connection between this finding and the slant of much of our established views about reading. It again reinforces the view that reading is seen as more important as a school activity than as an out-of-school activity.

Pupil attitudes to reported difficulties
The feelings of pupils about their difficulties with reading are hard to assess. In this investigation much of the evidence has been gathered by posing simple but straightforward questions such as: How much do you enjoy reading at school? The responses were broadly categorized into

Figure 3

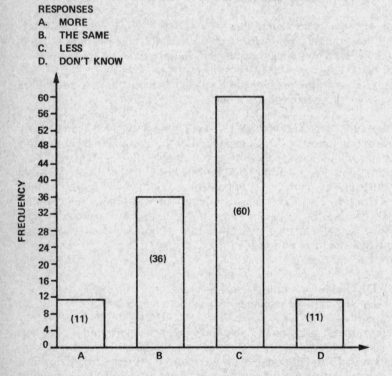

DO YOU THINK PEOPLE READ AS MUCH WHEN THEY HAVE LEFT SCHOOL AS WHEN THEY WERE STILL AT SCHOOL?

RESPONSES
A. MORE
B. THE SAME
C. LESS
D. DON'T KNOW

those who enjoyed reading and those who did not. While 45 per cent of the former answered, 'A lot', 73 per cent of the latter group replied, 'Not very much' or 'Very little'. Just less than two thirds of the sample claimed not to enjoy reading.

Each member of the group was asked to suggest why he felt this way. It became clear that a large number of those who did not enjoy reading felt this way because of an embarrassment or fear of ridicule. This feeling was by far the most commonly expressed, and it was also reported by the majority of the students in their reports on the interviews. There appears to be a genuine feeling of unease or embarrassment among poor readers. Many of them have an even greater fear of being mocked by their peers. This very real feeling of apprehension may not be appreciated by many class teachers and it certainly mitigates real progress in a classroom for these backward readers.

As a further indication of the pupils' feelings about their difficulties, each was asked: Does anyone make it easier for you with your reading? A variety of alternatives was given and the responses are shown in Figure 4 (page 284). Although the teacher is the most popular choice, the parents are chosen surprisingly often. In a sense this reveals something about how poor readers feels they are being helped. They attach considerable significance to the help given by their own parents. It would be useful to know if as much help as is indicated is actually given by parents. At a later stage in the present investigation an attempt at documenting this is made, but with a very much reduced sample. The apparent importance attached to the part played by parents has considerable significance for school and teacher practices.

Yet in very many schools, parents are seen to play little part in helping backward readers, perhaps for a variety of reasons: uncooperative parents, lack of material at home, lack of ability in parents, or a school decision that extra teaching should be the function of the teacher. At a later stage in this investigation some questions were asked of the teachers about parental involvement. Many seemed to suggest that such involvement was desirable, but in very few cases did it appear to happen.

Teachers' views

Although the larger part of this investigation has documented the views of poor readers about their own reading, some attention was given to the teachers of these pupils. Each class teacher and remedial teacher at primary-school level, and the English teacher and the remedial teacher at secondary school, were asked to fill in two forms. One asked for the teacher's views about an individual pupil in the sample, while the other was concerned with the teacher's feelings towards the teaching of remedial reading.

The teachers were asked to assess how true several statements might

Figure 4

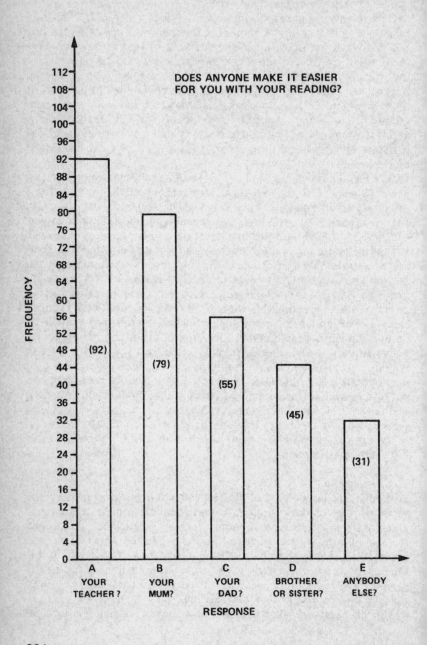

be when applied to each individual pupil in the sample. The statements referred, among other aspects, to the child being a good mixer in class, independent, full of life, disruptive in class, a pleasure to teach, obedient, responsive, etc. The responses to one of these statements – the child being a pleasure to teach – are given below:

As a pupil in class this child is a pleasure to teach

(a) Class teachers		(b) Remedial teachers
9	Certainly true	40
42	May sometimes be true	63
11	Certainly not true	6

Fewer of the class teachers completed forms for the sample pupils, but on most occasions the remedial teacher did. Even with a shortage of class-teacher responses, there appears from the above figures to be a marked difference (significant at 1 per cent level – chi square) between the judgment of the two types of teacher about the same pupils being a pleasure to teach. This leads to some important suggestions:

1 Often pupils with reading difficulties are seen as *other than* 'a pleasure to teach'.
2 Nevertheless, remedial teachers, both primary and secondary, see a significantly higher proportion of these pupils as 'a pleasure to teach' than do class teachers.

One implication of this finding is that children with serious difficulties are more likely to be easier to teach in remedial groups than in normal classes.

This also raises further questions. Are children no longer a pleasure to teach because they are seriously retarded in reading? *Or* do such children become more retarded because they are not a pleasure to teach? These questions may appear facile. The issues are complex, and no easy answers are available.

Earlier, some documentation of pupil reaction to their situation was given, indicating embarrassment, or feelings of uneasiness. Now it becomes clear that teachers also do not find every pupil altogether a pleasure. At the very least this combination of teacher and pupil attitudes in the classroom seems likely to operate against educational progress. At most, the combination could reflect the tenor of the latter question.

This investigation also set out to document some of the views teachers hold about backward readers with a view to establishing relationships between teacher and pupil attitudes. The teachers were therefore asked to judge how much of a problem various aspects of reading difficulty were to each child. There was a high degree of agreement between class teachers and remedial teachers as is shown in the example in Table 3.

Table 3 Teachers' views of identification of pupils' reading difficulty

Responses to 'Pupil resents identification of reading difficulty'

Category of teacher	A major problem	Only one problem among others	Not a problem
Class teachers	0	16	42
Remedial teachers	13	28	68

The responses are particularly interesting when compared with the corresponding area in the pupil interview. From the results shown in Table 3, it would appear that many class teachers and remedial teachers consider that backward readers' resentment of their identification just doesn't happen and therefore is not a problem, or that it does happen (i.e. they do resent being identified as backward readers), but that it is relatively unimportant. This contrasts markedly with the pupils' own views where they were most consistent in voicing fears and embarrassment at being identified in class as backward readers. It may be, therefore, that both class teachers and remedial teachers should consider again how their pupils feel about being identified as very poor in their own group.

Are teachers professionally informed?
The teachers were also asked to assess themselves in terms of being professionally informed about reading difficulties, (a) as a result of pre-service training; (b) from general inservice training; (c) from specialist inservice training, and (d) from their own reading. The results of this are shown below:

Class teachers

	Considerably informed	Slightly informed	Virtually uninformed
A	1	23	7
B	0	10	11
C	0	2	13
D	3	20	5

Remedial teachers

	Considerably informed	Slightly informed	Virtually uninformed
A	7	10	5
B	9	9	3
C	22	3	1
D	21	4	0

There were sixty-seven teachers altogether in the sample, thirty-eight of them being class teachers and the remaining twenty-nine being remedial teachers. Not all replied to each of the four possibilities, but the pattern which emerges is very clear. Remedial teachers consider themselves to be more informed than do class teachers about reading difficulties, even from their pre-service training. The general inservice training also appears to have been more fruitful in this area for remedial teachers than for class teachers, even though it could be argued that general inservice work is the most likely way in which class teachers can become more attuned to the needs of the backward reader. It is interesting to note, therefore, that the source of information most useful to class teachers is their own reading. The overall picture from these results must have some implications for those concerned with pre-service and inservice training of teachers.

A tentative summary of parents' views
Finally, an attempt was made to find out what parents felt about reading problems. Because this is a rather more 'sensitive' area, only a few schools were approached in the first instance. The result was that a simple questionnaire form was sent home to the parents of twenty-four of the sample pupils – twelve from primary-school level and twelve from secondary-school level. Only twelve forms were returned, and it is unwise to make any general statements about the outcomes. What can be said is that there is wide variation in the views which parents hold about the reading difficulties of their own children. Some parents accept that there are difficulties, others deny them; some parents think these difficulties will disappear with time, others that they may well be present for a long time; some parents feel they should be involved themselves in giving extra help, while others think it is entirely up to the school.

Summary and conclusions
This investigation sought to explore, by interview and questionnaire, the hitherto largely neglected area of 'attitude to reading failure', as revealed by pupils, teachers and parents. The topic is not only interesting, but pedagogically vital in that the Affective aspect (Bloom, Hastings and Madaus 1971) is a vital component of all learning.

Problems of the investigation
The investigation described here is basically an initial exploration revealing procedural difficulties as well as possible findings.

The informal approach has limitations in its use, although it provides some useful responses.

The problem of the validity of pupil responses remains a difficult one. It is significant that 42 per cent of the sample stated that they were at least average readers while 34 per cent did not admit to having persistent reading difficulties in school. There may be a category of pupils labelled by teachers as having reading difficulties but not personally conscious of this. The techniques used in this investigation may not necessarily have identified such a group as the face-to-face interview situation may affect responses in an unwarranted positive direction. Perhaps pupils are aware of an ideal self-concept in public and this includes 'no reading difficulties'.

Obviously more refined techniques would be required to seek more valid responses, perhaps incorporating an anonymous questionnaire with more detailed and probing questions.

A further difficulty, recognized from the outset, was contacting parents. Although only a few responses were obtained, the methods used were modestly successful. The help of the schools in issuing and collecting parental questionnaires is vital and required a careful cooperation with the headteachers. Only four schools in the present study were approached and three agreed to participate. In a future study all schools would be approached in the interests of obtaining a larger, although admittedly only fractional parents' sample.

Summary of the findings
1   A significant minority of the sample pupils, labelled by the school as 'having serious reading difficulties', stated that they had few or no reading problems.
2   The majority of the sample did not think they would have reading problems after they left school.
3   The majority considered that people read much less after they leave school.
4   Most, but not all, of the sample thought people needed to be able to read both at home and at work.
5   Almost two-thirds of the sample claimed not to enjoy reading at school, often because of embarrassment at being identified as poor readers.
6   While the sample indicated teachers as those giving most help with reading difficulties, parents were also seen by a majority as important in helping with reading.
7   Only a minority of the pupils were seen as 'a pleasure to teach' by teachers, although the remedial teachers accorded this description more often than class teachers.
8   By and large, teachers did not see that it was a problem for pupils to be identified in class as poor readers. This view contrasts markedly with the pupils' own views.
9   Remedial teachers considered themselves to be more informed professionally about the nature of reading difficulties than did class teachers. As a considerable amount of this information came from teachers' 'own reading', there appears to be room for a provision of more information in pre-service and inservice courses.

10 The small sample of parents (twelve) varied tremendously in their response. An initial impression is that some parents of such pupils are quite literate and eager to express their views.

Conclusion
This paper is based on selected findings from the investigation. A computer analysis of all the data collected is currently being undertaken. The indications from the data presented in this report are that 'attitudes to reading failure', although not easy to document, are in a rewarding area deserving further investigation.

References
BLOOM, B. S., HASTINGS, J. T. and MADAUS, G. F. (1971) *Handbook on Formative and Summative Evaluation of Student Learning* New York: McGraw Hill

PUMFREY, P. D. (1976) *Reading: Tests and Assessment Techniques* Hodder and Stoughton

PUMFREY, P. D. and DIXON, E. (1970) Junior children's attitudes to reading: comments on three measuring instruments *Reading* 4, 2, 19-26

31 Organization for remedial work in the secondary school

David Williams

The problem

'It is our central contention . . . that the provision of special help should be an automatic sequel to a screening and diagnostic programme.' (Bullock Report 17.3).

Benfield is an 11-18, ten-form entry, coeducational, urban comprehensive. Children come from a number of junior schools and we regard it as important that we build up as detailed a picture as possible about individual difficulties. During March, all prospective entrants are tested in their junior schools with a non-verbal IQ test and a reading comprehension test. The results are used to put children in mixed-ability classes, but the latter test has a screening function.

Most of the junior schools operate their own assessment system and detailed information is passed on when HOD Remedial visits them. The contact and feedback is via both verbal and written reports and is mutually beneficial.

Other important sources of information are as follows:

1 the LEA record card
2 remedial service reports
3 child guidance reports
4 contact with parents.

When the child gets to Benfield we already know a great deal about likely problems. On entry, all children attempt a standard reading test, write a few lines in their 'best' writing and write a few sentences in their own words. It is fairly easy to tell from these tests whether or not a child is going to have difficulties with reading, writing or spelling.

All children with a reading age of less than ten, or who have writing or spelling problems or were taught by the remedial service, or needed special help in their junior school, are interviewed by members of the department, in order to:

1 assess the extent of the child's difficulties
2 discover the child's interests and reading habits

3   establish the beginnings of a good, supportive teacher-pupil relationship

4   to persuade the child to look realistically at his problems.

Once we have identified the children who need help, we offer to withdraw them from English lessons for varying amounts of time. (Some children may be withdrawn from other lessons as well.)

Withdrawal is voluntary. We believe that compulsion is no aid to motivation and puts teacher and pupil in opposite camps. We realize that both our efforts and those of the child will fail if reading is only regarded as a 'school'-based activity.

Resources

At the mention of 'resources', most people would automatically think of books and equipment. My most important resources are the teachers who staff the department. They are crucial because success or failure often depends upon the relationship between child and teacher. We attempt to teach children as individuals and the teacher not only provides sympathy and support, but also modifies the general approach to deal with individual difficulties. It is the teacher's job to engineer successful experiences for the child and to provide him with feedback on his progress. Staff need:

1   sufficient time to prepare work
2   time and opportunity to discuss children
3   time and opportunity to discuss teaching problems
4   access to specialist advice
5   encouragement to evaluate self and work
6   opportunities to go on inservice courses (though I think much more is to be gained by visiting other schools and talking to teachers about their work).

It is very important that all staff working in the remedial department should be volunteers. At present, more staff want to work in the department than we can take.

Almost any human resource is valuable and we get help from students, sixth-formers and also encourage older slow readers to help the younger ones. (The act of ensuring that they keep one step ahead provides motivation, but such methods need close supervision.)

Finally, books, newspapers, comics, pop literature, magazines, functional signs and pupil-generated materials are all resources for reading. In my experience, machines do not justify the amount of time or money invested in them. (I exclude television, radio, tape recorders and typewriters from the last statement – they are useful and easily operated.)

In summary, my staff are a vital resource because they modify the general approach to the needs of the individual child.

The teaching framework

For the non-reader, we combine phonic training with a 'key words' approach. The child works on autobiographical material which is presented to him in many different ways. We develop a sight vocabulary based on the child's immediate needs. Almost all reading, writing and spelling is based on these words.

Once we feel confident of the child's success, we let the child read a basic reader. Usually we use *The Old House* (Inner Ring Series) – a simple, stark and realistic story. We try and ensure that the child reads the whole of the book at one sitting. This necessitates a 1:1 relationship; it is important that we avoid frustration and make the first book a pleasurable and successful experience.

Once the child can read Inner Ring and parallel series, phonics and whole words become less important. We concentrate on reading for meaning. We encourage fluency and comprehension. We encourage the prediction of word order and event sequencing and predicition. Above all, we encourage the child to review as he reads and hope to get to the point where the child recognizes his own errors and is able to correct them.

Relationships

The voluntary nature of the child's initial commitment sets the tone of the relationship with the teacher. Our approach is 'low key'; we recognize that reading failure has its emotional concomitants (and causes), and if a child comes to us in a disturbed state we are sympathetic and understanding, but we insist that they do not opt out. We avoid confrontation if at all possible. The understanding that hard work is expected is important in building up self-respect in the child, and a feeling of achievement is produced by repeated successful experiences. We feel that it is vital we be honest with the child over progress and problems, otherwise the child will not be able to assess himself in a realistic way.

It is necessary to stress that once the child has contracted to receive help, there's no backing out until we are satisfied that he can cope and will progress in normal English lessons. Usually, the return to normal English is gradual and the child's progress is followed up by remedial staff. We try to make return to lessons the cachet of maturity and success. Not all children accept this and some prefer the sympathetic, individually-based work of the department – but if the child is 'ready' to go back, the umbilical cord has to be severed!

Flexibility and evaluation

No organization should be static. Flexibility of organization, methods, criteria and relationship is vital. Both the extent and the nature of the problems may alter. Criteria may change. Methods may alter. Thus we are never dogmatic; there is no best way of teaching reading, writing and spelling.

We keep a cumulative record of each child's work and progress. Staff are expected to comment on the record sheets when they hear children read.

We evaluate our work in a number of ways: firstly, by testing children at yearly intervals; secondly, by looking at the child's performance in normal lessons. If, in the opinion of the class teacher, the child can cope successfully, then we've done our job. Thirdly, if we succeed in motivating the child to make a regular practice of reading at home, if only to find out what's on the television or who's in the local football team, we can be fairly confident of the child's future.

Responsibility

Responsible teachers should be self-aware and self-critical. A responsible department should constantly evaluate its overall performance and seek ways of improving its standards.

The department is accountable to the headmaster, to the governors, to the parents, to other staff, but above all to the children who are being helped. After all, if the children fulfil their part of the teaching contract, they are entitled to an improvement that is apparent to all. It is the remedial department's job to work to that end.

Note

The department has five full-time teachers, including two with a small commitment to other subjects, two part-time teachers, and three teachers offering a total of seven-and-a-half hours per week. It occupies six small classrooms; includes two units for disruptive children, although the term 'disruptive' is liberally interpreted; offers help to children with difficulties in reading, writing, spelling and number. We can teach the non-English speaker. We do offer to help children with learning difficulties in academic subjects.

32 Encouraging language development in slow learners

Richard Binns and Morag Hunter

In any secondary-school mixed-ability class there are likely to be some slower learners and amongst them there may be pupils who have great difficulty in reading, if indeed they attempt to read at all. These pupils are likely to have difficulty in a variety of areas of learning, including written language; yet in many school situations there will be little chance that they can be provided with individual help.

The workshop was intended to offer insights into teaching such pupils within the total context of the mixed-ability class. Participants in the workshop were provided with illustrated materials and guided through these by the speaker. The materials included:

1. a handout booklet of samples of pupils' jotter work
2. a length of overhead projector acetate on which there were guidelines for the pupils' work and rough sketches by the teacher and pupils (used as a starting point for dramatization and/or story writing)
3. an extensive wall display of samples of pupils' work over a year in the mixed-ability class
4. slides reviewing progress of one pupil acquiring skills of editing and self-correction
5. tape-recorded work, including selections of music used in a theme study and discussions between pupils.

The following report attempts to describe the approach, then to examine some of the underlying principles and major emphases, and to indicate possible extension of the uses of such an approach in teaching across the curriculum.

Description of the approach in practice

Individualized learning and diagnostic teaching are often assumed to depend on extensive individual initial testing. While test results can undoubtedly provide further insights and the possibility of describing work in terms of comparisons between and within individual pupils' achievement and those of wider normative samples, it is essential for most teachers to cope with the ongoing class-teaching situations either by using classwork itself as a means of evaluating progress and identifying difficulties, or by supporting their classwork observations by gradually building up diagnostic test-based information.

This approach focuses on coping informally with the ongoing problems of individual differences in ability, pace and interest in developing written language.

From this teacher's individual perspectives as an artist (his initial training prior to study of education) and related recognition of the importance of the process of drafting and redrafting (derived from sketching technique) there developed in the class a readiness to go on with the attempt to write and not to have any particular attachment to each draft in an ongoing process. It would appear that the possibility of continuity in work and progressively clarifying an idea is as fundamental to the success of the approach as the acceptance of every pupil's initial efforts in written language at whatever level he is willing to offer them.

This inevitably means that the extent of the class's range of attainment in basic skills is soon evident and the emphasis is gradually shifted from teacher-directedness to pupil-directedness in seeking assistance in order to sustain individual progress at all points across the range.

The individual teacher remains firmly in control, not only in the introductory phase while pupils are developing competence in drafting and redrafting, but in the selection and the organization of content-areas and management of the amount and what kind of help a pupil needs to keep him 'on the track' while he continues with the sorting out of his ideas.

How does it start?
The pupils must have a reason to write – one that is important to them. Some are motivated to pass examinations and keen to do whatever the teacher might suggest if this is seen as a means of helping towards examinations. Other pupils may have an equally strong desire to succeed but evidence it only in negative ways, showing their fear of failure. It is likely that this fear is associated with written work and that, short of painstaking copying, for some pupils the prospect of having to write is a sure sign of imminent defeat – another in a long series!

Step 1:   Talk and listen
Encourage the pupils to *talk*. Encourage them to *listen* to themselves as well as to each other. It is likely that one may be disorganized in speech as well as fearful in approach to writing, yet the verbal flow may be overwhelming.

Attention to what is actually being said will introduce the need to listen, and listening in turn will help to bring about some order in

295

thoughts, then speech.

Step 2: *Select vocabulary*

Select special words from talks and *write* them (or, if need be, copy them from a model provided by the teacher on the pupil's request). The emphasis here is on noting the most important words to convey impressions crucial to the pupil's meaning.

The awareness of the need to incorporate illustrations to provide a stimulating visual presentation for a newspaper article is evident. And selection from the range of ideas which emerged in discussion is clearly at work citing not only 'newsworthy' items of information but presenting these in a style approximately that of the eye-catching popular press.

The sequence of steps towards the first page of notes might involve a series of repeated attempts to talk, write, organize, edit and write again in a way more satisfying for the pupil's own purposes.

Step 3: *Use available resources to aid in word search*

This involves a further level of analysis of what the pupil actually wrote and what he actually meant. Frequently at this stage a pupil may be unable to re-read his own notes, or make spelling errors, or have difficulty in finding the exact words he wants. A satisfying step can be taken if the right material is available. In many cases a picture dictionary provides the necessary aid. The interest in precision of meaning as well as sounds and spelling of words can be furthered by flexible use of the dictionary. It can be a starting, middle or end point within the cycle of the drafting and re-drafting process.

Step 4: *Write the edited version so as to incorporate newly-selected words in a 'fluent language' style*

By this point, the pupil is likely to have come to value the purpose of listening to himself as he talks, attending to his own ideas as he sorts them out on paper and attempting to convey exactly the impression of meaning he has in his mind.

Discussion with others is an essential part of this process and maintaining his point of view, intention, or development of his ideas in and through discussion can lead to greater verbal fluency as well as clarity required for selecting ideas for writing and their presentation in an appropriate and relevant order.

To help with the organization into an appropriate order, a cartoon-style sequence of illustrations might be used and the pupil can benefit from talking about each picture as he makes it. The necessary slowing-down in order to represent the ideas in illustrated form is likely to have a beneficial effect in focusing on discrete steps, the story sequence, and hence the order of thinking for later writing.

A written statement cued by each picture is then easier to formulate and less likely to become scrawled and overdetailed or lose the point.

By joining a series of statements cued by the picture sequence, a story is likely to emerge with greater potential for fluency in written-language style than the attempts without the intervening stages of organizing the thoughts and editing unnecessary detail or pointing-up important information for appreciation of the writer's meaning.

It may be that the picture-cueing step suggests language development of a kind other than fluent prose to some pupils. Cast-lists for plays have been developed from this step interest, personal preferences in style have included a deliberate patterning of verbs and adverbs or of nouns. Syntactic as well as semantic features emerge and can be picked up and expanded informally by the teacher as long as the expansion is contributing to the pupil's purpose rather than deflecting from it. The teacher's role in encouraging reflection and consideration of the most appropriate forms from the range of linguistic and illustrative possibilities provides at the same time a challenge and reassurance for the pupil.

Step 5:   Use the jotter for 'organizing' and 'redrafting' by putting notes on the left-hand page and then working from them to develop a more fluent story on the right

This is a rather different use of a jotter as a drafting board than the frequent separation of exercises specifically intended for practice in an aspect of language skill or for either the 'rough copy' of an essay or story or for the 'finished version' which is often only slightly modified and largely copied from the rough version. The approach illustrated above allows for incidental language development in a context which encourages immediate internalization and application. It is thus not merely a means of improving one version of work, but of going beyond the first attempt to develop communication in a chosen direction. That first attempt on the left-hand page might include any or all of the following: cut-out magazine articles, pictures, drawings or words and phrases. Each pupil may take a different amount of time for his work on each page. Some may decide that a sequence of two pages is sufficient for their present topic, or others that six pages are required. The use of two pages tends to follow the pattern of left to right for most pupils. Some, however, may develop personal variations such as that illustrated above. The pupil clearly recognizes that the purpose of written language was for communication and added to the structure of developing from left to right by explaining in the note to the teacher the particular use of the pages. His note in the margin of the right-hand page indicates the acceptance of the teacher's position as someone interested in what he is writing.

Step 6.   Self-correction

It can be suggested to the pupils who are becoming familiar with the use of their jotter for drafting and redrafting that if they are not sure of a word, either of its spelling or appropriateness, they might put brackets around it. This sign will alert the teacher who can provide a helping hand by inconspicuously listing correct versions of bracketed 'mistakes' (placing a note on the back page of the jotter or indicating reassuringly that the pupil's attempt was in fact correct). As this step toward self-correction is made and practised the pupils may spontaneously develop their own correction code. When they begin to do this it is easier to decide on one shared code that has a variety within any class's jotter work. The following code was successfully used by one class:

( )	misspelling
P	punctuation
∧	omission
R	repetition or redundancy
NP	new paragraph

For some classes one introductory lesson on the use of these coded signs is sufficient for the pupils to begin to use the idea. With each pupil it is then necessary to use the specific code-signs most suitable for his needs.

The teacher's use of the code can be sensitively selective in directing the pupil's attention firstly towards an error or type of error which for him would be comparatively easy to correct, for example R. Then at a later stage, when the pupil is confidently identifying and correcting this error, another type of error can be drawn to his attention by use of the code. For example, to cut down on excessive use of 'and' in a story, the code sign 'R' for repetition can be introduced. The pupil can then use the same sign as a means of developing self-correction. This is achieved through attentive listening to himself as he reads and re-reads his notes either silently or aloud. (The quickest means of learning accurate use of this self-correction code was discovered to be the deliberate and careful reading aloud.)

Underlying principles
The guiding principle of this approach is the nature of drafting and redrafting as a process leading towards a point which will become clearer – only by devoted attention on the part of the writer to the task of communicating his ideas via the written word.

As a result of this process the *personal rewards for the writer are in achieving his own goal* by progressively reaching greater clarity of communication.

In order to maintain the *flexibility* of the principle of drafting and redrafting, it is essential to be ready to discard any early unsatisfactory draft if and when a later one is of greater value for the writer's purpose.

298

The wider interpretation of this need for flexibility includes those occasions on which a pupil might justifiably achieve his purpose in writing without requiring a series of redrafts.

The motivation to self-correct for the pupil is dependent on two factors:

1 recognition of a sense of relevance (achieved either with or without a series of redrafts)
2 the pupil's increasing realization that the internal coherence of his written language is not being communicated.

For the teacher the importance of looking at errors lies in *differentiating between the correction of surface features of written language and the sensing of the extent of the pupil's internal coherence of thought*.

Furthermore, once the differentiation has been made the analysis of error patterns can proceed. Some of these may be due to complex and not easily remediable language difficulties but the majority may prove to be amenable to modification if not complete eradication through the process of drafting and redrafting with the teacher's unobtrusive assistance.

As this procedure is followed the pupils learn more about *the way in which language works*. This knowledge is often formally presented through exercises and constructions for training in grammatical usage. It was found not necessary to introduce a single grammatical term; pupils could generate successively more complex grammatical structures and could use these appropriately.

The approach can and should help towards *independent* and self-directed learning. It can help the pupil to learn 'how to learn' by clarifying his thoughts and focusing his attention on selection and organization of his work.

The use of the left-hand/right-hand page and drafting approach has been tried in different subject areas across the curriculum and has been found to be an unobtrusive aid in learning for the able pupil as well as the slower learner.

Note: Sets of materials used in the workshop may be obtained from the authors.

33   A programme to develop reading for learning in the secondary school

Elizabeth P. Dolan

The school to which I was appointed Head of Compensatory Education in September 1975 was concerned to put into practice some of the recommendations of the Bullock Committee (DES 1975). It was felt that the onus for achieving this should not be placed solely onto the English department in the school, even if most of the expertise might be expected to be contained there. Staff in the school fully agreed with the Bullock Committee's assertion that 'English' has a subject content as equally definable as that of any other subject in the curriculum. At the same time, teachers from all departments felt that the problems presented by children who find reading difficult are small in comparison to those generated by general underachievement in children from across the full ability range. The immediate difficulty was one of tactics in planning a programme which would span the whole curriculum, and it was felt that my position might be an ideal one from which to launch a course of action which would influence the whole curriculum. Since colleagues had indicated agreement with the Bullock Report that all teachers have the responsibility for providing for all children in their care, this concern placed all members of staff in my department, and, conversely, me in theirs.

Most teachers, and especially those involved in the teaching of reading, would concur with the Bullock Committee's valuation of reading as a major strategy for learning. However, not all teachers would see the significance of the recommendation that a well-planned and systematic programme is vital for the greatest growth of reading competence; at least, not at secondary-school level. It has been my experience that most teachers in the secondary school feel that reading development is most rapid through being exercised in the context of curricular demands made in the course of the lessons set to children across the usual range of subjects, and that it is not really feasible to afford time from the timetable for 'reading' lessons. It is probably for this reason that the only specialist teachers of reading in the secondary school are usually those responsible for teaching in a remedial capacity.

The brief which established my department in school specified work across the curriculum with children of all abilities who find bookwork hard. The scope was considerable! I was interested in extending children's reading competence beyond the basic decoding level, in making pupils' use of reading more efficient for study purposes, and in encouraging children's sensitivity in selecting the most appropriate strategies to answer the demands of particular subjects. The school had been associated with the Schools Council Effective Use of Reading Project at Nottingham University. The project team's observations and the activities which they recommended seemed to point to a way in which reading could be extended systematically, and pupils' facility in using language in all its forms be increased. Activities which they had investigated were certainly not new but had still to be shown to be applicable to the various situations which characterize the range of subjects in the secondary-school curriculum. In addition, the techniques had not been used (to the writer's knowledge) as part of a structured programme with mixed-ability groups in secondary schools.

The programme
Each class is divided into three mixed-ability groups which rotate through a set of activities over a period of three weeks, one activity being completed by each group in every session. One group reads library books, which may be changed during the session; the second group completes an activity from instructions presented on a specially-prepared audio-tape; thus, the teacher is free to chair a third group activity with the remaining pupils. Materials are clearly labelled and easily accessible to pupils; seating positions are determined by each activity; pupils know the routine and come in and organize themselves with the minimum of fuss.

This pattern is similar throughout the first to fourth years, but is more regular and intensive in the first year. This choice of target pupils is deliberate and based on the notion that the wisest deployment of whatever time is available for this venture ought to be with year groups which might feel and display the impact of the programme over the longest time-span in the school.

A brief description of some of the activities
The activities included in the pilot programme have been fully described in the final report of the Schools Council project and will be published in 1977. Most of the activities have been used to an extent by teachers for some years. However, the format used in our programme means that the essential purpose of the activities is to use that which has been read to scrutinize arguments raised in small group discussion and to justify attempts at solutions to assigned tasks. Group prediction capitalizes on the novelty which children feel when they are placed in guessing-game situations and is derived from the work of Stauffer (1969) and Walker (1974). Group cloze derives from the Gestalt

tradition in psychology and its use as a means of exploring reading comprehension has been examined by Vincent and Cresswell (1976) for the NFER in England, and by Bormuth (1969) in the USA. Group sequencing may be traced to the old intelligence problem of rearranging into the most plausible order a set of statements which have been placed out of order. Group SQ3R uses the technique advanced by Robinson in the 1940s and described in several publications (Robinson 1961; 1962). The most succinct rationale for using the activities is probably to be found in Walker's book *Reading Development and Extension* (1974).

Group cloze

Children are faced with a text from which words have been deleted, the task being to think of words which may be inserted so that meaning is restored. A paragraph is left intact at the beginning of the passage, or a few sentences, in order to set the scene and portray the writer's style. Thereafter, words are systematically deleted in a regular numerical pattern, say, every fifth to twelfth word, depending on the difficulty of the text and the ability of the group. Occasionally, the regularity of the pattern may be broken so that words which are likely to promote discussion are deleted. The activity concentrates on developing the ability to read in units of word and thoughts, instead of individual words, by establishing linguistic relationships such as collocation, grammatical links and word patterns.

The procedure seems to have great potential for the teaching of technical vocabulary and terminology in context. Teachers may work from a class textbook or have a child tackle a summary of information about a topic taught over various stages of time. When used in the latter manner, group cloze seems an excellent revision exercise.

Once children have some proficiency in a foreign language, the passage may be presented in that language with subsequent discussion taking place in English. (With children of poor foreign-language ability, the teacher may also present the passage on an audio-tape to supplement the text. This technique is also used as an aid for children of poor reading ability.)

Group SQ3R

Booklets or documents may be specially prepared for this activity, or children may read a chapter or section of a book. In most lessons in this school, the activity is controlled through instructions presented on a specially prepared audio-tape which gives directions to the children to discuss this or that point. A child is selected to act as 'leader' and has the responsibility for switching off the recorder in response to signals on the tape, and for restarting the machine once discussion is completed. A group listening set with individual headphones for each child is sometimes used, although this is merely an effort to reduce distraction for children in other groups and is not essential for the exercise. The headphones are removed for discussion.

In the course of the activity, the children survey (S) the title, subheadings, illustrations, and first and last paragraphs. They aim to gain as much information as possible in a couple of minutes. An integral part of the activity is the encouragement of the children to raise questions (Q) about the content during the surveying process. At each stage, directions are given and the points raised by the children are discussed. Questioning is followed by a reading through (R1) of the text, reviewing (R2) – that is, picking out the salient points and making sure they are understood, and finally, reciting (R3), a consideration of the implication and application of what has been read, and a testing of recall.

The tapes have been carefully graded from the first 'survey-question' tapes to ones which involve notemaking, dictionary work, cross-referencing and a range of other assignments arising from the content of the passage.

Group sequencing
Several consecutive sections of the same passage, poem, set of instructions, workcard or a child's account of an event experienced by the group are prepared. Working in pairs, the children have to arrange the sections into an order which makes sense. Once an agreed order has been arrived at, one pair joins another or the group reassembles and discusses the respective orderings. Children frequently decide that several orderings are acceptable without the overall meaning being materially altered. The author's original order is usually revealed to the children and discussed. In performing the task, children may focus on punctuation and typographical clues, syntax constructions, units of meaning, the logic of the author's argument and the direction to which the passage is pointing.

A ready supply of duplicated sets of material has been found in multiple copies of newspapers and 'colour supplements', children seeming very interested in items of local events, football matches and in well-known advertisements. Each segment of a passage is typed onto card and covered with plastic film for greater durability, and each piece is numbered in an order which indicates to the teacher the original structure of the passage.

Group prediction
In this activity instalments of a passage or story are distributed one at a time to a group of eight to ten children. The children read the instalments silently, discuss its content with the chairman and try ot predict what is likely to happen in subsequent instalments. After each section has been discussed, the chairman (usually the teacher) summarizes the discussion then gathers in the instalments so that

children may no longer refer back to previous information. Pupils have to justify all predictions and comments, the general aims being to evoke judgments about the text and to develop the ability to support, to defend, to modify and to rethink judgments in the light of comments from others in the group and of further evidence from the passage. Discussion is most lively and predictions most forthcoming when there is an unusual short story which has an unexpected but plausible outcome. Such a story provides an opportunity for the teacher to heighten the suspense and to encourage the group to generate new ideas and to hypothesize developments. This is not to say that the activity lacks application in other areas of the curriculum. There, the content is deliberately chosen for its appropriateness to that aspect of the subject which it is desired to teach.

As the reading programme progressed and material of a wider variety was introduced, it became increasingly obvious that the activities were excellent 'teaching tools'. Concentration was so intense that pupils remembered much of what they had read for a considerable length of time. This was strong support for the claim of the activities for a place in the normal teaching and learning diet. It would be quite wrong, however, for the frequency of their use in the content areas to be as intensive as it is in the reading programme; this would run the risk of being as stultifying as an unrelieved series of worksheets.

Initially, those teachers who tried the activities had little to guide them and success was limited. The activities showed no advantages when tried with large groups, preparation was arduous, and there was a tendency for teachers to bypass discussion. To illustrate the use of the techniques, staff and university technicians cooperated in making videotapes of some lessons. These proved invaluable both in and out of school. During the first year, many refinements were made, as we found, for example, that it was vital to know the material thoroughly and to know how individual members of a group are likely to react in the group situation. This enabled the chairman to know which suggestions to emphasize, which to underplay and when to sit back and listen. Again, we found that it was imperative for teachers to try out all the activities several times before the efficacy of them was judged. This experience was necessary for teachers to refine their questioning technique, to modify modes of operation and to gain enough expertise to extract the maximum benefit. This 'code of conduct' applied even to very experienced teachers.

It was not possible to make an objective evaluation of the programme, but progress was considered sufficiently impressive in the first year to justify an extension of its size and range. Consequently, this year it has a place as a separate subject on the timetable. As yet, each first-year block of three classes has one 'study session' of one hour per week. There is the normal allocation of one teacher per class, but for the duration of a term, each teacher is responsible for conducting a set of activities instead of being responsible for a class. In this way, teachers gain indepth experience of the various aspects of the programme.

Many secondary-school teachers complain that pupils do not know how to gather information or to evaluate the merits of various books or pieces of information. They feel that pupils do not know how to make notes for future use and are unable to use reference and index systems. They insist that they do not have time to teach anything other than the content of their subject.

We are very conscious that, to be of any real value, the strategies exercised and developed during the study sessions must be applied in other lessons. To try and ensure that children and teachers develop a sensitivity to occasions for their use, certain measures have been adopted. Firstly, we draw upon material from all content areas; thus, we try to instil in children's minds that the strategies which have been made available to them are truly applicable to lessons in all subjects. Secondly, the sessions are sited in a resource centre, so giving ease of access to a wide variety of references. The school librarians play an important role as they have invaluable knowledge of the content of the resources areas and of the cataloguing systems in use. Thirdly, a system of inservice training has been instigated, the videotapes are used, workshops are held from time to time and staff from various content areas teach (and thereby learn) in the study sessions. In this way, not only do teachers understand and learn how to adapt the group activities to their subject lessons, but they also have first-hand awareness of the skills which children have at their disposal. Members of staff who take part are able to take back their experience to others in their departments. With this gradual infiltration of expertise we hope that the strategies gained by children and teachers in study sessions will be fostered and developed by means of an increased consciousness of reading and language processes, and that the techniques will be looked upon as fairly standard procedures of study across the curriculum.

References

BORMUTH, J. R. (1969) 'Empirical determination of the instructional reading level' in J. A. Figurel (ed) *Reading and Realism* 1968 Proceedings of the International Reading Association Newark, Delaware: International Reading Association

DES (1975) *A Language for Life* (Bullock Report) HMSO

ROBINSON, F. P. (1961) (revised edition) *Effective Study* Harper and Row

ROBINSON, F. P. (1962) (revised edition) *Effective Reading* Harper and Row

STAUFFER, R. G. (1969) *Teaching Reading as a Thinking Process* Harper and Row

VINCENT, D. and CRESSWELL, M. (1976) *Reading Tests in the Classroom* NFER

WALKER, C. (1974) *Reading Development and Extension* Ward Lock Educational

Part 7

International perspectives

34 Diagnostic-prescriptive teaching: a review of recent research and implications for education

Gilbert R. Gredler

Today there is great interest and emphasis in the diagnostic-prescriptive teaching of children with learning disabilities. The nature of the phrase 'diagnostic-prescriptive' implies the importance of differential diagnosis as well as the existence of valid educational strategies in helping children with learning disabilities.

Some specialists believe there are important psycholinguistic correlates of learning disabilities and that if such correlates are ascertained and strengthened, improvement in reading will result.

A number of individuals are now involved in schools within the USA in helping children with learning disabilities. Variously called educational diagnostician, diagnostic or prescriptive teacher, educational consultant, learning disability teacher-consultant, resource teacher, or reading specialist, they all have in common working with children who have academic problems and attempting to help them improve their performance in the classroom.

Our concern for the child with learning problems has led to a more careful delineation of factors involved in learning disorder. But in the search, the danger of dividing the child into smaller or more sterile components, which appear to bear on the child's reading retardation, is quite real.

One approach which has received substantial attention over the past few years is the relationship of modality functioning to the child's progress in learning. In attempting to ascertain how information is processed by the child an obvious question to raise is whether or not there is a preferential method of presenting reading material to him.

The modality concept received increased recognition as an important determiner of progress in learning from the work of the psychologist Joseph Wepman (1968). Wepman stressed the following points:

1 There is a preference by the child for use of one sensory channel or another.
2 Studies of neurologically-impaired children showed distinct differences in regard to input channel preferences.

3   Differential modality preferences appear to be closely related to the child's innate capacity.
4   The two major modalities (i.e. visual and auditory) reach a stage of full development and equalization by age nine. Lags are usually overcome by that age.
5   It is difficult to reduce the lag effects through training programmes. However, remediation needs to be attuned to the 'child's unique assets and liabilities'.
6   In the initial learning stages the perceptual factors inherent in the reading process need to be stressed: discrimination skills, retention and recall of sounds and letters, sequential ordering of letter units and the integration of such units.
7   The child will have difficulty in learning to read if we focus primarily on the conceptual level (i.e. comprehension skills). Later learning at the conceptual level may be faulty 'without a basic structure upon which the child can develop his linguistic skills' (Wepman, page 6).

Currently one important method used to assess learning modality preference is the Mills Learning Methods Test (Mills 1964). With this instrument a child's modality strength is ascertained through a process of teaching him to read a specified number of new words over a period of four days through each modality. Modality preference is based on a score reflecting performance on a test of immedate recall and a retention test.

Cooper (1969) modified the Mills test to include the use of nonsense words and used more precise guidelines for teaching these words.

It is seldom recognized that in measuring modality preferences by teaching new word units, there is no instrument which can provide a *pure* measure of a modality preference. Presenting material through a visual modality still involves utilization of some auditory cues.

Wepman also measures modality preference differently than Mills or Cooper. To ascertain visual modality competence, he devised tests which measure visual discrimination, visual memory and visual orientation. According to Wepman, when the results of all three are combined together 'the degree of visual competence in development indicates clearly those children who learn primarily through the visual modality' (Wepman *et al* 1975, page 11). While this is an important advance in Wepman's conceptualization of the attributes of the visual modality, note should be made that he includes no measure of visual sequential processing. Since sequential processing within the visual mode is one important facet of the visual modality concept, Wepman's battery is lacking in providing a complete picture of visual modality functioning. It must be recognized that the differences in approaches to measuring modality preference undoubtedly contribute to some of the variability of research findings in this area.

Cooper's study has been intensively analysed previously and will not be reviewed again (Gredler 1975). Suffice to say that in teaching new words to fifteen poor readers Cooper found that there were no differences in mean scores between one modality or another. However, in certain cases a poor reader was able to learn new words in significantly fewer trials through one modality rather than another modality.

To be able to state more conclusively that modality preference is of primary importance the child should be tested as to modality preference over a period of time to ascertain stability of this preference; poor readers should receive modality remediation over a substantial period of time, and comparison should then be made with a control group of poor readers as well as poor-readers groups subject to other remediation approaches.

There is a need to conceptualize more adequately a host of variables important to the reading process. It is quite possible that the modality preference approach is being overemphasized and that other variables are of equal or greater importance. That this possibly may be the case is seen in a study of the relationship of preferred learning modalities and conceptual tempo in first-grade children (Kalash 1972).

Kalash studied children in the New York City school system. Modality preference was ascertained from administration of the New York University Modality Test. Visual modality preference was defined as competence on tasks dealing with visual discrimination and auditory modality competence referred to auditory discrimination level. Teaching of words via a particular modality was not undertaken.

Kalash was interested in the relationship of preferred modality and conceptual tempo to reading readiness. The main task was to ascertain which factor was a more potent determiner of readiness status in the child. Concerning conceptual tempo, it is Kagan's thesis (1966) that the child whose learning style can be characterized as reflective, i.e. looking carefully at alternatives presented to him in a discrimination task, possesses a more helpful learning style than one who is impulsive, i.e. responding quickly and inaccurately.

Perhaps the most important finding of this study was that when Kalash compared reading readiness as a function of modality preference or conceptual tempo she found that impulsives, whether they indicated a visual or auditory modality preference, scored lower on the readiness test. Those children labelled reflective were able to obtain higher readiness scores whether showing a visual or auditory modality preference.

We need to assess carefully these results for their implications. While 31 per cent of the sample could be characterized as reflective (responding slowly and accurately) and 41 per cent as impulsive (responding fast and inaccurately), 17 per cent of the sample was found to be impulsive *and* accurate and another 5 per cent reflective *but* inaccurate. Thus 22 per cent of the children were subsequently dropped from further study. The fact that over one-fifth of this group did not fit into the conceptual tempo scheme as defined by Kagan cannot be forgotten. Such a loss of population sample indicates that Kagan's theoretical framework leaves something to be desired as a way of understanding children. For one in five children in this study this measure of cognitive style was not helpful as an assessment tool.

Despite the reservations, the importance of this study to the diagnostic-prescriptive specialist/remedial teacher is that here is a variable that must be investigated in some form or another when remediation help is offered. Since conceptual tempo is a primary factor of importance with many children and overrides the importance of modality preference, remediation which centres *only* on a strictly modality programme is insufficient as a structure for help.

Another way to determine the importance of a modality-based instructional model is to see if visual and auditory modality test-scores from *different* test batteries will reflect consistency of strength of that modality. This is precisely what Dubose (1972) undertook to investigate in her study. She used the Test of Modality Aptitude in Reading (TOMAR) which is an instrument similar in make-up to the Mills Test but in which children are taught words from a contrived alphabet by three different methods (visual, auditory and kinesthetic).

Dubose looked at the correlations among the following tests:

TOMAR – previously defined
MLMT – Mills Learning Methods Test
ITPA-V – Illinois Test – Visual Sequential Memory
ITPA-A – Illinois Test – Auditory Sequential Memory.

Results of her investigation are summarized as follows:

1   None of the correlations between *any* of the subtests of auditory modality functioning were statistically significant.
2   Only one of six intercorrelations between various visual modality subtests was statistically significant.
3   Substantial correlations were found between TOMAR-V and TOMAR-A and MLMT-V and MLMT-A. Such correlations indicate that these subtests are not pure measures of the functioning given.
4   The correlation of TOMAR-V and TOMAR-A was so high (.829) that Dubose correctly surmises that some common function underlies the performance requirements of both tasks. She feels that since the child must learn a new alphabet and then learn words made up of this new alphabet, the cognitive ability demand is the factor common to both tasks.

One interpretation of the results of this kind of study might be that when we talk of modality preference we are in fact dealing with a very fragile concept. Are there really such distinct modality differences and can we measure them precisely?

While Dubose established that the lowest intercorrelations were found between ITPA subtests (ITPA-V and ITPA-A) it is the writer's contention that a case can be made to administer both tests to a young child who is having difficulty in learning to read. Based on the findings of Hyatt (1968) we would expect a poor reader in first or second grade to perform poorly on both measures, *not* necessarily because he has both an auditory and visual modality weakness, but because he is poor in 'active listening and seeing'. Therefore such a child's lack of a positive learning style results in a low score on both modality/processing tests. This child's style of learning is found to be inadequate to meet the classroom situation. When a child is impulsive and distractible he is not tuned in to all the stimuli of the test situation. To perform adequately on the VSM the child must actively scan the visual stimuli and actively listen to the auditory stimuli when presented with the ASM test of the ITPA.

To go beyond the visual/auditory/kinesthetic modality emphasis we need to look at other variables of possible importance. Ffooks (1969) argues that the important factor is the relationship between quality of perception and memory storage. As the child's memory storage increases, his ability to sample and compare perceptual stimuli increases. The cortical cells increase in selectivity of response. Since memory storage is building up all this time the child does not need as many cues to decipher a perceptual stimulus as he once did. As Jaffee (1972) states: 'Once adequate long-term memories have been established, then a relatively low level of perception of a stimulus may be sufficient to trigger the associated memories.' (Jaffee, page 68).

The implication of this theory is that a low level of development *per se* in the auditory or visual perceptual area should not be automatically considered a deficit area to overcome. If the perceptual deficit is linked with deficit in long-term or short-term memory development, *then* we have a possible constellation of symptoms needing further analysis.

That Wepman, in writing of auditory modality functioning, now includes in his definition a measure of auditory memory, is significant.

As we look at the multitude of factors involved in the child's learning to read it becomes difficult to organize into a coherent pattern the significant factors which are important. Ffooks's comments suggest that it is the effective organization and interplay of a number of factors (i.e. adequate long-term memory and perceptual development) which are partially responsible for successful learning.

While diagnostic-prescriptive teachers eagerly plunge into working out a remediation programme for the child it appears that the task of adequate and accurate diagnosis is a much more difficult and involved process than has been presently conceived.

315

Other important factors which combine to produce effective learning have been studied in detail by Braught (1972) and Bakker (1971). Braught looked at the 'cognitive organization patterns' used by normal and learning disabled children when dealing with auditory, visual or haptic stimuli. She prefers to call these factors cognitive structuring tasks while Bakker refers to them as tasks involving temporal ordered perception.

Briefly, Braught investigated how seven to eight year old children learn to undertake a variety of cognitive tasks. She found the learning-disabled child was impaired in his ability to reconstruct auditory, visual and haptic tasks. She postulates long-term memory deficiencies hamper learning-disabled children when they are required to transpose and reconstruct tasks in the various modalities.

Braught suggests that further study of the cognitive structuring strategies used by learning-disabled children would indeed be a fruitful investigation. The learning strategies of the learning-disabled are indeed complicated, and analysis of intelligence test responses does not give us a sufficient answer as to why a child does not learn. Single instrument measures such as the ITPA, while frequently giving us additional data, are insufficient by themselves to describe the learning patterns of the learning-disabled child. Some educators, concerned that educational tests, which they once espoused, have not sufficiently helped, have either turned to simple conditioning techniques as a way of motivating the child to learn, or say that an analysis of the task into its simple component parts, is all that is necessary.

The adequate learner can deploy his attention and concentration in an effective manner. He can inspect the task in a systematic and structured, orderly manner. If emphasis is only placed on remediating learning-disabled children in a basic-skill deficit, such training may have a short-lived effect. If instead, emphasis is placed on a programme of trying to change, modify, expand the underlying cognitive structure, greater payoff may be expected (Braught 1972).

Because cognitive structuring strategies are so important, additional comments will be made on the work of Bakker (1971) which closely parallels that of Braught. Bakker investigated the ability of learning-disabled and of normal children to match auditory-temporal patterns with the same stimuli given in a visual-spatial dimension. Known also as a task of auditory-visual integration (Birch and Belmont 1964; 1965), the phenomenon has been generally studied by having a child match a rhythmic pattern presented auditorily with a number of alternatives appearing on a sheet in front of him. However, Bakker looked further – he asked the child explicitly for the sequential or serial position of the item presented. Thus with a TOVV (temporal ordering visual-visual) test children were presented with a series of three letters laid out in temporal succession. Then after removal of the letters the children were shown two of the letters visually and each child had to indicate the order in which he had perceived the two letters: first, second or last. By explicitly requesting the child to give the serial position via a reconstruction method Bakker has clearly gone beyond the usual request made in an auditory-visual integration task: that of imitation.

Bakker concludes that children with reading problems often have difficulty in sequential processing or temporal ordered perception. When verbal stimuli are presented, i.e. letters in a time scheme, a breakdown is readily apparent. The interaction between the 'time code' and the 'verbal code' is what is disturbed.

To summarize at this stage, it should be noted that an important reconceptualization is going on among psychologists and educators concerning how best to intervene with deficient learners. There is a small but growing shift from looking at narrow specific perceptual deficits to factors which can be considered cognitive in nature. Also a greater number of variables are being considered as having importance in the learning process.

Note should be made of how the diagnostic-prescriptive specialist works in the average school. She may be called in to administer a whole battery of tests in addition to the ones given by the school psychologist. She may just give the ITPA, note the deficit areas and give some general comments to the effect: 'spend more time on visual memory activities'. Often there is no coordinated programme of attending to specific cognitive deficiencies and to the emotional needs of the child.

While a more sophisticated programme approach towards learning materials is obviously needed, the need is just as great for creating a more humanistically-centred environment in which the child will feel comfortable to learn. Too often the 'deficit skill' building offered by the prescriptive teacher is a rigid, joyless process.

Summary

1 The modality approach for diagnosis and remediation needs to be approached with caution. Correlations of a number of modality instruments with each other are such as to raise questions as to the validity of the construct when certain instruments are used. When the auditory modality scores of instrument 'X' correlate more highly with the visual modality scores of instrument 'Y' than the auditory modality scores of both tests do with each other – then doubts can be raised as to the viability of the modality construct with *those specific instruments.*

2 Measuring modality preference by teaching new words to the child via methods emphasizing a certain 'pathway' is different from measuring modality preference through scores obtained on a number of subtests which reflect underlying psychological processes. We might therefore expect somewhat different results from such diverse research approaches.

3   While a definite case can be made for looking for psychological correlates of deficient reading performance, to say that a child has a modality weakness or psychological process weakness on the basis of a poor score on two subtests of the Frostig, or that he has a visual perceptual weakness because of his low scores on the test of spatial orientation or visual discrimination tests of the Wepman battery, is to misinterpret the nature of the problem.

4   Remediation based on such a narrow view of the psychological nature of the child will not be successful. The child with severe reading disability has a host of deficits in many psychological processes. What has occurred on the American educational scene is that a few deficits have been picked up and reified to a position of great importance. We have come to expect a remediation procedure based on the child's malperformance on a few tests to be able to ameliorate his poor reading, and all this to be accomplished within a short time period. This is the approach of a number of diagnostic-prescriptive specialists.

5   It should be noted that the conflict over the use of the term 'minimal brain dysfunction' has now been replaced with a conflict over the kinds of psychological tests to use to determine 'learning disabled' status. In addition some feel we should not use tests at all but apply behavioural reinforcement principles or task analysis. What is consistent is that conflict is still with us.

6   The degree of modality preference, competence or level of development is a partial reflection of the measurement technique used. If a specialist uses the ITPA-ASM, he is obtaining information on how the child performs on an *imitative* task involving the use of digits. With the ITPA-VSM a child is asked to *imitate* a task involving nonsense material. Bakker's studies indicate that differences in stimulus material (verbal *versus* nonverbal) is important in modal research. If the child is required to *reconstruct* the stimuli presented to him in either an auditory or visual framework, important differences in modality functioning between learning-disabled and normal children are obtained. Therefore if we are to understand precisely the modality process in the learning-disabled child we will have to find out how he performs on refined measures of sequencing ability.

7   In the enthusiasm for packaged programmes; concern for the child who is underachieving; and motivation to get one's viewpoint heard and accepted by others, confusion is naturally rampant in the general population. Modality treatment programmes have been applied to so many different groups of children of differing levels of reading retardation, different IQ levels and with different time periods for treatment that it is little wonder that a *smorgasbord* of results is

318

obtained that are conflicting and difficult to interpret.

8   Questions must also be raised in regard to the actual gains from prescriptive teaching because of the short time periods of remediation involved. In one study a combination of modality-remediation plus the use of reinforcement principles resulted in improved reading performance of the children as opposed to a control group and a group treated only with a reinforcement approach. Emphasis was placed on remediation of the child's psycholinguistic deficits through a planned modality programme. However, the total amount of remediation came to only eight hours distributed over a period of two months! (Hyatt 1968)

To emphasize the importance of a modality-based remediation approach; the severe deficits present in the child; that the remediation of such deficits was accomplished over a period of eight hours, raises some serious questions as to the severity of the deficits in the first place.

In a study reported by Pumfrey (1975) at a previous UKRA conference, two groups of poor readers with certain psycholinguistic deficits were given a structured remediation programme. One group was treated with an ITPA programme geared to the two main deficits shown by the poor readers; the other group worked with a general language programme built from the Peabody Language Kit. Both groups improved over the twelve weeks of remediation in academic achievement, and there were additional modest gains over the following twelve weeks.

Impressive results indeed, and Pumfrey correctly emphasizes that an aptitude and instruction interaction pattern is reflected by such results. However, it is important to note that it is an interaction built from a linguistic- and cognitive-type curriculum structured in approach. This is one aspect to which we need to attend and which appears to be an important factor. Pumpfrey's results suggest that we must recognize a diversity of cognitive programmes and approaches which can be of help to the learning-disabled child.

Instruction based solely on the diagnosis of preferential pathways of processing material (i.e. learning new words) and then noting performance gains is a method which is restricted in value because it offers too simplistic a model of cognitive factors important in the child's learning. While we may find that a child will perform best through 'X' modality, a successful remediation programme must take into account the child's learning strategies in other dimensions. Does he give up too easily before making an adequate attempt to deal with the material; does he react so impulsively that he continues to make errors? If he does react impulsively and scan the material inadequately, will remediation which is oriented towards productive learning styles be more helpful rather than just drill in the areas in which he performs poorly or remediation based on modality deficits? Over nineteen years ago Vernon strongly suggested that these factors might be centrally involved when she stated: 'The fundamental and basic characteristic of reading disability appears to be cognitive confusion and lack of system' (Vernon 1957, page 71).

It is up to us to spell out more precisely the specifics of the cognitive confusion as found in the learning disabled child. It is hardly likely that cognitive confusion can be cleared up through the simplistic prescriptions of the diagnostic-prescriptive specialist; or the token programme of the behaviour modifier.

When recommendations such as the following are made on reports written by the school psychologist: 'teach good listening habits' (for auditory perception problems); 'walk to a drumbeat with arms bent – quicken the beat to approach running speed and tempo' (to remediate gross motor coordination deficits), we can label such as amusing and quaint and realize they are borne of desperation over the fact of not being able to conceptualize and adequately plan for the child's learning difficulties.

Some would give up the search for finding valid and reliable measures of ascertaining the cognitive problems of the child who is having trouble in learning. They would say that instruction cannot be matched to the diagnostic strengths and weaknesses of the child (Ysseldyke 1973).

The call comes either to develop more reliable tests and/or reject standardized tests. Many American educators now tend to reject tests and say, 'task-analyse the behaviours involved in learning, assess skill development in very young children and programme material to remediate weaknesses in skill development' (Ysseldyke page 26).

However the problems with this approach are that all children do not utilize the same skills to the same degree; the skills identified by task analysis are not all found in good readers and missing in poor readers. Since measurement of these skills is done by criterion-referenced tests of a brief nature, their reliabilities are low and thus the child's performance may vary a great deal from one day to another; the skill development approach often results in a very rigid teacher-directed curriculum; and the presumption is made that a complete knowledge of the reading process is now at hand (Spache 1976).

Since each investigator of a skill or task analysis appears to have his own subset of skills needed for reading development, we are faced with the interesting situation that a child under one system need only show competency in 155 skills; under another system he must learn 277 skills and in still another system 450 skills are identified and must be covered before the child is considered an adequate reader! (Thompson and Dziuban 1973).

Thus the state of knowledge concerning skill development as practised by American educators and psychologists is somewhat precarious and needs to be taken with a grain of salt. The measurement syndrome, supposedly rejected by the task analysers has merely resurfaced with a vengeance in another form.

9   At the same time the learning-disability proponents say there are children who are severely learning-disordered and that they are restricted in number (1-2 per cent of the school population). They say that once they diagnose and treat, measurable improvement will definitely be forthcoming.

They are intimating and, in fact, practically promising gains over a short period of time with a part of the population which has been defined as having serious reading retardation. The net result of this kind of approach is that some parents will be disappointed, to say the least.

10   Few studies have been undertaken in the learning-disability area to measure the extent and permanence of performance gains of the children being remediated. To say that the field is so new and enough time has not elapsed is to sidestep the issue. We are talking of children called backward readers in school systems of other countries. There *is* a literature in existence which looks specifically at the success of remediation and the permanency of gains. An extensive British literature exists on the subject and needs to be replicated in America.

11   We cannot underestimate parental influence to the extent that the call for the learning-disabled class or resource room is a call for an organizational set-up so the child will have less pressure on him, and a more favourable teaching environment; then parents will continue to want to have their children partake of a situation which offers such a favourable teacher-child ratio and climate.

A number of children continue in a learning-disabled setting for more than one year. When this happens, we are conceding that the remediation of the learning-disabled child will take a fair time period before measurable gains are noted. However, we desperately need specific data on extent of improvement.

12   In a study of the remedial progress of retarded readers (Hughes 1975), it was found that two subgroups emerged – one group made adequate progress during remediation and continued to make gains when they returned to regular class. The other group progressed poorly in remediation and when returned to the regular class organization were never able to cope successfully. It is obvious that this second group needed additional diagnostic examination and treat-ment. The school certainly needs well-trained specialists who can give this kind of help.

13   The fact that the emotional atmosphere is important in remedia-

tion and brings some pay-off in improved academic performance alerts us to the fact that we must be more attuned to these nuances of the remedial or diagnostic/prescriptive process.

Lawrence's (1976) call for the introduction of a remedial teacher-therapist to help with the reading problems of a select group of backward readers is a step in the right direction. He has convincingly shown that the child's emotional life needs additional attention. Despite this fact, there is considerable resistance to combining aspects of these two jobs to help the learning-disabled child. In talking to a group of elementary guidance counsellors as to how they might specifically help in their counselling function within the elementary school, a large number rejected the idea of providing educational therapy wherein some principles of reading would be taught in a relaxed, positive atmosphere (Gredler 1974). 'It is not our job to teach reading' was the general reaction.

14   The deployment of the use of specialists within the US school system has reached a crisis stage. This is due to several factors: a tremendous influx of specialists from increased numbers of training programmes; loss of positions due to declining school enrolments and general poor economic conditions. Some specialist groups have grown recently at a faster rate than others. This occurs today when a particular group can obtain federal monies to be utilized for their specific goals. One such current case is that of providing federal monies for learning-disabled classes and specialists. The plight of the reading specialist is seen in the recent call by a national reading association asking for restrictions to be placed on the training of learning-disability specialists because of loss of positions of reading specialists (*Reading Today* 1976).

There are serious conflicts arising over the coexistence of learning-disability specialists and reading specialists within the school system. The general tone among many educators and psychologists is so negative that some parents are calling for drastic action to solve the problem. Many educators continue to make extreme statements which confuse the issues. One special educator (Newcomber 1975) rejects the use of any psychological tests, saying they tell us absolutely nothing; states we should forget aetiological conditions completely; that there is no neurological dysfunction we can legitimately ascertain; that remediation is simply the reteaching of reading and that the learning-disability specialist should take charge of the serious reading disabilities while the reading specialist can take responsibility for improving instructional techniques used in the regular classroom!

Such statements indicate the defensiveness and weakness of the learning-disability specialist. Those confident of their contribution to helping the child with a learning disorder do not have to make extreme statements about those in opposition to a particular point of

322

view.

Reference to Gredler's previous articles (1972, 1975) can provide a good springboard for understanding how psychoeducational diagnosis can be helpful; the kind of deficit performance which appears to reflect possible neurological involvement and need for a neurological examination; the importance of improving learning style as a condition of performance gain in reading; how a diversity of methods can be helpful – including behavioural reinforcement and structured materials; the value of games; the use of peers to reinforce positive learning experiences and behavioural gains, and the need to pay attention to aetiological conditions since the parent will be very concerned about causes – and legitimately so.

The conflict has gone so far that reorganization of special services will probably come about shortly in many schools. The tragedy is that every specialist wants to go his own way; insists he has the final answer, and states that what are really needed are more specialists of his own kind.

Details of a revised system of organizing and delivering effective educational services will be provided in a later paper. It has been the intent of this paper to look more searchingly at the diagnostic process and some important new developments in that area. In addition to raising questions about current American practices in the remediation field, new approaches to effective diagnosis and remediation have been described.

References

BAKKER, D. J. (1971) *Temporal order in disturbed reading* Rotterdam: Rotterdam University Press

BIRCH, H. G. and BELMONT, L. (1964) Auditory-visual integration in normal and retarded readers *American Journal of Orthopsychiatry* 43, 853–61

BIRCH, H. G. and BELMONT, L. (1965) Auditory-visual integration, intelligence and reading ability in school children *Perceptual and Motor Skills* 20, 295–305

BRAUGHT, L. R. (1972) *Cognitive structuring of first and second grade children with learning disabilities* Unpublished Doctoral Dissertation, Iowa State University

COOPER, J. D. (1969) *A study of the learning modalities of good and poor first grade readers* Unpublished Doctoral Dissertation, Indiana University

DUBOSE, R. F. (1972) *An investigation of auditory and visual modality preferences as a basis for determining reading instruction* Unpublished Doctoral Dissertation, George Peabody College for Teachers

FFOOKS, O. O. (1969) Neurophysiology and assessment of visual function *British Orthopaedic Journal* 26, 10–14

GREDLER, G. R. (1972) 'Severe reading disability – some important correlates' in J. F. Reid (ed) *Reading: Problems and Practices* Ward Lock Educational

GREDLER G. R. (1974) *Some new roles for the elementary guidance counsellor* Unpublished paper, Pennsylvania Elementary Guidance Counsellor Conference, Hershey, Pennsylvania

GREDLER, G. R. (1975) 'Reading disabilities: diagnosis and remediation' in D. Moyle (ed) *Reading: What of the Future?* Ward Lock Educational

HAYES, M. E. (1967) *Prescriptive teaching as a supplement to behaviour modification in the remediation of learning disorders* Unpublished Doctoral Dissertation, University of Southern California

HUGHES, J. M. (1975) *Reading and Reading Failures* Evans Brothers

HYATT, G. (1968) *Some psycholinguistic characteristics of first graders who have reading problems at the end of second grade* Unpublished Doctoral Dissertation, University of Oregon

JAFFEE, A. R. (1972) *Reading achievement and three aspects of auditory functioning in a second grade population with visual perceptual problems* Unpublished Doctoral Dissertation, Temple University

KAGAN, J. (1966) Reflection-impulsivity: the generality and dynamics of conceptual tempo *Journal of Abnormal Psychology* 71, 17–24

KALASH, B. D. (1972) *The relationship of preferred learning modalities and conceptual tempo to reading readiness of first grade disadvantaged children* Unpublished Doctoral Dissertation, New York University

KAUFMAN, A. M. (1975) *Assessment of preschool black children* Unpublished paper presented at a meeting of National Association of School Psychologists

LAWRENCE, D. S. (1973) *Improved Reading through Counselling* Ward Lock Educational

LAWRENCE, D. S. (1976) Same, but different *The Times Educational Supplement* 7 February, 17

MILLS, R. E. (1964) *The learning methods test* Miami: The Mills Center

NEWCOMBER, P. (1975) Learning disabilities: an educator's perspective *Journal of Special Education* 9, 145–9

PUMFREY, P. D. (1975) 'The Illinois test of psycholinguistic abilities in the diagnosis and remediation of reading failure' in D. Moyle (ed) *Reading: What of the Future?* Ward Lock Educational

READING TODAY (1976) Newsletter of International Reading Association, June, 2

SPACHE, G. D. (1976) *Investigating the Issues of Reading Disabilities*

Boston: Allyn and Bacon

THOMPSON, R. A. and DZIUBAN, C. D. (1973) Criterion referenced reading tests in perspective *The Reading Teacher* 27, 292–4

VERNON, M. D. (1957) *Backwardness in Reading* Cambridge University Press

WEPMAN, J. M. (1968) 'The modality concept' in H. K. Smith (ed) *Perception and Reading* Newark, Delaware: International Reading Association

WEPMAN, J., MORENCY, A. and SEIDL, M. (1975) *Visual Discrimination Test* Chicago: Language Research Associates

YSSELDYKE, J. E. (1973) 'Diagnostic-prescriptive teaching: the search for aptitude-treatment interactions' in L. Mann and D. A. Sabatino (eds) *The First Review of Special Education* Philadelphia: Journal of Special Education Press

35 A comparative study of successful practices and materials for teaching reading in the primary school as viewed by teachers in England and the United States

Robert E. Shafer

Introduction

Most Americans probably heard first about British primary schools with their concepts of 'open education', 'informal education', and 'collaborative learning', through Charles E. Silberman's book, *Crisis in the Classroom: The Remaking of American Education* (1970). Silberman's book was a widely-read volume which influenced many American parents and educators. It was the result of a three-and-a-half year study of American schooling supported by the Carnegie Corporation of New York. In general, Silberman condemned most American schools as 'grim, repressive, joyless places', documenting his observations with many examples from American schools. Silberman blamed the problem not on evil intent or ignorance, but on a rather widely-prevailing 'mindlessness', a failure 'to think seriously or deeply about the purposes or consequences of education'. Silberman went on to propose that the British primary schools he had visited during the course of the study were places which could be 'humane and still educate well'. He proposed that many of the British primary schools were simultaneously child-centred and subject- or knowledge-centred. He noted that they stressed aesthetic and moral education without weakening basic education. He proposed that the teachers who had changed to open education in both England and the United States found their major rewards in the quality of relationships with their students and in their new roles as independently responsible professionals. Silberman's book stimulated great interest among the American public in British primary education, an interest which was already being developed within professional education by such educators as Vincent R. Rogers (1970), one of the few American educators who had observed British informal schools at first hand before 1967 and who had returned to write on the subject. In the late sixties and early seventies Americans were subjected to an avalanche of writings generally concerned with the development of open schools, open classrooms, reforms in American school architecture to accommodate 'openness', and descriptions of methods and materials appropriate for open education. Books like Charles H. Rathbone's *Open Education: the Informal Classroom* (1971), Joseph Featherstone's *Schools Where Children Learn* (1971), E. Wallby Nyquist and Gene R. Hawes' *Open Education: A Source Book for Parents and Teachers* (1972), and Alexander Frazier's *Open Schools for Children* (1972), became influential in American education.

In England, growing from the influential Plowden Report (DES 1967), books like Leonard Marsh's *Alongside the Child: Experiences in the English Primary School* (1970), and many others continuing through the 1970s brought about a variety of developments in open and informal education. Within the United States, specialists in open education were brought from England to give inservice training to teachers in states like North Dakota and Maryland. Model open schools opened in a variety of school districts. In some states, new elementary schools were built on the open plan and teachers inserted in them whether they had specialized training or not. Hordes of visiting Americans descended on British primary schools. Indeed, 'open education' and 'informal education' caught on and became a virtual 'Bandwagon'. In England, informal education continued as a viable educational philosophy, but opposition was crystallizing. In a collection of papers known as *The Black Papers* (Cox and Dyson 1971) a more conservative voice was heard.

Reaction
Although various moves towards 'accountability' had been developing in the United States throughout the mid- and later 1960s, the 'accountability movement' had only begun to reach the majority of teachers in the United States in 1972. True, the National Assessment of Educational Progress had begun its work in the mid-sixties and more and more state legislatures were passing laws to develop statewide assessments of language and reading, and teachers were being asked to write behavioural objectives. But the conflicts between open education and accountability in the United States were yet to occur. When the National Foundation for Educational Research in England and Wales published *The Trend of Reading Standards* (Start and Wells 1972), it established that 'there is a high probability that reading comprehension standards of juniors had declined somewhat since 1964, and on the combined bases of both WV and NS6 tests, the mean scores of juniors and seniors had undergone no significant rise or fall since 1960/61.' In speculating why these standards in junior schools had declined and the standards for secondary schools remained static, the authors of the report speculated as to whether the amount of curriculum time for reading had changed or whether the

methods of instruction had changed. They speculated as to the preparation of infant and junior teachers, and they also speculated as to whether the 'less formalized methods' that had been introduced into the schools in the last two decades would not *necessarily* mean that less time was devoted to reading. They quote the then President of UKRA, Mrs Vera Southgate, that 'there has been a declining interest in reading, especially in the "infant classes" ', where she noted a decrease in the acceptance of the importance of learning to read. The authors of *The Trend of Reading Standards* quoted further research by Keith Gardner indicating that 'the attention to reading has changed between 1961 and 1967, as in the former years some 25 per cent of the first-year primary-school pupils in his sample of 2,000 had not started to learn to read and this percentage increased annually until in 1967 it had reached 40 per cent'. Start and Wells went on to cite other research indicating that there seemed to be less emphasis on the teaching of reading for probationary primary teachers in various parts of England, which led to an increased demand for inservice training at various active reading centres. It seemed to suggest that the 'less formal methods' which had come into play in teaching reading in the fifties and sixties were ultimately resulting in a decline in the reading ability of children in primary schools in England. Although this was an educational research report it created headlines in the popular press. Sir Alan Bullock, on a trip to Japan, received a call from Margaret Thatcher, then Secretary of State, who upon seeing the headlines decided that a national committee of inquiry should be established to look into 'all aspects of teaching use of English, including reading, writing and speech', concerned with 'how present practices might be improved and the role that initial and inservice training might play', and 'to what extent arrangements for monitoring a general level of attainment in this skills could be introduced or improved; and to make recommendations'. Sir Alan Bullock accepted the offer to chair the Committee of Inquiry and we have before us some four-and-a-half years later the now famous Bullock Report, *A Language for Life* (DES 1975).

In the United States, drops in scores on the Scholastic Aptitude Test have been offset by reports that show no decline, but instead tell of a slight rise in the performance of high-school juniors and a similar rise for lower-grade students on a variety of standardized tests. The mixed results on tests of reading and language skills have lead to continuing controversy and some research into the implications of using criterion-referenced testing and other forms of evaluation and measurement, rather than commercially-produced standardized tests. Few of the researchers in either country have gone directly to teachers to ask them their own views concerning the effects of various methods and materials on the 'realities' of the child in the school, and in the particular society. In this study, the data was obtained directly from teachers in interviews usually conducted in their own schools.

The schools, the teachers and the setting

No statistically representative sample was formally developed for this study. Nevertheless, the data was collected in both countries representing a definite cross-section of England and of a major metropolitan community in the United States – Los Angeles, California. Twenty-three teachers were interviewed in twenty-one schools in England, and twenty-five teachers were interviewed representing twenty-five schools in the greater Los Angeles area. In the case of England, the schools were chosen on the recommendation of specialists in language arts and reading, including advisers from local school authorities, HMIs, and university personnel from teacher-education programmes who were familiar with the schools. In the United States similarly, supervisors, reading specialists and university personnel of teacher-education programmes were used to recommend schools and teachers. In England, recommended schools ranged throughout the Greater London area, the Midlands, East Anglia, Devon, Buckinghamshire, Berkshire, Yorkshire, and Lancashire. In the case of Los Angeles, most of the schools were confined to the Los Angeles City Schools, ranging from the city centre to Orange County on the south, and Culver City on the west. In both countries teachers represented a variety of ages, of geographical and social origins, and of length of service in the teaching profession. In England, headmasters and headmistresses, and deputy headmasters and headmistresses who taught children at least part of the time, were included in the sample; but in the United States, principals, since none were found who actually taught children, were excluded.

Procedures

In each case, the school was visited for a period of at least one day by the researcher. In most cases, the teacher was interviewed either in his or her school or at a nearby university. Teachers were asked whether or not they would object to having their classes observed, and in most cases the classes of all teachers interviewed were observed. An interview schedule was developed, field tested, and eventually used in conducting the interviews. (The Appendix, on page 340, contains the interview schedule used in both countries.) The interviews were recorded and analysed for significant trends.

Teachers' comments: methods and materials

The data was coded with respect to comments made by teachers in both countries concerned with methods and materials. No statistical analysis of the data has been undertaken for this paper. Rather, teacher-comments have been used to illustrate the views of teachers of children of comparable age levels from the two countries. Although most of the data for this paper emerged in answer to question number five of the interview schedule ('What teaching materials do you consider most effective in the development of language power?'), other comments related to methods and materials emerged in answers to some of the other questions and in various other interview probes. Where appropriate, these have been included. In addition, comments related to the teachers' pre-service and inservice training have been included as this training relates specifically to methods and materials. Although all the data in the total study could not be included, enough illustrative comments have been included to demonstrate various trends which emerged in the analysis of the data.

Teachers of five to seven year olds

English teacher one: Reading comes the first thing in the morning. My idea is to listen to children's experiences and to make the first period a time for helping them. They decide what they are going to do and I allow them responsibility to do the activity. They can develop their own experiences. My idea is that they take responsibility for themselves in doing the various work of formal English. We then have a break and a quiet time where we can talk to one another and then we do formal English. I hear them read. Each child has a file with his name written on it in colours. I do an initial assessment when the children first come to me as six-and-a-half to seven year olds. I give them the Schonell Reading Test since they have already had some early mechanics such as studying initial consonants. We work on the structure of words and use class dictionaries. We take words both from the dictionaries and from their own experience. Also I put in new words using formal techniques. Generally, I work from their experience around some theme. We talk about it, and then we do some reading and writing as well as poetry and drama, all around a particular theme. We do a lot of sharing of reading with other children and we ultimately make a class book. We use a language scheme called *Breakthrough*. I use flashcards to develop a coverage with basic words. It then gets placed in his folder. We then refer back to that flashcard and eventually the children begin to use their own language using *Breakthrough* but they still continue to have their own personal words in one section of the folder. Gradually they begin to build sentences. When they know the sentences they can begin to share the sentences with each other and begin to make storybooks. We start using the folders, then we ultimately get past the folders. At some point the teacher must know when to stop using the child's folder and the language scheme and begin to develop creative writing. When children know enough words they can begin to work their way into creative writing. We have *Nippers*, a reading scheme, but it has working-class language in it and some of the parents objected. But mostly these were working-class parents who had just made it into the middle-class.

English teacher two: We give the Schonell Test at age seven years and from that we can see who is going to need help in reading. The Head usually does it herself. The Head monitors the whole test. The teacher and the Head listen to the child read orally and eventually we monitor the whole school. We eventually give both forms A and B of the Schonell. We do not use a reading scheme but we use the *Breakthrough Language Scheme* which was known as the *Initial Literacy Scheme* and consisted of some 'home-made stuff' which came out of a Schools Council study done by Brian Thompson and David Mackay. It has been published by Longmans as *Breakthrough* and it does help us to use the child's language to help him to recognize words and eventually make sentences.

English teacher seven: I teach in an infant school and we have to work very hard to get to know a child when he comes to school. We need to get a one-to-one relationship with him. Ten per cent of the children are really deprived in this school and 60 per cent need a teacher's personal attention almost all the time when they are beginning to learn to read. I realize that many of the children understand very little of what I am saying to them. Many of the middle-class kids who have had books around the home understand me. We do all sorts of expression activities, painting, modelling, drawing – creative things. I encourage them to get their hands in glue and paint, to express rhythm, jingles, to bring in animals like hamsters and rabbits, and then we draw and write about these things. I do the writing and they read what I write. They begin to copy the letters and to make their own books. That sort of activity goes on for almost a year with some, and with others for only a few weeks. Some will move fairly rapidly from writing single words to writing a sentence like, 'Daddy go to work', or 'Where is my milk?'

English teacher ten: The children come in from the home and when we see the parents' ability to communicate we can tell almost immediately whether the children will be fluent or not. Sometimes the children will point and not speak at all, or will get another child to speak for them. If we had playgroups or nurseries in this community the children would come into school with more language. Sometimes they have two ways of speaking, the playground way and the school way. Some children have great difficulty in listening when they come to school. We generally feel that reading cannot begin until speech has developed. We begin to have the children handle materials when they first come into the school. We don't believe that any part of the school day can be disassociated from any other part. We try to stimulate conversation around various activities such as a water tray. We have an activity time at the beginning of the day. We try to make it a calming influence and listen to everyone for a while. We have news time and children will tell news or bring something from home. I usually ask them a question to stimulate their interest. We have colour-coded words and we have a different colour for each day. We use a pre-primer called *My Little Book*, which is part of the *Janet and John Reading Scheme*. I start on the big cards leading into the series, read them as a whole and use flashcards as we move into the books. I don't believe in pushing the children and we do not have any set point for all of them to be at a certain age. We do prereading activities such as noting similar shapes.

Most children are from the working class in this school (there are only four whose parents own their own homes), and I notice a significant difference between the experiences of children from the working class and children from the middle class.

American teacher one: We use a basic reading series which is adopted by the state and by our board of education. The problem is that with thirty-three children in a class, a few of the children already know how to read and have read the whole reader, and others are having trouble recognizing any of the words or doing any reading at all. I have to group them because there are so many differences in ability but that leaves me a very limited time to try to stimulate the ones who already can read. We have very few materials or good children's books that children who can already read can be referred to. Some of the children come to school speaking Black dialect and this seems to interfere with their reading. I have a few Spanish-speaking children and it is virtually impossible for them to do any of the reading in the reader when they first come. I have managed to get a teacher's aide who is Spanish-speaking and she works with these students but they mostly work on recognizing English words and it is important for them to be in an English-speaking environment.

American teacher two: I teach second grade and although we have a state-adopted basic reading series which we are supposed to make each child go through, I found after teaching three years in the school that it simply didn't work for some of the children. I use a combination of language experience and keyword vocabulary with some children because they simply do not respond to the reader. Although the principal does not like us to depart from this reading series he has confidence in me and I have produced as well on the *California Third Grade Reading Test* as did any of the ones in any of the other second-grade classes. What this means to me is that the language-experience approach would work for more children if we were allowed to use it.

American teacher twelve (Black): Most of the children who come to this school have almost no incentive to read. Very few of the parents do much reading, and there are very few books or magazines in the home. The reader is the first book that most of these children have ever encountered. Of course we use the pre-primers, flashcards and experience charts, and we try to relate the reading in the pre-primers to the words that the children use and know. It is clear that the primers and the other books in the reading series do not really represent much that these children have experienced in life so far.

Teachers of eight to eleven year olds

English teacher six: I use a variety of materials to get students interested in reading. We rely on the class library and the county library. I use *Sound Sense* for remedial readers and the SRA Power and Rate cards and the SRA library as well as diaries, puppet plays, poems and stories. We also do a great deal of dictionary work which I make into crosswords such as lexicon crosswords, and we use the *Ladybird* cards for word building. We have also used television programmes and the *British Trader Alphabet Journal*. As a part of English they make a choice from this journal as to a trade that they would like to investigate. Then they visit a local shop and get extra material. They then make their own books related to the topic they chose. We work on these from September to Christmas. We have competitions for prizes and give certificates for the winners. This is very good for junior children.

We have many visiting speakers, talking for example on road-safety tests. Every morning the children start the day writing in their diary (no one looks at it). We also have watched the TV programme *A Year's Journey*, which is shown all around England. The children from advantaged homes where books are accepted are more sure of themselves. They are usually very ready to read and enter into discussions more freely. The children from less advantaged homes seem less sure of themselves, less free and are uncertain about joining in discussions. It takes a lot longer to help them get the right book. I can tell right away if a child comes from 'the old village' or from the council estates. If they come from the council estates their English usage is usually not very good. They also have a different accent and you can occasionally tell from their clothing.

I have made my own automatic flashcard machine and my own tachistoscope for the children who are slow-learners. I notice that those who can speak freely and clearly are usually keen readers and able writers, but many quiet, shy individuals are avid readers and able writers as well. Some of the chatterboxes are retarded. The social class in this school comes out in the puppet plays. Children will have their parts written on paper. By and large, the good readers not only read but speak their parts fluently. They don't keep having to look at their paper, and will *ad lib* more readily. This is usually a class thing and the children from the working class are much less good at this sort of thing.

We administer the Schonell Test for Reading in September, February, and in July, and also the NFER Sentence Reading test. We use a continuous form of assessment with the SRA. I believe that there is a necessity to utilize any out-of-school activity to the fullest advantage in oral work and writing. I tell them to walk down to the river and use their eyes, not just report what happens, but tell how they feel and what struck them and then to come back and draw and illustrate what they have seen and felt. We are just beginning a project on the effects of the M5 coming in through W—. We are taking photos to illustrate how it is now and we will show the turmoil as it is coming through and then we will also photograph how it looks after it has come through. We are doing a whole community study on this.

English teacher seventeen: In this school we believe that the school is a powerhouse of language. We build language into the school where we can. We hit them with language in the hall from the time they enter the school. Any adult converses with the children. We can bring more adults into the school with our open setting and we bring many parents into the school and try to tie the home and school together all the way along. We feel that it is necessary for speech fluency to come before reading, but we like to begin having students enjoy words for words' sake. We even do the chanting of some silly riddles and rhymes with the younger children earlier in the school, and as they get older we work on a project. You saw the volcano and the castle. Our language develops as a result of working on the concepts which are developed when working on the project. The children first study the historical approach and find out words which are associated with castles and volcanoes. They have to do things like describe a volcano erupting and develop a whole vocabulary around whatever project we are doing. For materials we use junk materials which are talking-points to explore language. We use sandpaper, stones, shells, rabbits that children keep in the back of the school, reading games that teachers have made up themselves, and maths games. We think that the reading schemes in some cases do the exact opposite of what they are supposed to do and inhibit language. For example, we have never had a child say anything like 'jump, jump, jump,' which is a sentence you can find in the reading schemes. Of course there are some good imaginative reading schemes. Some schemes are better for some areas than others, for example. Our goal is to gear the material to the child's home language. We need to find out about his home language by talking with him and with his parents and then find books for each child which are geared absolutely for that child. Some of the teachers do like to tick off the phonics that are in the reading scheme with the various children. I make an initial assessment with the Stott Pre-Reading Scheme, *Flying Start*, and go through the scheme with them. I believe that the open school helps language development and the assessment of language development. We use the Neale Analysis of Reading Ability at the end of every year which gives the child's reading age.

American teacher five: Our principal really was enthusiastic about the open-school concept and when we moved into our new building there were practically no walls in it. We did put up some dividers and began to get the things organized to do team teaching. The problem was that some of the people on the teams didn't like some of the other people on the teams. It ended up with some teams that we divided the open spaces up into three classrooms and simply taught our classes the way we would have if there had been no open school built. My team worked out very well because we all get along together and we keep being afraid that the principal will break us up for some reason. I think he trusts us and therefore we can get away with a lot such as not following the reading series or the district policy on teaching grammar. We really try to build a new curriculum and try to put reading, language and literature all together. The problem is that if everybody in fifth grade isn't using the same books, and we use a book that a sixth-grade teacher is going to use, that teacher is upset with us.

American teacher eighteen: I am committed to individualizing instruction particularly in reading. The problem is, it takes so much time. Also I don't have nearly enough books for the thirty-three children and there is no library in my school. Our district does not insist that we stick to a prescribed programme, but the parents feel that the children should get basic skills. We are very much a part of the 'back to the basics' movement, and with the statewide tests in reading coming in grades three and six there is no doubt that we have all become apprehensive and somewhat more structured in our teaching.

American teacher twelve: Our district supervisor actually comes around and checks which page of the grammar book we are on. The worst problem is that the kids really hate the books we are using. The *Roberts English Series* is a beautiful set of books but it just doesn't work with the kids in this school and I've heard other teachers say the same thing. I have bits and pieces of poetry but there is no way that I can get the kids to go through the book page by page. Most of the books we have available for language and reading are like the Roberts Series. We depart from it every chance we get and use films, plays, field trips, and a variety of other projects to get kids interested in reading. The big problem is to make them aware that there are books that will really hold their interest.

Conclusions and analyses
Although no statistical analysis of the data for this study has been

335

attempted in this paper, it seems that several major trends emerge. Most of the English teachers in the study were in informal, open schools by American standards which they took for granted as the normal way of schooling. Most of them used a language-experience approach which they called 'teaching reading', which generally drew language from the experience of the children and bridged into reading in various contexts, although most stated that reading schemes existed in their school. No English teacher interviewed in this study would admit to relying upon a reading scheme as the basic material for teaching reading in any English school. In contrast, 90 per cent of the American teachers interviewed indicated that not only did a reading series exist in the school, but that it was the basic material used for reading. Many said that supervisors and principals monitored where teachers were in the particular series and some stated that parents took a considerable interest in the placement of students not only in the various tests, but within the actual books of the series. Some American teachers stated that they felt sufficiently free to depart from the series to initiate activities on their own which they felt would be good for the particular students they were teaching. Most American teachers felt that they were asked to rely heavily on a reading series or language series with younger children, and that this trend continued with the teachers of older children as well. Although a number of American teachers indicated that they were in sympathy with the concept of open education, they clearly saw external testing, both statewide and commercial, as interfering with experiments in team teaching and open education. Many, expressing the same view as American teacher five, stated that the pressures of accountability had resulted in putting the walls back up in what had originally been planned as an open school.

Few English teachers relied on reading schemes to any great extent and seemed much more inclined to take various stories and phonics charts and other elements out of reading schemes and use them for whatever purpose they felt necessary. Many English teachers noted that the children were engaged in conversation by all of the adults in the school and that there was a heavy stimulus on oral language development before reading was begun, and as reading continued. In fact, most stated that reading was based on oral language.

Many American teachers noted the influence of the Principal in forcing the dictates of the school district with respect to implementing various reading series. Fewer English teachers noted that the Head used such influence but all knew that the Head had such influence. One English teacher stated that the Head had decided to use a particular test and monitored that test for the whole school. Generally, English teachers seemed to be less concerned with the restrictions placed upon them by the headteacher or by the LEA than did American teachers. Most of the American teachers interviewed in this study seemed to see the bureaucracy consisting of the Principal, Supervisor, School Board, parents, etc. engaged in a kind of conspiracy to prevent them from working effectively with children. Many of them clearly resented the onset of various accountability measures and there was indeed always the hint that these accountability measures were being used for teacher evaluations rather than evaluations of children's achievement. With regard to the use of materials, two major conclusions emerged from this study:

1 With few exceptions the English teachers interviewed tended to use the child's natural language in beginning reading and continued to derive reading from language-related activities throughout the primary-school years. Reading schemes were not used as the primary means of instruction but rather were used as they fit the means of a particular child at a specific time.
2 Ninety per cent of the American teachers interviewed in this study noted that a reading series was the basic means for instruction in reading in their school. None of them used the language-experience approach primarily, but some of them used the child's language to develop reading activities where the series did not seem to be appropriate.

Open education and accountability
At least half of the American teachers interviewed in this study had had direct experience with open education either in their training or in actual practice. Approximately 20 per cent of the teachers interviewed had been in what might be called 'open' situations of some sort. As the comments of American teacher five indicated, because of lack of preparation of teachers and lack of harmony on many teaching teams thrown into open situations, some teachers and principals became dissatisfied with open education. In addition, various accountability measures, for example statewide testing programmes and national assessment programmes, have tended to make American teachers feel less experimental and generally forced them into a position of relying on traditional methods and materials. In addition, some research has shown that children in traditional schools make better scores on standardized tests than do children in open schools (Wright 1975). Although such research is not conclusive, it adds weight to what already seems to be a significant trend away from open education in the United States.

In England, despite the conditions which brought about the formation of the Bullock Committee and its ultimate report, *A Language for Life*, there is now no question that the committee did not come up with evidence to support the fact that there were wholesale declines in standards of reading and literacy which were the result of open education or informal education. It is striking to an American observer and to many teachers caught up in accountability struggles in the United States to see that neither the Bullock Report, nor any subsequent commentary, has proposed a major shift away from informal education and that the report itself stressed the importance of oral language in the early years of schooling and proposed that 'monitoring should employ an array of techniques of a kind that will make assessment both reliable and valid'. Further, Watts (1975) observed that the Bullock Report seemed to offer many teachers 'a basis for a shift of emphasis in English teaching . . . away from the fragmentary and mechanical, away from the conception of literacy that merely linked certain skills, away from the notion of high culture with many poor relations; it is a shift towards the promotion of competence and enjoyment in an increasingly broad field of linguistic activities, differentiated but firmly related, uniting language with literature, concerned with learners of all ages and abilities'.

So there seems to be little evidence from the conclusions and from reactions to the Bullock Report or from the reports of teachers interviewed in this study that there is dissatisfaction with the basic philosophy of open or informal education as it is currently being applied in England. Naturally, teachers express needs for more materials, lighter teaching loads and more assistance to enhance their own effectiveness. Reactions to the Bullock Report in England have noted the mixing of definitions of reading from a psycholinguistic model to a behaviouristic model which essentially means that the writers of the report were not able to agree on the relationship between reading and language although the stress on oral language and on using children's language experience in reading is clearly present in the report (Spencer and McKenzie 1975). Many teachers interviewed in this study seemed to have mixed language attitudes concerning children from the working class and children from the middle class, and the fact that these are prevalent in England, whether in an informal or traditional setting, is explained very well, not only by the comments of some of the English teachers in this study, but by the work of Harold and Connie Rosen, who in their report of the Schools Council Project on Language Development in the Primary Schools (Rosen and Rosen 1973), noted:

> However much the old style of teaching of grammar is discredited, nothing will ever stop teachers conveying to children often in very subtle ways what their attitudes to language are. They may write in red ink in the margin, 'slang!' or stop to correct a child's speech or enjoy with a class an invented word. These deeply-held attitudes will have a considerable effect for better or for worse and there is no escaping them. Anyway, children are, not surprisingly, interested in language but not in the kind of language teaching we have traditionally provided. They will play with words as they play with anything else. They make up

nonsense, which is linguistic experiment, and the child's own oral culture, as the Opies showed so dramatically, is rich with language awareness and experiment. The playground and the street has its own verbal culture . . . (pages 253-4).

The English teachers in this study seemed to find the materials for instruction within the language and the child. This was true of some of the American teachers interviewed although for the most part the American teachers in this study seemed more like victims who, together with their children, are being oppressed by a vast array of tests, assessment techniques, and commercial publishers who continually erect a barrier between the child and the language.

Acknowledgement

I would like to thank the headteachers, principals and staffs of the schools in England and the United States who cooperated in the preparation of this study.

References

COX, C. B. and DYSON, A. E. (1971) *The Black Papers on Education* Davis-Paynter

DES (1967) *Children and their Primary Schools* (Plowden Report) HMSO

DES (1975) *A Language for Life* (Bullock Report) HMSO

FEATHERSTONE, J. (1971) *Schools Where Children Learn* New York: Riveright

FRAZIER, A. (1972) *Open Schools for Children* Association for Supervision and Curriculum Development, Washington D.C.

GARDNER, K. (1968) 'The state of reading' in N. Smart (ed) *Crisis in the Classroom* IPC

MARSH, L. (1970) *Alongside the Child: Experiences in the English Primary School* New York: Harper Colophon Books, Harper and Row

NYQUIST, E. W. and HAWES, G. R. (1972) *Open Education: A Source Book for Parents and Teachers* New York: Bantam Books

RATHBONE, C. H. (1971) *Open Education: the Informal Classroom* New York: Citation Press

ROGERS, V. R. (ed) (1970) *Teaching in a British Primary School* New York: Macmillan

ROSEN, C. and H. (1973) *The Language of Primary School Children* Penguin

SHAFER, R. E. (1976) National assessment: backgrounds and projections *English Education* 7, 2, 67-78

SILBERMAN, C. E. (1970) *Crisis in the Classroom: The Remaking of American Education* New York: Random House

Spencer, M. and McKenzie, M. G. (1975) 'Learning to read and the reading process' in H. Rosen (ed) *Language and Literacy in our Schools: Some Appraisals of the Bullock Report* University of London Institute of Education

Start, K. B. and Wells, B. K. (1972) *The Trend of Reading Standards* NFER

Watts, J. (1975) 'A Language for Life' – a comment on the Bullock Report from the National Association for the Teaching of English *English in Education* 9, 3, 9-10

Wright, R. J. (1975) The affective and cognitive consequences of an open education elementary school *American Educational Research Journal* 12, 4, 449-68

Appendix

Interviews with teachers

1 What do you consider to be the most important reasons for the development of language power?

2 What have you observed in your pupils about the development of their language power?

3 What do you consider to be the most important classroom activities to develop language power?

4 From your observations, what relationship seems to exist between the development of oral language ability and reading and writing?

5 What teaching materials do you consider most effective in the development of language power?

6 How do you evaluate progress?

7 What did you learn about developing children's language in your initial preparation to teach or subsequently? To what extent have you been able to use effectively in the classroom what you did learn?

36 The relationship between language and reading in Nigeria

Bolarinwa Balogun

Introduction

While it is true to say that a little child starts washing his hands before eating as soon as his parents decide that it is time to begin training in personal cleanliness, it can only be said that a child begins to speak no sooner and no later than when he reaches a given stage of physical maturation. Individual variations occur in language development especially when age correlation is considered but it is of particular significance that in language development there is a better correlation with motor development than with chronological age. As a correlation between the variable language development with the variables chronological age and motor development is possible, so it is possible to relate it to the physical indications of brain maturation such as the gross weight of the brain or the changing weight proportions of given substances in either grey or white matter (Lenneberg 1970).

Language is a critical factor in cognitive development and the child's progress in language during the preschool years is astounding. For example, between the ages of three and five, the child adds over fifty new words to his vocabulary each month on average, and data collected during the 1920s indicated that 'the average two year old had an effective vocabulary of 272 words, the average three year old 896 words, the average four year old 1540, and the average five year old 2000 (Mussen *et al* 1969). This situation has not been static. A more recent study conducted in the late 1950s showed that children possessed larger vocabulary and talked in lengthier clauses and sentences than those thirty years before them. Thus, four year olds in 1930 used 4.3 words per 'sentence' on average as contrasted with 5.3 words in 1957 (Mussen *et al* 1969). Although it is not easy to explain this kind of increase in sentence length it has been said by McCarthy (1959) that this may be due to: 'the advent of radio and television, the rise of nursery schools affording more opportunities for language stimulation outside the school for formerly underprivileged groups of children, more leisure time for parents to spend with their children and better economic conditions allowing parents even in lower income brackets to provide more stimulating environments for their children'.

The child's cognitive abilities undergo radical modifications as his facilities in language improve by leaps and bounds. The child of four perceives, thinks, reasons and solves problems in ways that are quite different from a child of two. When the basic understanding of language is acquired, subsequent learning becomes increasingly controlled and regulated by words. It has been pointed out (Luria 1975) that:

> in the early stages of child development, speech is only a means of communication with adults and other children ... Subsequently it becomes also a means whereby he organizes his experience and regulates his own actions. So the child's activity is mediated through words.

Teaching may be defined as the process of supplying the conditions favourable to learning. The teaching of reading is no exception. As De Boer and Dallman (1964) point out, the conditions needed by children to make maximum progress in learning to read include physical health, mental health, sight and hearing, intelligence, background experience, *knowledge of language*, desire to read, purpose for reading, interest in reading and reading skills. As luck would have it, nearly all children come to school already equipped with most of these elements in differing degrees. It is true that some children learn to read in spite of the lack of some of these elements and that blind children, deaf children, and sick children do learn to read. 'But to the extent that children are lacking in the elements named, they will be handicapped in the process of learning to read.' (De Boer and Dallman 1964, page 27).

At this stage, the most relevant of these elements is *knowledge of language*. As there is no question that direct experience is a substantial aid to reading, it follows that this experience must be accompanied by an adequate fund of experience with language. That a good knowledge is necessary in preparation for reading experiences illustrates the close interrelations of the various aspects of language communication. There is enough evidence to confirm the fact that there is a strong relationship between linguistic ability and reading achievement, and that a child's ability to understand and use language orally is an important factor in beginning reading (Hildreth 1948). Since we know that children's learning points to the interrelatedness of the four factors of language, i.e. reading, writing, speaking and listening, we can conclude that wide experience with all kinds of language, including extensive contacts with words and sentences in meaningful situations, contributes effectively to the improvement of reading. For reading to flourish, therefore, a rich, diversified and stimulating language environment and a curriculum which makes room for highly-motivated language experiences is imperative.

In rounding up this part of the paper, we may interpret reading as 'the process of translating from alphabetical symbols to that form of language from which the native speaker can already derive meaning' (Venezky *et al* 1970). To teach reading, therefore, is not to teach language, because by the time the normal child comes to the reading task, he already speaks a language and has also mastered a system of signals for communicating in a meaningful way with other people (Lenneberg 1967).

Language and reading in Nigeria

All that has been said so far about language and reading are universal 'truths' which apply to all languages, particularly where the language acquired in infancy is the same as that to be used for formal reading. In Nigeria, this is not exactly the situation. There are various local languages which are distributed on a geographical basis. These local languages are the first to which the child is introduced and it is the vocabulary of these languages that the child acquires as he matures. Formal reading in the school is done in another language, and throughout Nigeria this language is English. In essence, the language with which the Nigerian child grows and which he uses during his preschool years and the vocabulary of which he has accumulated is not the same as that he will use when he begins to read in school.

It is necessary to explain the relationship between reading and English in the curriculum of the Nigerian school. In almost all cases, reading is taught only as an adjunct of English. In other words, the teacher of English is also the teacher of reading and whatever is said in the following pages about the teacher of English is also valid for the teacher of reading.

Being a Yoruba, and that language being my mother tongue (MT) all my examples will be taken from it. However, what I say for Yoruba goes for almost all other Nigerian languages. But before going on, one point needs to be made. During the Nigerian child's early school days, some of his lessons are taught in the MT. The medium of instruction in this case is the 'standard' Yoruba as opposed to the local dialect of it spoken in that particular geographical location where the child is born. The result is that the child has to operate in three 'languages' – his dialect of Yoruba, the 'standard' Yoruba and English. The least one can say is that to a younger learner, this is a very confusing situation. This confusion can be traced to a variety of causes.

First, the sound patterns of most Nigerian languages sometimes show a major contrast to the sound systems of the English language. For example, there are no dental fricatives *th* as in *thin*, *the* as in *this* in Yoruba language. The tendency then is for the reader or learner to substitute *t* for *th* and *d* for *the* (Dunston 1969).

Problems also arise in the area of cultural usage of language which is not the same in the Yoruba and English languages. For instance, in

Yoruba the plural form of pronouns is often used for the singular as a form of respect for elders. Consequently, *won* (they/them) and *e* (you) which are plural forms are used for singular pronouns, and are known as the 'plurality of respect'. The tendency, therefore, is to carry this cultural usage of the MT over to the English. Thus, to a Yoruban reader 'They are coming' (Won nbo) may mean 'He is coming' (O mbo); and 'I saw them' (Mo ri won) may mean 'I saw him/her' (Mo rii).

One fact which is incontrovertible is that language, even when it is introduced into another culture as a foreign or second language (English in Nigeria) is intricately interwoven with the culture of the 'donors' as well as the 'recipients'; and since semantic status of words derive their potency from the experience of the background of the users, it only follows that when a foreign language is introduced into another language environment, there is the tendency for the child to give a MT equivalent to such foreign words and concepts. For example, the Yoruba word 'dun' can describe a wide variety of situations in English, though to the Yoruba child, the only English equivalent is 'sweet'. In Yoruba 'dun' is correctly used in 'Inu mi dun' (*I feel happy*); 'O dun' (It is *sweet*); 'Ere na dun' (The play is *interesting*); 'Orin na dun' (The song is *melodious*). So a Yoruba child learning to read English and whose single word 'dun' can mean sweet, happy, interesting or melodious (and many other words), is bound to experience a lot of difficulty because his single word covers a lot of situations in the language in which he is expected to function.

In the same way, when one word in English language stands for an idea, the Yoruba speaker may have varied vocabularies for the purposes of distinguishing different meanings intended. For example, 'dead' is literally 'ku' in Yoruba. But then, the Yoruba speaker will go on to say 'Ofo se' (a little child is dead). 'Oba wo ja' (the king has disappeared/i.e. is dead); 'Ojo se alaisi' (Ojo is no more/dead). The concept of death, at least semantically, is problematic to a Yoruba child learning to reading English because it raises a number of varieties of usage which may not be necessary in the new language being learnt. It is then not very difficult to appreciate under what hazard a Yoruba child operates when he tries to read English and translate what he has read into concepts and ideas for which the MT has varied distinctions.

Despite the enormity of the problems of the MT in relation to reading in English, it is impossible to completely ignore it without dire consequences in the total education of the Nigerian child. The MT furnishes the conceptual substance from which the child builds new creations of thought, and the signal with which he can direct himself (MacCainite 1969, page 688 *ff*). To the Nigerian child, therefore, the MT he uses in the preschool days and with which he learns in his first six years of life is not like a garment that he can put off when he dons his school uniform. It is indeed a part of the stuff of which his mind is built; it embodies the ideas and attitudes he has gained from his environment; it is the language through which he has acquired the earliest experience of life; it is the language through which he thinks, dreams, cherishes, loves, scolds and learns (Sharma 1957).

There is evidence to show that adequate training of the child in the MT is a precondition to adequate training in the non-MT like English or French, if the proper tool should be provided for the child to function successfully in the present world and face the challenge of the future. As a matter of fact, it has been shown in the South Pacific that it is not only advantageous but also largely essential to teach the MT for the effective understanding of the non-MT. Here experiences tend to show that when pupils were taught the MT, a better knowledge of English, the non-MT, was subsequently acquired in a comparatively short time with a comparatively small expenditure of effort (Platten 1953). In Hong Kong and Malacca, further verification has been made possible through the comparison of the efficiency attained as a result of teaching in the MT and non-MT. The conclusion reached here was that the results in English (the non-MT in these areas) were better for the pupils who had first of all been taught in the MT than for those who started their studies in English, the non-MT (Verbake 1966).

Conclusion

An attempt has been made to discuss the general nature of language and reading. Some of the reading problems which the learner of English as a second language faces have also been examined. In addition, the fact that local language cannot be 'eliminated' without making the learning or reading of the essential language, English, more difficult has been spotlighted. It only remains to enumerate some of the steps which may be taken to integrate the MT experience into the language and reading curriculum of the schools and the training colleges for the teachers of English.

There is an urgent need for a comprehensive contrastive study of the major languages of Nigeria and English. From such exercises, materials needed for writing workbooks for teachers and pupils, particularly in areas where interference, be it semantic, structural or phonological, may occur.

Teachers of English and in effect teachers of reading, particularly where they are non-Nigerians, should be able to appreciate the problems which the Nigerian child faces in learning English because of the MT experience. Opposition to the teaching or usage of the MT by such teachers can only add to the problems with which the child has to contend.

Courses in the various aspects of the MT should be offered to teachers of English/reading with a view to understanding its cultural, syntactic, lexical, phonological and semantic systems as compared with English.

Finally, there will be a rich return for any investment made on compiling an error analysis of the pupil's use of English, spoken and written, which could be traced to the MT influence. This will be a tremendous advantage to both the teacher and his pupils.

References

DE BOER, J. and DALLMAN, M. (1964) *The Teaching of Reading* New York: Holt, Rinehart and Winston

DUNSTON, E. (ed) (1969) *Twelve Nigerian Languages* Longman

HILDRETH, G. (1948) Interrelationships among the language arts *Elementary School Journal* 48, 538-49

LENNEBERG, E. (1967) *Biological Foundations of Language* New York: Wiley

LENNEBERG, E. H. (1970) in D. V. Gunderson (ed) *Language in Reading* Center for Applied Linguistics, Washington D. C.

LURIA, A. R. (1975) 'The role of language in the formation of temporary connections' in B. Simon (ed) *Psychology in the Soviet Union* Stanford: Stanford University Press

MacCAINITE, W. M. (1969) Language development *Encyclopedia of Educational Research* New York: Macmillan 688

MCCARTHY, D. (1959) Research in language development: retrospect and prospect *Child Development* 24, 5, 3-24

MUSSEN, P., CONGER, J. and KAGAN, J. (1969) *Child Development and Personality* New York: Harper and Row

PLATTEN, G. J. (1953) The use of vernacular in teaching in the South Pacific *South Pacific Commission Technical Paper* 44

SHARMA, G. R. (1957) 'The Teacher of Hindi, *Shiksha*' cited by J. Dakin *et al* (1968) *Language in Education: The Problem in Commonwealth Africa and the Indo-Pakistan Sub-continent* Open University Press

VENEZKY, P. L., CALFEE, R. C. and CHAPMAN, R. S. (1970) pp. 38-9 in D. V. Gunderson (ed) *Language and Reading* Center for Applied Linguistics, Washington D. C.

VERBAKE, R. (1966) Language vehiculaires de l'enseignement Afrique *International Review of Education* 12, 4, 450-66

37 Classroom teachers' procedures in teaching Finnish to school beginners

Kari Tuunainen

Introduction

Teaching the mother tongue is in the very centre of the classroom teacher's interests when she teaches the first and second graders (in Finland seven and eight year old children). As we all know mastering language is very important for every field of the child's mental development. The child needs his native tongue not only for communication with his environment but also for getting along with himself, i.e. for thinking. But the trouble is that it is not clear whether or not school can do enough to speed up that important process. School seems to have many old traditions that tend to move the focus of attention to other and often minor matters.

In order to get a better view of the problem and to start making curricula and methods better we must obtain more knowledge about the ways the teachers actually conduct their roles as mother-tongue teachers. That is not an easy task. To obtain really reliable and valid knowledge on the matter we should arrange a study where many highly-skilful observers could take notes about all the actions of the teachers in their classrooms. With the very limited grants that we nowadays get (in Finland) that kind of study would not be possible. So we have to be satisfied with cheaper and less accurate ways: directly asking the teachers what they do when they teach their pupils the mother tongue. Even this is a new approach in Finland. In this paper I shall attempt to introduce a study on the procedures and the points of emphasis of thirty-two Finnish classroom teachers in the mother tongue teaching to first and second graders. In the last section I try to draw some general comments and suggestions.

The study

A questionnaire containing questions about sources of information on the pupils, supportive teaching, and differences in emphasis and attention given to different areas in teaching language was presented to thirty-two first- and second-graders' classroom teachers, all women, from the city of Joensuu. Nearly half of them (47 per cent) had spent their whole career with the school beginners, 29.4 per cent had taught for more than twenty years, 44.2 per cent for between ten and twenty years, and 26.4 per cent for less than ten years. Younger teachers had got their teacher training in universities and had significantly more extra training than the older ones who had been trained in small teacher-training colleges (seminaries) before the whole thing was transferred to the universities.

The question blank for teachers was designed using a judgment method. Ten teacher-trainers, previously classroom teachers, picked up the most important objectives out of the 1970 National Curriculum Plan for the Elementary School, and put them into order of importance. The importance of being honest was greatly stressed in the instruction and the participating teachers remained anonymous during the study. This was done to reduce the numbers of socially desirable answers.

What follows now is a short account of the most significant points in the results of the study. I first present the division of the answers and then the mean scores and the dispersals on the right.

1 Sources of information about the school beginners

The first cluster of questions was presented in order to find out the sources of information about the pupils. Table 1 (below) shows the situation with information of time before school and Table 2 (page 349) during school. The teachers were given mainly ready-structured alternatives. but room and encouragement for free answers were also given. Neighbours, friends, etc., were left out of the results, because there is not much that could be done to improve the flow of information from these sources, while those 'official' sources can be activated, if needed. If the information does not flow, the 'officials' can be blamed and forced to release more knowledge.

Table 1   **Sources where the teachers obtained information about their pupils concerning time before school**

Source	Percentage of teachers according to the amount of information they obtained				
	None	Some	Plenty	$\overline{X}$	S.D.
Kindergarten teacher	(19) 76.0%	(5) 20.0%	(1) 4.0%	1.2	0.5
Parents	(11) 35.4%	(16) 51.6%	(4) 12.9%	1.7	0.6
Maternity and child-care clinic	(19) 79.7%	(5) 20.3%	—	1.2	0.4
Educational psychologist	(19) 82.6%	(4) 17.4%	—	1.1	0.3

Generally, teachers seem to obtain very little information about their pupils' preschool lives. Parents are the main source, but not for every teacher, since more than one-third claimed not to have obtained any information from parents either. The other sources are quite dry, and to get information from them seems more like an accident. On the other hand, the teachers may have been too passive to go and get it.

Table 2 Sources of information about pupils during their school years

Source	Percentage of teachers according to the amount of information they obtained				
	None	Some	Plenty	$\overline{X}$	S.D.
Kindergarten teachers	(17) 73.9%	(6) 26.1%	—	1.2	0.4
Parents	(1) 3.1%	(26) 81.2%	(5) 15.6%	2.1	0.4
Health record (in school)	(11) 36.7%	(18) 60.0%	(1) 3.3%	1.6	0.5
Educational psychologist	(13) 52.0%	(12) 48.0%	—	1.4	0.5

Most children had been in a day nursery (80 per cent) and in a kindergarten (75 per cent).

During the school years parents' importance as a source of information has grown and the health record in care of the school nurse has come into the picture. When looking at the figures above it must be kept in mind that they only show the teachers' subjective opinions about the situation and that the real amount and depth of the information flow cannot be measured with this method, nor its relation to different pupils. One of the most interesting points is that the gap between kindergarten and school is very wide. In forming a mental picture of a pupil the classroom teacher appears to be alone.

2 *Supportive teaching*

In Finnish schools (elementary and junior-high levels) in addition to special education some supportive teaching is arranged for those ordinary pupils who have minor difficulties in learning. The importance of the mother tongue and its major place in the curriculum is reflected in the amount of supportive teaching which is given during the first and second grades. Attending the supportive lessons is mostly voluntary and hence shows active interest from the pupil's and parents' side. But since information about the new remedial arrangements is essential in the efforts to get parents' and pupils' attitudes favourable to the programme, the amount of the supportive teaching also shows the effectiveness of the information between school and home besides the activity of the teacher.

The question 'What proportion of the total available supportive teaching do you use with your pupils?' was presented to the thirty-two classroom teachers. The division of the answers was as follows:

		f	%
1	Gave no supportive lessons	—	—
2	Used less than half of the maximum	16	50.0
3	Used more than half of the maximum	13	40.6
4	Used the whole maximum	3	9.4

Teachers can give two hours of supportive lessons per week for which additional payment is made. Half of the respondents gave supportive lessons less than half of the maximum. All teachers said that they gave these lessons to their own pupils.

3 Teaching Finnish (language)

The main categories of the questionnaire covered the areas of language stated in the 1970 National Curriculum Plan. They were:

(a) speech and listening
(b) reading
(c) writing
(d) knowledge of the language (grammar).

It was seen best to give the respondents ready-structured alternatives for answers. As we know, this brings some problems, but still it was considered more reliable than dealing with a large variety of unclassified answers. The given alternatives are items (sub-areas) drawn out of either the sub-categories or the instruction text in the 1970 N.C. Plan book. Then these items were arranged according to the judgments of the ten teacher-trainers mentioned above. The question with every item was: 'How often do you pay attention to the item given? Please mark your answer under the number most suitable to

Table 3 **Division of teachers according to the sequence of attention to different items in speech and listening**

Speech and listening	Attention paid					$\overline{X}$	S.D.
	1	2	3	4	5		
Estimation of child's vocabulary	—	4	14	10	4	3.4	0.8
Vocabulary of the Finnish language	1	1	4	20	6	3.9	0.8
Errors in the quality of voice	—	1	8	16	7	3.9	0.7
Errors in pronunciation	5	6	15	6	—	2.6	0.9
Willingness to express through language	—	1	8	16	7	3.9	0.7
Auditory sorting ability	—	—	10	14	8	3.9	0.7

your way of teaching.' The alternatives were 1 (never), 2 (seldom), 3 (sometimes), 4 (often), and 5 (all the time). The same arrangement applies to Tables 3, 4, 5 and 6.

The mean scores show that only errors in pronunciation are generally lacking attention with $\overline{X}$ = 2.6 (between seldom and sometimes) and five teachers paying no attention at all. Four items got the mean score as high as 3.9 which means that attention is paid often and is very good also for the children who have lingual disabilities.

Table 4 Division of teachers according to the sequence of attention to different items in reading

Reading	1	2	3	4	5	(32-n)	$\overline{X}$	S.D.
	\multicolumn{5}{c}{Attention paid}			
Hardness level of the text	—	3	10	10	8	(−1)	3.7	0.7
Individualization of the text	1	5	10	14	2		3.3	0.9
Understanding the text	—	—	1	6	25		4.7	0.5
Text's quality in enlarging vocabulary	—	2	10	14	3	(−3)	3.6	0.7
Clarity of pronunciation	—	1	7	17	7		3.9	0.7
Reading in chorus	—	7	11	11	3		3.3	0.9
Rhythm of speech and reading	1	1	8	18	4		3.7	0.8
Poems, prattles, etc.	—	3	17	7	3	(−2)	3.3	0.8

All items in the reading area reveal high mean scores. Understanding the text received most attention all the time ($\overline{X}$ = 4.7). Next come the clarity of pronunciation exercises ($\overline{X}$ = 3.9). Relatively less attention is devoted to individualization of the text, reading in chorus and poems, prattles, etc. ($\overline{X}$ = 3.3 for each). In general, there seem to be many different factors under teachers' attention at the same time in reading lessons. The above items are not clear-cut factors, but overlap each other to some degree.

Table 5 Division of teachers according to the sequence of attention to different items in writing

Writing	1	2	3	4	5	(32-n)	$\overline{X}$	S.D.
	\multicolumn{5}{c}{Attention paid}			
Hand motor control	—	—	2	11	19		4.5	0.8
Neatness and carefulness	—	—	2	21	9		4.2	0.5
Smoothness of handwriting	—	3	4	18	7		3.9	0.8
Lessening muscular tensions	1	1	5	16	9		3.9	0.9
Active relaxation	—	3	11	12	6		3.6	0.9
Breathing habits	6	11	11	4	—		2.4	0.9

Hand motor control and neatness and carefulness show the highest mean scores. Relaxation, smoothness of handwriting and lessening the muscular tension are often under teachers' attention. Breathing habits do not get much attention ($\overline{X} = 2.4$).

Table 6   Division of teachers according to the sequence of attention to different items in knowledge of the language (grammar)

Knowledge of the language	1	2	3	4	5	(32-n)	$\overline{X}$	S.D.
Child's sense of sentence	—	—	7	12	13		4.1	0.7
Sentence structure of the text	—	2	12	12	4	(−2)	3.6	0.8
Versatility in the use of language	—	—	12	14	5	(−1)	3.7	0.7
Grammatical standard	—	6	11	13	—	(−2)	3.2	0.7
Contents (meaning) of the text	—	1	6	17	6	(−2)	3.9	0.7

It appears that all items in the area of knowledge of the language receive a lot of attention. Answers concentrate heavily inside classes 3 and 4 (sometimes and often). We cannot obtain accurate knowledge about time devoted to each item or the real nature of the teacher's actions. The results seem to contradict some points in Table 4 (reading), because efficient work with pupils' sense of sentence and their versatility in the use of language needs individualization of the text in reading as well.

4   *Relative importance order of the areas in teaching native tongue*
Scores on items (sub-areas) in all areas of language were rather high, and the items that really received most attention cannot be easily discriminated. This fact raised further questions. The teachers were asked to put the four main areas of language into the order of relative importance.

Table 7   Areas of language in the order of relative importance (for the first and second graders)

	(Most) 1	2	3	(Least) 4	$\overline{X}$	S.D.
Speech and listening	21	3	6	2	1.6	1.0
Reading	10	19	3	—	1.7	0.6
Writing	1	9	20	2	2.7	0.6
Knowledge of language	—	1	3	28	3.8	0.45

The answers of each teacher were interrelated, because the areas of language had to be put into an order of relative importance. The teachers considered the knowledge of language the least important almost unanimously. Speech and listening was placed first, followed closely by reading but with greater dispersal. Hence the items that generally receive most attention in language teaching can be found in the areas of speech and listening and reading. The following six may be the ones that teachers favour most:

1 understanding the text
2 vocabulary of the Finnish language
3 errors in the quality of voice
4 willingness to express
5 auditory discriminative ability
6 clarity of pronunciation exercises

but not necessarily in this order.

Summary and comments

Methodologically this questionnaire seems to give realistic knowledge, although certainly on a rather general level. On the other hand, systematic observation in the classroom which would have given much more specific information is too hard and expensive a method for this kind of study. This straight approach gave knowledge about the thoughts of teachers and their preferences, no matter how well they are able to carry their ideas through in everyday work.

Because throughout this study the dispersals of the answers are small, it appears that in Finnish language teaching all teachers act very much the same way along with some old traditions. Apparently most attention and time is devoted to understanding texts through vocabulary growth and to pronunciation with some emphasis on auditory abilities and motivation to oral expression. Most confusion that remains in mother-tongue teaching seems to be in the area of grammar. The newest sociolinguistic teaching methods have not yet taken shape in the Finnish ways of school work, particularly in grammar, for example the situational method and Halliday's and Wilkins's forms of thinking.

Perhaps the most alarming discovery is the wide information gap between the classroom teacher and her co-workers in the field of education. Information does not seem to flow between kindergarten or day nursery and school, child-care clinic or psychological clinic and school. Classroom teachers have to struggle alone with many difficulties, perhaps often not seeing some of the problems. In addition to straight questions on the sources of information, the fact that half of the teachers use less than half of the maximum amount of supportive teaching strongly indicates this information gap.

Another information gap exists between investigators and teachers.

This is partly due to differences in the spoken and written languages and partly because both work in different worlds, thinking different thoughts. Investigators and educational planners should be able to form a clear concept of a real learning process in the classroom. They should learn to know the paths that teachers' thoughts travel, and they must cooperate more with all workers in the field of education. Practice can be described with theory, but practice will remain primary. Pedagogic practices in mother tongue contain a very rich experience, perhaps all that we need. But we must make it systematic, form it so that it can be related to new generations of teachers, and at the same time question the relevance and efficiency of old traditions. Then we would not need to start right from the very beginning all the time and to use the trial and error method, which we so annoyingly often do.

38 The impact of research in reading upon the classroom: aspects of the American experience

E. Jennifer Monaghan

No single subject in the United States has been the target of so much research as has reading. By 1943, over 8,200 studies in reading had been undertaken (Betts and Betts 1945). At present, the total must be at least 15,000. And the trend is for more research studies in reading, not fewer. The *Reading Research Quarterly*, which publishes annually a summary of all the reading research studies undertaken in the preceding academic year, reported 302 studies for the year 1971-2; 369 for the year 1972-3; 431 for the year 1973-4; and an all-time high, 558 studies for the academic year 1974-5 (Weintraub *et al* 1973; 1974; 1975; 1976). No doubt, when the total number of studies in reading for this past year is totted up, the number will be found to be up again.

Given this embarrassment of riches, it is of crucial importance to determine the relationship between research in reading and its practical applications, if any, in the American classroom. This paper seeks to examine certain features of American classroom practice, chosen somewhat arbitrarily from stretches of time during the past seventy-five years, and relate them to research. If we find that classroom practice has not been systematically influenced by the results of research, we shall then try to ascertain what the predominant influences were, or are.

The periods to be discussed are three in number; first, we shall take a look at the late teens and early twenties of the twentieth century. This time period represents, in many ways, the first time that research in reading has been conducted in bulk. Our second period will be a span of time which was notable both for the uniformity of its instructional approaches and for the mutual agreement of its textbooks: a period running roughly from 1930 to 1965. Our last period will be the 1970s – a period fraught with pitfalls, because it is so difficult to do justice to one's own time, lacking, as one does, the advantage of perspective that only the passage of time can bring. Nonetheless, I shall argue that some of the characteristics of the earlier periods may be found in our own times. I should also add that the periods I shall discuss should not in any way be taken as a summary of seventy-five years of the American experience. As I have said, they are chosen rather arbitrarily, essentially for their value as tales from which one may draw a moral.

We open, then, with the first of our three periods: the late teens and early twenties of this century. We shall have to put this time into its historical context in order to have a clearer idea of where reading research fitted into the picture.

There were two major forces at this time in American education. The first, of course, was the philosophy of John Dewey; its educational aspects came to be known as 'progressive' education. The second was the so-called scientific movement, where the statistical concept of the normal curve was being applied for the first time in the assessment of variables such as intelligence, spelling and reading.

As far as the first of these influences was concerned, reading occupied a pretty small place in Dewey's great scheme of things. Learning to read in a 'progressive' school was a casual affair, begun late rather than early, and subordinated to the overall activity or project with which it was involved. If there was anything structured enough to be called a method, it was the language-experience approach (Monaghan 1976). Words were presented whole to children as they needed them. Dewey himself paid little attention to reading and writing, except to chastise the national preoccupation with them as a 'primary education fetich' (Dewey 1898). (For a description of reading in two progressive schools, see Huey 1968, pages 289-300.)

The scientific movement, on the other hand, was very much concerned with the 'tool' subjects of reading, writing and arithmetic. The birth of the 'scientific movement' is usually dated 1910, the year when Edward Lee Thorndike produced his handwriting scale (Smith 1965, page 157). In essence, the scientific movement in education was a measurement movement. To Thorndike, after all, had the remark been attributed that everything that existed existed in quantity and could be measured (*cf* Cremin 1964, page 114). The era was, as one observer described it, an orgy of tabulation. The first time the new measurement techniques were applied to reading was in 1914, when William S. Gray produced a 'Tentative Scale for the Measurement of Oral Reading Achievement' as his Master's thesis for Columbia University (Gray 1914).

In actuality, these two forces in American education in the early decades of this century were thoroughly incompatible. It took genius on the part of men like Carleton Washburne to assimilate the one with the other: by using measurement techniques to measure individual differences, and by planning programmes tailored to the individual, Washburne managed to be both 'progressive' and 'scientific' (Washburne 1932). A more typical contrast between the two influences may be seen in the twentieth yearbook of the National Society for the Study of Education, published in 1921. The NSSE devoted the first part of this yearbook to a report on the 'project' method – which had a characteristically progressive flavour – and the second part to the report of their committee on silent reading (Whipple 1921).

One of the discoveries of research on reading had been that children read both faster and, apparently, with better comprehension when they read silently than when they read orally. One of the spin-offs from the progressive movement in education was that children should understand what they were doing. From the point of view of reading, this gave a new importance to the status of comprehension. Indeed, it became a cliché that all the efforts in teaching reading in the nineteenth century had ignored comprehension, and that the great contribution of the brave new world of the twentieth century was to stress comprehension.

Silent reading fitted nicely into these perceptions, for, as Ernest Horn of the University of Iowa put it (Watkins 1922, page 6), there was:

> a common agreement today that more care should be taken to insure proper comprehension in the reading exercises in the primary grades. This inevitably leads to an increase of emphasis upon silent reading, since in oral reading it is impossible to tell with any degree of accuracy whether or not the pupil understands what he has read.

There was a spate of silent reading textbooks published after 1920, which rejoiced in such titles as *The Silent Readers*, *The Silent Reading Hour*, and, with a title that scored on every count, *The Progressive Road to Silent Reading* (cited in Smith 1965, page 175). Emma Watkins published her study on *How to Teach Silent Reading to Beginners* in 1922, and claimed that by the end of first grade a child could progress from reading silently a simple command like 'hop' to the instruction: 'Tell that man sitting by the window that the spinning wheel over in the corner is older than the telephone, electric light, railroads and the United States' (Watkins 1922, page 13).

From our point of view, the important question is how much this shift in classroom instruction was indebted to research. The conventional view of that time and since was that it was greatly influenced by research. (Stone, in 1926, subtitled his work *Silent and Oral Reading* 'a practical handbook based on the most recent scientific investigations' *cf.* Smith 1965, pages 158-63.) In this case, I think that the conventional view is correct. The publicity given to the findings of eye-movement studies and so on, however, was probably as influential as the research itself.

It is fair, then, to point to the influence of research in promoting the popularity of silent reading as an instructional technique. But it is also true that the new enthusiasm for silent reading would probably not have caught on had not silent reading fitted in so nicely with the temper of the times.

357

The second period that we shall look at may be taken as extending from 1930 to about 1965. In 1930, William S. Gray co-authored the new version of the *Elson Readers*, which became known as the *Scott Foresman* series, and which dominated the American basal reader market for over thirty years.

Children – using *Scott Foresman* or a similar series – started by learning words whole by the 'sight' approach. These words were introduced slowly, with ample provision for repetition. After the child had mastered some fifty or more words whole, he then supplemented the sight approach by using a variety of 'word attack' skills. William S. Gray called them 'clues', and they were most familiar to teachers from his influential book *On Their Own in Reading* (Gray 1948). These word attack techniques included picture clues, configuration clues, context clues, structural clues and finally, if all else failed, phonic clues. Phonics was regarded as a slow method of word attack, and one that detracted from attention to meaning. Meaning, the experts held, then as now, was the ultimate goal of reading. (For a list of the experts who supported this 'combined' approach to word recognition, see Tinker and McCullough 1962, page 138. The list reads like a *Who's Who* of the reading profession.)

If we take a closer look at the years between 1950 and 1965, we find the same agreement in textbooks aimed at teachers. Indeed, it is difficult to exaggerate the unanimity of the advice proferred teachers in all the textbooks of those years. They follow the same format: first, reading is defined as a complex skill, and eulogized; then there follows a list of the physical and mental characteristics that a child has to possess in order to be ready to read; a discussion of reading readiness itself; a review of teaching at different grade levels, which follows the pattern we have described above; and finally a pep-talk on adjusting to individual differences (e.g. De Boer and Dallmann 1964; Dawson and Bamman 1959; Hester 1964).

Research studies do not play a large part in this type of book. When research is cited, it is often represented by a few classic studies such as the finding that phonic readiness was not achieved until the mental age of seven (Dolch and Bloomster 1937, cited in Tinker 1952, page 93), or that children were not ready for reading before they had a mental age of six and a half (Morphett and Washburne 1931, cited in Gans 1963, page 55).

Now there are several things that are odd about these particular citations. Take the finding that children had to have a mental age of six and a half in order to start reading, for example. Other research had long contradicted this. Arthur Gates, colleague of Edward Lee Thorndike, had done a nice little study in 1937, and found, at least to his own satisfaction, that a child could be taught to read as young as the age of five, provided that instruction was geared to his level (Hunnicutt and Iverson 1958). The reason for Gates's research being ignored in favour of the other must be that the author of the first study was Carleton Washburne. While Gates was becoming a dominant figure within the reading profession, Washburne had emerged as the spokesman for progressive education as a whole.

But the most curious fact of all about the relation of research to classroom practice and teacher training was one that emerged from Rudolf Flesch's book *Why Johnny Can't Read – and What you can do about it*: namely, that the reading profession had ignored the results of a large portion of their own research. For, thundered Flesch, the research had shown the overwhelming advantage of phonics over whole-word instruction (Flesch 1955). When Jeanne Chall examined the same research, she came to the same conclusion, although she put it in more temperate prose (Chall 1967).

There were certainly flaws in this research – Chall herself said it left much to be desired – and a later study showed greater differences within methods than between methods (Bond and Dykstra 1967). Nonetheless, the point still remains that this body of research was all that the reading professionals had to go on at the time, in assessing the respective merits of phonics and the word method. We are forced, therefore, to conclude that the professionals did indeed choose to ignore what did not fit in with the suppositions of the time. Although this is not a situation that is likely to occur again, it is important to see if we can discover why it occurred in the first place.

Now, the whole-word method, contrary to popular belief, was not the child of reading experts like William S. Gray and Arthur Gates. They had inherited the method from the early progressive movement (*cf* Huey's remark in 1908 (Huey 1968, page 272) that the word method was used by 'progressive teachers' from 1870 onwards). The word method had been adopted by the progressives partly because it seemed so much easier for the child to use, and partly because of the cliché, already in vogue by 1925, that phonics detracted from comprehension (Stone 1926, page 54). Once the word was established as the unit of instruction, it was seized upon joyfully by the measurement movement, because, in part, words lend themselves so readily to being counted. Edward Lee Thorndike himself had produced the basic vocabulary list for teachers in his *Teacher's Word Book* of 1921. The word approach *per se*, then, was not a product of the 1930s, 1940s or 1950s. But the multiple approach to word recognition (context clues and so forth) undoubtedly was.

One of the reasons given by critics for the triumph of this conventional wisdom was that there was too close a link between the teachers of teachers and the publishing industry (Blumenfeld 1973). Almost all the basal readers of the forties and fifties were authored by some prestigious figure in the reading profession (*ibid* page 121). Now, while there is no reason why one should not turn theory into practice, it must be remarked that the basal reader is an instrument of extraordinary power. This was particularly true in the United States in the 1940s and 1950s, when statewide adoptions were the rule. If the teacher-trainer is also the author of the basal reader, there is a danger of the self-perpetuating orthodoxy. Moreover, it must be hard to retain one's objectivity, as a professional, under such circumstances.

A further reason for professional unanimity is that the profession, at least as early as 1949, was increasingly on the defensive (Monaghan 1976). One textbook of the period even mentioned that it could be used as a resource by teachers 'confronted by parents who do not understand modern methods' (Hester 1964, page 9). There is no doubt that a great many parents were upset by the prevalence of the whole-word approach, and that these were the public that kept *Why Johnny Can't Read* on the bestseller list for fourteen straight weeks in 1955. The profession was closing its ranks against a hostile lay public.

Be that as it may, and leaving aside other reasons for professional unanimity for the moment, we shall now turn to the third of our time periods: the present day. It is marked by a refreshing lack of agreement. As I see it, there are three major types of material in the American classroom today. (And if I talk about classroom material, rather than classroom practice, it is because, in the United States, so much classroom practice seems to be dictated by classroom material.)

The first type of classroom material is the most remarkable, because it owes so little to anyone in the reading profession. Indeed, it represents a reaction to the conventional wisdom of the 1950s, and stems from what is usually called the 'back to basics' movement. The basal readers that are inspired by these sentiments employ systematic phonics, which have been used but rarely in the United States since the *McGuffey Readers* went out of style (for example, *Lippincott's Basic Reading*; *Open Court Correlated Language Arts Program*. See also Terman and Walcutt 1958).

While these reading materials for children owe little to our own profession, a second group of materials derive from a viewpoint that was once radical but is now becoming positively establishment. The psycholinguistic view, at least as interpreted by Kenneth Goodman and Frank Smith, holds that writing is not just speech written down, and that fractionating language – as phonics undoubtedly does – kills both language and reading (Goodman 1975; Smith 1973). Materials embodying this concept include the newest edition of the *Scott Foresman* series, co-authored, among others, by Kenneth Goodman.

The third and last of our classroom materials derive from skill- , or objective-based instruction. The student's needs are identified by testing, and appropriate learning activities prescribed from a bank of some 400 or 500 instructional objectives. The key to all this is individualization (for example, *Wisconsin Design for Reading Skill Development*; *Westinghouse Learning Corporation School Curriculum Objective-Referenced Evaluation*).

Once again, we have to ask how research fits into all this. As far as the first type of material – the systematic phonics basals – is concerned, not at all. As the systematic phonics advocates have not been drawn from the ranks of our profession, they are not, so far as I know, conducting research on their own particular approach; they are publishing these materials because they firmly believe that the way for a child to learn to read is to decode written material into his own spoken language. Although other people's research is relevant and available to them (for example, Venezky's study of letter-sound correspondences, Venezky 1970), they have not, apparently, availed themselves of it.

Our second group, who believe that language should be taught as a whole, not in bits, are indeed engaged in research. Goodman, for example, is well known for his imaginative research into dialects and miscues. But it is important to note that, here again, the type of materials produced for children by those working along these lines are not themselves validated by research, but justified on intellectual and philosophical grounds as to what written language is, and how it should be taught.

Similarly, the skills, or instructional objectives, of those in our third group are not validated by research, even though they may be sponsored by those actively engaged in research on skill-based instruction. On occasion, promoters of skill-based instruction are disarmingly frank about how they arrived at their skills: they took contemporary classroom procedures, assessed the areas of agreement, and divided them up into skills (for example, Otto *et al* 1971, pages 121, 144, 181, 209). As a result, it comes as no surprise that it is the conventional wisdom of the forties and fifties that appears in its new guise as a series of instructional objectives.

There are, I believe, several useful parallels that can be drawn between our own times and the earlier periods that we have discussed. The first is that classroom materials today are as little motivated by research as they were in the heyday of Dick and Jane, and rather less so than in the heady days of the silent reading craze. Research may fill in some of the details, but the overall thrust of a given piece of reading material derives from a philosophical stance, not an experimental one. Second, reading experts, including those engaged upon research, are still closely identified with classroom materials. And, once again, teacher-training is being undertaken by many who have authorised programmes, which presents the dangers of the self-sustaining methodology.

A third parallel is the conflict between the holistic, natural viewpoint on reading instruction on the one hand, and the skills-oriented approach on the other. It is tempting to see these as echoing the early conflict between the progressives and the measurement people. In fact, the frankly behaviouristic cast of the skills approach is not too dissimilar to Thorndike's connectionism. The difference today is that the two groups make no attempt to accommodate one another! Fourth, there are still statewide adoptions of textbooks, which makes the basal reading market worth the loving care and attention of not only publishers, but some of the United States' largest businesses.

Other factors are at work, for which it is harder to find earlier parallels. The influence of the government – the types of programmes or research projects that are being funded by government money – is a dark and neglected area that badly needs a little sunlight and spring-cleaning. On the brighter side, there has been a fresh infusion, since 1960, of researchers: cognitive psychologists who are not identified with any programmes, but who are examining the reading process in new ways (Gibson and Levin 1975).

My conclusion, then, is that the real influence upon the American classroom has been, and still is, the prevailing philosophy – or philosophies – of the day. Research can always be mustered to support a given viewpoint, because the kinds of questions we ask will dictate the sorts of answers we shall get. Moreover, the very questions that we ask are themselves strongly influenced by the larger philosophy of education that we hold. Prevailing philosophies produce materials, and the American teacher is often distressingly susceptible to the latest fad. My moral is that we should encourage the teacher, much more than we do now, to make her own choice of what she believes reading to involve, and how the child should learn, so that she is master of classroom materials, and not their slave.

References

BETTS, E. and T. (1945) *An Index of Professional Literature on Reading* New York: American Book Company

BLUMENFELD, S. L. (1973) *The New Illiterates* New Rochelle: Arlington House

BOND, G. amd DYKSTRA, R. (1966-7) The cooperative research program in first-grade reading instruction *Reading Research Quarterly* 2, 4, 5-142

CHALL, J. (1967) *Learning to Read: The Great Debate* New York: McGraw-Hill

CREMIN, L. (1964) *The Transformation of the School: Progressivism in American Education, 1876-1957* New York: Vintage Books

DAWSON, M. A. and BAMMAN, H. A. (1959) *Fundamentals of Basic Reading Instruction* New York: Longman Green

DE BOER, J. J. and DALLMANN, M. (1964) *The Teaching of Reading* New York: Holt Rinehart and Winston

DEWEY, J. (1898) Primary Education Fetich *Forum* 25, 315-28

DOLCH, E. W. and BLOOMSTER, M. (1937) Phonic Readiness *Elementary School Journal* 38, 201-205

FLESCH, R. (1955) *Why Johnny Can't Read – and What you Can Do About It* New York: Harper and Row

GANS, R. (1963) *Common Sense in Teaching Reading* Indianapolis: Bobbs-Merrill

GIBSON, E. and LEVIN, H. (1975) *The Psychology of Reading* Cambridge, Massachusetts: MIT Press

GOODMAN, K. S. (1975) Do you have to be smart to read? Do you have to read to be smart? *The Reading Teacher* 28, 625-32

GRAY, W. S. (1914) *A Tentative Scale for the Measurement of Oral Reading Achievement* Unpublished Master's Thesis, Columbia University

GRAY, W. S. (1948) *On Their Own in Reading* Chicago: Scott Foresman

HESTER, K. B. (1964) *Teaching Every Child to Read* New York: Harper and Brothers

HUNNICUTT, C. W. and IVERSON, W. J. (eds) (1958) *Research in the Three 'Rs'* New York: Harper and Brothers

HUEY, E. B. (1968) (first published in 1908) *The Psychology and Pedagogy of Reading* Cambridge, Massachusetts: MIT Press

MONAGHAN, E. J. (1976) *The Impact of Psychology upon Reading Methodology in the United States, 1880-1960* Unpublished paper, presented at Bowling Green State University

MORPHETT, M. V. and WASHBURNE, C. (1931) When should children begin to read? *Elementary School Journal* 31, 496-503

OTTO, W., CHESTER, R., MCNEIL, J. and MYERS, S. (1971) *Focused Reading Instruction* Reading, Massachusetts: Addison-Wesley Publishing

SMITH, N. B. (1965) *American Reading Instruction* Newark, Delaware: International Reading Association

SMITH, F. (1973) *Psycholinguistics and Reading* New York: Holt, Rinehart and Winston

STONE, C. R. (1926) *Silent and Oral Reading: A Practical Handbook of Methods Based on the Most Recent Scientific Investigations* Boston: Houghton Mifflin

TERMAN, S. and WALCUTT, C. C. (1958) *Reading: Chaos and Cure* New York: McGraw-Hill

TINKER, M. A. (1952) *Teaching Elementary Reading* New York: Appleton-Century-Crofts

TINKER, M. A. and MCCULLOUGH, C. M. (1962) *Teaching Elementary Reading* New York: Appleton-Century-Crofts

VENEZKY, R. L. (1970) *The Structure of English Orthography* The Hague: Mouton

WASHBURNE, C. (1932) *Adjusting the School to the Child* Yonkers-on-Hudson, New York: World Book Company

WATKINS, E. (1922) *How to Teach Silent Reading to Beginners* Philadelphia: J. B. Lippincott

WEINTRAUB, S., ROBINSON, H. M., SMITH, H. K. and PLESSAS, G. P. (1973) Summary of investigations relating to reading, 1 July, 1971 to 30 June, 1972 *Reading Research Quarterly* 8, 241-440

WEINTRAUB, S., ROBINSON, H. M., SMITH, H. K. and ROSER, N. L. (1974) Summary of investigations relating to reading, 1 July, 1972 to 30 June, 1973 *Reading Research Quarterly* 9, 3, 247-513

WEINTRAUB, S., ROBINSON, H. M., SMITH, H. K., PLESSAS, G. P. and ROWLS, M. (1975) Summary of investigations relating to reading, 1 July, 1973 to 30 June, 1974 *Reading Research Quarterly* 10, 3, 267-543

WEINTRAUB, S., ROBINSON, H. M., SMITH, H. K., PLESSAS, G. P., ROSER, N. L. and ROWLS, M. (1976) Summary of investigations relating to reading, 1 July, 1974 to 30 June, 1975 *Reading Research Quarterly* 11, 3, 217-565

WHIPPLE, G. M. (ed) (1921) *The Twentieth Yearbook of the National Society for the Study of Education* Bloomington: Public School Publishing Company

The contributors

Helen Arnold, B.A., M.A., Dip.Ed.
Research Associate
Schools Council Project: Extending Beginning Reading
School of Education
University of Manchester

Bolarinwa Balogun, Ph.D.
Lecturer
Department of Language Arts
University of Ibadan
Nigeria

Wyn Barrow, D.A.F.E. (Reading)
Area Advisory Teacher
Bradford

Richard H. F. Binns, B.Ed., B.A. Hons., Dip.Fine Art.
Principal Teacher, Remedial Education
St Mungo's Academy
Glasgow

Rene Boote
Teacher
Stockport

Asher Cashdan, M.A., M.Ed., F.B.Ps.S.
Senior Lecturer in Educational Studies
The Open University

L. John Chapman, Dip.Ed., M.Sc., Ph.D.
Sub-Dean, Faculty of Educational Studies
The Open University

Margaret M. Clark, Ph.D.
Reader in Psychology
University of Strathclyde

Alan Cohen, M.A., M.Ed.
Lecturer in Education
Institute of Education, University of Durham

John Cole, M.A.
Project Officer
Schools Council Project: Effective Use of Reading
University of Nottingham

Peter Davies, B.Ed., B. Lings.
Assistant Research Officer, N.F.E.R.

Elizabeth P. Dolan
Head of Compensatory Education
Christ the King Comprehensive School
Arnold, Nottinghamshire

Terry Dolan, M.Phil.
Lecturer in Education
School of Education, University of Nottingham

James M. Ewing, B.Sc., M.Ed.
Lecturer in Psychology
Dundee College of Education

Bruce A. Gillham, B.A., A.C., Dip.Ed., M.Ed.
Senior Lecturer in Education
Newcastle Polytechnic

John Gilliland, B.A.
Lecturer in Education
Institute of Education, University of Durham

Gilbert R. Gredler, Ph.D.
Professor of Psychology
University of South Carolina, U.S.A.

Hans U. Grundin, Ph.D.
Department of Educational Research
Teachers' College
Linköping, Sweden

Colin Harrison, B.A., M.Phil.
Project Officer
Schools Council Project The Effective Use of Reading
University of Nottingham

Morag Hunter, M.Ed.
Lecturer
Post-Experience Course
The Open University

366

Robert J. Kedney
Adviser
Bolton Metropolitan Borough

Fergus McBride, B.A., M.Ed.
Principal Lecturer in Education
Moray House College of Education, Edinburgh

Tom MacFarlane, Dip.Ed.
Curriculum Development Leader for Adult Literacy
Manchester

Christopher P. Marshall, B.A., M.Ed., Dip.Ed. Psych.
Principal Educational Psychologist
Northamptonshire County Council

James Maxwell, M.A., M.Ed.
Former Director Reading Research Unit
Queen Mary College
Edinburgh

John E. Merritt, B.A., A.B.Ps.S.
Professor of Education
The Open University

E. Jennifer Monaghan, M.A.
Corrective Reading Teacher
New York, U.S.A.

Joyce Morris, B.A., Ph.D.
Language Arts Consultant
London

Donald Moyle, M.A., L.C.P., L.T.C.L.
Reader in Education
Edge Hill College of Higher Education
Ormskirk

David A. Pendleton, B.A.
Lecturer in Psychology of Education
Leeds Polytechnic School of Education

Peter D. Pumfrey, M.Ed., Dip.Ed. Psych.
Senior Lecturer in Education
University of Manchester

Anthony K. Pugh, B.A., M. Phil.
Staff Tutor, Faculty of Educational Studies
The Open University

H. Alan Robinson, Ph.D.
Professor of Reading
Hofstra University
New York, U.S.A.

Susanne M. Shafer, Ph.D.
Professor of Education
Arizona State University
Tempe, U.S.A.

Robert E. Shafer, Ph.D.
Professor of English
Department of English
Arizona State University
Tempe, U.S.A.

Christopher H. Singleton, Ph.D.
Lecturer of Psychology
University of Hull

Kari Tuunainen
Assistant Professor
University of Joensuu, Finland

Denis Vincent, M.A., B.Ed.
Research Officer, N.F.E.R.

Alma Williams
Education Officer
Consumer Association

David Williams, B.A.
Head of Remedial Department
Benfield School, Newcastle upon Tyne

Sheila Wolfendale, B.A., M.Sc.
Educational Psychologist
Croydon Borough Council